*Under the edi*

DAYTON D. McKEAN

*University of Colorado*

∗

# OTHER TITLES IN THE SERIES

\*

# The Indian

# Political System

SECOND EDITION

NORMAN D. PALMER

UNIVERSITY OF PENNSYLVANIA

HOUGHTON MIFFLIN COMPANY · BOSTON

NEW YORK · ATLANTA · GENEVA, ILLINOIS · DALLAS · PALO ALTO

COPYRIGHT ACKNOWLEDGMENTS

To Harper & Row, Jonathan Cape Limited, and Amaury de
Riencourt for passages from *The Soul of India* by Amaury
de Riencourt. Copyright © 1960 by Amaury de Riencourt.
Reprinted by permission of Harper & Row and of Jonathan
Cape Limited.

To The John Day Company, Inc., and the Right Honourable Indira Gandhi, Prime Minister of India, for *The Discovery of India* by Jawaharlal Nehru. Copyright © 1946
by The John Day Company. Reprinted from THE DIS-
COVERY OF INDIA by Jawaharlal Nehru by permission
of THE JOHN DAY COMPANY, INC., publisher.

To Little, Brown and Company and Rajni Kothari for
*Politics in India* by Rajni Kothari. From Rajni Kothari,
*Politics in India*. Copyright © 1970 by Little, Brown and
Company (Inc.). Reprinted by permission.

PRINTED IN THE U.S.A.

Library of Congress Catalog Card Number: 77–151750
ISBN: 0–395–11926–X

# CONTENTS

# PREFACE

For students of politics India is perhaps the most important of all the newer nations of the so-called "underdeveloped world." Its long and complex past, its vast population (one-seventh of the human race, greater than that of Africa and Latin America combined), and its present position give India a special importance that can be acknowledged without doing an injustice to any other nation.

India is a particularly significant laboratory of political, economic, and social development and change. It is a static society, with a political system grounded in orthodox and conservative traditions, but one paradoxically in the process of change. Although it is common and convenient to speak of India's "political system" — and for these reasons I have chosen to do so throughout the book — it is not quite accurate. In the strictest sense of the term India has perhaps not yet evolved a real political system at all; but it has a well-established framework of government and law which is a working reality, although to be sure this sometimes operates in peculiar ways and is currently under extraordinary stresses and strains.

Since the first edition of this book appeared in 1961, India has experienced a series of traumatic events and developments. These include the border war with China in October–November, 1962, which had a profound effect on the entire Indian scene; the death, in May 1964, of its "tallest" leader, Jawaharlal Nehru; three successions to the prime ministership, in 1964, 1966, and 1967; three general elections, in 1962, 1967, and 1971, and a mid-term election in five states in 1969; two years (1965–67) of severe drought and crop failure; the beginnings of the "green revolution," which is already having far-reaching political and social, as well as economic, consequences; a split in the dominant Congress Party in 1969, which has led to a minority government at the Center and a growing number of coalitions and other unstable forms of government in the States; frequent periods of President's Rule in several States; and an alarming deterioration in law and order and an increase in communal and other forms of violence.

During the past decade, also, some significant new contributions, in theory and in substance, have been made to the study of comparative politics, political systems, and political development. Many of these are quite germane to the Indian political system. More sophisticated contributions have been made to the study of this system, in books, articles, and special studies of both a macroscopic and microscopic nature. I have tried to take account of these contributions, as well as of all major political developments since 1961, in this new edition.

At long last, it seems, the study of Indian politics is being given the attention it deserves, by both Indian and foreign scholars who are well trained in the techniques of modern political analysis and who are familiar with the Indian political scene. This is a welcome development indeed.

This brief volume presents a comprehensive view of the evolving Indian political system at a critical period in its development. It calls attention to the need for studying the system as a whole, as well as for subjecting it to minute analysis. As Arnold Toynbee has observed: "India is a whole world in herself; she is a society of the same magnitude as our Western society."

In the early years of the decade of the 1970's, a profound pessimism seems to grip most Indian, and many foreign, observers of the Indian scene. Gloomy predictions of India's future are frequently voiced. While there are ample grounds for such pessimism, there is also good reason for confidence in India's basic capacity to survive and to cope with its gigantic problems. As Chester Bowles once remarked: "Prophets of gloom and doom have long been predicting India's collapse. While the prophets fall by the wayside, India endures." It may be that the Indian political system, like Indian society as a whole, is more firmly based than it appears to be. It is also possible that some other kind of political system may be more suitable to India's needs and conditions.

For whatever merit this volume may possess I am particularly indebted to the many friends whose knowledge of Indian politics and society has aroused my lasting envy and admiration. Among these friends who know India so well, I would single out the following for special mention: a remarkable group of older Indian scholars, mostly political scientists, whom I first met in India many years ago, notably A. Appadorai, D. N. Banerjee, R. Bhaskaran, Nirmal Bhattacharya, C. J. Chacko, Mohammad Habib, S. V. Kogekar, Mukhut Behari Lal, V. K. N. Menon, Ishwari Prasad, B. M. Sharma, M. P. Sharma, Gurmukh Nihal Singh, R. U. Singh, J. P. Suda, and M. Venkatarangaiya; M. S. Rajan, Bimal Prasad, K. P. Misra, and others at the Indian School of International Studies (now the School of International Studies of the Jawaharlal Nehru University); Rajni Kothari, Gopal Krishna, Ramashray Roy, Bashir Ahmad, and other able scholars at the Centre for the Study of Developing Studies in Delhi; Harnam Singh, J. S. Bains, and colleagues in the Political Science Department of Delhi University, where I was a visiting professor in 1952–53; S. P. Varma, Iqbal Narain, and others in the Political Science Department and the South Asia Studies Centre of the University of Rajasthan; Aloo J. Dastur, Usha Mehta, S. P. Aiyar, and colleagues in the Political Science Department of Bombay University; Shanti Kothari, former Member of Parliament and Director of the Centre of Applied Politics in New Delhi; M. V. Pylee, Director of the School of Management Studies, University of Kerala; V. M. Sirsikar of Poona University; P. N. Sheth of Gujarat University; C. Satyapalan of S. N. College, Quilon, Kerala; several Members of Parliament and Members of Legislative Assemblies of many parties; a number of able civil servants in the central government and in the governments of several States; some outstanding Indian and foreign journalists, including Krishan Bhatia, Girilal Jain, Frank Moraes, N. Nanporia, Selig S. Harrison, and Neville Maxwell; a number of public-spirited citizens of India, distinguished in several walks of life, notably A. D. Gorwala, G. L. Mehta, M. K. K. Nayar, A. G. Noorani, P. Kodanda Rao, and M. A. Sreedhar; several outstanding non-Indian students of Indian politics, notably W. H. Morris-Jones, Richard L. Park, and Myron Weiner; and colleagues in the Political Science and South Asia Regional Studies departments of the University of Pennsylvania.

I am especially grateful for the cooperation and tolerance of Dayton D. McKean of the University of Colorado, general editor of the series in which this volume appears; Frank Shelton, editor of political science texts in the College Department of Houghton Mifflin Company, who guided the manuscript through all stages leading to publication; and Shirley Quinn, who skillfully edited the manuscript and helped me to reduce it to a length that was barely tolerable to Houghton Mifflin and well-nigh intolerable to me.

This Preface was completed on January 26, 1971, on the twenty-first anniversary of the inauguration of the Indian Constitution and the Republic of India, and just before the fifth general elections. Although the Indian political system has impressive achievements to its credit, it is clearly a political system in transition, and its future is quite uncertain.

NORMAN D. PALMER

Leopard Lake
Berwyn, Pennsylvania

# *  1  *

# The Nature of
# Indian Politics

Contemporary India is a fascinating laboratory of political, economic, and social change. It is clearly a major example of a transitional society. It has a complex political system in an even more complex social order. "The model on which India is set is one of modernization of an ancient and highly plural society in the context of an open polity."[1] To comprehend this model one has to draw upon the methods and approaches of comparative politics and interdisciplinary studies, using primarily a "developmental approach"; but he also has to become deeply immersed in the study of one of the longest civilizations and most complex societies known to man. "There *is* nothing simple in so vast and complex a society as India's."[2] This is certainly true of the Indian political system, which is deeply rooted in Indian society and which functions within a framework of identifiable institutions and processes in various peculiar and subterranean ways.

## Political Perspectives

In conventional terms, the general nature of the Indian political system is easy enough to describe. It is a system of parliamentary democracy, based largely on the British model but with many differences in structure and even more in spirit; it is a federal system, with strong

[1] Rajni Kothari, *Politics in India* (Boston, 1970), p. 12.
[2] Philip Mason, "Unity and Diversity: An Introductory Review," in Philip Mason, ed., *India and Ceylon: Unity and Diversity* (London, 1967), p. 3. For an excellent discussion of various elusive but important themes in Indian politics, see Ashis Nandy," The Culture of Indian Politics: A Stock Taking," *The Journal of Asian Studies*, XXX (November, 1970), 57–79.

centralizing and decentralizing features and shifting balances; it is an increasingly open polity, in a society which is still basically rigid and hierarchical. In David Apter's terms, it is a reconciliation rather than a mobilization system, although it is faced with the recurring problem of achieving mobilization goals with reconciliation techniques.

India today is clearly in a multiple-crisis stage, and it is not well geared, institutionally, materially, or psychologically, to cope with its pyramiding crises. It is facing simultaneously all the crises which students of political development have described, including, to adopt the terminology of Professor Lucian Pye, the crises of identity, legitimacy, penetration, participation, integration, and distribution.[3] The Indian political system has already shown a high degree of flexibility and accommodation, and a considerable capacity to promote such basic goals as national and social integration, economic development, and human survival at higher levels of existence. But it is greatly handicapped by inadequate human and material resources. "Politics in India is the politics of scarcity, and everything else, including the nature and particular sequence of events, follows from this basic fact."[4]

In studying Indian politics special attention should be given to many basic, and often contradictory, themes: unity and diversity, perhaps the central theme in India's long history; tradition and modernity; continuity and change; consensus and conflict; centralization and decentralization; alienation and identification; secularization and religious values; political participation and aversion to or isolation from politics; political socialization and social fragmentation; Westernization and Indianization; pragmatism and ideological commitments; and innumerable contradictions between goals and achievements, theory and practice, ideals and realities. In the Indian system, as an astute Indian scholar has observed, "the traditional, charismatic, and secular forces conjointly obtain and operate. This, we suggest, is due to transitional anomie, the relative insignificance of any set of norms which regulate behaviour."[5]

In his important study of the Indian Parliament, Professor Morris-Jones warned that in approaching the study of Indian politics the Western student "is well advised to be on his guard. He should not assume, for instance, that institutions with familiar names are necessarily performing wholly familiar functions. He should be ready to detect political trends and forces in what he will be tempted to set aside as nonpolitical movements. He should be prepared to find the behaviour of

---

[3] Lucian Pye, *Aspects of Political Development* (Boston, 1966), pp. 63–66.

[4] Aneeta Ahluwalia, review of Mason, ed., *India and Ceylon,* in *Seminar,* No. 107 (July, 1968), p. 40.

[5] T. K. Oomen, "Transitional Anomie in Indian Politics" (unpublished paper), p. 10.

those who hold apparently familiar political positions conditioned by considerations which he would not normally associate with such places."[6] Hence, special consideration should be given to the non-political factors in India, which often will prove to be more potent in shaping Indian political behavior than trends and institutions which are clearly political.

**The Languages or Idioms of Indian Politics.** Two other concepts emphasized by Professor Morris-Jones are also highly relevant and useful. The first relates to the languages or idioms of Indian politics, the second to levels of politics. He finds three main languages or idioms, which for want of better terms he calls the "modern," the "traditional," and the "saintly."[7] They might also be called three different political styles.

The "modern" language or idiom is the most apparent and the most obvious, especially at the national level. Indeed, "it is so widespread in India that it has seemed possible to give comprehensive accounts of Indian political life without moving outside its terms," although deeper analysis would soon reveal how superficial and misleading such an approach would be. "This modern language of politics is the language of the Indian Constitution and the courts; of parliamentary debate; of the higher administration; of the upper levels of all the main political parties; of the entire English Press and much of the Indian language Press. It is a language which speaks of policies and interests, programmes and plans. It expresses itself in arguments and representations, discussions and demonstrations, deliberations and decisions."[8]

At the State, district, and local levels, throughout most of India, politics are largely carried on in the "traditional" language or idiom. This is "the language of a host of tiny worlds," the worlds of the villages, of caste — especially as expressed in terms of the innumerable sub-castes, highly localized in nature (*jati*), not in terms of the so-called four main castes (*varna*) or local political groups and leaders.

"The third language of saintly politics is to be found 'at the margin' of Indian politics. By this is meant the fact that it is in some quantitative sense relatively unimportant, spoken only by a few and occupying a definitely subsidiary place on the political page";[9] but it has a wide-

---

[6] W. H. Morris-Jones, *Parliament in India* (Philadelphia, 1957), p. 2.

[7] Professor Morris-Jones has presented this conceptualization of India's political languages or idioms in several of his articles and books. See, for example, "India's Political Idioms," in C. H. Philips, ed., *Politics and Society in India* (New York, 1962), pp. 133–154; and *The Government and Politics of India* (Garden City, N.Y., 1967), pp. 40–49.

[8] Morris-Jones, *The Government and Politics of India*, p. 41.

[9] *Ibid.*, p. 47.

spread appeal to many sections and people in India. It was one of the many political languages of Mahatma Gandhi, as it is today of Jaya-prakash Narayan. It seems to be the main political idiom of Vinoba Bhave, India's "walking saint," sometimes described as the leading "spiritual heir" of Gandhi. Many Indian political leaders, including the most "modern" among them, often speak in this idiom, or at least pay lip service to it. It has permeated the vocabulary, if not the prac-tice, of Indian politics at every level.

These three languages or idioms are distinct, but in varying degrees all may be found at all levels of Indian politics and in almost all Indian political groups and leaders. There is obviously a high degree of inter-penetration among them. "It is the mixing up of languages which gives Indian politics its distinctive character."[10] Together they shape and largely account for India's distinctive political style.

**Levels of Politics.** Professor Morris-Jones has also called attention to two main levels of politics in India, one reflecting mainly the impact of Westernization and modernization (the two terms are not necessarily synonymous), conditioned by the British heritage and carried on largely by the Westernized Indian elite, the other deeply rooted in Indian so-ciety and traditions.

Because it is less familiar and less immediately obvious it is particu-larly important to recognize what Morris-Jones has called "the presence in Indian politics of a manner of political thought and behaviour which it is difficult to regard simply as a local modification of some aspect of Western politics. It draws its inspiration from religious teachings and represents a development of an aspect of Gandhian politics. It leads its own life, alongside and not wholly unconnected with the world of 'normal' politics, but largely independent of it. It is possible to say that it is not politics at all; in that case the Western pattern (of course, with its modifications) is left in sole command as the only pattern of political conduct available. But it seems more in keeping with the facts to allow that it is politics, even if it is of a kind quite distinct from that of mod-ern Europe."[11]

The levels of politics approach may also be used in another, but re-lated, sense to embrace the kinds of politics carried on at different ver-tical and horizonal levels, vertically from the international and national to the State, district, sub-district, and village levels, horizontally to in-clude comparisons and contrasts between political entities and formal and informal groupings in different regions and States of India. Particu-lar attention should be given to the politics of the different Indian

[10] W. H. Morris-Jones, "Behaviour and Ideas in Political India," in R. N. Spann, ed., *Constitutionalism in Asia* (Bombay, 1963), p. 83.

[11] Morris-Jones, *Parliament in India,* p. 37.

States, the main units or subsystems of the Indian political system, and to the different types and styles of politics in urban and rural India.

**Contemporary Indian Political Thought.** The political values and ideas which govern the thinking and approach of the political leaders and thinkers of modern India are an uncertain mixture of many ingredients, drawn from Hinduism, Gandhism, and other indigenous sources (which were not unaffected by outside ideas), as well as from liberal democracy, non-Marxist social democracy, Marxism, and other modern "isms."[12] The values or ideologies most frequently mentioned by spokesmen of the Indian Government are those of nationalism, democracy, socialism, and secularism (along with nonalignment in foreign affairs, which perhaps should not be classified as an ideology). Each has to be considered within the Indian context, in the light of characteristic Indian interpretations and emphases, as well as within a general theoretical and historical framework.

**Leaders and Leadership.** Considerable insight into the nature of a society may be obtained from a study of the traditions and types of leadership which have characterized it. The leadership principle has been particularly strong in India, reinforced by the traditional aspects of Indian life and social organization. It is reflected in the great classics of the early Hindu period, in the rigidly structured caste system, in the authoritarian patterns which have prevailed throughout the centuries, in the long experience with foreign conquerors and rulers, in the organization of the villages and other units of rural society, in religious practices and groupings.

In modern India leadership has continued to be of surpassing importance. Of special importance are the influence of religious mystics like Ramakrishna, leaders of the Hindu Renaissance like Vivekananda, great literary figures like Tagore, the unique and all-encompassing leadership of Mahatma Gandhi, the work of the men who are trying to carry on the Gandhian spiritual tradition, notably Vinoba Bhave, and the dominant role in the post-Gandhian era of Jawaharlal Nehru.

India has been fortunate in the character and stature of its leaders. Gandhi, Nehru, Vallabhbhai Patel, and in an earlier generation Tagore, Gokhale, and Tilak would rank among the great figures of the past century in any country. One of India's outstanding assets has been what Dr. Paul Appleby called "extraordinary national leadership."[13]

Many of India's leaders could truly be described as charismatic

[12] Norman D. Palmer, "Indian and Western Political Thought: Coalescence or Clash?," *The American Political Science Review,* XLIX (September, 1955), 755.

[13] Paul H. Appleby, *Public Administration in India: Report of a Survey* (Delhi, 1953), p. 3.

leaders. These include persons of such diverse character and personality and ideals as Bal Gangadhar Tilak, Mahatma Gandhi, Subhas Chandra Bose, Vinoba Bhave, Chakravarti Rajagopalachari, and Jawaharlal Nehru. Some of these leaders, notably Gandhi and Bhave, have also been characterized as "unconventional" political leaders, although it is difficult to determine what in the Indian political and social environment is conventional and what is unconventional.

Writing in 1963 an English observer noted: "In effect, there are two coexistent patterns of political leadership in India. There is the basic democratic, party-political pattern, borrowed from Britain, to which the great majority of educated Indians are attached. Beside it, intersecting it at many points, there exists an older, semi-religious pattern of personal authority."[14] These two patterns still exist, but the most striking trend in political leadership in India today is the change from the dominant role of charismatic leaders and the Westernized elite to the growing importance of new, more generally representative, leaders, especially at State and local levels. Even at these levels, however, the traditional and ascriptive criteria are becoming less, and achievement criteria more significant.[15]

The nature of India's new leaders is well characterized by Rajni Kothari:

> The electoral and democratic process has shifted the levers of power from the hands of the first generation leadership to those in charge of state and district organizations, caste federations, and rural panchayats and cooperatives. . . . The new organization men . . . are to be found . . . in small towns and district capitals, closer to the traditional social order, and exhibiting a new style in Indian politics. They are pragmatic men, less oriented to the modernist idiom but modernizers in their own way, men who understand the subtleties and nuances of local society, powerful persons who have taken time in coming up, and who are therefore confident of their own strength. . . . Some of them are popular leaders, others ruthless managers, but they control the vote. The focus of power has shifted.[16]

On the national level, India today faces a crisis of leadership that raises grave questions for the future. The generation of outstanding

[14] John Mander, "Indian Autumn," *Encounter,* CXIII (February, 1963), p. 21.
[15] See *Seminar,* No. 51 (November, 1963). The entire issue is devoted to the topic: "The Emerging Leadership."
[16] Kothari, *Politics in India,* pp. 127–128, 282. See also V. M. Sirsikar, "Political Leadership in India," *Economic and Political Weekly,* March 20, 1965.

leaders that piloted India to independence along nonviolent lines has passed from the scene. Their successors are men and women of lesser stature, or at least of lesser reputation. There seem to be few, if any, truly all-India leaders; the new leaders have not yet demonstrated their capacity for national leadership. They are less well educated and less oriented toward the West; but because they are, in a sense, the new modernizers, if not modernists, and because they have regional or local standing, they may achieve a new synthesis between Indian and Western ways and find new sources of strength in India's traditions and peoples.

**The Politics of Agitation and Mass Violence.** The late 1960's and early 1970's witnessed an alarming increase in communal and other incidents, and in the general level of violence. The forms of protest are many and varied, and some are peculiar to the Indian scene. "An important aspect of the crystallization of oppositional strength in India is the confident use made of protest demonstrations and strikes. To these are added new Indian versions of opposition against authority, often spontaneous, sometimes organized, and by and large endowed with legitimacy gained during the nationalist movement and since. These are hunger strikes and fasts, *bandhs* (general strikes in whole cities or states), *gheraos* (condoning [*sic*] of men in authority), and *dharnas* (sit-in strikes before offices or homes of public figures). Such opposition is sometimes directed against state governments, sometimes against the central government, and sometimes against specific managements or officials."[17]

These and other forms of protest are being resorted to with increasing frequency, and the more violent forms are causing increasing disruption, destruction, and casualties. No doubt, as Rajni Kothari has stated, "the instruments of gherao, bandh, and dharna will remain an important part of the armory of oppositional politics in India, and in their own way contribute to the opening of the system."[18] But if communal incidents continue to increase in frequency and in intensity, and if almost continuous acts of violence seriously disrupt the conduct of governmental, economic, and personal affairs, as has been happening for some time in West Bengal, the threat to the social fabric and to the political system may grow to major proportions.

### Politics and Society

**Dilemmas and Trends.** As Professor Morris-Jones has pointed out, "the relationship between politics and society in the new states is often of a kind which for Western students of politics is novel and arresting.

---

[17] Kothari, *Politics in India,* p. 219. For an excellent collection of articles on mass violence in India, see S. P. Aiyar, ed., *The Politics of Mass Violence in India* (Bombay, 1967).

[18] Kothari, *Politics in India,* p. 221.

. . . Without attention to social forces the study of such politics is peculiarly partial and even misleading."[19] This is particularly true in the case of India, an ancient society in which, until recently, society was largely apolitical and relatively unaffected by any but the most pervasive political developments and pressures. In ancient India "the problem of isolating political concepts from the main body of Hindu philosophy and from the all-pervasive influence of spiritual and religious teachings and beliefs" was almost insuperable.[20] Throughout most of India's long history, politics was confined mainly to the elite few, and to foreign conquerors. The masses of the people were often the victims of, but seldom active participants in, the political process.

Conditions have been perceptibly changing in recent years, leading to "a closing of the gap between political organization and the social structure of rural India, along with the downward shift of power within the government and the ruling party." This development, in the opinion of Rajni Kothari, "underlines a tremendous transformation in the power relations of Indian society."[21] Society is becoming politicized, and the social base of the political order is widening. "There is thus a clear trend towards increasing participation in the political process by sections of society which have hitherto been excluded from positions of power."[22] Many of the political parties and groups on national, regional, State, and local levels draw their main support from certain segments of Indian society and are in effect political manifestations of deep-rooted social institutions and practices.[23]

India is still wrestling with the dilemma of establishing an open, secular political system in a society that is not open and is essentially nonsecular.

**Tradition and Modernity.** In a speech in Montevideo, Uruguay, in September, 1968, Prime Minister Indira Gandhi said: "India lives in many layers. Many centuries co-exist in our land. Parts of India are as advanced as you will find elsewhere in the world. The rest are bound in tradition." The elements of tradition and modernity in In-

---

[19] Morris-Jones, *The Government and Politics of India,* pp. 37, 38.

[20] Palmer, "Indian and Western Political Thought," p. 753.

[21] Kothari, *Politics in India,* p. 128.

[22] André Béteille, "The Future of the Backward Classes: The Competing Demands of Status and Power," in Mason, ed., *India and Ceylon,* p. 110. See also *Seminar,* No. 107 (July, 1968). The entire issue is devoted to the topic of "Politics and Society."

[23] "The phenomena of traditional society and the politics of the Rightist Parties are so closely related that one cannot be studied or understood without a proper understanding of the other." C. P. Bhambhri, "Rightist and Traditional Society in Rajasthan: A View Point," *Political Science Review,* University of Rajasthan, 1963. The terms "rightist" and "leftist," though often used, are sometimes quite confusing and even meaningless in the context of the Indian political system.

dian society and politics are fascinating subjects for study and observation. For long they were regarded as rather separate and, in fact, contradictory, phenomena. Now they are being analyzed in terms of synthesis, as well as antithesis. Students of the Indian scene are speaking of "the modernity of tradition" and "the traditonalization of modernity." Tradition is clearly being affected by modern trends and pressures, and in the Indian setting, at least, so-called modernity often reveals traditional characteristics. One detailed study, for example, has indicated that elected officials in development blocks — i.e., at local levels — are more modern in their orientation than the appointed officials assigned to the same blocks, who are affiliated with a presumably modern bureaucracy.[24] Members of Parliament and of the central Cabinet and top leaders of national parties often show in their speech and behavior, as well as in their social and family life, the strong hold of tradition upon them.

The role of tradition and modernity in the changing Indian scene has been well analyzed by Rajni Kothari:

> The Indian approach to development may be characterized as one in which the exposure to modernity led to a renewed awarenes and quickening of traditional identity, its reinterpretation and rejuvenation, and its consolidation in the framework of new institutions and ideas. The Indian response to modern stimuli consisted of asserting the Indianness of India, reformulating this Indianness, and giving it a modern character. The model of those who conceive of modernization as a rejection of traditionality and a "transformation" on modern lines does not apply to India. Nor does the opposite model of those who deny potency to modern institutions and values and simply assert the durability and resilience of traditionalism. . . . the need is to discern the peculiar "mix" that emerges when an ancient society comes to terms with the demands of a new age, seeks its continuity essentially through change, and achieves a new identity without destroying either its rich diversity or its other, antecedent identities.[25]

Thus it is apparent that the search for the "traditional" and the "modern" in India, while a fascinating exercise, can lead to misleading conclusions and impressions. In any event, it cannot suffice to explain

[24] This was the finding of the International Studies of Values in Politics project. For a preliminary report, see Philip E. Jacob, Henry Teune, and Thomas Watts, "Values, Leadership and Development: A Four-Nation Study," *Social Science Information,* VII (April, 1968), 49–92.

[25] Kothari, *Politics in India,* pp. 85–86. See also Lloyd I. Rudolph and Susanne Hoeber Rudolph, *The Modernity of Tradition: Political Development in India* (Chicago, 1967).

the dichotomies in the Indian political scene. "Apparently a process of socialization has occurred and is proceeding which is apparently bridging the gap between the 'modern' or 'modernizing' and 'traditional' elements in the Indian political system, perhaps even to the extent of creating new disparities because of unequal rates of change in different parts of the political system."[26]

**Problems of Social Communication.** Indian society is still characterized by a considerable lack of mobility and by the primacy of local interests over larger considerations. Distances, geographical and social, are great in India. Fewer than 30 per cent of the people are literate. Most of the great decisions are made by a small educated elite whose members for the most part speak English, are familiar with Western thought and institutions, hold most of the important positions in business, government, and the professions, and are often out of touch with the masses of the Indian people. Mass illiteracy, social conservatism, geographical distances, extreme localism, and a fairly rigid social structure cut off the great majority of the people from effective participation in the political life of the country.

Social communication is difficult in India, and many of the channels of communication commonly available in Western countries are relatively unimportant in the Indian setting. Illiteracy and regional and linguistic differences lessen the influence of such media of mass communication as the press and the radio. Informal channels of communications are especially important, and personalities are important in Indian life generally, including politics.[27]

**Public Opinion and Pressure Groups.** In spite of the mass illiteracy and relative lack or social communication, public opinion is potent in India, even though the study of it as a political force is still quite undeveloped.[28] In India, as elsewhere, various publics may be discerned. The most obvious publics are the uneducated many, whose role in influencing public policy is largely negative and general, and the elite few, who control the effective channels of access and who exercise most of the power. Within each of these publics many subdivisions may be found, especially on particular issues. Divisions between North and South, between regional and linguistic groups, between the literate and

[26] Marshall M. Bouton, "Role and Politics in India: A Study of Elected and Appointed Officials in Panchayat-I-Raj" (unpublished M.A. thesis, University of Pennsylvania, 1968), p. 127.

[27] Gene D. Overstreet and Irene Tinker, "Political Dynamics in India" (a paper prepared for the Modern India Project, University of California, March, 1957), pp. 10–11.

[28] The most extensive continuing surveys of public opinion in India are to be found in the *Monthly Public Opinion Surveys* of the Indian Institute of Public Opinion.

the illiterate, between villagers and townspeople, between communal and caste groups have a profound effect on political life and behavior.

Pressure groups also are to be found in India, although perhaps to a lesser degree and in different forms from those in Western states. "Three main types of pressure groups may be distinguished in the Indian setting: (1) special-interest organizations of fairly recent origin representing modern bases of social and economic association familiar to the Western observer, such as trade unions and business groups, social welfare agencies, or youth and women's organizations; (2) organizations representing traditional social relationships, such as caste and religious groups, and (3) organizations representing the Gandhian ideological heritage,"[29] such as the Sarva Seva Sangh, the main agency of the Sarvodaya movement, whose outstanding activity is the Bhoodan Yagna movement of Vinoba Bhave. The exact role of these pressure groups is hard to determine, but they obviously exert considerable influence on particular issues.

**New Leadership Classes.** In traditional Hindu society the classes that mattered were the high-caste Hindus, notably the Brahmans and the Kshatriyas. In Mogul times a new ruling class of Muslims governed the country, but they made relatively little impact on the masses of the people, who were mostly Hindus. The British became a new ruling aristocracy, and they trained and associated with them a group of Western-educated and Western-oriented Indians, who formed a new class in economic and political life, if not so obviously in Indian society generally. This Western-educated group split up into various classes. Some continued to the end as loyal servants of British rule, while others furnished the top leadership of the nationalist movement.

Gandhi raised up another new class of persons of various castes and backgrounds who were more clearly identified with the masses of the people and with Indian traditions and outlook.

A different new class may now be emerging, with deeper roots in local and regional society — a class neither as Westernized in education or outlook as the new classes which developed in the days of British rule nor as devoted to India's past traditions as some of the more conservative followers of Gandhi or some of the many thousands of *sadhus* and other "holy men" who presumably devote their lives to nonmaterial things.[30] This new class — perhaps one should say this new generation — may be able to achieve a more satisfactory synthesis of the many values, foreign and indigenous, which compete for the loyalties of Indians today.

[29] Overstreet and Tinker, "Political Dynamics in India, p. 11.
[30] See Selig S. Harrison, *India: The Most Dangerous Decades* (Princeton, N.J., 1960), pp. 77–95.

**Consensus and Synthesis.** An interesting problem for exploration would be the extent to which a genuine political consensus exists in India today.[31] Some students of Indian history and politics would insist that a remarkable degree of consensus has existed throughout Indian history and that this consensus still exists on fundamentals. Historically, it arises out of the unifying forces in Indian social and religious life, notably Hinduism and the caste system. At the present time it is reinforced by the common experience and challenge of building a new nation, by the widespread acceptance of the basic decisions which have been made regarding the nature of the new state, including the decision to build a modern secular and democratic state, and above all the decision to establish a "socialist pattern of society." It is also reinforced by an almost unparalleled continuity and quality of national leadership. Undoubtedly Nehru himself, the chief political spokesman for India for a generation and the dominant figure in the Indian scene generally from the assassination of Gandhi early in 1948 to his death in 1964, was a great unifying influence, and did much to develop a high degree of political consensus, even in "a fragmented society."

For all the traditional emphasis on consensus and for all the current emphasis on India as a unified nation, many scholars would agree with Professor Morris-Jones that Indian society today is, both in appearance and in reality, "a fragmented society, a society with an absence of a basic consensus." This " 'absence of consensus' theme," states Professor Morris-Jones, "has been central to an understanding of modern Indian politics."[32]

Among the finest traditions of Indian society have been those of assimilation, tolerance, and synthesis, as illustrated in the two great religions (or religio-philosophical systems) which originated in the Indian subcontinent, Hinduism and Buddhism. These qualities have given a distinctive flavor to Indian life and culture. They help to explain how over the centuries India tolerated and to a large degree absorbed many different racial groups and cultures.

"The tradition of India," in the view of a profound student of Indian history, K. M. Panikkar, "has always been one of synthesis . . . a singular ability to absorb the culture of others and assimilate it without losing her own identity. It is the synthesis of Aryan and Dravidian

---

[31] For the importance of the idea of consensus in Indian political and social life, see Susanne Hoeber Rudolph, "Consensus and Conflict in Indian Politics," *World Politics,* XIII (April, 1961), 385–399, and W. H. Morris-Jones, "The Unhappy Utopia—JP in Wonderland," *The Economic Weekly,* June 25, 1960.

[32] W. H. Morris-Jones, "The Exploration of Indian Political Life," *Pacific Affairs,* XXXII (December, 1959), 419.

that laid the basis of Hindu civilization. . . . The prolonged contact with Islam had profound significance for every aspect of Indian life."[33] India later became the "meeting-ground of the East and the West." Indeed, as G. K. Gokhale observed in 1911 at the Universal Races Conference in London, "whereas the contact of the West with other countries had only been external, in India the West had so to say entered into the very bone and marrow of the East."[34] Arnold Toynbee has pointed out that the Western impact on India was more intimate than on any other part of Asia, although of all the major Asian civilizations the dominant civilization of India, the Hindu, is most alien to the civilization of the West.[35]

**Caste and Politics.** In Hindu society the caste system was the dominant social institution, and even though it is undergoing many changes, it is still the most pervasive influence in Hindu life and behavior. As a leading authority on the subject, Professor M. N. Srinivas, pointed out, "caste is so tacitly and so completely accepted by all, including those who are most vocal in condemning it, that it is everywhere the unit of social action."[36] Professor Srinivas speaks of caste as "a series of local systems of interacting *jatis* linked in an all-India framework by means of the idea of *varna*" (referring to the so-called four main castes). It is in this sense, of caste as meaning hundreds of separate and localized *jatis* rather than the four main *varna*, that caste has permeated Hindu society and has more recently had a considerable impact on politics. As Adrian C. Mayer noted, "caste means different things at different levels. . . . one must specify the level about which one is talking, and the kind of caste unit to which one refers, before one can speak of caste's role in politics."[37]

At any level, but especially at the rural and local levels, those most directly affecting the vast majority of the people of India, caste is obviously a most important factor in Indian politics, and will probably remain so for the indefinite future. Jayaprakash Narayan once remarked that "Caste is the most important political party in India." This is obviously an overstatement, but it does contain a large measure of truth. One of the most important developments in Indian politics is the growing consciousness, activity, and assertiveness of large numbers

[33] K. M. Panikkar, *The State and the Citizen* (Bombay, 1956), p. 19.

[34] Quoted in *ibid.*

[35] Arnold Toynbee, *The World and the West* (New York and London, 1953), Chapter III ("India and the West").

[36] M. N. Srinivas, "Caste in Modern India," Presidential Address to the Fourth Indian Science Congress, Calcutta, 1957; reprinted in *The Radical Humanist*, Nov. 10 and 17, 1957.

[37] Adrian C. Mayer, "Caste and Local Politics in India," in Mason, ed., *India and Ceylon*, p. 139.

of lower caste voters, who thus profoundly affect the balance of political power in many parts of India and at almost all levels of politics,
and greatly broaden the base of the Indian political system. Caste considerations are given great weight in the selection of candidates and in
the appeals to voters during election campaigns.

Much of the story of Indian politics, particularly at State levels and
below, could be told in terms of caste. Profesor Srinivas' famous concept of Sanskritization, which he defines as "the process by which a
'low' caste or tribe or other group takes over the customs, rituals, beliefs, ideology, and style of life of a high and, in particular, a 'twice-
born' (*dwija*) caste,"[38] is helpful in connection with studying the growing political influence of lower castes. Professor Srinivas has argued that
"the power and activity of caste had increased in proportion as political
power passed increasingly to the people from the rulers."[39] In a sense,
therefore, although caste seems to be declining in importance as a social
factor, it is increasing in importance as a political factor. But if this is
an accurate general assessment, it needs to be qualified in many ways.
In the political arena caste is only one of the factors determining political choices and political behavior, and often not the most important
determining one. In this arena caste undergoes many changes and takes
on new dimensions. Particular attention has been given to the role of
caste associations and caste federations, which "have provided an important infrastructure of politics in India."[40]

A common observation is that caste has become politicized; another
is that caste has communalized politics. Professor Rajni Kothari insists: "It is not politics that gets caste-ridden; it is caste that gets politicized."[41] But another comment by the same close student of Indian
politics may be more relevant: "Where caste itself forms a political
category, it is futile to argue as to whether caste uses politics or politics
uses caste."[42]

The caste system is indelibly linked with traditional Hindu society.
One would assume, therefore, that it operates in politics, as in society,

[38] M. N. Srinivas, "The Cohesive Role of Sanskritization," in Mason, ed.,
*India and Ceylon,* pp. 67–68.

[39] Srinivas, "Caste in Modern India," *The Radical Humanist,* Nov. 10,
1967, p. 558.

[40] On caste associations see Lloyd I. Rudolph and Susanne Hoeber Rudolph, "The Political Role of India's Caste Associations," *Pacific Affairs,*
XXXIII (March, 1960), and Rudolph and Rudolph, *The Modernity of Tradition,* pp. 30–36, 52–54, 61–64, 125–126. On caste federations, see Rajni
Kothari and Rushikesh Maru, "Federating for Political Interests: The Kshatriyas of Gujarat," in Rajni Kothari, ed., *Caste in Indian Politics* (New Delhi,
1969).

[41] Kothari, *Politics in India,* p. 240.

[42] *Ibid.,* p. 226.

as a traditional force and is an impediment to modernization and political development. There is certainly plenty of evidence, as any first-hand observer can testify, of the reactionary and stultifying influence of caste. But some students of Indian politics hold that in the political arena, where it assumes new dimensions and operates in different ways, caste is becoming a significant force for modernization and social change.[43] This is an intriguing thesis, one that still has to be tested in the crucible of Indian political life.

Many observers warn against attaching too much importance to caste as a factor in Indian politics. It is obviously important, but it is often overshadowed by others. Rajni Kothari refers to "the emerging world of secularism in which caste is only one of many components entering into the political process," and he states that "caste has turned into just another variable in politics, along with many other variables."[44] But even if caste is demoted from a "determinant" of Indian political behavior to just an "ethnic variable," it is still an important variable indeed. No serious student of Indian politics can afford to overlook or neglect it.

**Scheduled Castes and Tribes.** More than one-fifth of the population of India today belongs to scheduled castes and scheduled tribes. According to the Census of 1961, 14.2 per cent belonged to the former, and 6.8 per cent to the latter. They constituted over one-third of the population of Orissa and Madhya Pradesh, and were also particularly numerous in Rajasthan, West Bengal, and Assam. Kerala and Kashmir, on the other hand, had very few members of scheduled tribes, and less than 10 per cent belonging to scheduled castes.

The scheduled castes are the untouchables of Indian society. Gandhi called them Harijans, "Children of God," and did much to contribute to their political as well as social uplift. They still suffer innumerable social restrictions, and their influence in politics is by no means in keeping with their numbers. Some scheduled castes, notably the Mahars in Maharashtra, have become significant political forces. Untouchables have served as Chief Ministers, members of the national and State Parliaments, Presidents of the Congress Party, and members of the central Cabinet.

The scheduled castes have their own party, the Republican Party, the successor to the Scheduled Castes Federation, founded and led for many years by India's most famous untouchable, Dr. B. R. Ambedkar. Toward the end of his life, Dr. Ambedkar, discouraged by the slow progress of untouchables within Hinduism, led many of them, espe-

---

[43] This seems to be a central theme of Rudolph and Rudolph, *The Modernity of Tradition,* and to some extent it is also endorsed by Kothari.
[44] Kothari, *Politics in India,* p. 241.

cially his fellow-Mahars, in a mass conversion to Buddhism. Some of these are today known as neo-Buddhists.

Scheduled tribes have been especially active, politically speaking, in Bihar, especially through the Jharkhand Party; in Assam, where they have had their own party, the All-Party Hill Leaders' Conference, and where, in 1970, they were given their own "autonomous" state of Meghalaya; and in Orissa and Madhya Pradesh. The State of Nagaland, the specially-administered territory of NEFA, and the Union Territories of Manipur and Tripura, are almost wholly tribal units.

There is still considerable controversy over the proper policies to follow with respect to tribal communities. Isolation, assimilation, and integration have been proposed as possible alternatives. One authority deplores "the widespread unwillingness to face the fact that the 30 millions of aboriginals will for a long time to come form a separate and unassimilated element within the Indian nation."[45] Another, however, points out that "The tribal people everywhere are being drawn increasingly into wider social, economic, and political networks."[46]

**Factionalism.** "To understand India's 'politics and society' one has to realise the significance of 'factions' in the process of mediating between the Indian social structure and the specialized processes of government, law and politics."[47] Factions, which may be defined as "vertical structures of power cutting across caste and class divisions," have been a traditional and pervasive feature of Indian society and politics. At the village level, as almost every village study has indicated, factions have almost always existed, and they have often been more important than caste, although they are, of course, more unstable and less cohesive groups. Opposing factions, sometimes including members of the same castes or even of the same families, have often divided entire villages into two or more antagonistic groups.

In State politics factionalism has been rampant, and in the States of the north Indian heartland — Bihar, Uttar Pradesh, Madhya Pradesh, Haryana, and the Punjab — it seems to have become chronic.[48] "Bipolar factional politics at the State level is quite often denominated as the 'ministerialist group' and the 'dissident group.' The first group is led by the faction leader in power, the Chief Minister, and the second

[45] Christoph von Fürer-Haimendorf, "The Position of the Tribal Populations in Modern India," in Mason, ed., *India and Ceylon,* p. 212.

[46] Béteille, "The Future of the Backward Classes," p. 115.

[47] Shashishekhar Jha, "Factionalism," *Seminar,* No. 107 (July, 1968), p. 36. Oscar Lewis, *Group Dynamics in a North Indian Village* (New Delhi, 1954); and D. F. Miller, "Factions in Indian Village Politics," *Pacific Affairs,* XXXVIII (Spring, 1965), 17–31.

[48] See Paul R. Brass, *Factional Politics in an Indian State: The Congress Party in Uttar Pradesh* (Berkeley, Calif., 1965).

group is led by the opposing factional leader who may or may not be a minister. The situation is marked by fluidity."[49]

Factionalism is also prevalent in national politics. The Congress Party, long the dominant party in Indian politics, has been troubled by factions for many years, although these were kept under control while Jawaharlal Nehru was alive. Since his death the divisions within the Party, largely of a factional nature, have become more obvious, and were the main factors in the split in the Party in 1969.

**Religion and Politics: Secularism and the Communal Divide.** As the homeland of two of the world's great religions, Hinduism and Buddhism, with the third largest concentration of Muslims in any country, with small but significant pockets of Sikhs, Parsis, and Christians (of several varieties), and with large numbers of tribals and others whose religious views are more akin to animism than to any formal religion, India is inescapably a land of religious pluralism. But it is primarily a land of the Hindus, who constitute some three-fourths of the population and who dominate Indian politics just as they dominate social and religious life.

For many centuries, from the coming of the Aryans in the second millennium B.C. until the consolidation of Muslim control over much of the subcontinent some 3,000 years later, Hindu dominance was virtually unquestioned. In recent years, after some four centuries of Muslim and British rule, it has been reasserted. The partition of the subcontinent and the creation of a separate Islamic state of Pakistan have left the Hindus in clear command in the new Indian state. (The Muslims who remained are a relatively impotent, but numerically large, minority.)

One of the most dangerous issues that plagues India today is communalism, whose major expression is Hindu-Muslim communalism.[50] Various developments in recent years have led to the growth of communalism, which has been particularly virulent since 1967 and almost as pervasive as caste and factionalism. It was, for example, apparently the main factor leading to widespread rioting and bloodshed in Ahmedabad and elsewhere in Gujarat in September 1969 — in Gandhi's part of India and almost on the eve of the centenary of his birth — and in central Maharashtra in May 1970. According to the Indian Home

[49] Jha, "Factionalism," p. 37.

[50] Communalism "is the term given in India and Pakistan to the sense of insecurity which any community feels and the accompanying action it takes to protect itself and further its own interests. It is applied in different localities to groups differentiated by religion, language, region, historical origin, occupation. . . . It is above all applied to the ill-feeling existing in Hindu-Muslim relationships." W. Norman Brown, *The United States and India and Pakistan* (Cambridge, Mass., 1953), pp. 112–113.

Ministry, in 1969 there were 519 communal incidents in India, an increase of 50 per cent over the previous year.

Like caste, communalism has had a profound impact on Indian politics. It has been strongly condemned by leaders of the Government and of most political parties, but it is closely related to Indian political behavior and practice. "Universal adult suffrage and regular elections have placed power in the hands of the illiterate masses who are still highly susceptible to appeals to communalism and caste loyalties."[51] Evidence of this susceptibility can be found in every part of India, as a study of the activities of political parties and of elections will starkly reveal.

Several Indian political parties are organized mainly along communal lines and rely mainly on communal appeals. These include the Akali Dal, a Sikh political and social organization in the Punjab, and the Muslim League, which has considerable support in northern Kerala. The Jana Sangh, one of the so-called national parties, has often been described as a communal party. It denies the accuracy of this description, but it has become "the chief spokesman for Hindu interests in Indian politics" and "it has been heavily dependent on a close link with the Rashtriya Swayamsevak Sangh (RSS), a group completely committed to the communalist Hindu Rashtra ideology."[52]

Gandhi, Nehru, and other leaders of modern India have spoken out strongly against communalism. Hindu-Muslim unity was one of the passionate desires of Gandhi. In fact, he was assassinated in January 1948 by a Hindu fanatic who resented his attitude toward the Muslims. Most of the Indian leaders, especially Jawaharlal Nehru, have been strongly devoted to the principle of the secular state. Secularism was one of the fundamental principles of the Indian Constitution and of the Indian state. Some observers regard it as Nehru's greatest contribution to his beloved India and to the Indian people.

In many respects India is one of the most unlikely and unpromising places for the establishment of a secular state.[53] It is a religiously impregnated society. Religion is the warp and woof of its very being. Yet the conscious dedication of India's leaders to secularism, however much it is violated in practice, is a fact of great importance. It may yet overcome, or at least bring under tolerable control, the communal virus which is still such a serious threat to India's existence as a unified state.

**Regionalism and Language.** Much of the politics of India has centered around questions of regionalism and language. These questions

[51] Donald E. Smith, "The Political Implications of Asian Religions," in Donald E. Smith, ed., *South Asian Politics and Religion* (Princeton, N.J., 1966), pp. 24–25.

[52] *Ibid.,* p. 25.

[53] See Donald E. Smith, *India as a Secular State* (Princeton, N.J., 1963).

are particularly difficult, for they have deep historical and cultural roots and relate to some of the deepest divisions in Indian society and in India's historical experience. Like most Indian problems, they are multi-dimensional.

India's regions may be delineated in various ways. Geographically the obvious divisions are the Himalayan regions to the far north, the vast Gangetic plain in the north, center, and east, and the Deccan plateau and surrounding coastal regions in the south. Culturally and historically, and to some extent geographically, the divisions are much more complex, centering mainly on different racial, ethnic, and cultural groupings. The main divide here is that between north and south, between the Hindi-speaking heartland and the non-Hindi-speaking coastlands, between Aryan and Dravidian India.

India is preeminently a multinational nation, with many subnations with different historical, cultural, and linguistic characteristics and experience. Many of these subnations can be identified from a geographic, cultural and linguistic point of view. Thus one can speak of a Bengali, a Tamil, a Maratha, and a Sikh "nation" or "subnation." These "subnations" are very conscious and very proud of their own history, culture, and identity and are rather suspicious of any real or imagined efforts to dominate them from the outside, especially from the Hindi-speaking "imperialists" (often regarded as culturally inferior even though they are numerically larger) of north India.

One of the main barriers to the achievement of national integration in India is the strong hold of subnational loyalties and the difficulty of developing a hierarchy of loyalties, granting preeminence to loyalty to the nation.

Problems of regionalism are clearly related to those of language. Since the States Reorganization Act of 1956 the Union of India has been divided largely into linguistic States. This process was consolidated, if not completed, by the division of Bombay State in 1960 into the States of Gujarat and Maharashtra, each with its own dominant language, and the division of the already divided Punjab in 1966 into Haryana (Hindi-speaking) and the Punjab (thus giving the Sikhs, not primarily a linguistic group, a "homeland" where they can develop their own identity and perhaps cultivate their own language as well). Thus all of the fourteen main languages of India, as specified in the Eighth Schedule of the Indian Constitution of 1950, except Sanskrit and Urdu, are dominant in one or more of the Indian States, and all except one of these twelve (Hindi) are dominant in only one State.

The language question was the subject of lengthy, and sometimes bitter, debates in the Indian Constituent Assembly. The result of these debates was a compromise embodied in the Constitution, designating fourteen "languages of India." (Sindhi was later added as a fifteenth recognized language.)  Hindi was the "official language" for all purposes but English could be used for at least fifteen years.  In 1955, in accordance with Article 344 of the Constitution, the President of India appointed an Official Language Commission, which two years later recommended, with some major dissenting votes, that Hindi should progressively replace English, with a suggested official changeover on January 26, 1965.  The Official Languages Act of 1963 embodied this recommendation.

Despite Nehru's personal "assurances" that the Act would not be implemented in a manner prejudicial to the interests of the non-Hindi-speaking peoples, fears of Hindi domination remained, and after Nehru's death led to strong protests and violence culminating in the self-immolation of two political leaders in Madras City in 1965.  After further agitated debate and protracted negotiations, a "three-language formula," apparently more acceptable than that set forth in the Official Languages Act, was endorsed in a resolution of the national Parliament in 1965.  This formula provides for the continued use of Hindi and English on the national scene and gives regional languages recognized status in the States and to some extent on the national level as well.

In terms of numbers of speakers, Hindi is clearly the predominant — but not the dominant — Indian language.  According to the Census of 1961 Hindi was the main language of 30.4 per cent of the population, and if the main related languages of the Hindi group — Urdu, Panjabi, Bihari, and Rajasthani — are included, of 54.4 per cent.  Moreover, many more millions can speak, or at least understand, Hindi, whether they will admit it or not.  No other language is spoken by more than 8 or 9 per cent of the population, although about 25 per cent speak Dravidian languages (Tamil, Telegu, Kannada, and Malayalam).  The *Linguistic Survey of India,* published in 1927, listed 1,652 "mother tongues," including 179 "languages" and 544 "dialects," and the Census of India of 1961 recorded speakers of 1,018 different "languages." India is obviously a land of many tongues where 73.3 per cent of the people, based on the 1961 Census, speak Indo-Aryan languages, and 24.5 per cent Dravidian.  Of the whole population, 87 per cent have one of the fourteen "languages of India" listed in the Indian Constitution as their "mother tongue."

With such a linguistic mosaic it is obviously difficult, if not impossible, to find a suitable national language.  The problem is greatly complicated by the strong historical, cultural, and regional aversion to Hindi and the fears of Hindi "imperialism" in the non-Hindi-speaking States, especially in Tamil Nadu (whose DMK leaders have banned the use of Hindi in the schools of the State!).  Regional languages are being developed in many ways, and the dangers of linguistic isolationism and provincialism are increasing. On the other hand, knowledge of both Hindi and English is also increasing, and some of the most ardent champions of linguistic autonomy are also proving to be good citizens of India.[54]

## Prospects for Democracy in India

One of the greatest experiments in human history is going on in India today. Many millions of people are trying to attain a tolerable standard of existence and decent political, economic, and social institutions, in the face of tremendous obstacles from within and from without, and to achieve these goals in a democratic way.

The factors which militate against democracy are indeed formidable. India's political traditions and most of its social systems and conventions are far more authoritarian than democratic. India is still bedeviled by local and regional loyalties. There is still little real sense of national unity. On the one hand, India is still in search of national unity, and centrifugal tendencies are strong; on the other, the Central Government has assumed an increasing amount of authority and power, although since Nehru's death the trend seems to have been mainly in the other direction. Thus democracy is threatened by both centrifugal and centripetal tendencies.

Pressures from without also place India's experiment in democracy in peril. The general world situation, especially as it affects Asia, is not conducive to genuine democracy. Pressures from Communist China have already added greatly to India's problems.

Democracy does not seem to flourish in Asian soil. Most of the new states of Asia adopted democratic forms, but in almost all of them these forms have been superseded by various types of authoritarian rule. Thus far India is a conspicuous and almost solitary holdout against the erosion of democracy in the new Asian states.

In 1969 a concerned observer wrote: "The subcontinent offers the worst possible nursery for democracy. It has one of the world's lowest standards of living, widespread illiteracy, a living powerful tradition of feudalism, massive unemployment and almost insuperable poverty which combine to deny its population more than a fraction of its rising expectations."[55] The test of India's democratic system will be its capacity to find ways to meet the growing demands of more and more people under continuing conditions of scarcity. If India's leaders, who have deliberately chosen the democratic way, fail to meet these needs, they will be forced to give way to other leaders who will take India

[54] Kothari, *Politics in India*, p. 331.
[55] Derek Davies, in the *Far Eastern Economic Review*, LXV (May 15, 1969).

along authoritarian paths, in the direction of communalism, military rule, or some form of totalitarianism.

As India entered a period of greater political instability in the post-Nehru era, more and more foreign and Indian observers began to express doubts about the stability, and even about the prospects for survival, of parliamentary democracy in India.[56] In 1969, Nirad C. Chaudhuri, a noted iconoclast, declared flatly that the party system, and along with it parliamentary democracy, had failed, and that "We must now think of an alternative method by which the government of the country may be carried on";[57] and on January 1, 1970, he wrote of the "breakdown of the parliamentary system of government based on the party system, and the growth of lawlessness throughout the country."[58] In 1967, shortly before the fourth general election, Neville Maxwell, a long-time correspondent of the London *Times* in India, wrote an article entitled "India's Disintegrating Democracy," and in an article in the *Sunday Times* of November 30, 1969, he called attention to the growing weakening of the central Government of India and to many evidences of governmental "impotence." "Indians," he wrote, "are now beginning to ask the question outsiders posed some years ago: Can the parliamentary system withstand the country's unstable conditions?"

Obviously Mr. Maxwell fears that the answer will be in the negative. Hence he also posed the question, "What alternatives are there?" and he confessed that he saw no clear answer or answers to this question. The alternatives which he listed were a Communist takeover, probably spearheaded by Maoists; or a military regime, with the Army in direct or indirect control; or "a limping version of the present system," which would be "the post-Moghul pattern — or the broken-back State." "What is in prospect," he believes, "is not a coup but a steady decline of the civil authority which seems likely to create a need ultimately for an alternative centre of power."[59]

Other alternative scenarios have been proposed. These include various Gandhian-type systems of extreme political decentralization, inverting the pyramid of political power so that real power rests with the villages and other units at the base of the pyramid and relatively little with the central authorities at the apex. A version of this alternative

[56] See, for example, Harrison, *India: the Most Dangerous Decades* and Amaury de Riencourt, *The Soul of India* (New York, 1960).

[57] Quoted in Joseph Lelyveld, "Indian Democracy, under Continuing Pressure, Nears a Test of Survival," *The New York Times,* June 1, 1969.

[58] Nirad C. Chaudhuri, "The Anarchic Indian at Decade's End," *The Statesman,* Jan. 1, 1970.

[59] Neville Maxwell, "Parliamentary System on Trial in India," *Sunday Times,* Nov. 30, 1969.

would be the system of "partyless democracy," which Jayaprakash Narayan has long championed. Another alternative that is often predicted is political fragmentation, i.e., the disintegration of the Indian Union. Still another is the establishment of a kind of Hindu Raj, a Hindu-dominated India in which non-Hindus would be tolerated so long as they did not challenge the essentially Hindu, nonsecular basis of the State. The RSS, and to some extent the Jana Sangh Party, which has close ties to the RSS, seem to have this kind of India in mind.

Many other scenarios conceive of the breakdown of democracy and the establishment of some kind of authoritarian regime of the Left or Right. Another, and less drastic, alternative that is sometimes advocated is to change from a parliamentary to a presidential system, either by reinterpreting the present Constitution so as to strengthen the central Government by resorting more freely to the emergency powers of the President, or by using electoral or other means to end the parliamentary system and to establish a strong presidential system, perhaps along the lines of Pakistan under Ayub Khan, or France under de Gaulle.

The system will obviously be severely tested during the period of readjustment and recurrent crises that lies ahead. The era of coalition politics has already begun. This will witness almost continuous instability, defections, and shifting alliances. Under such conditions, which will probably be aggravated by inept leadership, inadequate performance, internal divisions and cleavages of many kinds, and mounting levels of agitation and violence, the prospects for Indian democracy are none too bright. A well-established democratic system would be severely tested by these problems, and the Indian system of democracy has not yet developed deep roots. One cannot rule out the possibilities of "either prolonged instability and stagnation or an ideological polarization that would lead to chaos."[60] India may indeed become "a broken-back State," or come under some kind of authoritarian rule.

However, the prospects for democracy in India have immeasurably heightened by the success of the Indian political experiment during the first decades of independence. As has been pointed out, India has been fortunate in its leadership. On the whole, the Constitution is working well. Economic and social changes have for the most part been conducive to greater social mobility and to greater participation by the people in the life of the nation. The Five Year Plans have contributed to the process of economic development, and some aspects of them, such as the Community Development Program, the National Extension Service, and Panchayati Raj, have had a direct appreciable impact on millions of people. The basic decisions have been made, and the great task

[60] Kothari, *Politics in India,* p. 190.

ahead is to preserve past gains and to make independence meaningful for the masses of the people.

Fortunately there is a great deal of room for compromise, change, accommodation, participation, and reconciliation within India's present system of "bargaining federalism." It is a flexible system, which can be adapted to considerable changes in the locus of power. As Michael Brecher observed in 1967, "the all-India segment of the Indian political system is stable, mature, sophisticated, and resilient. Its survival potential is high, in the absence of overwhelming disturbance of the system from outside, notably massive invasion or unremitting economic crisis."[61] India has a way of confounding its "prophets of doom," and there are grounds for hope that the Indian political system will continue along essentially democratic lines.

[61] Michael Brecher, "Succession in India 1967: The Routinization of Political Change," *Asian Survey,* VII (July, 1967), 443.

# 2

# Hindus, Moguls, and John Company

The Indian subcontinent, with the possible exception of the Chinese mainland, has been the center of the oldest high-level civilization in the world. This fact should be constantly borne in mind in any discussion of contemporary India. If India is a new nation, it is a very old land. As Jawaharlal Nehru wrote in *The Discovery of India:* "We are very old, and trackless centuries whisper in our ears."[1]

Discoveries in the present century at various places in the Indus valley, notably at Mohenjo-daro, Kot Diji, and Harappa, have revealed the existence of an advanced urban culture as early as 2500 or perhaps even 3000 B.C. Thus the Harappa culture of the Indus valley is apparently as old as the civilizations of the Tigris-Euphrates and the Nile valleys, and may have been "the most extensive civilization of the pre-classical world."[2] According to Sir Mortimer Wheeler, the Indus civilization covered an area of nearly half a million square miles, and its two main centers, Harappa in the Punjab and Mohenjo-daro in Sind, were more than three miles in circumference. "It is tempting," wrote Sir Mortimer, "to infer something like an imperial status for so uniform a civilization. . . . If at any rate the underlying influence is correct, . . . then the Indus Civilization exemplifies the vastest political experiment before the advent of the Roman Empire."[3]

A Western student of Indian history is constantly baffled by the length and complexity of the story; by the strange intermixture of leg-

[1] Jawaharlal Nehru, *The Discovery of India* (New York, 1946), p. 144.
[2] Sir Mortimer Wheeler, *Early India and Pakistan to Ashoka* (rev. ed., New York, 1968), p. 94.
[3] *Ibid.*, p. 98.

end, religion, and history; by the mystical otherwordliness and life negation of the Hindus; by the lack of reliable written records until well into the medieval period; by a long series of invasions; by the rise and fall of innumerable petty kingdoms, "states," and "republics," with little concept of political unity and no actual unity, except to a limited degree in a few scattered periods; by the strange patterns of life and thought that developed in the subcontinent; and by the general lack of a true historical outlook among the Indian people.[4]

For modern India and Pakistan are the products of centuries of evolution and the experiences of the many racial groups that have either amalgamated or coexisted in the subcontinent. Their history has been marked by three main periods of very unequal length: the Hindu period, beginning with or soon after the Aryans came to India nearly 3,500 years ago and extending until the decline of Hindu culture after the tenth or eleventh century A.D.; the Muslim period, beginning with the first major invasions by the Muslims not long after the death of Mohammed and reaching both its apex and its age of decline under the Moguls; and the British period, lasting about two hundred years from the consolidation of British power in the middle of the eighteenth century until the British withdrawal in 1947. Two of these periods merit special attention: the early Hindu, when Hindu culture reached its zenith and Hindu society, institutions, and beliefs were largely shaped; and the British, when the impact of Western ideas and institutions had a great effect on the development of modern India and Pakistan. The Harappa culture of the pre-Hindu period, as we have seen, was also of importance, and of course the years since independence, even though only an instant in historical time, are the most important of all for the student of contemporary affairs.

It should be noted that this periodicization of Indian history is artificial and is used here simply for the purposes of convenience. It was popularized by British writers, notably James Mill, in the first half of the nineteenth century, and has been strongly objected to by some In-

---

[4] There is considerable controversy over the oft-repeated claim that Indians lack "a true historical outlook." The author of a profound but highly controversial interpretation of Indian history wrote; "If the history of the Indians is as shadowy as has already been pointed out on more than one occasion, it is largely because, of all the people on this earth, they were the least interested in history. . . . The key to an understanding of Indian culture lies precisely in this total indifference toward history, toward the very process of *time.*" Amaury de Riencourt, *The Soul of India* (New York, 1960), p. 15. For a different point of view, see C. H. Philips, ed., *Historians of India, Pakistan and Ceylon* (London, 1961), and Majumdar, "A Defence," *Seminar,* No. 39 (November, 1962), pp. 13–17. This entire issue of *Seminar,* under the general title of "Past and Present," is devoted to a symposium "on the attitudes and approaches to a study of history."

dian historians as historically misleading and even invalid. To describe the long centuries between the coming of the Aryans and the rise of Muslim power as the Hindu period is not very informative and may create misunderstandings regarding the complexity of Indian history over a period of nearly three millennia. To characterize later periods as Muslim and British is even more misleading, for the labels refer only to the temporarily ruling minority groups and not to the whole gamut of India's historical experience during these five centuries.[5]

## The Hindu Period

We may think of the Hindu period as extending roughly for 1,500 years before and after the beginning of the Christian era. The coming of the Indo-Aryan people, apparently from south central Asia, in the second millennium B.C. was more of a folk movement than an invasion. The Aryans spread out over much of the western and northern part of the subcontinent. The Dravidians were forced into the south. Over the centuries a good deal of intermixture has occurred between Aryans and Dravidians, but even today the dominant racial stock of south India is Dravidian while that of most of the north and west is Aryan.

The two great religio-philosophical systems which developed in the Indian subcontinent, Hinduism and Buddhism (as well as Jainism), began to emerge shortly after the coming of the Indo-Aryan peoples.

**Hinduism.** Hinduism is perhaps more philosophy, or metaphysics, than religion in any specific sense, although it may also be used as a term to apply to a wide range of religious beliefs and postures, ranging from something akin to animism to monotheism, with a strong emphasis on pantheism in most instances. Most Hindus do not regard themselves as monotheists, although they do recognize Brahma, the creator, the source of all things, as one of the holy triad of Hinduism, along with Vishnu, the preserver, and Shiva, the destroyer. Vishnu appears in many incarnations (avatars), the most popular of which is in the form of Krishna. Shiva, with his many arms, his many fierce incarnations, and his terrible consort, Kali, has always exercised an irresistible fascination for many Hindus.[6] "The story of Shiva," suggests Frank Moraes, "is symbolic of the emotional and contemplative mosaic which enmeshes Hindu thought and character."[7] Cults dedicated to the worship of Vishnu or Shiva, or their various incarnations, have flourished and still flourish in many parts of India.

[5] See Romila Thapar, Harbans Mukhia and Bipan Chandra, *Communalism and the Writing of Indian History* (Bombay, 1969).
[6] See A. L. Basham, *The Wonder That Was India* (3rd rev. ed., New York, 1968), pp. 302–313.
[7] Frank Moraes, *India Today* (New York, 1960), p. 4.

Most of the basic beliefs and doctrines of India have their origin in Hindu ideology. Among these are the so-called four ends of life: *artha, karma, dharma,* and *moksha.* It is impossible to give meaningful English equivalents of these terms; they symbolize, respectively, material gain, the pursuit of love and pleasure, duty, and salvation. These concepts have had a central place in Indian thought and action — or inaction.[8] Other concepts, such as *maya,* illusion, and *ahimsa,* nonviolence, are inextricably associated with Hinduism, although *ahimsa,* which Gandhi made one of his motivating doctrines, is emphasized even more in Buddhism and in Jainism. *Ahimsa,* in the opinion of W. Norman Brown, is "the most dynamic concept of Indian ethics since the days of Buddha and Mahavira, 2500 years ago."[9]

Hinduism is also associated with more formal systems of philosophy, stemming many centuries ago from Brahmanism and from the influence of great Hindu philosophers, such as Shankara. The best known of all the formal systems of Hindu philosophy are the Saddar-Shana, or the six doctrines or schools, namely Nyaya, Vaishesika, Samkhya, Yoga, Mimamsa, and Vedanta.[10] They have all had a profound impact on Indian thought, and in various ways are still influential. This is especially true of Yoga and Vedanta. Yoga — a word which means union — emphasizes the discipline of the body and the mind. Vedanta, stemming from Brahmanism and from the classic Upanishads, was developed into a system known as Advaita Vedanta, or nondualist Vedanta, several centuries later by Shankara. Noted Nehru, who professed to be an agnostic although his traditions were Hindu: "It is this philosophy which represents the dominant philosophic outlook of Hinduism today."[11]

For a Western student Hinduism offers special problems of understanding and interpretation. It is a most complicated and varied religious-philosophical-metaphysical creed, ranging from ideas which seem to be without form and almost without substance to some of the most rigid and systematic of philosophic systems. It does not have generally accepted interpreters, and it is one of the most tolerant and absorptive of religions or philosophies. Because Hindus believe that while truth is one, there are many roads leading to it, they tend to react negatively to advocates of a proselytizing religion, like Islam or Christianity. It is

[8] See William Theodore de Bary, ed., *Sources of Indian Tradition* (New York, 1958), I, 206–361.

[9] "Indian National Ideals Today," Mary Keatinge Das Memorial Lecture, Columbia University, Nov. 28, 1955.

[10] See Basham, *The Wonder That Was India,* pp. 325–331.

[11] Jawaharlal Nehru, *The Discovery of India* (New York, 1946), p. 182. See also de Bary, ed., *Sources of Indian Tradition,* I, 295–302.

particularly hard for Westerners to grasp the intricacies of Hinduism, whether viewed as an inchoate body of folk beliefs, or as a complicated and subtle pattern of philosophic systems, or as the worship of various cults dedicated to Vishnu, Shiva, or their incarnations. Yet there is no escaping the importance of Hinduism in the Indian experience. As T. Walter Wallbank has pointed out, "Hinduism, or the Hindu way of life, is one of the most important historical ingredients of modern India."[12]

**The Caste System.** Any study of Hindu society must give special attention to the caste system, one of the most rigid social systems ever evolved in any part of the world. It emerged in India, along with Hinduism itself, many centuries ago, and was chiefly associated with the Indo-Aryan invaders. It developed its distinctive features and its rigidity over the centuries. It became in fact "the central feature of Hindu society. . . . Throughout the centuries the caste system gave Indian society stability, and so partially compensated for the lack of large-scale political genius displayed in much of the Hindu period."[13]

In ancient India four main castes emerged: the Brahmans, the highest caste, the scholars and "priests" of Hinduism; the Kshatriyas, the nobles and warriors, to which most of the rulers of various kingdoms and small "states" belonged; the Vaisyas, the merchants and traders; and the Sudras, the workers. Members of the three upper castes were the "Twice-Born," the elite of Hindu society. In one way or another most of the more than 2,000 castes and subcastes in India today have stemmed from the four basic castes, but the pattern has become hopelessly complicated, at least for the outsider.

At the bottom of the social scale were the untouchables, people without caste, although even among this large group there were grades and variations. The untouchables of India became "the largest subordinate racial group in the world";[14] they were subject to all kinds of discrimination and were forbidden to have any but the most rigidly circumscribed dealings with caste Hindus. Today there are some

[12] T. Walter Wallbank, *A Short History of India and Pakistan* (New York, 1958), p. 37.

[13] Sir Percival Griffiths, *Modern India* (New York, 1957), p. 31. See also M. N. Srinivas, *Caste in Modern India, and Other Essays* (London, 1962); M. N. Srinivas, *Social Change in Modern India* (Berkeley, Calif., 1966); A. C. Meyer, *Caste and Kinship in Central India* (London, 1960); M. Singer and B. S. Cohn, eds., *Structure and Change in Indian Society* (Chicago, 1968).

[14] Louise Ouwerkerk, *The Untouchables of India* (London, 1945), p. 3. The term "untouchable" has virtually disappeared from the Indian vocabulary, although untouchability has by no means disappeared from Indian life. The official designation of the untouchables is "Scheduled Castes." Gandhi referred to them as "Harijans," meaning "Children of God."

60,000,000 untouchables in India. Most of them still live in segregated areas and do menial tasks. In villages, the strongholds of Hindu orthodoxy, many of the old taboos still exist. But untouchability is now officially illegal, and untouchables have more opportunities than they have ever enjoyed in the past. They are given special opportunities in schools and certain professions, and today a few untouchables occupy high positions in government and business. But they are still considered untouchables, and will so remain until a profound change occurs in the minds of the caste Hindus.[15]

The caste system itself is still a powerful influence in India, although it is changing rapidly.[16] Along with the joint family system,[17] another traditional Hindu institution, it determines the patterns of life of most Hindus: how they live, what they eat, whom they marry, what professions they enter, what societal obligations they must accept. Gandhi, although strongly opposed to untouchability, saw some social values in the caste system; but many of the leaders of modern India have rejected this notion. Nehru, a high caste Brahman of Kashmiri descent, stated flatly that "in the social organization of today it has no place left"; the "aristocratic approach based on traditionalism" on which it was based "has to change completely, for it is wholly opposed to modern conditions and the democratic ideal."[18]

**Buddhism and Jainism.**    Buddhism, with its emphasis on "the noble eightfold path" to *nirvana*, is an offshoot of Hinduism. Siddhartha Gautama, who became known as the Buddha ("the enlightened one"), was a Kshatriya, son of the chief of a tribe occupying a small territory in the Himalayan foothills, who lived in the sixth and fifth centuries B.C. At the age of 29 he renounced a life of ease, spent many years as a hermit and wanderer, and finally attained "the great enlightenment."

Buddhism is less formal than Hinduism, and places greater emphasis on self-denial and compassion. Its fundamental teaching is embodied in the famous "Sermon of the Turning of the Wheel of Law," which the Buddha is said to have preached to his first disciples in a deer park near Varanasi (Benares). This contains the "four noble truths" — exis-

---

[15] See J. Michael Maher, ed., *The Untouchables in Contemporary India* (Tucson, Arizona, 1970).

[16] See Singer and Cohn, *Structure and Change in Indian Society.*

[17] The joint family system is a traditional larger family unit within the Hindu caste framework. "Within the caste the traditional unit has been the 'joint family,' which consists of a man, his wife (or wives), and all his descendants except the married females, living in a common household, the earnings of each member being in some measure the property of all. . . . This system has largely broken down in modern India as the economic structure has been changing." W. Norman Brown, *The United States and India and Pakistan* (Cambridge, Mass., 1953), pp. 32–33.

[18] Nehru, *Discovery of India,* p. 532.

tence is sorrow or suffering, which arises from desire or passion and which ceases when desire or passion ceases; such a state can be achieved by following the "noble eightfold path" (right views, right resolves, right speech, right conduct, right livelihood, right effort, right recollection, and right meditation). Buddhism employs the "middle way," a concept which is often said to characterize many aspects of Indian life, thought, and conduct, and even domestic and foreign policy. It teaches that suffering can be stopped by the sublimation of desire, "by taking a middle course between self-indulgence and extreme asceticism and leading a normal and well-ordered life." The final goal of man is to escape from existence into a state of blissful non-existence — *nirvana* (a Sanskrit word meaning annihilation).[19]

Buddhism flourished in India for centuries, even after reaching its height in the third century B.C. Many *stupas* — mounds over the divided ashes of the Buddha or the remains of local saints and ascetics — and monasteries were built. At an early period Buddhism was carried outside of the Indian subcontinent, and it became the dominant religion of much of Southeast and East Asia.

By the time of the Guptas (fourth to sixth century A.D.) or shortly thereafter, Buddhism as a whole was in a state of decline. In many parts of India it lost its identity as a separate religion; but some of its monasteries, notably Nalanda, one of the greatest centers of Indian medieval learning anywhere in the world, continued to be important until the Muslim invasions. After the fifteenth century Buddhism virtually disappeared from the Indian scene. In the twentieth century it experienced a modest revival, with some significant political overtones, as in the mass conversion to Buddhism in 1956 of some 250,000 Hindu untouchables, and in the formation of a political party whose members are mostly untouchables or neo-Buddhists, known first as the Scheduled Castes Federation and later as the Republican Party.

Jainism, another offshoot of Hinduism, was founded, according to Jainist tradition, by twenty-four Tirthankanas (saints), of whom Mahavira — contemporary of the Buddha — was the last. Jainism emphasizes asceticism and self-discipline. Each *yati* (ascetic) must take five vows: to injure no living thing, to speak the truth, to abstain from stealing, to renounce all worldly goods, and to practice sexual continence. This ascetic religious system never attracted large numbers of followers, but it exercised an influence in India far out of keeping with its numbers. Gandhi, for example, was profoundly influenced by it. Today there are some 2,000,000 Jains in India. Unlike Buddhism, it never spread beyond India.[20]

[19] See Basham, *The Wonder That Was India*, pp. 270–271.
[20] See de Bary, ed., *Sources of Indian Tradition*, I, 35–89; and Basham, *The Wonder That Was India*, pp. 289–297.

**The Classics of Hinduism.**   The great classics of Hinduism, as well as of Buddhism and Jainism, date from the Hindu period. Most Hindu literature was written in Sanskrit, most Buddhist writings in Pali or Prakrit, and most Jainist tracts in Prakrit. The best known and most important of Hindu classics are the Vedas, the Upanishads, and the epics. The Vedas, the sacred scriptures of Hinduism, date back to a time shortly after the coming of the Aryans; they were apparently written in Vedic, a parent language of Sanskrit. The oldest and most famous of the Vedas is the *Rig Veda*, some one thousand hymns of praise of different gods, often called the oldest of all the great works of literature and religion known to man. The Upanishads, poetic dialogues on metaphysics, were written after the Vedas, and were in part derived from these earlier classics; they were the source of the major systems of Hindu philosophy, and therefore have been of continuing importance.

The two great Sanksrit epics are the *Mahabharata* and the *Ramayana,* apparently composed sometime between 200 B.C. and 200 A.D. The *Mahabharata,* perhaps the world's longest epic, is a fabulous account of dynastic struggles. In the course of the account of a great battle the philosophical discourse on right action and duty known as the *Bhagavad Gita* appears. *The Bhagavad Gita* is perhaps the most famous piece of Hindu literature. Every student of Indian civilization should read and try to understand this little gem of Hinduism.

The other great epic, the *Ramayana,* is far shorter and more unified than the *Mahabharata.* It tells of the adventures of Rama, who allied himself with Hanuman, king of the monkeys, and fought a mighty war in Ceylon. When he was restored to his Indian kingdom, he subjected his wife, Sita, to various ordeals to test her virtue. The *Ramayana* has been a source of legends, dramas, and folk tales throughout the centuries.[21]

**Hindu Political Thought and Institutions.**   Most of this ancient literature is essentially religious in character and contains little which would normally be classed as political thought. Exceptions are Kautilya's *Arthasastra,* the Manusamhita, the laws of Manu, the most influential Hindu legal work, and the Santiparvan of the *Mahabharata.* These "provide material which can clearly be labeled political thought as distinct from philosophy in general."[22] Ancient Indian political

[21] See Basham, *The Wonder That Was India,* pp. 342–345, 401–417; and W. Norman Brown,"Varieties of Religious Mythology in India," in Samuel Noah Kramer, ed., *Mythologies of the Ancient World* (New York, 1961), pp. 287–304.

[22] Norman D. Palmer, "Indian and Western Political Thought: Coalescence or Clash?", *The American Political Science Review,* XLIX (September, 1955), 755. See also A. S. Altekar, *State and Government in Ancient India* (3rd ed., Delhi, 1958), pp. 1–3.

thought "deals with many subjects which have bulked large in the political theory of the Western world. Among these are the nature and origin of the state, types of states, the relation of state and society, the forms of government, the origin of kingship, the duties of kings, royal authority and its limitations, power politics, diplomacy, and administration. Perhaps we should also include theories of the state of nature, the social contract, and sovereignty, possibly even international law. Conflicting theories of international relations can be found in ancient India as well as in the modern world. The doctrine of *mandala* or circle of states was a kind of Hindu theory of the balance of power, and the doctrine of *sarvabhauma* suggests modern theories of world federation or a world state."[23]

There seems to be general agreement that *dharma* is the central concept of Hindu political thought; indeed, Radhakrishnan has called it the most important concept in Indian thought generally. *Dharma* cannot be defined precisely, but it refers to a man's moral obligations or duty. "In the context of the *dharmashastras* (or Hindu Political Science) the word *dharma* came to mean 'the privileges, duties and obligations of a man, his standard of conduct as a member of the Aryan community, as a member of one of the castes, as a person in a particular stage of life.' "[24] Thus "*dharma* is relative to time, place, circumstances, sex, age, temperament, vocation." Everyone has his *dharma*.

Another basic Hindu political concept is that of the *saptanga,* or the "seven limbs" of the state. These are *svamin* or sovereign, *amatya* or minister, *janapada* or *rastra* referring to territory with people, *durga* or fortress, *kosa* or treasury, *danda* or *bala* meaning sceptre or army, and *mitra* or friends or allies. This doctrine of *saptanga,* in the opinion of Benoy Kumar Sarkar, "constitutes the basis of all political speculation among the Hindu philosophers."[25]

The political systems and institutions which emerged in the Hindu period were varied and complex.[26] Monarchy was the prevailing pattern. Rulers, usually Kshatriyas, often claimed to rule by right, but they

[23] Palmer, "Indian and Western Political Thought," p. 755. See also John W. Spellman, *Political Theory of Ancient India* (Oxford, 1964), pp. 156–159.

[24] K. P. Mukerji, *The State* (Madras, 1952), p. 327. See Appendix I (pp. 321–346), "The Hindu Conception of Dharma." See also Sarvepalli Radhakrishnan, *Indian Philosophy* (New York, 1922), I, 52; Nehru, *Discovery of India,* p. 77; and Spellman, *Political Theory of Ancient India,* pp. 98–107, 211–216.

[25] Benoy Kumar Sarkar, *The Political Institutions and Theories of the Hindus* (Leipzig, 1922), p. 167.

[26] See Spellman, *Political Theory of Ancient India;* Basham, *The Wonder That Was India,* Chap. IV; Altekar, *State and Government in Ancient India;* U. N. Ghoshal, *A History of Indian Political Ideas* (Bombay, 1959); K. P. Jayaswal, *Hindu Polity* (3rd ed., Bangalore, 1955).

were usually subject to certain sanctions, including even a kind of right of rebellion if they abused their power. There were some germs of "democratic" practices in ancient India, chiefly in the existence of a number of so-called republics, the institution of the *panchayat* (council) in many villages, and the recognition of the obligations of rulers to act in the interests of the people; but the dominant tradition was authoritarian.

Ancient India was never brought entirely under a single political state. Two great dynasties, the Mauryan from the fourth to the sixth century B.C. and the Gupta from the fourth to the sixth century A.D., extended their sway over a large part of the subcontinent, except the far south; and one later ruler, Harsha, who reigned over an important north Indian kingdom for more than fifty years in the seventh century, succeeded in extending some measure of control over much of the subcontinent. Kautilya, the author of the classic of Arthasastra writings, was apparently a minister at the court of Chandragupta, the founder of the Mauryan Empire. Kautilya has been called "not only a kingmaker, but also . . . the greatest Indian exponent of the art of government, the duties of kings, ministers, and officials, and the methods of diplomacy."[27] His *Arthasastra* is a very practical manual of statecraft, which has often been compared with Machiavelli's *The Prince*.

The most famous of the Mauryan rulers was Asoka, who ruled in the third century B.C. (c. 268 B.C.–c. 232 B.C.). Asoka has been called "the greatest and noblest ruler India has known,"[28] and was indeed one of the enlightened rulers of history. He is particularly renowned because after long campaigns of conquest, he became a devout Buddhist and devoted himself to the welfare of his subjects and to the arts of peace. His famous edicts, engraved on rocks and pillars throughout his far-flung kingdom, "are the oldest surviving Indian documents of any historical significance."[29] He had a highly organized civil service, and he kept a close watch on it and on all of the affairs of state.[30]

The best known of Gupta rulers was Chandragupta II, who reigned in the late fourth and early fifth centuries A.D. and extended his empire over most of north India. The Gupta period was the golden age of Hindu culture, as exemplified by the dramas and other works of Kalidasa, the cave paintings at Ajanta, and the cultural contributions of

---

[27] J. F. Fleet, Introductory Note in *Kautilya's Arthasastra,* trans. by R. Shamasastry (4th ed., Mysore, 1951), p. v.

[28] Basham, *The Wonder That Was India,* p. 53.

[29] *Ibid.*

[30] See *ibid.,* pp. 53–58; and Wheeler, *Early India and Pakistan to Ashoka,* Chap. IX.

several great universities, the most famous of which was Nalanda, whose scholars later played a large part in spreading Indian culture abroad.

**Contacts with China and Southeast Asia.** India has experienced many waves of invasions by peoples of varying racial and cultural characteristics who have come into the subcontinent through the mountain passes in the west-northwest. Some of these invasions, such as those by Alexander the Great and by many bands of marauders from inner Asia, were brief and had little impact. Others, notably those of the Aryan peoples, had a profound effect upon the racial composition and civilization of India. All the major invading groups which remained in India mingled with the peoples they found there, and were absorbed into the dominant Hindu culture.

In the early Christian era extensive contacts developed with China and Southeast Asia. Buddhist monks and traders traveled by hazardous overland or sea routes to China, and hundreds of Chinese pilgrims and scholars came to India.[31] "It is a striking fact," observes Amaury de Riencourt, "that in all relations between the two Civilizations, the Chinese was always the recipient and the Indian the donor."[32]

From this time, also, dates the Indian impact on Southeast Asia, so great that it is sometimes known as "the Indianization of Southeast Asia" and the area itself is often called "Greater India." "From the first to the ninth centuries A.D., from the zenith of Indian Civilization to its petrifaction, four great waves of colonization hit the southeast, every one of them organized by some powerful South Indian state." These waves of organized colonization were supplemented by the work of Buddhist monks, by a flourishing commerce, and by individual settlements. "Between the second and fifth centuries A.D., Indian kingdoms were founded in Malaya, Cambodia, Vietnam, Sumatra, Java, Bali, and Borneo. Everywhere, Indian influence prevailed over the Chinese, and for evident reasons: an undoubted cultural superiority owing to much greater philosophic and religious insight (China itself fell under the spell of Buddhism), and also to a far more flexible script. Furthermore, Indian Civilization respected the political autonomy of its colonies and the cultural freedom of all its units, and, on the whole, worked through peaceful penetration." Indian influence, dating back to this early period, and accentuated by modern contacts and immigration,

[31] "The most famous of the Chinese travelers to India was Hsuan Tsang, who came in the seventh century when the great T'ang dynasty flourished in China and Harshavardhana ruled over an empire in north India." Nehru, *The Discovery of India,* p. 187. Another famous Chinese pilgrim was Fa Hsien, who came to India in the fifth century and studied at Pataliputra University. See *ibid.,* p. 187, and Basham, *The Wonder That Was India,* p. 67.

[32] De Riencourt, *The Soul of India,* p. 141.

can be found in most of Southeast Asia today, with the exception of Vietnam where Chinese influence predominates.[33]

**Hindu India in Decline.** After the Gupta period Indian influence continued in Southeast Asia, but in India itself the great days of the Hindu era were over. "The Indian political world went back to its anarchic medley of quarreling states and countless dynasties. . . ."[34] In the north, which had been the center of most of the important Hindu empires, only one empire, that of Harsha in the seventh century, seems to have rivaled the mighty empires of the past; and we would know little even about the great Harsha had it not been for the Chinese pilgrim, Hsuan Tsang, who left voluminous records of his work.

The center of power and of culture shifted to the south, which had been the source of the colonizing efforts in Southeast Asia. There important empires rose, flourished, and declined even after the Gupta period. Notable among these were the Pallavas and the Cholas. The Pallavas were the dominant power in the Deccan from the fourth to the ninth century, but they were weakened by incessant wars and fell to the rising Chola power around 1000 A.D. For some two centuries the Cholas were the great power of South India, reaching their zenith in the late tenth and early eleventh centuries. They became a formidable naval power, capturing Ceylon and sending a great expedition to various parts of Southeast Asia. But in the thirteenth century they were torn apart by civil war, and by the following century their empire had completely disintegrated.[35] India in the post-Gupta period was in a state near anarchy. "What India lacked was political unity and social solidarity. Her leaders counted by hundreds; her energy was frittered away in petty squabbles between the various states. She may correctly be described during this period as merely a geographical expression."[36]

To the extent that it was held together at all, Indian society survived because of the unifying force of Hinduism as a philosophic and cultural power and the caste system, and because of the persistence of those institutions of local government which over the centuries had provided some element of stability and protection and even of popular expression amid the tendencies toward absolutism or anarchy.

Thus far Hindu India had been able, for all its lack of unity and fissiparous tendencies, to absorb foreign invaders and to survive despite its political weaknesses. From the thirteenth century on it was faced

[33] *Ibid.,* pp. 142, 159, 161.

[34] *Ibid.,* p. 142.

[35] See K. A. Nilakanta Sastri, *A History of South India from Prehistoric Times to the Fall of Vijayanagar* (Bombay, 1955).

[36] Iswari Prasad, quoted in Sir Percival Griffiths, *The British Impact on India* (London, 1952), p. 29.

with its greatest internal and external challenges, arising from the unwelcome necessity of dealing with foreign invaders more powerful than
any that had yet come into India, who, unlike their many predecessors,
could not be absorbed into the basic Hindu life-stream, and from the
equally unwelcome necessity of adapting to the modern world. For a
time it seemed that Hindu India might disappear under these powerful
new and alien pressures. It is a remarkable tribute to the basic strength
and staying power of the ideas and institutions that developed in the
heyday of the Hindu period that Hindu traditions are still predominant
in modern India.

### The Muslim Period

The Muslim period was of much shorter duration than the long era
of Hindu ascendancy, and its impact was much less profound; but the
millions of Muslims in India and Pakistan today — the largest concentration of the followers of Islam to be found anywhere in the world —
look to it as the golden age. It did mark the beginning of a new era
in Indian history, during which large numbers of Muslim invaders came
into the subcontinent, established themselves as rulers of most of the
area, developed a great political and administrative system under the
Moguls, converted hundreds of thousands of Hindus, and coexisted
rather than amalgamated with the Hindu majority.

Islam and Hinduism represented not only two different religions, but
two different civilizations. Muslims came to India as invaders and conquerors. In the great days of the Delhi Sultanate and even more in
those of the Mogul Empire they were definitely the dominant political
force in India, as far as overall control was concerned. Their impact
on local government and institutions even in those parts of the subcontinent over which they ruled was slight, and their impact on the masses
of the people was even less, although many Hindus were converted to
Islam by force or persuasion. Most of the more than 160 million Muslims in India and Pakistan today are descendants not of Muslim invaders or rulers but of converted Hindus. Thus the greatest of all the
communal problems that have bedeviled the subcontinent was introduced and the basis laid for the partition of the subcontinent and the
formation of the Islamic state of Pakistan.

**Before the Moguls.**[37] Followers of the new religion of Islam appeared in Sind as early as the eighth century. In the late tenth and early
eleventh centuries the great Afghan ruler, Mahmud of Ghazni, made
many destructive raids into India and maintained control for some time

[37] See S. M. Ikram, *Muslim Civilization in India,* edited by Ainslie T. Embree (New York, 1964), Part One: "The Early Invasions and the Delhi Sultanate 712–1526."

of much of western India.  In 1206 an Afghan general founded the
Delhi Sultanate, which at the height of its power in the late thirteenth
and early fourteenth centuries ruled over a large part of India, except
Kashmir and the extreme south.  In 1398 Tamerlane or Timur, a Mon-
gol conqueror who claimed to be a descendant of Genghis Khan, sacked
Delhi and ended the Delhi Sultanate.  (Although the Sultanate was
revived in the middle of the fifteenth century and lasted for another
seventy-five years, it never regained its former influence.)

"For five hundred years the Muslims failed to build up a stable polity
. . . and in general the early Muslims in India displayed no more constructive political genius than had their Hindu predecessors."[38]  For a
time in the fourteenth, fifteenth, and sixteenth centuries the Hindu
Empire of Vijayanagar, which at the height of its power controlled
nearly all of India south of the Krishna River, seemed to present a
formidable challenge to the growing Muslim power; but the forces of
Vijayanagar were defeated by Muslim armies in 1565, and the capital
of the Empire was destroyed.  By this time the Muslim rulers were
strongly entrenched in the north.  In 1526 a descendant of Tamerlane,
Baber, captured Delhi and founded the Mogul (or Moghul or Mughal)
Empire.

**The Moguls.**[39]  The greatest of the Mogul rulers, Akbar (1556–
1605), was a contemporary of Queen Elizabeth of England, and had
an even longer reign over a much larger empire; in his time the Mogul
Empire was probably stronger and more important than was England
under Elizabeth.  Next to Asoka, Akbar is the best known of all the
rulers of India.  He fought many wars to consolidate his great empire;
he developed an effective administrative system; although he was himself illiterate, he made his courts at Delhi, Fatehpur Sikri, and Agra
centers of culture and learning, as well as of architectural magnificence;
he was remarkably tolerant of all religions, and spokesmen of many
faiths — Hindus, Parsis, Jains, Jesuits, as well as Muslims — explained
and defended their beliefs at his court; he even tried, unsuccessfully,
to develop a new religion, the *Din-i-Ilahi,* which would be a synthesis
of Islam and other faiths.

Mogul administration in the time of Akbar, according to Sir Percival
Griffiths, had five main characteristics.  It was "in origin a foreign
domination. . . . Akbar was as much a non-Indian by birth and early
training as were Clive and Hastings."  It was a "complete despotism,"
in which "the emperor's will was law in the most literal sense."  It was
established along military lines, and "even officials employed wholly in
civil duties were graded in the military hierarchy."  Akbar himself said

---

[38] Griffiths, *The British Impact on India,* p. 30.
[39] See Ikram, *Muslim Civilization in India,* Part Two: "The Mughal Period, 1526–1858."

that "a monarch should be ever intent on conquest lest his neighbors rise against him," and this aim of conquest "necessarily conditioned his organisation of the system of government." A fifth characteristic of the Mogul Empire "was the complete absence of an hereditary aristocracy." This had unfortunate effects when lesser men than Akbar were emperors, but in the days of the Great Mogul it "gave Akbar a free hand to refashion administration in a scientific manner."[40]

Akbar perceived that even he, with all his power and might, had to depend upon many people to govern his vast empire, populated mostly by non-Muslims. For this reason he made friends with powerful Rajputs, who had resisted Muslim inroads for decades, and he enlisted the services of thousands of Hindus. Some of his wives, chief officials, and military commanders were Hindus. Unfortunately his successors — Jehangir, Shah Jehan, and Aurangzeb — were lesser men, lacking his ability, integrity, prestige, and tolerance. Although the Mogul empire reached its greatest extent under Shah Jehan and Aurangzeb, it decayed because of internal difficulties caused by inefficient rule and religious intolerance and because of the growing challenge from the Sikhs and the Marathas. The Sikh religion was founded by Nanak, the first *guru,* shortly before the beginnings of Mogul rule, and the tenth and last *guru,* Govind Singh, was a contemporary of Aurangzeb. So was the great Maratha leader, Shivaji, who declared his independence of the Mogul empire and from his capital in Poona launched a number of expeditions against the Moguls and conquered a considerable part of central India.

The Mogul Empire really came to an end after the death of Aurangzeb in 1707, but theoretically it continued until 1862, under a series of puppet emperors. Its weaknesses became more and more apparent after the strong hand of Akbar was removed. "The Mogul Empire," Vincent Smith observed, "like all Asian despotisms, had shallow roots. Its existence depended mainly on the personal character of the reigning autocrat and on the degree of his military power. It lacked popular support, the strength based on patriotic feeling, and on the stability founded upon ancient tradition."[41]

### The British Period to 1857: In the Days of "John Company"

For the past four and a half centuries and more the people of India have been subject to the growing impact of the West. During this long

---

[40] Griffiths, *The British Impact on India,* pp. 123–127. Griffiths has two excellent chapters on Mogul administration (pp. 122–142). See also Sir Jadunath Sarkar, *Mughal Administration* (Calcutta, 1935).

[41] Vincent Smith, *The Oxford History of India* (2nd ed., London, 1923), p. 465.

period, which a distinguished Indian scholar-diplomat, K. M. Panikkar, has called "the Vasco da Gama epoch of Asian history," a new India emerged under the impact of the West, especially of the British, which in turn produced various kinds of Indian responses.

For some two centuries Western contacts with India were relatively few and inconsequential, confined largely to the efforts of Portuguese, Spanish, French, and British explorers, and trading companies, chiefly British and French.

**The Consolidation of British Control in India.**   The most important of all the trading companies was the British East India Company. Formed in 1600, the Company was at first concerned only with trade and commerce and had only limited contacts with India, chiefly through the ports of Calcutta, Madras, and Bombay. Gradually, however, faced with the necessity of dealing with pirates, protecting its interests in India, and competing with other trading companies, the Company became involved in political and military activities, which in time made it in fact the leading power in India. As early as 1687, during the reign of Aurangzeb, the Directors of the Company instructed their chief representative in Madras "to establish such a politie of civil and military power, and create and secure such a large revenue to secure both . . . as may be the foundation of a large, well grounded, secure English dominion in India for all time to come."[42]   "In 1715 the Company sent an embassy to the Mogul court and wrested from the weak ruler extensive privileges throughout the Empire, including the right to trade in Bengal free of all duties, to rent additional territory around Calcutta, and the right to coin money in Bombay and to circulate it throughout India. The *firman* of 1716–1717 became known as the 'Magna Charta' of the Company, the major step in the establishment of this new type of politico-commercial power on Indian soil."[43]

Even though the central power of the Moguls was weakening, the British East India Company did not have a clear field for its expanding activities. Other possible successors to the Moguls were also active in the early eighteenth century, notably the French, the Muslim rulers of the states of Mysore and Hyderabad, the Marathas, the Rajputs, and the Sikhs, with powerful invaders from Persia and Afghanistan also constituting no small threat. One by one, however, the British eliminated or cut down the power of their chief rivals.

The struggle between the British and the French in India in the early eighteenth century was a phase of the overall struggle between the two powers, which was waged on the European continent, in North Amer-

[42] Quoted in R. C. Majumdar, H. C. Raychaudhuri, and K. Datta, *An Advanced History of India* (London, 1946), p. 639.

[43] De Riencourt, *The Soul of India*, p. 199.

ica, and on the high seas, as well as in India. The French East India Company, formed by Colbert in 1664, established trading posts in Pondicherry, Chandernagore, and elsewhere in Bengal and along the Coromandel coast. For a time, under the brilliant and determined Dupleix, it threatened to oust the British from South India. This threat was finally eliminated by Robert Clive, an official of the British East India Company, through a combination of military operations and wily diplomacy, during the Indian phase of the Seven Years War (1756–1763), which, among other results, ended effective French influence in India.

Control by the Company over the subcontinent may be dated from the decisive triumphs over the French, acknowledged in the Treaty of Paris of 1763, and the granting of the *diwan* — the right of collecting revenues — for Bengal, Bihar, and Orissa to the Company by the Mogul emperor in 1765. The work of Clive was continued by the famous Warren Hastings, who was Governor-General from 1774 to 1784, and by Lord Wellesley, who may in a sense be regarded as the first true British imperialist in India.[44]

One of the first acts of Lord Wellesley as Governor-General (1798–1805) was to enter into an alliance with the Nizam of Hyderabad and the Peshwa, the Brahman chief minister of the Maratha Confederacy, against Tipu Sultan, ruler of Mysore, who was defeated and killed in 1798. "By the beginning of the nineteenth century British forces were maintained in Mysore, Hyderabad and Oudh, and either in this way or by direct rule Britain controlled large areas of India."[45] By brilliant campaigns and by profiting from internal conflicts among member states of the Maratha Confederacy, Lord Wellesley effectively broke the power of the Marathas and forced them to enter into the British system of subsidiary alliances, and a decade later the Peshwa was deposed, the main Maratha rulers were brought within the orbit of the British alliance system, and a great deal of territory was ceded to the British East India Company.

In the 1840's the Sikhs, who had established firm control and a proud military tradition in the Punjab, took the initiative against the British. After two Sikh wars they were decisively defeated, and the Punjab was added to the territories under the direct control of "John Company." In 1856, during the Governor-Generalship of Lord Dalhousie, the vast kingdom of Oudh was also annexed.

Thus by the middle of the nineteenth century most of India was controlled by the British — either directly by the British East India Company or indirectly through the system of alliances and resident agents

[44] Griffiths, *The British Impact on India,* p. 88.
[45] *Ibid.,* p. 90.

in a multitude of princely States. Many of the former Indian States were annexed by the Company under the "doctrine of lapse," which forbade rulers to follow the long-recognized practice of adopting an heir if they had no natural one. This was developed during the Governor-Generalship of Lord Dalhousie (1848–56).

**"John Company" and the British Government.** When the political power of the British East India Company was solidly established, the British Parliament began to exercise an increasing control over its activities, although until 1858 the British Government left the major task of governance in India to the Company. The Regulating Act of 1773 was the first of a long series of acts of the British Parliament which set the limits for the operations of the Company. After 1773 the British Government continued to appoint the Governors-General, but they ruled India for the East India Company. The Amending Act of 1781 provided that all dispatches from the Company concerning political and certain other matters had to be submitted to the British Government. Some of the leading orators in the Parliament, in a day of great orators, turned their fire on the Company — on alleged patronage, corruption, perfidy, greed, and ill-gotten gains. Fox called the Company's administration "a system of despotism unmatched in all the histories of the world." Burke in 1784 denounced the Company as "one of the most corrupt and destructive tyrannies that probably ever existed in the world."

Pitt's India Act of 1784 and a series of supplementary measures in the decade that followed established a clear chain of control through the British Parliament and the Board of Control to the Governor-General and Council of Bengal to the Governors and Councils of the Bombay and Madras Presidencies. Several Charter Acts progressively whittled down the other powers of the East India Company. The most important of these was the Charter Act of 1833, which put an end to the commercial activities of the Company, leaving it as a purely administrative body, and gave more power to the Governor-General and Council.

The East India Company was in effect the successor to Mogul rule in India; consciously and unconsciously it served as the agent of British imperialism. Thus its activities profoundly affected the course of Indian life and development, for good and for ill. It is impossible to chronicle the many steps which were taken by the various representatives of the Company, from Robert Clive and Warren Hastings to Lord Dalhousie, over a period of nearly a century; it is even more impossible to assay the effects of the steps which were taken and of the impact of "John Company" on the Indian scene.

Consider, for example, the actions of Lord William Bentinck, Governor-General from 1828 to 1835. Some of the reforms which he sponsored were truly spectacular, striking directly at long-established practices: the abolition of suttee (the practice of widow-burning); the suppression of thuggee (ritual strangling by worshippers of the goddess Kali); and efforts to end the practice of female infanticide. Other measures taken by Bentinck attracted less attention, but were perhaps equally noteworthy. These included many administrative reforms, reduction in the costs of government, and stricter supervision of the Indian States. The Charter Act of 1833 was passed while Bentinck was Governor-General.

Perhaps the most far-reaching of all Lord Bentinck's reforms was the decision to adopt English as the medium of instruction in Indian education. This represented a great victory of the "Anglicists" over the "Orientalists" in England. Lord Macaulay, then Law Minister in the Board of Control for Indian affairs, was the leader in the movement to make English the medium of instruction in India and thereby, as he wrote in his famous "Minute on Education," in 1835, to train "a class of persons, Indian in blood and colour, but English in taste, in opinions, in morals, and in intellect,"[46] and who would be faithful allies of the British in governing India.

For more than a century this policy was a brilliant success. Generation after generation of Westernized Indians served as "clerks" and lesser civil servants in British employ and made it possible for the British to run a vast country with remarkably few English troops and officials. In the long run, of course, the Westernized Indians, trained in English and in Western ways, were the leaders of the movement for independence from the British. In a dim way Macaulay foresaw this eventuality, but he did not shrink from it. "When it comes," he declared, "it will be the proudest day in English history."

The long-run significance of this decision has been clearly stated by Amaury de Riencourt:

> From 1835 on, European learning through the medium of the English language was patronized by the Anglo-Indian government and revolutionized the whole educational system of India with far-reaching effects on the social and political structure of Indian society. . . . For all its defects, it is this education and the use of the English tongue that gave actual coherent *unity* to India. If this had not happened, if the British, in a more diabolic mood, had concentrated on developing the vernaculars, there is no doubt that there would not have been *one* Indian nationalism, but *several.*[47]

[46] For the text of the "Minute on Education," see de Bary, ed., *Sources of Indian Tradition,* II, 44–49.

[47] De Riencourt, *The Soul of India,* pp. 252, 290. Italics in original.

**The British Impact on India.**   One of the most important and generally unfortunate results of the domination of India by a trading company turned imperial ruler was the virtual destruction of the economic institutions on which Indian society had been based, including village communities, the system of landholding, and cooperative associations and industries. As a result of British policies in England and in India and of the prevailing economic philosophy in Britain, a flourishing Indian trade and commerce virtually collapsed, and the growing middle class collapsed also. The effects on the system of landholding were equally disastrous.

The Permanent Settlement of Bengal, introduced by Lord Cornwallis during his first Governor-Generalship (1786–94), and subsequent measures in other parts of India interposed a new class of middlemen, who had come into existence in Mogul times, between the state and the farmers. These middlemen, generally known as *zamindars,* collected land revenue and paid agreed-upon amounts to the State. In time they became in effect hereditary landowners; they dominated the land system of most of India for more than a century and a half, until the system which they represented was largely ended by acts of the independent Governor of India and the constituent States.

The British impact on India was more profound than that of any invader since the coming of the Aryans; "through their new-found political power, they were able to carry out a profound social transformation through redistribution of economic power."[48] Modern India reflects this impact; but it also reflects the tremendous staying power of old institutions and traditions, especially in the social and religious or philosophical realms.

Indian nationalists emphasized the negative and unfortunate effects of British rule, such as the conscious or unconscious suppression of indigenous customs and institutions, the economic "drain" and the exploitation of India for the benefit of a foreign power and foreign interests, the divisive effects on Indian society, the favoritism shown to English-educated and English-speaking Indians who supported foreign rule, the loss of dignity and identity, and, in short, all the less happy consequences of imperialism at its zenith. Englishmen and their supporters stressed the manifold contributions of British rule to India, including a degree of unity virtually unknown in the many centuries of Indian history; fair, just, and efficient government; an effective system of administration, education, law and order, and defense; assistance to Indians in rediscovering their own past heritage and traditions; and a guided entry into the modern world. There was considerable truth in

[48] *Ibid.,* p. 209.

both points of view, and also considerable exaggeration and selection. Clearly the overall verdict on British rule and influence in India must be an ambivalent one.

By the beginning of the second half of the nineteenth century it seemed that the British had established a pattern of control that would endure for a long, long time, and that they had brought a new India into being. But the century that followed began with a major uprising against the British, witnessed the consolidation and nadir of British rule and the rise of an increasingly powerful independence movement, and ended with the independence of India and Pakistan. The British set in motion forces which were more powerful than they themselves realized, and it is these forces, rather than the British policies and influence, which really created modern India.

# 3

# The British Century

Approximately a century elapsed between the zenith of the British East India Company during the Governor-Generalship of Lord Dalhousie (1848–1856) and the end of British rule in India in 1947. The beginning of this century was highlighted by the "Mutiny" of 1857 and the assumption in the following year of direct control of India by the British Government. The century ended with the withdrawal of the British and the independence of two new states in the subcontinent, India and Pakistan. The great events of the century were the consolidation of British rule, which resulted in the establishment of a pattern of colonial administration probably more highly developed than that in any other colonial area at any time; the increasing association of Indians in the work of government, below the policy-making level; various steps in the direction of self-government, from the Indian Councils Act of 1861 to the Government of India Act of 1935; the rise of a strong nationalist movement, led by the Indian National Congress and by the Muslim League; and eventually, with increasing concessions by the British and increasingly successful techniques of resistance by the Indians under Mahatma Gandhi, the last days of British rule in India.

The century prior to 1947, therefore, witnessed new techniques of colonial rule and new techniques of resistance to that rule. It may properly be called the British century, for the British did govern India in this period in a real sense; but while it witnessed the apogee of British power in India, it also marked the final phases of the British part of the Indian story. The British impact on India, however, did not end with independence in 1947.

## The "Mutiny" and Its Consequences

In conventional histories of India by British or other foreign writers the "Sepoy Mutiny" of 1857 is presented as an uprising of disaffected

46

Indian "Sepoys" (Indian soldiers in British employ), chiefly in a few cities and cantonments in north India, limited in scope and operations, and suppressed after a few months' desultory fighting without undue difficulty. Today, in both India and Pakistan, the "Mutiny" is described rather generally as "the War of Independence," and any suggestions that it was not this in fact are usually resented. In *The Discovery of India,* written several years before independence, Nehru himself declared: "It was much more than a military mutiny, and it spread rapidly and assumed the character of a popular rebellion and a war of Indian independence."[1]

Unquestionably the "Mutiny" was prompted by causes much more deep-seated than revulsion against the use of greased cartridges, and it led to many significant results. It was in fact a watershed in modern Indian history, "in general terms, the violent meeting of two dying systems, of British India as a 'country' power — an essentially oriental government with strong European overtones — and of traditional India, trembling with unresolved and frequently unstated fears, obsessed with the past and unable or [un]willing to accept the modernizing tendencies of the British."[2] According to one perceptive Indian writer it was prompted basically by a "revulsion against western influence." "The repeated annexation of territories by a foreign power, the spread of western modes of education and new ideas of life — all combined revealed to the Hindu mind a consistent effort to substitute a western for a Hindu civilisation."[3] The British position in India was never the same after the "Mutiny," although for a time it seemed that British rule was never more firmly entrenched.

Two of the most immediately significant results were the end of the East India Company and the assumption of direct control by the British Government. These momentous changes were incorporated in the Act for the Better Government of India, which received the Royal assent on August 2, 1858. The main responsibility for the government of India was vested in a parliamentary minister, the Secretary of State for India, assisted by an advisory Council for India. All the powers of the East India Company, and all the military forces of the Company, were transferred to the Crown.

An even older, and once even more powerful, institution also came to an end shortly after the "Mutiny." This was the Mogul Empire,

---

[1] Jawaharlal Nehru, *The Discovery of India* (New York, 1946), p. 324.

[2] Michael Edwardes, *British India, 1772–1947* (New York, 1968), p. 152. For differing interpretations of the "Mutiny," see R. C. Majumdar, *The Sepoy Mutiny and the Revolt of 1857* (2nd ed., Calcutta, 1963), and S. B. Chadhuri, *Theories of the Indian Mutiny (1857–59); A Study of the Views of an Eminent Historian on the Subject* (Calcutta, 1965).

[3] S. N. Ray, "The Sepoy Mutiny of 1857," *The Radical Humanist,* XXI (May 12, 1957), 237.

which theoretically existed until the death of the last "emperor," Bahadur Shah II, in 1862, although it had of course long been "the shade of a shadow of a shade." The British had allowed successors of Akbar and Aurangzeb to retain the title of Emperor, but some years before the "Mutiny" the British Government decided that after the death of Bahadur Shah II "the imperial rank should no longer be recognized." So ended the Mogul Empire. Some twenty years later and with great fanfare, a different kind of imperial rank was recognized. By the Royal Titles Bill of 1876, sponsored by Benjamin Disraeli, Queen Victoria was made "Empress of India."

Other consequences of the "Mutiny" were less obvious but perhaps even more significant. Actually, many of the new developments in India after 1857 were occasioned not so much by the "Mutiny" itself as by the changing circumstances in England, India, and the world as a whole, which helped to account for the many significant developments in British-Indian relations during the "British Century." Certainly, for various reasons, relations between British and Indians became more distant after 1857, even though British rule was more efficient, more extensive, and probably more benevolent, and even though increasing numbers of Indians were associated with the administration of the subcontinent. The British were particularly careful that the ratio of British to Indian troops in the British Indian Army should never again be such as to make possible another formidable uprising. They were careful to keep Indians in lesser positions in administration, and to keep them out of policy-making positions. They were likewise careful to keep Muslims out of positions of trust and responsibility, for they remembered the seemingly uncooperative attitude of Muslims in the past, and they believed that Muslims had been involved out of proportion to their numbers in the uprising of 1857.

### The Pattern of British Rule

During the ninety years of direct rule in India, the British developed an effective administrative system. It is important to understand how India was governed by the British, because the system developed by the British has been in large measure continued by the Indians themselves since independence.

In the heyday of British rule all of India was controlled either directly or indirectly by the British authorities. The subcontinent was divided into two main parts: British India, and the India of the princely States. Since there were 562 of these princely States at the time of partition, some as large as major states of Western Europe (notably Jammu and Kashmir, Hyderabad, and Mysore), and since they existed in all parts of the subcontinent and covered nearly two-fifths of the total area, a political map of India prior to partition looked like a crazy quilt. In each of the princely States the British had a resident who was usually the effective source of power, although to the fullest extent possible every deference was paid to the pomp and customary privileges of the hereditary rulers, especially to major potentates like the Maharajas of Jammu and Kashmir and of Mysore or the Nizam of Hyderabad.

British India was divided into provinces, of which there were eleven at the time of independence in 1947. The main centers of British rule were in Calcutta, Madras, and Bombay. The Governor-General, called also the Viceroy when he was acting on behalf of the British Crown, maintained headquarters in Calcutta until the early 1920's when the capital of British India was moved to the new city of New Delhi, now the capital of independent India. The Viceroy was responsible to the Secretary of State for India, who headed the India Office in Westminster, and through him to the Cabinet and the British Parliament. After the establishment of direct telegraph communications between England and India in 1870, the administration of affairs in India was subject to more direct and effective control from London.

The provinces of British India, which were very large in size, often embracing more people than most of the independent states of the world, were divided for purposes of administration into divisions, districts, and subdistricts usually called *tahsils* or *talukas.* The district was the most important of these administrative units, and the officer in charge, usually known simply as the District Officer, but sometimes also called the District Magistrate or the Collector, was the key man in the whole system of local administration. Most members of the Indian Civil Service (I.C.S.) served for a time as District Officers. As the various titles given to him suggest, he had many functions, both official and unofficial. Officially, he was charged with the overall tasks of administering the affairs of his district, preserving law and order, dispensing justice, and collecting revenue. He represented the British Government in rural India. Unofficially, his duties and symbolic importance were even greater.[4] He symbolized the power and splendor of the British Raj, as well as the unwelcome aspects of all-powerful and all-pervasive government. Of all the British representatives in India he had the closest contacts with the Indian masses; he was the man to whom the people looked for protection, guidance and advice. In the latter days of the British period more and more Indians, usually Indian members of the I.C.S., served as District Officers, thereby gaining valuable experience in the administration of their own country.

The British always ruled India with remarkably few administrators, military personnel, and others from the home country. But during this century and before hundreds of Englishmen, often of England's most

[4] See R. Carstairs, *The Little World of an Indian District Officer* (London, 1912).

distinguished families, served in India — as political representatives and advisers, as members of the top ranks in the Indian Civil Service, as officers and soldiers in the British Indian Army. These were the men who built and maintained an empire, the men of whom Kipling wrote, the "guardians" whom Philip Woodruff has described.[5] Their services, sufferings, privileged existence, and experiences on the frontiers of empire in India have been told in innumerable memoirs, monographs, novels, and other writings. Less well-known are the services, sacrifices, and contributions of the far larger number of Indians who helped Britain govern a mighty empire.

Particularly noteworthy was the Indian Civil Service, the "steel frame" of British administration in India, which gained for itself a well-deserved reputation as perhaps the finest and most incorruptible civil service in the world. Members of the I.C.S., carefully recruited and trained and held up to the highest standards of efficiency and integrity, manned most of the key administrative posts in India in British days. They were often criticized for developing a spirit of elitism and an exaggerated sense of their own importance, but no one could deny that they measured up impressively to the responsibilities entrusted to them.

From its establishment in the eighteenth century until well into the twentieth century few Indians were recruited for the I.C.S. As late as 1892 only 21 of the 992 members of this Service were Indians; in 1903 only 94 out of 1307 I.C.S. Officers were Indians. Toward the end of the British period, however, the number of Indians in the I.C.S. increased greatly, so that eventually they outnumbered the British members. Several hundred non-British I.C.S. Officers were available to India at the time of independence, and somewhat less than 200 to Pakistan. These men did yeoman service in carrying on the work of government and administration in the early stages of nation-building. Today the ranks of the former I.C.S. Officers have been thinned by death, resignation, and transfer to other duties; but even today those few former I.C.S. Officers who are still in active service in India or Pakistan hold key positions in central and local administration, in diplomacy, and in various trouble-shooting roles. They are still the most professional of the professionals in the subcontinent.

## Steps Toward Self-Government: From 1861 to 1892

At the beginning of the British century little thought was given by the British to any future for their Indian empire other than its indefinite

---

[5] See Philip Woodruff (pseud. of Philip Mason), *The Men Who Ruled India*. Vol. I, *The Founders of Modern India* (London, 1953); Vol. II, *The Guardians* (London, 1954); John Masters, *Bugles and a Tiger* (New York, 1956).

continuation. Even though the objective was clear, the British found it advisable, both for external and internal reasons, to associate increasing numbers of Indians with the work of administration and to make concessions looking toward greater self-government of the Indian realm. These steps toward self-government during the British century did much to determine the course and nature of British rule, and they helped to prepare Indians for the assumption of full political responsibility in 1947. The fact that this was not the objective in the beginning is perhaps of only incidental importance.

The story of the steps toward self-government during the British century is a complicated one, involving a few major landmarks, innumerable lesser steps, and a bewildering variety of men, motives, and events. The major landmarks were at least six; the three in the latter half of the nineteenth century prepared the way for the even greater ones in the first half of the twentieth. The six were: the Indian Councils Act of 1861; the increased attention to local government symbolized by and stemming from Lord Ripon's famous Resolution on Local Self-Government of 1882; the Indian Councils Act of 1892; the Morley-Minto Reforms of 1909; the Montagu-Chelmsford Reforms of 1918 and the Government of India Act of 1919; and the Government of India Act of 1935. Some knowledge of the nature and significance of these major landmarks is essential to an understanding of the government and politics of independent India.

The Indian Councils Act of 1861 enlarged the Council of the Viceroy (as the Governor-General was henceforth known) and the Council of the Governor of each Presidency (Calcutta, Madras, and Bombay) for purposes of legislation, although the Governor-General was empowered to veto any measures proposed by the enlarged Council, and the general authority of the British Crown and Parliament was strictly preserved. Even before 1858 the executive and legislative authority in India was vested in the Governor-General-in-Council. In 1853 six members were added to the Council for legislative purposes. The enlarged Council was known as the Legislative Council, although it had no independent powers. Nevertheless, it established the framework within which the Government of India functioned in the following decades and has been described as marking "the modest beginning of a parliamentary system in India."[6] A year after its passage three Indians were appointed to the Legislative Council as nonofficial members, the first Indians to be associated with the higher councils of the Government of India in the British period.

Before the 1880's "the principle of local self-government had been put into practice only in the cities of Calcutta and Bombay, and in a few

[6] R. C. Majumdar, H. C. Raychaudhuri, and K. Datta, *An Advanced History of India* (London, 1946), p. 849.

of the towns of the Central Provinces and North-Western Provinces. Elsewhere, although a framework of local administration and local taxation existed, control was firmly in the hands of servants of the government." Lord Ripon, a liberal-minded Viceroy, was responsible for the famous Resolution on Local Self-Government of May 18, 1882, which set forth "the general principles which were to govern the future development of local representative institutions" in India.[7] The purpose of the resolution was clearly stated: "It is not primarily with a view to improvement in administration that this measure is put forward and supported," although "in course of time, as local knowledge and local interest are brought to bear more freely upon local administration, improved efficiency will follow." Instead, "it is chiefly designed as an instrument of political and popular education," and as an outlet for the talents and ambitions of the growing numbers of educated Indians. The resolution advocated the development of Local Boards in subdivisions of districts, both urban and rural, with a majority of elected nonofficial members wherever possible. Even when these Local Boards were established, however, they were still under the supervision of District Boards, which in turn were largely controlled by the District Officers, who served as chairmen.

Shortly after the issuance of the resolution, Local Self-Government Acts were passed in several of the provinces of British India; but in general progress in the direction of genuine local self-government, especially at the subdistrict level, was disappointingly slow. In 1906 G. K. Gokhale observed that local government "still remains all over the country where it was placed by Lord Ripon a quarter of a century ago, and in some places it has even been pushed back."[8] The Report of the Royal Commission upon Decentralisation in 1909, which has been called "the watershed in the history of local government" in India, made recommendations similar to those of the Resolution of 1882,[9] but again the results were disappointing.

The Indian Councils Act of 1892 was the result of expressions of dissatisfaction by the Indian National Congress and liberal spokesmen in India and in England over the operations of the Legislative Councils as provided for in the Indian Councils Act of 1861. It increased the number of members in the Central and provincial Legislative Councils, and it provided that the nomination of nonofficial members should be on the basis of recommendations by the Calcutta Chamber of Com-

[7] Hugh Tinker, *The Foundations of Local Self-Government in India, Pakistan and Burma* (London, 1954), pp. 42, 44. For the text of the Resolution on Local Self-Government of 1882 see P. Mukherji, ed., *Indian Constitutional Documents* (Calcutta, 1918), I, pp. 638–651.

[8] *Collected Speeches of the Hon. G. K. Gokhale* (Madras, n.d.), Appendix, p. 149.

[9] See Tinker, *Foundations of Local Self-Government,* Chap. IV.

merce and the nonofficial members of the Legislative Councils of Madras, Bengal, and Bombay Presidencies, and the North-Western Province, in the case of the Governor-General's Council, and by local bodies such as the municipalities and chambers of commerce in the case of Governors' councils. "In this (indirect) acceptance of the principle of election lies the momentous character of the change made by the Indian Councils Act of 1892." The Act also enlarged the powers of the Legislative Councils. Thus while the Act of 1892 "was not meant to mark the beginnings of [a] parliamentary system" in India, "nevertheless, it is a definite milestone on the road that led to the establishment of parliamentary government later on."[10]

### Steps Toward Self-Government: From 1892 to 1918

From 1899 to 1905 Lord Curzon, one of the greatest of British colonial administrators, was Viceroy of India. A man of great energy and organizing skill, he ran the Government of India with a firm hand. Even today some of the tangible evidences of his great contributions are still manifest. But he was also an imperious and autocratic man, and he alienated his superior authorities in England and influential elements in Indian society alike. Two of his acts provoked widespread resistance in India — his attempt to strengthen state control and responsibility for university education through the Indian Universities Act of 1904, and the partition of Bengal in 1905. His successor, Lord Minto, was a very different type, who cooperated with the Secretary of State for India, the famous liberal statesman and author, Lord Morley, in a series of reforms. The Morley-Minto Reforms were embodied in the Indian Councils Act of 1909 and the rules and regulations promulgated in implementation of this Act. They also included the appointment of two Indians to the Council of the Secretary of State for India and of the first Indian Law Member of the Viceroy's Executive Council.

The Indian Councils Act of 1909 greatly expanded the membership and functions of the Legislative Councils in India. It also empowered the Viceroy to create Executive Councils for the Governors in the larger provinces and to enlarge the Executive Councils that already existed in Madras and Bombay. Members of the Legislative Councils continued to be of three main types: officials, nominated nonofficials, and elected nonofficials. The electorates created by the regulations under the Act were divided into three main classes: general, class, and special.[11]

[10] J. P. Suda, *Indian Constitutional Development and National Movement* (Meerut, 1951), I, pp. 31–32.

[11] Of the 27 elected members of the Viceroy's Legislative Council 13 were to be elected by general electorates, mostly nonofficial members of the provincial Legislative Councils, 6 by special landowners' constituencies in six provinces, 6 by Muslim constituencies, and 2 by special electorates, one each by the Chambers of Commerce of Bombay and Bengal.

These regulations introduced for the first time the principle of communalism into official Indian political life by providing for separate electorates for Muslims. In one sense this was a factor which had existed for a long time, and therefore only the official recognition was new; in another sense, it was an additional divisive factor in Indian politics, which had all kinds of unfortunate consequences and which undoubtedly helped to pave the way for the eventual division of the subcontinent and the creation of the Islamic state of Pakistan. In October 1906 in response to a hint conveyed through the Private Secretary to the Viceroy, a deputation of leading Muslims, led by the Aga Khan, waited upon the Viceroy, Lord Minto, at Simla and presented him with a carefully prepared Address. The Address asked for separate Muslim electorates and outlined an elaborate scheme of Muslim representation. It based its request on the ground that "the position accorded to the Mohammedan community, in any kind of representation, direct or indirect, and in all other ways affecting their status and influence, should be commensurate not only with their numerical strength, but also with their practical importance and the value of the contribution which they make to the defence of the Empire" and with due regard to "the position they occupied in India a little more than a hundred years ago."[12] Lord Minto expressed his sympathy with this request, which in effect amounted to an official acceptance of the principle of communal representation.

While the germs of later concessions were embodied in the Indian Councils Act of 1909, the intention of its framers and supporters was to make certain limited concessions to Indian sentiment without in any way affecting the predominant position of the British rulers. In a speech in the House of Lords when the Act was being considered, Lord Morley said: "If it could be said that this chapter of reforms led directly or indirectly to the establishment of a parliamentary system in India, I for one would have nothing to do with it." Three years later Lord Crew, then Secretary of State for India, confirmed this position by asserting that "the experiment of extending a measure of self-government practically free from parliamentary control to a race not our own is one which cannot be tried." Yet only five years later, on August 20, 1917, another Secretary of State for India, Edwin Samuel Montagu, in an historic pronouncement declared that the aim of the British Government was "the progressive realisation of responsible government in India."

What were the reasons for this significant change in British policy and outlook? They are to be found in many developments between the

[12] Muslim Delegation to Lord Minto, Oct. 1906; quoted in *Indian Statutory Commission* (the Simon Commission), 1930, IV, 130–131.

years 1909 and 1917, including the dissatisfaction of most Indians with the aftermath of the Morley-Minto reforms, the agitation of the Indian National Congress and the Home Rule movement, and, above all, the consequences of World War I for India. During the war the British were particularly concerned with securing the cooperation of Indians in the war effort, and the Indians expected and even demanded further concessions from the British as the price of such cooperation.

On August 20, 1917, Mr. Montagu made a statement in the House of Commons which became "the basis of all subsequent legislation by the British Parliament in relation to India."[13] The statement included the following significant declaration:

> The policy of His Majesty's Government, with which the Government of India are in complete accord, is that of the increasing association of Indians in every branch of the administration and the gradual development of self-governing institutions with a view to the progressive realisation of responsible government in India as an integral part of the British Empire. . . . I would add that progress in this policy can only be achieved by stages. The British Government and the Government of India, on whom the responsibility lies for the welfare and advancement of the Indian peoples, must be the judges of the time and measure of each advance, and they must be guided by the co-operation received from those upon whom new opportunities of service will thus be conferred and by the extent to which it is found that confidence can be reposed in their sense of responsibility.[14]

The Secretary of State for India also announced that he would soon go to India at the head of a mission, for purposes of consultation and enquiry. After consultations with the Viceroy, Lord Chelmsford, and other officials and with some influential Indian spokesmen, investigations of prevailing conditions in India, and consideration of several proposals for reforms, the Montagu mission, on July 8, 1918, issued the Report on Indian Constitutional Reforms, popularly referred to as the Montagu-Chelmsford or the Montford Report. It accepted the principle of Montagu's declaration of August, 1917, that the aim should be "the progressive realisation of responsible government in India." It

[13] Suda, *Indian Constitutional Development*, p. 125.

[14] *Report on Indian Constitutional Reforms, 1918* (Montagu-Chelmsford Report), p. 1. Since Mr. Montagu made it clear that "the British Government and the Government of India . . . must be the judges of the time and measure of each advance," and that India would remain "an integral part of the British Empire," it is obvious that he used the terms "responsible government" and "self-governing institutions" in a much more limited sense than they have come to signify in contemporary Western political science.

laid down four fundamental objectives for future constitutional advance: (1) "popular control in local bodies and the largest possible independence for them of outside control"; (2) establishment in the provinces, in which "the earlier steps towards the progressive realisation of responsible government should be taken," of "the largest measure of independence . . . of the Government of India which is compatible with the due discharge by the latter of its own responsibilities"; (3) enlargement of the membership and functions of the Indian Legislative Council and increase of its representative element; and (4) relaxation of the control of Parliament and the Secretary of State for India over the Government of India and the provincial governments.[15]

## Government of India Act of 1919

On the basis of the Montford Report, and the recommendations of three committees set up to complete its work, the Government of India Act of 1919 was drafted. This act is a major landmark along the road to self-government in India. It made significant changes in the machinery for the government of India, both in London and in India. It increased the number of Indian members of the India Council, a group of advisers to the Secretary of State for India, and it provided for the transfer of some of the Secretary's functions to a new official, to be known as the High Commissioner for India. It also increased the degree of Parliamentary control over the administration of Indian affairs. In India it radically modified the nature of the central legislative body, providing for a new legislature of two chambers, a Council of State and a Legislative Assembly, to be made more representative than the previous unicameral Indian Legislative Council. The Council of State was to consist of 60 members, 34 of whom were to be elected — 20 by general electorates, 3 by European Chambers of Commerce in India, and 11 by communal electorates. Of the 144 members of the Indian Legislative Assembly, 103 were to be elected — 51 by general constituencies, 32 by communal constituencies, and 20 by special constituencies. The new central legislature was given a wide field of activity, but the Viceroy, still directly responsible to the Secretary of State for India and the British Parliament, exercised a veto power over any of its enactments.

In the provinces of British India the Government of India Act of 1919 introduced such novel changes that they are of continuing interest to students of government — a dual system of government known as "dyarchy."[16] Provincial subjects were divided into two classes — the

[15] *Ibid.,* p. 123.
[16] See Lionel Curtis, *Dyarchy* (Oxford, 1920); A. Appadorai, *Dyarchy in Practice* (London, 1937); and "Kerala Putra" (pseud. of K. M. Panikkar), *The Working of Dyarchy in India* (Bombay, 1928).

"Reserved" and the "Transferred." Reserved subjects, including finance, land revenue, justice, and police, remained the responsibility of the Governor, acting as the representative of the British Government. Responsibility for transferred subjects, including local self-government, education, health, and public works, was entrusted to the voters of the provinces, through the Legislative Councils, which were enlarged in membership and functions and made more representative of various communities and interests. Thus "the government of each Governor's Province was divided into two parts — the Governor in Council in charge of the 'Reserved Departments' and the Governor acting with Ministers in charge of the 'Transferred Departments' — each part accountable to separate and distinct sets of people — the British electors in the one case and the provincial voters in the other."[17]

"Dyarchy was not only a novel but also a clumsy experiment in constitution-making," and it is hardly surprising that, in the unfavorable environment which existed in India in 1919 and after, it proved to be a failure. "It was a failure in the sense that the objective for the sake of which it was introduced was not realized; there was no real transfer of power to the people, no genuine responsible government even in the limited sphere of transferred subjects. The absence of stable political parties, the presence in the legislatures of a large bloc of officials and nominated non-officials, and of persons returned from communal and special constituencies, the joint purse, the powers of the Governor to override the advice given by the ministers, the rights of the services: all these factors combined together to prevent the growth of responsible government in the provinces."[18]

Another consequence of the Montague-Chelmsford Reforms was the improvement of the machinery for cooperation between British India and the Indian States. Relations between the British and the rulers of the Indian States had gone through many stages in the previous century and a half, ranging from noninterference to a policy of "subordinate isolation." While paying considerable deference to the princes, the British Government left no doubt that it was the paramount power in all of India. Its general position was thus summarized in the Montagu-Chelmsford Report: "The States are guaranteed security from without; the Paramount Power acts for them in relation to foreign powers and other States, and it intervenes when the internal peace of their territories is seriously threatened."[19] The report recommended the creation

[17] Gurmukh Nihal Singh, *Landmarks in Indian Constitutional and National Development,* Vol. I, 1600 to 1919 (3rd ed., Delhi, 1952), pp. 293–294.

[18] Suda, *Indian Constitutional Development,* pp. 173, 181–182.

[19] *Report on Indian Constitutional Reforms, 1918,* p. 190.

of a permanent "Council of Princes," with "a small Standing Commit-tee to which the Viceroy of the Political Department might refer." The Government of India Act of 1919 contained no provisions regarding the Indian States, but the recommendations of the Montford Report were not forgotten. Its proposals were considered at a Conference of the Ruling Princes in January 1919, and a more definite scheme, based on the proposals, and sponsored by the Viceroy and the Secretary of State for India, at another Conference of Princes in November 1919. The decision to constitute the Chamber of Princes was announced by Royal Proclamation, and the Duke of Connaught formally inaugurated the Chamber in February 1921.

## The Simon Commission and the Round Table Conferences

The Government of India Act of 1919 provided for a review of the political situation in India every ten years. Well before that time, in November 1927, the Viceroy, Lord Irwin, announced the appointment of an Indian Statutory Commission, under the chairmanship of Sir John Simon. Although the Commission, composed exclusively of English-men, visited India twice and made every effort to discharge its duties faithfully, its work was greatly hampered by the hostile reception it received in India. It was boycotted not only by the Indian National Congress but also by almost all sections of Indian opinion, including the Indian Liberals. Its report was not released until May 1930. By this time the situation in India had changed, and few people paid much attention to the Commission's recommendations, which included pro-vincial autonomy, with safeguards, and the possibility at some future date of a federal constitution which would embrace both British India and the Indian States.

Doubtless the Simon Report deserved a better fate. Coupland de-scribed it as "the most complete study of the Indian problem that had yet been made."[20] Many of its recommendations were eventually in-corporated into the Government of India Act of 1935. But C. F. Andrews expressed the prevailing view in India when he said that it dealt more "with that old India which I knew when I first went out nearly thirty years ago, before the national movement had started; it shows little understanding of the Young India which we see rising to-day on the tide of national upheaval."[21]

While trying to justify the exclusion of Indians from membership in the Simon Commission, Lord Birkenhead, Secretary of State for India, had challenged Indians of varying shades of opinion to produce

[20] See R. Coupland, *The Indian Problem* (New York, 1944), Vol. I, Chap-ter VIII, "The Simon Report," pp. 97–112.
[21] C. F. Andrews, *India and the Simon Report* (London, 1930), p. 40.

an agreed-upon proposal for constitutional reform. Indian leaders accepted this challenge and organized an All-Parties Conference in 1928. This Conference appointed a subcommittee under the chairmanship of Motilal Nehru, father of Jawaharlal Nehru, with a distinguished membership representing different groups in the Indian National Congress, the Liberals, and some Muslims, to draft a constitution. The Nehru Report recommended full responsible government for India along the lines of the self-governing Dominions as "the next immediate step" and left some scope for those who insisted on complete independence as the immediate goal.[22] Although it was endorsed by the All-Parties Conference in August 1928, the report encountered considerable opposition in some of the affiliated organizations. Some members of the Muslim League wanted to reject the report completely, on the ground that it was slanted in favor of Hindus. Even within the Congress some younger members, led by Subhas Chandra Bose and Jawaharlal Nehru, were reluctant to endorse any recommendation which did not demand complete independence. After the intervention of Mahatma Gandhi, the Congress agreed on a resolution promising to "adopt the Constitution if it is accepted in its entirety by the British Parliament on or before the 31st of December, 1929." Otherwise the Congress announced its intention to organize a campaign of nonviolent noncooperation.

On October 31, 1929, Lord Irwin issued a proclamation, containing the following commitment: "I am authorized on behalf of His Majesty's Government to state clearly that in their judgment it is implicit in the declaration of 1917 that the natural issue of India's constitutional progress . . . is the attainment of Dominion Status." The proclamation also announced that a Round Table Conference would be held in London soon after the publication of the Simon Report to consider the recommendations of that Report and other proposals for Indian constitutional reform.

Events were moving toward a showdown between the Indian National Congress and the British Government. At the annual session of the Congress in 1930, held in Lahore, Mahatma Gandhi moved a resolution which declared: "This Congress . . . declares that the word Swaraj in . . . the Congress constitution shall mean Complete Independence . . . This Congress authorises the All India Congress Committee, whenever it deems fit, to launch upon a programme of civil disobedience." In March and early April Gandhi made his famous salt march, which was the signal to start a massive civil disobedience cam-

[22] See *All Parties Conference, 1928: Report of the Committee Appointed by the Conference to Determine the Principles of the Constitution for India* (Allahabad, 1928).

paign. When the First Round Table Conference met in London in November 1930, Gandhi and thousands of Congress supporters were in jail. Fifty-seven nominated delegates from British India and sixteen representing the Indian States attended the Conference. Upon its conclusion in mid-January 1931, the British Prime Minister issued a declaration of policy, favoring "the advance of India through the new Constitution to full responsibility for her own Government," and pledging to take steps to enlist the cooperation of those who were engaged in civil disobedience. Shortly thereafter the leaders of the movement were released from jail. Gandhi thereupon entered into negotiations with Lord Irwin, which led in March to a settlement known as the Gandhi-Irwin Pact. Gandhi agreed to suspend the civil disobedience campaign in return for certain concessions from the British. This pact was quite unpopular with the younger group in the Congress, but it was ratified at a meeting of the Congress in Karachi.

Gandhi attended the Second Round Table Conference in the latter part of 1931, as the sole representative of the Congress. It proved to be a trying experience for him; in fact, he himself described it as a "long, slow agony." The representatives of the British Government and of various communal interests in India joined in postponing consideration of basic questions, such as the communal problem, and spent endless hours in considering minor matters. Gandhi returned to India in a melancholy frame of mind and found that the situation had deteriorated even during his short absence. The British authorities took the initiative in preventing a renewal of civil disobedience; by the end of April all of the top leaders and nearly 70,000 persons, including more than 5,300 women, were in prison. In the autumn Gandhi embarked on his most famous fast in successful protest against a proposal by the British Government to create separate electorates for the untouchables. In May 1933, he was released from prison just as he had started another fast. On his release he advised the suspension of the civil disobedience campaign, and after another period of imprisonment he recommended the abandonment of individual civil disobedience as well.

In November–December 1932, while the Congress leaders were in prison, a Third Round Table Conference was convened. After this session, which was even boycotted by the British Labor Party, the British Government issued new proposals for India in a White Paper. These proposals were disappointing to Indians. They were made even less satisfactory after the deliberations of a Joint Committee of the British Parliament, which considered the Indian problem for eighteen months. Out of these deliberations came the Government of India Act of 1935, the last and most important of the great landmarks along the road to self-government and eventual independence for India.

## Government of India Act of 1935

Briefly stated, the Act of 1935 may be regarded as a constitution for a federal state in India, in which both British India and the Indian States would be joined. It abolished dyarchy in the provinces and provided instead for provincial autonomy and full responsible government. It envisioned a kind of dyarchy at the Centre,[23] with some of the central subjects to be administered by the Viceroy with the advice and assistance of his ministers, responsible to the Central Legislature, and other subjects to be administered by him subject to the overall control of the British Crown.

The federation provided for in the Act of 1935 was a most peculiar one. Since it was never really established, it is impossible to say whether it would have been a workable arrangement. However, it served as a model for the federal state which India established in the Constitution of 1950. There is a striking similarity between the Government of India Act of 1935 and the Indian Constitution of 1950. It is a remarkable political fact that the major legislative contribution of the British to the government of India, a contribution which was widely criticized and in large part rejected by Indians at the time of its passage, should have been so largely accepted fifteen years later by independent India, less than two and a half years after it had gained its freedom from British rule.

According to the Act of 1935, the federation of India was to consist of the eleven Governors' provinces and the six Chief Commissioners' Provinces which constituted British India and those Indian States whose rulers agreed to accede to it. The federation was to be brought into being only when and if the rulers of Indian States representing not less than half the total population of the States and entitled to not less than half of the total number of seats allotted to the States in the upper chamber of the federal legislature had agreed to join the federation.

In dealing with four federal subjects, namely foreign relations, defense, ecclesiastical affairs, and tribal areas, the Viceroy would be responsible only to the Secretary of State for India and the British Parliament; he would not be constitutionally bound to consult his ministers at all. For the remaining federal subjects he was to act after consultation with the Council of Ministers, but in many instances even here he was not bound to accept the advice of the ministers. He was empowered to appoint the ministers, in consultation with the leader of the majority group in the House of Assembly. He could dismiss the ministers at his pleasure, although they were also responsible to the legisla-

[23] In India the Central Government is almost invariably referred to as the "Centre," and this common usage is adopted in this volume.

ture. He would still have a wide variety of discretionary powers and special responsibilities.

The federal legislature was to consist of the British sovereign, represented by the Viceroy, and two Houses to be known as the Council of States and the House of Assembly. The Council of States was to be composed of 156 representatives of British India, 150 of whom were to be elected on a class or communal basis, and not less than 52 nor more than 104 representatives of the Indian States, nominated by the rulers. The House of Assembly was to consist of 250 representatives of British India, 105 to be elected from general constituencies, and the remainder from class and special constituencies, all through a system of indirect election, and not more than 125 representatives of the Indian States, to be nominated by the rulers. The powers of the federal legislature, while extensive, were severely limited by the control which the Viceroy, as the representative of the British Crown, was to have over it.

In the provinces the Act of 1935 provided for a considerable measure of autonomy and responsible government, instead of the system of dyarchy introduced by the Government of India Act of 1919. The executive of a province was to consist of a Governor and a Council of Ministers responsible to a legislature. Six of the provinces were to have bicameral legislatures, and the rest a single chamber to be known as the Legislative Assembly. Of the 1585 seats provided for in the Legislative Assemblies, 959 were general seats (including 151 reserved for scheduled tribes and classes), 482 were Mohammedan seats, and the remainder were reserved for other class and communal and special groups. When elections were held for the Legislative Assemblies in 1937, some 35 million people, including more than 6 million women, were given the right to vote — a fivefold increase over any previous franchise in India.

As in any federal constitution, the distribution of powers between the central government and the constituent units of the federation was a matter of great interest and delicacy. The Act of 1935 spelled out these powers in great detail, and in a most ingenious way. It attempted to place every possible subject of legislation in one of three lists: a Federal List, a Provincial List, and a Concurrent List. The 59 subjects on the Federal List included defense, external affairs, central finance, central communications, and customs. Among the 54 subjects on the Provincial List were justice, police, land tenure and acquisition, local self-government, public health, education, agriculture, provincial finance, and tolls. Both the federal and provincial legislatures were empowered to pass legislation relating to any of the 26 subjects on the Concurrent List, which included criminal and civil procedure, control of the professions, and labor matters.

The Act also made certain changes in the "Home" Government of India to conform to the grants of additional political power to the proposed new Indian federation and its constituent units. A notable change was the abolition of the India Council, which had been the advisory body to the Secretary of State for India since 1858.

Most federations are formed by agreement among smaller political units and their representatives. The federation envisioned in the Government of India Act of 1935 was proposed by the British Government and represented the concessions which that Government was willing to make, or felt obliged to make, to public opinion at home, to the Indian nationalist leaders, to spokesmen of Indian communal groups, and to the rulers of the Indian States. In India the Government of India Act of 1935 received a frigid reception. If it had been enacted a generation before, it would have been hailed as a welcome step along the road to self-government. In the mid-1930's, with the nationalist movement a growing force, the Act was regarded as wrongly motivated and inadequately conceived. The Indian National Congress, the Muslim League, and other parties were hostile to it, though for different reasons. Jawaharlal Nehru, in *The Discovery of India,* written in 1944 while he was confined in a British prison, reflected the attitude of Congress toward the Act.

> This provided for some kind of provincial autonomy and a federal structure, but there were so many reservations and checks that both political and economic power continued to be concentrated in the hands of the British government. Indeed in some ways it confirmed and enlarged the powers of an executive responsible solely to that government. The federal structure was so envisaged as to make any real advance impossible, and no loophole was left for the representatives of the Indian people to interfere with or modify the system of British-controlled administration. . . . The act strengthened the alliance between the British government and the princes, landlords, and other reactionary elements in India. . . . The whole complicated structure of government remained as it was.[24]

Since the federal provisions of the Act could not be put into effect because of the reluctance of the Indian princes to accede, the British Government decided to proceed with the implementation of those provisions relating to responsible government in the provinces, and it announced that general elections would be held early in 1937 for the members of the provincial legislature. After considerable debate the

[24] Nehru, *The Discovery of India,* pp. 368–369.

Congress decided to participate in the elections, as did the Muslim League.

The Congress scored a notable success in the elections, winning clear majorities in six provinces, and pluralities in three others. After these electoral successes the Congress leaders announced that they would not approve the formation of Congress ministries "unless the leader of the Congress party in the Legislature is satisfied and able to state publicly that the Governor will not use his special powers of interference or set aside the advice of ministers in regard to their constitutional activities." Not until June 21, 1937, did the Viceroy make a public statement which was regarded as satisfactory on this point. Soon afterwards Congress ministries were formed in eight provinces. The Congress created considerable resentment on the part of the Muslim League and certain minority groups by deciding against participation in coalition ministries in provinces where no party had a clear majority, and by refusing to include non-Congressmen in provincial cabinets where they had a majority.

The Congress ministries made a creditable record in most of the provinces of British India.[25] The Congress experience in provincial responsibility, however, was short-lived. In October 1939, on instructions from the party's high command, all the Congress ministries resigned on the war issue, which led to a definite parting of the ways between the main wing of the nationalist movement and the British Government.[26]

### The Transfer of Power

Protracted negotiations between British representatives and spokesmen of the Indian National Congress failed to find a way out of the impasse that had developed over fundamentally different approaches to the issue of participation in the war. In August 1940, the Viceroy pledged that the British Government, after the war, would agree to

[25] For a detailed analysis of the record of the Congress and non-Congress governments in the provinces in the period 1937–39, see Coupland, *The Indian Problem*, II, pp. 22–157.

[26] Many Indians at the time and subsequently thought that the resignation of the Congress ministries was a serious mistake. V. P. Menon has stated this view most forcefully: "Had it [the Congress] not resigned from its position of vantage in the provinces the course of Indian history might have been very different. By resigning, it showed a lamentable lack of foresight and political wisdom. There was little chance of its being put out of office; the British Government would surely have hesitated to incur the odium of dismissing ministries which had the overwhelming support of the people. Nor could it have resisted a unanimous demand for a change at the Centre, a demand which would have been all the more irresistible after the entry of Japan into the war. In any case, it is clear that, but for the resignation of the Congress, Jinnah and the Muslim League would never have attained the position they did." V. P. Menon, *The Transfer of Power in India* (Princeton, N.J., 1957), p. 152.

convene a representative body to frame a new constitution for India, and he appealed for such unity in India "as would enable her to make the fullest possible contribution in the world struggle against tyranny and aggression." The Congress view was that it was impossible to co-operate in any "world struggle against tyranny and aggression" when India was not free and when it was faced with "an arrogant imperialism which is indistinguishable from Fascist authoritarianism," to use the language of a resolution of the Congress Working Committee in December 1941. In the meantime the Muslim League had issued its Lahore resolution in 1940, demanding a separate Pakistan, and the Indian Communists, after denouncing the "imperialist war," changed their position completely, to conform to the international party line after the Nazi assault on the Soviet Union in June 1941.

In March–April 1942, Sir Stafford Cripps, known as a friend of India, came to India to investigate ways and means of giving effect to the British offer of August 1940. In late March he issued some general proposals, and in a broadcast on March 30 he said: "Let us enter upon this primary task of the defence of India in the now sure knowledge that when we emerge from the fire and the travail of war it will be to build a free India upon foundations wrought by the Indian people themselves." Neither the Congress nor the Muslim League would accept his proposals, and Sir Stafford abruptly terminated his negotiations and admitted failure. Shortly thereafter the Congress high command, following Gandhi's advice, demanded an immediate end to British rule, and threatened "a mass struggle on non-violent lines on the widest possible scale" if this demand was not met. The reply of the British Government was to imprison Gandhi, Nehru, and virtually all the other important leaders of the Congress, and to declare that the Congress committees were unlawful associations.

In June 1945, after extended negotiations in India and England, the new Viceroy, Lord Wavell, broadcast proposals "to ease the present political situation and to advance India towards her goal of full self-government." He announced his intention to hold a political conference at Simla, to which twenty-one Indian leaders would be invited. The Simla Conference brought together representatives of all the major political groups in India, but it did not produce a meeting of minds. The Viceroy himself described it as a failure. "The Simla Conference," as V. P. Menon has observed, "afforded a last opportunity to the forces of nationalism to fight a rear-guard action to preserve the integrity of the country, and when the battle was lost the waves of communalism quickly engulfed it. Only the Hobson's choice of partition was left."[27]

Soon after this unhappy event a Labor Government came into power

[27] Menon, *The Transfer of Power in India*, p. 215. Chap. VIII, pp. 182–215.

in Britain and World War II ended with the surrender of Japan. These developments created a more favorable atmosphere for determining India's political future and also made the need of some lasting solution even more urgent. On September 16, 1945, the Viceroy announced that elections to the central and provincial legislatures would be held during the winter, and that he would "convene as soon as possible a constitution-making body." Elections to the central Legislative Assembly were held in late 1945 and resulted in decisive victories for the Congress and the Muslim League, proving that they "were the only parties that counted in the country."[28] This fact was confirmed in elections to provincial legislatures, which were held early in 1946. As a result of the provincial elections Congress ministries were formed in six provinces. The Muslim League did not fare so well, but it did form ministries in Bengal and Sind.

In March 1946 a British Cabinet Mission, consisting of Lord Pethick-Lawrence, Secretary of State for India, Sir Stafford Cripps, President of the Board of Trade, and A. V. Alexander, First Lord of the Admiralty, came to India to confer with Indian leaders and to consider various proposals for the solution of the "Indian problem." After several meetings with Gandhi, Maulana Azad, Jinnah, and other Indian leaders, the members of the Mission invited representatives of the Congress and the Muslim League to confer with them at Simla. The conference served only to dramatize the gulf that existed between the Congress and the Muslim League. Since it could not bring the main parties into agreement, the Cabinet Mission issued its own proposals. Rejecting the demand of the Muslim League for partition, the Mission proposed a Union of India, embracing both British India and the Indian States, with a Constituent Assembly consisting of representatives of the provincial legislatures and divided into three sections.

After further negotiations both the Congress and the Muslim League accepted the Cabinet Mission plan, with many conditions and reservations. Later the League, charging that the Mission had "played into the hands of the Congress," revoked its acceptance of the plan and raised again the demand for a separate Pakistan. However, the League did participate in the elections for members of the Constituent Assembly and won all but five of the seats allotted to Muslims. The Congress won all the general seats save nine.

The British Government decided to go ahead with its interim plans, even without the cooperation of the Muslim League. On August 6, 1946, the Viceroy invited Nehru to form an interim Government. This Government was sworn in on September 2nd. In mid-October the

28 *Ibid.*, p. 226.

Muslim League reversed its previous decision and agreed to participate, chiefly in order to prevent the Congress from consolidating its position to the detriment of the League's interests. But when the Viceroy issued invitations for the first meeting of the Constituent Assembly, Jinnah announced that the League would not join in.

In spite of the League's refusal, the Constituent Assembly met on December 9th. Dr. Rajendra Prasad, later President of the Republic of India, was elected President. Nehru immediately introduced an important "Objectives Resolution," which envisaged the Indian Union as "an independent Sovereign Republic," and the Congress insisted that the League should either participate in the Constituent Assembly or withdraw its representatives from the interim Government.

Confronted with this dilemma, the British Labor Government made a momentous decision. On February 20, 1947, Prime Minister Attlee announced in the British Parliament that the Government intended to take the necessary steps to transfer power into Indian hands by June 1948. If no agreement had been reached among the Indian parties by that time, his Government would then consider whether it would transfer power "as a whole to some form of central Government for British India, or in some areas to the existing provincial Governments, or in such other way as may seem most reasonable and in the best interests of the Indian people." The Prime Minister also announced that Lord Mountbatten would go to India as Viceroy, charged with the task of implementing the historic decision. This announcement was generally hailed in India and in Britain, although in both countries there were those who greeted it with the direst forebodings. In the debate on the announcement in the House of Commons, former Prime Minister Winston Churchill made his famous and, fortunately, ill-founded prophecy: "In handing over the Government of India to these so-called political classes we are handing over to men of straw of whom in a few years no trace will remain."

Lord Mountbatten arrived in India on March 22, 1947. He quickly concluded that the date for the transfer of power should be moved up, and that the decision between one or two states should be referred to the Indians themselves. On June 3 the British Government's new plan was announced in London and New Delhi. It provided for the handing over of power before the end of the year to one or two governments, each to have Dominion status. In broadcasts over All-India Radio that evening Nehru, Jinnah, and the Sikh leader Baldev Singh joined with the Viceroy in explaining and endorsing the new plan, although Nehru, at least, did so with a heavy heart.

Less than two and a half months elapsed between the announcement of the British Government's plan for the final transfer of power and the inauguration of the new nations of India and Pakistan. In this short time, in an atmosphere of growing tension and under a spirit of great urgency, was carried out what Lord Birdwood called "the greatest political and military operation in history."[29] "There was so much to be done within such a limited time. The verdicts of the provinces had to be ascertained; parliamentary legislation had to be hurried through; if partition were decided upon, the administrative services and armed forces had to be divided, assets and liabilities to be apportioned and the boundaries in the disputed areas to be settled — all these tasks had to be carried through more or less simultaneously."[30]

When the results of the decisions in the crucial provinces, obtained by votes in the legislative assemblies or by referenda or other ways, became known, there was no longer any doubt that the subcontinent would emerge from its long period of dependence as two nations, not one.[31] Once this basic decision had been confirmed, the Indian Independence Bill was introduced in the House of Commons on July 4. Although it was properly labeled by the Secretary of State for India as "a Bill unique in the history of legislation in this country," it was passed by the House of Commons on July 15, by the House of Lords on the following day, and received the Royal Assent on July 18. On August 14 the necessary adaptations of the Government of India Act of 1935 were put into effect by the India (Provisional Constitution) Order, 1947. "By August 15th the rulers of all the States geographically contiguous to India, with the exception of Hyderabad, Junagadh and one or two States in Kathiawar with Muslim rulers, had signed the Instrument of Accession and the Standstill Agreement. The fundamental unity of the country having been ensured, India became one federation with the provinces and the States as integral parts."[32]

Thus in August 1947, less than two years after the war, two new Dominions, India and Pakistan, emerged in the Indian subcontinent. This remarkable achievement in liquidation and rebirth required a high level of statesmanship and forbearance on all sides, especially on the part of the new Labor Government and the Parliament in Britain and on the part of responsible leaders of Indian opinion in the Congress, the Muslim League, and elsewhere.[33] On August 14, in Ka-

[29] Lord Birdwood, *India and Pakistan: A Continent Decides* (New York, 1954), p. 34.

[30] Menon, *The Transfer of Power in India*, p. 387.

[31] In effect East Bengal, West Punjab, Sind, Baluchistan and the North-West Frontier Province voted for Pakistan.

[32] Menon, *The Transfer of Power in India*, p. 413.

[33] For the details of the developments in 1945–47 leading to the transfer of power, see *ibid.* and E. W. R. Lumby, *The Transfer of Power in India, 1945-7* (New York, 1954).

rachi, the capital of the new Islamic state of Pakistan, with Lord Mountbatten on hand to perform his last official duty as Viceroy, Jinnah was sworn in as Governor-General and Liaquat Ali Khan as Prime Minister. On the following day, in New Delhi, Lord Mountbatten, having given up his post as British Viceroy, was sworn in as Governor-General of free India, and he in turn swore in a new Cabinet, headed by Nehru.[34] The British century was over. The destiny of India was henceforth primarily in Indian hands.

[34] See Leonard Mosley, *The Last Days of the British Raj* (London, 1961), pp. 238–242.

# 4

# Toward Independence: The Nationalist Movement

Along with the organizing skill and the military power which enabled the British to conquer and to rule India for many decades came the ideas which eventually liberated it. "British imperialism in India had two contradictory sets of features. In some respects, it had a revolutionary character. In others it was reactionary in the extreme. But in both its phases, British rule encouraged and provoked the rise and development of the nationalist struggle for justice and independence."[1]

While the British were consolidating their power in India, they were also, unwittingly, laying the bases for Indian independence. Their contributions were manifold: political, administrative, legal, economic, social, cultural, educational, and psychological. Politically, they assumed effective power in India at a very low period in Indian history — the Mogul dynasty was hardly more than a shell of its former self; the Hindu revivalism under the Marathas had fallen far short of its avowed goals; and other Western powers, notably France, were rivals for trade and influence in the subcontinent. The British gave India a greater degree of national unity and solidarity and a better form of government than it had ever enjoyed, save perhaps during a few periods in its long history. *Administratively,* the British developed a pattern of government which is still followed in its basic outlines by free India. This administrative system extended through British India, even to the village level, and indirectly affected the princely States as well. By associating Indians in increasing numbers in the administrative services, the British helped to train generations of capable administrators. *Legally,*

[1] Santosh Trikha, "Political Parties in India" (unpublished doctoral dissertation, University of Saugar, Sagar, India, 1955), p. 56.

70

they gave India something close to a uniform code of justice, a revolutionary departure from the previous patterns of regional and local "justice" and communal differences. They also gave India a concept of liberty under law. *Economically,* they destroyed the base of existence of village India and undoubtedly "milked" India for British ends, but they introduced new forms of land tenure, they tied the country together economically as well as politically, they helped to create new economic classes and interests, and they developed systems of trade and finance which have prevailed to the present day. *Socially,* they helped to ameliorate some of the worst abuses of the strongly entrenched caste system, and they created new standards and practices of social behavior. *Culturally,* they brought India into contact with the West and helped India to rediscover its own past as well as the riches of other cultures. *Educationally,* they made great progress in achieving the objective recommended by Lord Macaulay in his famous Minute of 1835: "to form a class who may be interpreters between us and the millions whom we govern; a class of persons, Indian in blood and colour, but English in taste, in opinions, in morals, and in intellect."[2] The existing educational system in India is largely constructed along British lines, with certain concessions to the advocates of a *sarvodaya* (welfare, equality, and uplift of all) society, the demands of champions of linguistic reforms, the goals of free, compulsory education on a mass scale, and the needs of an independent state in the modern world. *Psychologically,* the British were themselves victims of a superiority complex which gave them great confidence and prestige but which often blinded them to the real conditions and attitudes of the Indians whom they ruled. Conversely, the Indian reaction to British superiority was a blend of inferiority complexes, an aping of their rulers, resentment of foreign rule, Hindu or Muslim revivalism, esoteric movements of many kinds, and a determination to shape their own future.

Whatever the British may have contributed to India, and however successful they may have been in training many generations of Indians to help them rule the subcontinent, there was always a fundamental conflict of interests between Britain and India. Briefly stated, the British were interested in ruling India primarily for British interests, which by a process of rationalization they often interpreted as being for India's best interests as well; whereas the Indians were primarily concerned with Indian interests, whether they accepted British rule as the best thing for them or whether they espoused the cause of indepen-

[2] Thomas Babington Macaulay, *Prose and Poetry* (Cambridge, Mass., 1952), p. 729. The text of Macaulay's "Minute on Education" is given in Wm. Theodore de Bary, ed., *Sources of Indian Tradition* (New York, 1958), II, 44–49.

dence. This basic conflict of interests explains many developments in the modern history of India. As Toynbee has pointed out, the Western impact on India was greater than that on any other part of Asia, but the gulf between Western civilization and the predominant Hindu civilization of India was extreme.[3] The Indian acceptance of British rule, except among a relatively few individuals, was always tentative and rather negative; and the Indian response to this rule took many forms.

## Characteristics of Indian Nationalism

The most vigorous Indian response was the rise of an increasingly effective and popular nationalist movement. As an organized movement, nationalism in India dates from the latter half — and indeed from the last fifteen years — of the nineteenth century; but it had its roots in certain movements and in the works of certain individuals of the early nineteenth century. To be sure, some precursors of nationalism in India might be sought on a regional level. The Marathas are an outstanding example, for they cherish the memory of a great leader — Shivaji, a mighty Maratha chieftain of the seventeenth century — and of days of greatness in the last seventeenth and early eighteenth century when Maratha power dominated a large part of western and central India.[4]

Some features of Indian nationalism are common to nationalist movements and feelings everywhere; others are characteristic of Asian nationalism; others are peculiar to India itself. The nationalist movement in India was a political movement with strong economic, social, and religious aspects. It was essentially a creation of and a reaction against foreign rule — a movement of protest which eventually became a movement of revolt. Before 1885 it lacked effective organization and focus, but after that date the Indian National Congress became its spearhead.

The first leaders of the Congress were moderates steeped in the traditions of Western liberalism. They favored the continuance of British rule and concentrated on relatively mild requests for greater participation of Indians in the political life of the country. Shortly after the turn of the century the leadership of the Congress was divided between moderates and an increasingly influential and vocal group of more mili-

[3] Arnold Toynbee, *The World and the West* (London, 1953), Chapter III, "India and the West."

[4] In 1784 Warren Hastings wrote: "The Marathahs possess, alone of all the people of Hindostan and Deccan, a principle of national attachment, which is strongly impressed on the minds of all individuals of the nation, and would probably unite their chiefs, as in one common cause, if any great danger were to threaten the general state." Quoted in Jawaharlal Nehru, *The Discovery of India* (New York, 1946), p. 270.

tant nationalists, sometimes called extremists. These new leaders were more critical of British rule and more militant in their demands.

Shortly after World War I the Congress came under the domination of Mahatma Gandhi, who remained the most powerful voice in the nationalist movement from that time until the achievement of Indian independence. Under Gandhi the Congress, which had been largely a movement of intellectuals with some broadening of leadership and support under the extremists, became a genuine mass movement. It embraced more radical elements and included in its ranks socialists of all hues, peasants' and workers' organizations, the Radical Humanists, and even Communists. By the 1930's the Congress was flatly demanding complete independence, although it was not clear on the timetable for achieving that goal. In fact most of the Congress leaders were surprised when the British actually did set a date for independence and even more surprised when the British moved up that date and transferred power completely and with considerable grace.

Nationalism is a complex phenomenon wherever it is encountered, but in India it was particularly complex because of the environment in which it arose and because of the many forces, internal and external, which affected it. In the nineteenth and twentieth centuries India experienced a great reawakening, produced no doubt by the Western impact upon it and by the search to find its own identity. Nationalism was powerfully stimulated by the work of many persons and organizations whose efforts were directed to the rediscovery and revitalization of the past and to the preservation of basic ideals and faiths. Even movements which were essentially nonpolitical and reactionary in their fundamental outlook contributed to the development of a nationalist upsurge. A very powerful impetus was given by the Ramakrishna movement, inspired by one of the great religious mystics of modern India and organized and developed by his leading disciple, Vivekananda. Vivekananda preached that India should undertake a spiritual conquest of the world and was associated with the Hindu Renaissance of the late nineteenth and early twentieth centuries, which contributed in various ways to the growth of nationalism.[5]

Nationalism eventually permeated all sections of the subcontinent, but for some time it was confined largely to British India. Most of the early leaders of the nationalist movement were Bengalis or Maharashtrians. Bengal, the homeland of Rammohun Roy, Ramakrishna, Vivekananda, Surendranath Banerjea, Bankim Chandra, Chatterjee, Aurobindo Ghose, Bipin Chandra Pal, Chitta Ranjan Das, Rabindranath

[5] See de Bary, ed., *Sources of Indian Tradition*, II, 85–107; and Charles H. Heimsath, *Indian Nationalism and Hindu Social Reform* (Princeton, N.J., 1964), pp. 42–45, 331–336.

Tagore, Subhas Chandra Bose, and a host of great leaders of modern India, had a long tradition of both intellectual and revolutionary activity. There the contacts with the British were longest and closest, for Calcutta was the main center of British rule in India throughout most of the British period. The British ruled with the cooperation of hundreds of Bengalis who were trained for administrative service; but the British never did win over the Bengalis, and after the partition of Bengal that province became a center of disaffection and sometimes extreme nationalist agitation.[6] The experience in Maharashtra was quite different. Although the Bombay presidency was another center of British power, the Marathas had a proud tradition of independence from both Mogul and British control, based on the successes which they achieved against Aurungzeb and their resistance to British encroachments until the early years of the nineteenth century. They cherished memories, based in part on chauvinistic exaggeration, of the great days when they controlled a large part of western India and when they seemed about to extend their influence still farther, at least until the British became the dominant power in the subcontinent. Although few were Marathas, some of the greatest leaders of Indian nationalism came from Maharashtra (including Bombay) and were influenced by this tradition. They include Pherozeshah Mehta (a Gujarati); Dadabhai Naoroji (a Parsi); and M. G. Ranade, G. K. Gokhale, and Bal Gangadhar Tilak (all Chitpavan Brahmans). Despite the special role of the Brahmans in the nationalist movement, the greatest of all modern Indians, Mahatma Gandhi, did not belong to this caste. Gandhi was also neither a Bengali nor a Maharashtrian. He was a member of the Vaisya or merchant caste and was a Gujarati from Saurashtra.

The nationalist movement in India was always dominated by Hindus. This is not surprising, for the great majority of Indians were Hindus. Moreover, under the British the Muslims lost much of their position and influence, and the Hindus benefited more from the opportunities opened up by the British to enter the trades, professions, and governmental and educational service. Muslims were further alienated by the many evidences that in the minds of some of the nationalist leaders the struggle for *swaraj* (freedom) in its various forms was linked with a revival or reaffirmation of Hinduism. Vivekananda advocated a revival of Hindu virtues and Tilak gave a strong Hindu cast to all of his efforts. Even Gandhi was suspect by many Muslims; while he made Hindu-Muslim unity a major plank in his program, he spoke of the need for a *ram rajya* — a Hindu conception of an ideal kingly rule; he

[6] See J. H. Broomfield, *Elite Conflict in a Plural Society: Twentieth Century Bengal* (Berkeley, Calif., 1968).

opposed partition and the establishment of a separate Muslim state; and he was, after all, a Hindu. Although many Muslims were active in the nationalist movement (some, like Maulana Azad, held high positions in the Indian National Congress and later in the government of independent India), the majority remained aloof from the Congress, especially at the beginning of its activities when their great leader, Sir Syed Ahmad Khan, advised them to have no part in it, and in the years just preceding independence when most joined the Muslim League. In short, while there was a kind of all-India nationalism, at least in the negative sense of opposition to foreign rule and of the demand of "India for the Indians," it would be more accurate to refer to two types of nationalism in India — Hindu nationalism, headed by the Congress, and Muslim nationalism, eventually led by the Muslim League.

The greatest spokesmen of Indian nationalism in its final phases constantly sought to promote what Jawaharlal Nehru called a "real or Indian nationalism" — "something quite apart from these two religious and communal varieties" (Hindu and Muslim).[7] While they were ardent nationalists in the sense that they wanted not only freedom from foreign rule but economic, social, and human freedom as well, they also had a world outlook which was almost nonnational, or even antinational. "It is surprising," wrote Nehru in *The Discovery of India,* "how internationally minded we grew in spite of our intense nationalism. No other nationalist movement in a subject country came anywhere near this."[8] Tagore denounced the evils of modern nationalism, and in one of his best-known poems, included in his Nobel Prize-winning volume, *Gitanjali,* he expressed the hope that his country would awake into a "heaven of freedom . . . where the world has not been broken up into fragments by narrow domestic walls." Gandhi declared: "I do want to think in terms of the whole world. . . . I want the cultures of all lands to be blown about my house as freely as possible." Nehru warned that nationalism "is a narrowing creed," and he insisted that "we seek no narrow nationalism." All three of these great nationalist leaders were bent on freeing India not only from the British yoke but, as Gandhi once declared, "from any yoke whatsoever." Yet all of the nationalist leaders of India came gradually to accept the view that political independence for India was an essential step, if only the first step, toward the kind of freedom which they envisaged for their country and their people.

Thus nationalism was a major force in the India of the nineteenth and twentieth centuries. In *The Discovery of India* Nehru wrote:

[7] Jawaharlal Nehru, *Glimpses of World History* (4th ed., London, 1949), p. 720.

[8] Nehru, *The Discovery of India,* p. 427.

"Nationalism was and is inevitable in the India of my day; it is a natural and healthy growth. For any subject country national freedom must be the first and dominant urge; for India with her intense sense of individuality and a past heritage, it was doubly so."[9]

## Main Stages of the Nationalist Movement

The story of the nationalist movement in India may be divided into five stages, with the terminal dates of each succeeding stage being 1885, 1905–1907, 1919–1920, 1934–1935, and 1947, respectively. An analysis of each of these stages will throw some light on the historical evolution of the struggle for independence and on the characteristics of Indian nationalism.

**1. The Formative Stage, to 1885.** Until recently the beginnings of the Indian nationalist movement were usually dated from the founding of the Indian National Congress in 1885. Now more attention is being given to the formative period of Indian nationalism, prior to 1885. Among the highlights of this period are the manifold activities of Raja Rammohun Roy in the early nineteenth century; the contributions of other liberal reformers, especially in Bengal and Maharashtra; the influence of many politico-religious organizations, such as the Brahmo Samaj and the Arya Samaj; British policies, such as the introduction of a British pattern of education; the beginnings of the enlisting of Indians in the civil service; the first Indian Councils Acts; the circumstances leading to the transfer of power in India from the British East India Company to the British Government; the "Mutiny" of 1857 and its aftermath; the growing awareness of certain British and Indian leaders of the need for an organization to serve the dual purpose of siphoning off mounting Indian unrest and of presenting to the British authorities the just grievances of the Indians, including their desire for greater representation in political and economic affairs; the formation of several societies, notably the Calcutta Indian Association, which were in effect precursors of the Indian National Congress; and the early efforts of many persons, including Surendranath Banerjea and Dadabhai Naoroji, who were to become prominent leaders of the Congress in its early phases.

Raja Rammohun Roy (1772–1833), a Bengali Brahman, is often called not only "the Father of Indian Nationalism" but also "the Father of Modern India." A man of universal interests and tremendous energy, Rammohun Roy acquired a remarkable knowledge of both Western and Indian civilization. After a successful career in the Bengal Civil Service, Roy retired at the age of 42 to devote his energies to his

[9] *Ibid.,* pp. 40–41.

political and other interests. An admirer of the liberal ideas of the West and of the teachings of Christ, he also saw much value in the lessons of the Vedas and in India's past; but he found many things to criticize in both Western and Eastern civilization. He was critical of such Indian practices or institutions as the caste system, child marriage, and widow-burning. He believed that British rule was a good thing for India, and he hoped that his fellow-countrymen would take advantage of the opportunities afforded them by the British. He founded and edited newspapers in Bengali, English, and Persian, and he established several secondary schools. In 1828 he organized the Brahmo Samaj (Society of God), a society which "was to exercise a deep influence on the social and religious life of modern India,"[10] and which has been described as "the pioneer of the nationalist movement."[11]

Many other organizations founded well before 1885 contributed directly or indirectly to the development of a spirit of nationalism. Prominent among these were the British India Society (1843), the British Indian Association (1851), the associations organized in Bombay, Madras, and Calcutta to present representations to the British Government at the time of the renewal of the Charter of the East India Company in 1853, and the Arya Samaj, founded in Bombay in 1875 by Dayananda Saraswati, a Gujarati Brahman. Dayananda, "the Luther of India," regarded the Vedas as infallible, and the Arya Samaj, with its slogan of "Back to the Vedas," advocated a kind of militant Hinduism which alienated Muslims and many Hindus as well; but many nationalist leaders were associated with it, and its contributions to the cause of Indian nationalism have continued until the present day. Its main stronghold has been in the Punjab.[12]

The "Mutiny" of 1857 also contributed to the growth of Indian nationalism, although, as has been noted, it was far from being a nationalist uprising. Before 1857, as Dr. R. C. Majumdar, one of India's leading historians, has pointed out, India "had not yet developed any general idea of either conscious nationalism or true patriotism."[13] After the "Mutiny" the nationalist idea was promoted by many individuals and organizations, and within two decades it began to take on institutional form.

The immediate precursor and "true prototype" of the Indian National Congress was the Indian Association, founded in Calcutta in

[10] De Bary, ed., *Sources of Indian Tradition,* p. 572.
[11] A. R. Desai, *Social Background of Indian Nationalism* (London, 1948), p. 265. See also Heimsath, *Indian Nationalism and Hindu Social Reform,* pp. 73–76.
[12] See *ibid.,* Chap. V ("Dayananda Saraswati and the Social Reform Movement in Northern India").
[13] Quoted in the *Radical Humanist,* XXI (June 30, 1957), 319.

1876. Its leading spirit was Surendranath Banerjea, a Bengali Brahman whose dismissal from the Indian Civil Service in 1874 led him to devote the remainder of a long life to "redressing our wrongs and protecting our rights, personal and collective."[14] A powerful orator, Banerjea made three highly successful lecture tours in various parts of India — in 1877, 1878, and 1884. At the All-India Durbar in Delhi in 1877, convened by the Governor-General, Lord Lytton, to celebrate the conferring of the title of Empress of India on Queen Victoria, representatives of Indian organizations advanced the idea of a national organization of Indians to voice the sentiments of the Indian people. This idea intrigued Surendranath Banerjea, who attended this Durbar, and was apparently taken up by the Indian Association. Under the auspices of the Association a National Conference was held in Calcutta in 1883. This was "the first effort of its kind in India" and "must be regarded as the true forerunner of the Congress of 1885."[15]

Other Indians who were soon to play a prominent part in the work of the Indian National Congress began their active work in the 1870's and early 1880's. By the year 1870 Dadabhai Naoroji, who was later known as the grand old man of the Indian nationalist movement and who was the first Indian to be elected to the British Parliament, had formulated his famous theory of "economic drain" as a result of British rule and foreign exploitation. "It was this theory of economic drain which may be considered to have laid the foundation for the political agitation of Indians from 1885 onwards."[16] It profoundly influenced the thinking of several generations of Indians, and it is still widely held, even by eminent Indian economists. Before 1885, also, Justice Ranade began his lifelong work for economic and social reforms and "laid the foundations of what later came to be called Indian political economy."[17] Naoroji and Ranade differed in their outlook and in their policies. Ranade espoused views which appealed to the moderates in the Indian nationalist movement, whereas Naoroji's approach, a more direct and critical one, found favor with the group which is often referred to as the extremists.

[14] Surendranath Banerjea, *A Nation in the Making* (London, 1925), p. 33.

[15] Nandalal Chatterji, "The Forgotten Precursor of the Indian National Congress," *Journal of Indian History*, XXXVI (April, 1958), 13. See also Michael Edwardes, *British India, 1772–1947* (New York, 1968), pp. 276–278. Wilfred Scawen Blunt, a well-known British journalist, referred to it as "the first session of the Indian Parliament," in *India Under Ripon: a Private Diary* (London, 1909), p. 118.

[16] From an unpublished précis of S. D. Javadekar, "Adhunik Bharat (Modern India)," a treatise in Marathi, p. 13. See also William R. Smith, *Nationalism and Reform in India* (New Haven, 1938), p. 140.

[17] Javadekar, "Adhunik Bharat," p. 13.

Muslim nationalism can also be traced to the years prior to 1885. In part this took the form of harking back to the great days of Muslim rule in India; in part it was a reaction against the difficulties which the Muslims experienced after the consolidation of British rule and particularly after they failed to hold their own with Hindus in the economic and political field. They suffered further as a result of the "Mutiny," for which the British Government held them largely responsible. Yet in the years following the "Mutiny," when Muslim fortunes and spirits seemed to be at a low ebb, a change in their political, if not economic, status set in.

The leading spirit in this Muslim revival was Sir Syed Ahmad Khan (1817–1898), who urged his fellow-Muslims to overcome their superstitions and bigotry, to cease feeling sorry for themselves, to work for their moral and material improvement, and to cling to the fundamentals of their faith while at the same time preparing themselves more adequately for the demands and needs of the contemporary world. Two cardinal points in his creed were cooperation with the British and the preservation of Muslim identity against the Hindus. He did much to reconcile the Muslims to British rule and to remove British suspicions and contempt for Indian Muslims. He advised the Muslims to remain aloof from the Indian National Congress, on the ground that it would inevitably come under Hindu domination. He argued that the Muslims should not identify themselves with the Hindus, but should instead seek their own salvation along different lines. Sir Syed believed that the best way to preserve the Muslim way of life was for the Muslims to become better educated. This included education in Western culture as well as in the Indian and Islamic past. In 1877 he founded the Anglo-Oriental College at Aligarh, which later developed into the Muslim University. The Aligarh movement, of which Sir Syed was the moving spirit, contributed to the regeneration of the Muslims in India and laid the basis for a more active Muslim political movement at a later period.

**2. The Indian National Congress: Moderates versus Extremists.** In 1885 the nationalist movement entered its second and more organized phase with the founding of the Indian National Congress. From that date until 1947 the Congress was the chief voice of Indian nationalism, and almost all of the prominent spokesmen of nationalism were at one time associated with it.

The British authorities in India looked with favor upon the new organization. One of its chief founders was an Englishman, Allan Octavian Hume, and several Englishmen and one Englishwoman (Mrs. Annie Besant, the famous theosophist) were Presidents of the Congress. Hume conceived of the Congress as a constructive channel for the growing discontent in the subcontinent. The object of the Congress was not at first separation from Great Britain, but continued association with it; the views of the Congress were presented in moderate terms, and they were confined largely to requests for administrative reforms and for the greater participation of Indians in the British-controlled administration and in local and national elective bodies. Surendranath Banerjea, one of the early leaders of the Congress, declared as late as 1895: "It is not severance that we look forward to — but unification, permanent embodiment as an integral part of that great Empire that has given the rest of the world the models of free institutions."[18]

During the first two decades of its existence the Congress was under the direction of Indian liberals, who were English-educated and admirers of Western ideas and institutions, and it drew its support from a small but influential group of the intelligentsia and the commercial classes. Among its early leaders were Dadabhai Naoroji (1825–1917), Surendranath Banerjea (1848–1926), Justice M. G. Ranade (1842–1901), and Pherozeshah Mehta (1845–1915). Toward the end of this period the leading figure in the Congress was G. K. Gokhale (1866–1915), a disciple of Ranade, who devoted his life to the public service. In 1885 he joined the Deccan Education Society, and he taught for several years at Fergusson College in Poona, which the Society established in the year in which he became associated with it. In 1905 he founded the Servants of India Society, an organization dedicated to the public welfare, which Gandhi once tried in vain to enter. Gandhi, however, regarded Gokhale as his "political *guru*." For the last thirteen years of his life Gokhale was a member of the Imperial Legislative Council. While he believed in cooperation with the British and in a policy of gradualism, he did not hesitate to criticize British policies. His annual speeches on the imperial budget in the Imperial Legislative Council were brilliant exposés of the economic shortcomings of British rule.

From the 1890's on more and more criticisms of the British were voiced in Congress ranks and certain policies of the British authorities and the rise of a more extremist group within the Congress tended to create a rift between the Congress and the Government. The partition of Bengal and several other developments in 1905–1907 widened the rift and ushered in a more militant phase of Indian nationalism. The British authorities tried to curb the activities of the Congress, and they warned against the consequences of what they regarded as growing

[18] From Presidential Address to the Indian National Congress in 1895; quoted in Desai, *Social Background of Indian Nationalism*, p. 294.

radicalism within Congress ranks. Apparently they believed that their policies and warnings were bearing fruit in a weakening of the Congress. In 1900 Lord Curzon wrote to the Secretary of State for India: "My own belief is that Congress is tottering to its fall, . . . and one of my ambitions while in India is to assist it to a peaceful demise."[19]

While the policy of the British Government toward the Congress was hardening, the control of the liberals within the organization was being challenged by a younger but very active group of more militant nationalists. This group drew its chief support from Bengal, Maharashtra, and the Punjab. In Bengal the leaders were Bepin Chandra Pal and Aurobindo Ghose, in the Punjab the chief leader was Lala Lajpat Rai, and in Maharashtra the more militant school of nationalism was led by Bal Gangadhar Tilak.

Tilak turned to India's past for inspiration, and he sought to induce a spirit of pride and self-respect in his fellow-countrymen. He revived the cult of Shivaji (the great Maratha warrior of the seventeenth century) and the Ganapati festivals, and used these for political purposes. Later, during his years of exile and confinement in Mandalay (1908–1914), he wrote a lengthy commentary on the *Bhagavad Gita,* in which he reinterpreted that great Indian classic as preaching a philosophy of political and religious action.

The British journalist, Valentine Chirol, called Tilak "the Father of Indian Unrest." Undoubtedly the policies which he championed were twisted by more extremist followers into a philosophy of justifiable violence, and his own attitude toward the many acts of violence which agitated Bengal after 1908 was always rather paradoxical. But he was not himself an apostle of violence. He was a spokesman of the extremist or nationalist group within the nationalist movement which emphasized the political struggle rather than social and economic reforms, which distrusted the British rather than believed in the importance of cooperating with the foreign rulers, and which advocated stronger pressures than the moderates were willing to endorse. "Political rights," argued Tilak, "will have to be fought for. The Moderates think that these can be won by permission. We think that they can be got by strong pressure." He held that the so-called extremists were not in fact very extreme. He brought the demand for *swaraj* squarely into the center of the nationalist agitation. In ringing words, quoted over and over again throughout India, he declared: "*Swaraj* is my birthright and I will have it." He was perhaps the first nationalist leader who had great mass appeal. In a sense he foreshadowed the great work of

[19] Quoted in Leonard Mosely, *Curzon: The End of an Epoch* (London, 1960), p. 88.

Mahatma Gandhi in this respect. He is still referred to today by the name by which he was best known during his lifetime: "Lokamanya" — "Honored by the People."[20]

Tilak and others in the extremist group preached a kind of Hindu revivalism which gave new life to the nationalist movement, but which at the same time alienated many Muslims from the movement. The separation of Muslim from Hindu nationalism became more marked as a result of the formation of the Muslim League in 1906, the famous deputation of Muslim spokesmen, led by the Aga Khan, to the Viceroy in 1906 to petition the British authorities for separate electorates for Muslims in elections, and the endorsement of the principle of separate electorates in the Morley-Minto reforms of 1909.

**3. The Era of Gokhale and Tilak.** Thus the third period of Indian nationalism was ushered in by agitation, extremism, and separatism. At the annual session of the Indian National Congress in 1905, a nationalist party was formed within the Congress, under the leadership of Tilak, with strong support from Lala Lajpat Rai and B. C. Pal — a triumvirate popularly referred to as Lal-Bal-Pal, or the "national trinity." At the 1906 Congress session Dadabhai Naoroji, then 80 years old, exhorted leaders of both moderate and extremist groups to work together for the goal of *swaraj*. But this was not to be. At the historic session of the Congress at Surat in 1907, Tilak and Aurobindo Ghose led a movement of extremists to gain control of the Congress; this effort failed amid scenes of wild disorder, and for several years thereafter the control of the Congress remained in the hands of the moderates.

This was a low period in the nationalist movement as a whole. The extremists were accused of complicity in various acts of violence, and their chief leaders were removed or retired from active political life by the British Government. In 1908 Tilak was tried and sentenced to six years of confinement in Mandalay. Lala Lajpat Rai was deported from the Punjab. Aurobindo Ghose was imprisoned briefly for alleged complicity in the terrorism that was flaring up in Bengal, and after his release he was a changed man. In 1910 he abandoned Bengal and his wife, and retired to the French possession of Pondicherry, where he spent the remaining forty years of his life.

A very different Bengali voice — that of Rabindranath Tagore — was heard in protest against the wave of violence in Bengal. In disgust at the terrorism in his native province, Tagore virtually withdrew from political activity. He continued to write stirring poems and other works which made him at once one of the greatest apostles of Indian national-

[20] See M. A. Buch, *Rise and Growth of Indian Militant Nationalism* (Baroda, 1940); D. V. Tahmankar, *Lokamanya Tilak* (London, 1956); de Bary, ed., *Sources of Indian Tradition*, pp. 717–724.

ism and one of the greatest critics of modern nationalism. Later, in the Gandhian era, he again played a more direct role in the nationalist movement.

The position of the extremists, greatly weakened by the arrest or retirement of their chief leaders, was made more difficult by British concessions, including the Morley-Minto reforms and the abolition of the partition of Bengal in 1911. However, for some five years after the return of Tilak from Burma in 1914, the extremists were in the ascendancy, although even Tilak seemed to be more moderate than in former days. From the time of his return, and particularly from 1915 when he became more active again and when his great rival, Gokhale, died, until his death in 1920, he was the unquestioned leader of the nationalist movement.

During the years of World War I the movement gained strength and cohesion. The 1915 session of the Congress passed a compromise resolution which paved the way for Tilak and his followers to re-enter the national organization. At the 1916 session in Lucknow, the reunion of moderates and extremists was consolidated. Another important development at the Lucknow Congress was the endorsement of the so-called "Lucknow Pact," for cooperation between the Congress and the Muslim League.

As Tilak had predicted many years before, "the Extremists of today will be Moderates tomorrow." Moderates, extremists, and Muslims could unite on the demand for a large measure of self-government after the war. The extremists, to be sure, developed other organizations, notably the Home Rule League, in which Tilak and Mrs. Annie Besant were particularly active. A campaign of *swadeshi*[21] and of national education was also launched. Some of the liberals in the Congress, feeling unhappy with the radical trend of the main nationalist party, seceded and formed the Liberal Federation. Within the Congress Tilak formed a Congress Democratic Party to agitate for self-government through a policy of "responsive cooperation."

The British Government made sweeping concessions to Indian demands in the Montagu-Chelmsford Reforms of 1918 and the Government of India Act of 1919. The Congress in 1919 passed a resolution labeling these reforms "inadequate, unsatisfactory and disappointing" and urging the British Parliament to "take early steps to establish full Responsible Government in India in accordance with the principles of self-determination." However, the resolution also declared that "Pend-

---

[21] *Swadeshi:* a Hindi word derived from Sanskrit, meaning "homemade." Refers to the "buy home goods movement," a kind of economic boycott which the Indian National Congress used effectively in its resistance to British rule, especially in the Gandhian era.

ing such introduction, the Congress trusts that, so far as may be possible, the people will so work the Reforms as to secure an early establishment of full Responsible Government."

Dissatisfaction with the "inadequate, unsatisfactory, and disappointing" British concessions was deepened by tensions arising from various repressive acts and policies of the British authorities. Among these were the notorious Rowlatt Acts, the arrest of Mrs. Besant and other Congress leaders (Mrs. Besant was elected President of the Congress in 1917, while she was still interned), the shooting of several hundred Indians in Amritsar in April 1919, on the orders of the British General, Dyer (the Jallianwala Bagh massacre), and the alleged failure of the British to redeem their wartime pledges to India. Moreover, in 1920 the nationalist movement was given greater depth and a new direction under its greatest leader, Mahatma Gandhi.

**4. The Gandhian Era.** In 1915 Mohandas Karamchand Gandhi returned to India after twenty years in South Africa. In South Africa, where he had gone upon completing his studies in England (where he was admitted to the bar), he developed ideas and a philosophy of action which represented his individualistic blend of Western and Indian ideas and practices. Notable among these were his concepts of *satyagraha,* which he often translated loosely as "soul-force," his emphasis on the doctrine of *ahimsa,* or nonviolence, and his theories of the relation of ends and means. For some months after his return to India he traveled about the country and observed conditions at first hand. Then he began to take an active part in the independence movement, through the Congress and the Home Rule Leagues and through limited experiments in the technique with which his name is forever associated — that of nonviolent noncooperation.

After the death of Tilak in 1920 Gandhi became the unquestioned leader of the nationalist movement, although some nationalist leaders, Hindu as well as Muslim, did not approve of his methods and although he sometimes openly disagreed with Congress policies. But whether his advice was followed at a given time or not, and whether he was in the forefront of the nationalist struggle or in prison or in "retirement," he gave the struggle the imprint of his powerful personality. Gandhi had the courage of his convictions, and he won a following among the masses of the people that is unparalleled in the long course of Indian history. It is impossible to exaggerate his contributions, not only to the nationalist cause but to the rebirth of modern India in far more than a political sense.

The Congress might have lost much of its momentum if it had not come under the influence of a man who could bring the different factions together and give the movement a mass base, a new technique of political action, and a deeper meaning. Gandhi taught that *swaraj* should be the goal, and *satyagraha* the means, but first the people of India should understand the means and be worthy of the goal. "The English have not taken India," Gandhi declared; "we have given it to them. . . . It is Swaraj when we learn to rule ourselves." Again he wrote: "Our noncooperation is a retirement within ourselves. . . . In order to be fit to save others, we must try to save ourselves. Indian nationalism is not exclusive, nor aggressive, nor destructive. It is health-giving, religious, and therefore humanitarian."[22]

The fourth phase of Indian nationalism, from 1919–1920 to 1934–1935, witnessed three major campaigns of nonviolent noncooperation along the lines recommended by Gandhi. It also saw the end of the loose alliance between the Congress and the Muslim League, after the Khilafat issue (see page 269) had ceased to have much significance; considerable dissatisfaction within the Congress with some of Gandhi's techniques; and efforts by the British Government to find another formula for making further concessions to India in the light of growing nationalist pressures and the unsatisfactory working of the experiment in dyarchy under the Government of India Act of 1919.

Shortly after his return from South Africa, Gandhi gave an effective demonstration of his technique of civil disobedience. When he was ordered to leave a district in Bihar where he was investigating the conditions of workers on indigo plantations, he refused to obey the order, was arrested, and pleaded guilty at his trial. So great was the outcry over his arrest that he was released without punishment. In 1919, when the British imposed restrictions upon civil liberties, Gandhi asked the people of India to join in a campaign of nonviolent noncooperation. This campaign was endorsed by the Indian National Congress in the following year and was launched in 1921. For a time it seemed to go well, even though thousands of Indians were imprisoned for their nonviolent resistance; but when some Congress followers resorted to violence, Gandhi called off the campaign, saying that he had made a "Himalayan miscalculation" in believing that the people of India were ready for this new form of resistance. Many of the Congressmen who had been imprisoned as a result of the campaign, including the young Jawaharlal Nehru, disapproved of Gandhi's action, but it was endorsed by the Working Committee of the Congress. In March 1922, shortly after the civil disobedience campaign had been suspended, Gandhi was arrested on charges of sedition and sentenced to six years' imprisonment. He was released two years later.

With Gandhi in prison the nationalist struggle lost much of its focus. Even after his release in 1924 the controversies inside the Congress continued. Communal tensions became more serious, and socialist and

[22] Quoted in de Bary, ed., *Sources of Indian Tradition*, pp. 809, 822.

Communist groups and several working class organizations were formed outside the Congress. A number of prominent Congress leaders, including C. R. Das, Motilal Nehru (the father of Jawaharlal Nehru), and Vithalbhai Patel, formed the Swaraj Party to press for the immediate achievement of Dominion status for India. This party was for a time given charge of much of the political work of the Congress. Under its influence the historic Madras session of the Congress in 1927, for the first time and over Gandhi's objections, passed a resolution declaring that independence was the goal of the Congress. In 1928 a committee of the Congress, headed by Motilal Nehru, outlined a scheme of constitutional government. This report was not approved by Gandhi; it was attacked by the Muslims, who objected to its stand against separate electorates and who claimed that it was a Hindu document, and by a group of younger men within the Congress, including Motilal's son, Jawaharlal, and Subhas Chandra Bose, who demanded immediate independence as a goal. The Congress session in Lahore in 1929 adopted a resolution defining *swaraj* as complete independence and adopting January 26 as "Independence Day." It is no mere coincidence that the Constitution of the Republic of India became effective twenty years later on the same day, which is celebrated each year in independent India as "Republic Day."

Gandhi's salt march in 1930 ushered in the second mass campaign of civil disobedience and demonstrated the driving power of his techniques of peaceful noncooperation. The Mahatma selected the simple act of making salt from the sea, in defiance of British laws, because the salt tax affected almost every Indian villager. "As the independence movement is essentially for the poorest in the land," he explained, "the beginning will be made with this evil." As a result of his decision salt, as Nehru said, "suddenly became a mysterious word, a word of power." On April 6, 1930, after a 24-day march of 240 miles from Ahmedabad to Dandi, Gandhi defied the British by taking a small amount of salt from the sea. At first he was not arrested, although thousands of his fellow-*satyagrahis* were; but in early May, after he had notified the Viceroy that he intended to lead a raid on a government salt depot, he too was taken into custody. Even though nearly 100,000 Indians were imprisoned, the civil disobedience campaign went on. Thousands of humble people engaged in passive resistance activities, and they kept their discipline in spite of charges of the police and other forceful measures against them.[23]

In January 1931, Gandhi and the members of the Working Committee of the Congress were released, and two months later Gandhi

[23] For an excellent analysis of the salt *satyagraha,* see Joan V. Bondurant, *Conquest of Violence* (Berkeley, Calif., 1965), pp. 88–102.

agreed to the suspension of the noncooperation campaign and to his participation in the Second Round Table Conference in London in late 1931 as the sole representative of the Congress. From his point of view the conference was a complete failure, and upon his return to India he found that many Congress leaders were back in jail. In January 1933, he was again arrested. Shortly thereafter he began a "fast unto death" against a British decision to grant separate electorates for untouchables. The fast ended a week later when the British Government reversed its decision.

With this dramatic demonstration of the power of *satyagraha* a third mass movement of civil disobedience gained momentum. By April 1933, 120,000 Indians were in jail. In May Gandhi embarked on another fast, which soon led to his release. A short time later he suspended the noncooperation campaign. This action was criticized by many leaders of the Congress, some of whom were becoming dissatisfied with the methods which Gandhi was using in shaping the nationalist movement. Subhas Chandra Bose and Vithalbhai Patel, who were in Europe at the time, declared in a joint statement: "We are clearly of the opinion that Mr. Gandhi as a political leader has failed. The time has come for a radical reorganization of the Congress on a new principle, with a new method, for which a new leader is essential." Gandhi resigned his membership in the Congress because of the growing criticisms of his leadership.

**5. The Achievement of Independence.** Thus the fourth period in the history of Indian nationalism ended with the Congress Party at a rather low ebb, after spectacular victories in the nonviolent noncooperation campaigns, and with the British Government capping real concessions to Indian demands with the Government of India Act of 1935. But by this time the nationalist movement, thanks largely to Gandhi, had won mass support, and had even stimulated some political consciousness in the Indian States. It was no longer directed toward an increasing measure of self-government within the British Empire. The goal now was complete independence.

Since the early 1920's, and especially after the return of Jinnah from several years' residence in England in 1934, Muslim nationalism had been developing apart from the main nationalist movement. Most politically conscious Muslims had tended to accept the view of Sir Syed Ahmad Khan that the Muslims of India should remain aloof from the Congress and should look to their own interests. The formation of the Muslim League in 1906 and the granting of separate electorates in the Morley-Minto reforms of 1909 tended to emphasize the political as well as the social and religious distinctiveness of the Indian Muslims. In Mohammad Ali Jinnah they found an able leader.

Gradually the idea developed that wherever possible the Muslims should have a separate political status, within or without the British Empire. Much of the credit for this idea goes to the great Muslim poet-philosopher of the subcontinent, Muhammad Iqbal. In his presidential address at the 1930 session of the Muslim League, Iqbal said: "I would like to see the Punjab, North-West Frontier Province, Sind and Baluchistan, amalgamated into a single state. Self-government within the British Empire or without the British Empire, the formation of a consolidated North-West Indian Muslim State appears to me to be the final destiny of the Muslims at least of North-West India." Iqbal made no suggestions for the parts of Bengal which contained a Muslim majority.

The establishment of Congress governments in most of the provinces in 1937 was only one of the developments of the late 1930's which strengthened the Muslim League and which led it to demand a separate Muslim state. The League Congress in Lahore in 1940 passed an historic resolution, placing the League on record for the first time in favor of a separate state of Pakistan.

During World War II the League profited from the favors bestowed upon it by the British, because its position regarding the war was, from the British viewpoint, far more sympathetic and cooperative than was that of the Congress, which opposed the war effort. While the leading Congressmen spent most of the war years in jail, the leaders of the Muslim League were able to pursue their ends with little competition. After the war the League was in a relatively impregnable position, and Pakistan became in fact the price of independence.

The leaders of the Congress and the Muslim League differed fundamentally regarding the nature of Indian society and the kind of political system which should be established with the withdrawal of the British. The Congress was dedicated to what later came to be called the idea of the secular state, whereas the spokesmen of the League, faithful to the principles of Islam, argued that religion and politics could not be separated. They also charged that the Congress was a Hindu organization in which the Muslims would never be given a fair voice. In 1937 Jinnah declared, with reference to the failure of the Congress to associate Muslims with their provincial ministries: "On the very threshold of what little power and responsibility is given, the majority community have clearly shown their hand that Hindustan is for the Hindus." Jinnah became an advocate of a theory that had been held by other prominent Muslims before him, namely that the Muslims of India were not just a minority group but were in fact a separate "nation." In his presidential address at the Lahore session of the Muslim League in 1940, which adopted the Pakistan resolution, Jinnah asserted: "Mussalmans are a nation according to any definition of a nation and they must have their homeland, their territory and their state." This "two-nations" theory was anathema to the leaders of the Congress and above all to Mahatma Gandhi, who once wrote: "The 'two-nations' theory is an untruth . . . Hindus and Muslims of India are not two nations. . . . My whole soul rebels against the idea that Hinduism and Islam represent two antagonistic cultures and doctrines."

By the time the Muslim League had come out flatly for Pakistan the Congress was locked in a struggle with the British Government over the issue of India's proper role during World War II. When, upon the outbreak of the war in Europe in September 1939, the British Government declared that India too was at war with the Axis powers, the Congress, under the influence of Mahatma Gandhi, again strongly protested. (In 1939 Subhas Chandra Bose had been elected President of the Congress over a candidate supported by Gandhi; but most of the members of the Working Committee resigned after this election, and Bose, unable to reach an agreement with Gandhi, resigned the presidency. Subsequently he formed the Forward Bloc within the Congress, but soon he left India, to reappear in Nazi Germany and later in Japan and Southeast Asia, where he became identified with the puppet Indian government established with the support of the Japanese, and with the Indian National Army.)

The Congress protest against involvement in World War II was contrary to the advice of Nehru and other Congress leaders, but Gandhi argued that India could cooperate with the British in a fight for freedom only if it were granted freedom immediately. Otherwise it must withhold its support. This position of the Congress greatly hampered the British and Allied operations in the Asian theater and led to increasingly strained relations between the British authorities and the Congress. The impasse became complete with the passage of the "Quit India" resolution in 1942. Most of the Congress leaders spent the rest of the months of the war in prison. Gandhi himself was released in 1944 because of ill health, but Nehru and most of the Congress leaders were kept in confinement until a few weeks before V–E Day.

Independence came to India in 1947. Two independent nations came into existence on the Indian subcontinent, which had never achieved real unity during the entire course of its long history, and which had come closest to this unity under foreign rule.

The winning of independence came about as a result of many developments, in India and elsewhere. Certainly the nationalist movement in India placed increasing pressure upon the British. "The eventual achievement of Indian independence in 1947 was the outcome of a combination of circumstances — probably the most important being the weakening effect of two world wars on Britain's power and prestige in Asia — but the presence of a disciplined political organization under a revered leader greatly facilitated the transfer of power."[24] Power was transferred to two nations instead of one, because the Muslims of India chose not to identify themselves with the main nationalist movement. After 1947 the basic problems facing both new nations were the consolidation of independence, making that independence meaningful, learning how to co-exist with each other and how to exist in the world of the mid-twentieth century.

[24] De Bary, ed., *Sources of Indian Tradition*, p. 802.

# * 5 *

# The Nature of
# the Indian State:
# The Basic Decisions

India paid a heavy price for independence. In the final stages the hopes for freedom were jeopardized not by the opposition of the British but by the widening gulf between the Indian National Congress and the Muslim League. Because of this communal rift two new nations emerged, not one, and from the beginning of their independent existence these new nations were at odds with each other.

Even today many of those who were involved in the freedom struggle look back on the months prior to independence and wonder whether partition could have been avoided, or what the consequences would have been in the long run if they had refused to pay this price for independence. In a much-discussed book, published posthumously, the most famous of all the Muslims who cast their lots with India, Maulana Abul Kamal Azad, wrote: "If we had remained steadfast and refused to accept partition, I am confident that a safer and more glorious future would have awaited us."[1] This would almost certainly have delayed India's independence indefinitely. Lord Wavell, the Governor-General prior to Lord Mountbatten, had in fact recommended that the British should not set a date for their withdrawal, and when the new Labor Prime Minister, Clement Attlee, did not agree, Lord Wavell resigned. "Looking at the events after ten years," mused Maulana Azad, "I sometimes wonder who was right. . . . Perhaps history will decide that the

[1] Maulana Abul Kamal Azad, *India Wins Freedom* (Calcutta, 1959), p. 226.

wiser policy would have been to follow Lord Wavell's advice."[2] Instead, in February 1947, the British Government announced its "definite intention to take the necessary steps to effect the transference of power to responsible Indian hands by a date not later than June, 1948," and then in June, on Lord Mountbatten's advice, moved the date up to August 15, 1947. By this time most of the Congress leaders had accepted the inevitability of partition, although their hearts were heavy. Even Gandhi, who had steadfastly opposed the division of the country, urged acceptance of the plan.

Thus the demand for a separate Pakistan, which the Muslim League had first officially made in 1940, was granted. In view of the separate paths and ways of life of Hindus and Muslims over the centuries, and especially in view of the events of the decade prior to independence, including the increasing hold of the Muslim League on the Muslims of the subcontinent and the growing feeling of most Muslims that they would fare badly in a Hindu-dominated state, there was probably, in the last days, no choice other than partition. Even if the British had stayed on for a longer time, it is doubtful that the Muslim League could have been reconciled to a single Indian state.

V. P. Menon summarized clearly the major considerations which led most of the leaders of the Congress to acquiesce in partition:

> The Congress had accepted the division of the country on two considerations. In the first place, it was clear from the unyielding attitude of the Muslim League that a united India would either be delayed or could only be won at the cost of a civil war. Secondly, it was hoped that the establishment of a separate Muslim state would finally settle the communal problem which had for so long bedevilled Indian politics and thwarted all progressive aspirations, that India and Pakistan would thereafter live in peaceful relations with each other, and that all men of goodwill on either side would be free to concentrate on improving the economic conditions of the common people.[3]

### The Aftermath of Partition

The aftermath of partition was bitter. Instead of averting a communal struggle, the division of the subcontinent occasioned one of the major internal disasters of modern times. Hundreds of thousands of people on both sides of the new frontiers, especially in the divided Punjab, were massacred. The rejoicing over independence soon gave way

[2] *Ibid.*, pp. 177–178.
[3] V. P. Menon, *The Transfer of Power in India* (Princeton, N.J., 1957), p. 440.

to horror at the murders, riots, and innumerable lesser acts of violence which accompanied the mass uprooting of people. By June 1948, some five and a half million Hindus and Sikhs had crossed from West Pakistan into India, and about an equal number of Muslims had moved the other way, abandoning most of their worldly possessions. This mass movement of people created a major refugee problem, which has never been fully resolved, especially since the movement of refugees has continued in both directions ever since, although on a much lesser scale.

Lord Mountbatten and nearly all responsible leaders of the National Congress and the Muslim League were confident that the dislocation which would inevitably accompany partition could be kept under control and that there would be no major acts of violence or undue suffering.[4] They could not have been more wrong. Even today memories of the horrors of the weeks following partition are etched into the hearts of those who lived through those trying times. Indians certainly did not foresee such a tragedy. At a press conference in February 1959, Nehru said: "When we decided on partition I do not think any of us ever thought that there would be this terror of mutual killing after partition. It was in a sense to avoid this that we decided on partition. So we paid a double price for it, first, you might say politically, ideologically; second, the actual thing happened that we tried to avoid."

After a few weeks the worst excesses were over, and the new Government of India began to bring the situation under control. Thus at the very outset it faced and overcame a major crisis. As V. P. Menon recalled:

> The communal holocaust, the two-way exodus of refugees, their protection and the rehabilitation of those who had come to India — all these provided the Government of India, at a time when the administrative machinery was already out of joint as a result of partition, with a task which was as stupendous as any nation ever had to face. If in its initial stages the situation had not been controlled with vigour, the consequences would have brought down the Government itself.[5]

Among the other developments in the early weeks of independence which cast a pall over the new state, two may be singled out for spe-

[4] As V. P. Menon wrote, many years later: "It is true that the situation was full of fear and foreboding; but we had not expected to be so quickly and so thoroughly disillusioned." Menon, *The Transfer of Power in India*, pp. 417–418. Maulana Azad records that on May 14, 1947 Lord Mountbatten told Gandhi: "At least on this one question I shall give you complete assurance. I shall see to it that there is no bloodshed and riot." *India Wins Freedom*, p. 190.

[5] Menon, *The Transfer of Power in India*, p. 434.

*Kashmir*

*Assassination*

cial mention. In October 1947, tribal raiders moved into Kashmir, and Indian troops were airlifted to Srinagar to drive them back, after the hasty last-minute accession of the Hindu Maharaja of Kashmir to India. In 1948 Indian and Pakistani troops engaged in armed clashes in Kashmir, and the two new nations nearly came to the brink of war. Although a cease-fire was agreed upon on January 1, 1949, through the good offices of the United Nations, the Kashmir question has been the major issue in dispute between India and Pakistan ever since.

The second event seemed even more portentous. On January 30, 1948, while he was conducting a prayer meeting on the lawn of the Birla mansion in New Delhi, Mahatma Gandhi, then 78 years of age, was killed by three bullets fired at close range by a member of the Hindu Mahasabha from the State of Maharashtra, who violently objected to the Mahatma's policy of Hindu-Muslim unity and brotherhood. Thus Gandhi was a victim of the very communal forces which he had fought for so long. It was in a grim way fortunate that his assassin was a communalist Hindu and not a Muslim; for if he had been killed by a Muslim, India might have witnessed another blood bath far greater in horror than that which had darkened the early days of independence. The assassination of "the Father of the Nation" so soon after the nation had been born raised grave doubts about India's future and plunged the people of India into the darkest despair, mingled with pride in the little man who had been the greatest among them. Nehru voiced the feelings of his fellow-countrymen when he spoke, in broken tones, over All-India Radio shortly after Gandhi's death:

> Friends and comrades, the light has gone out of our lives and there is darkness everywhere. . . . Our beloved leader, Bapu as we called him, the Father of the Nation, is no more. Perhaps I am wrong to say that. . . . For the light that shone in this country was no ordinary light. The light that has illumined this country for these many, many years will illumine this country for many more years, and a thousand years later, that light will still be seen in this country and the world will see it and it will give solace to innumerable hearts.

In a sense, Gandhi had completed his work, although its full fruits will not be manifest until and unless many radical changes occur in Indian life and thought. In his last months, he was increasingly disturbed by the many signs that his teachings were being neglected or even ignored. He was distressed by the orgy of communal fury, which ran counter to everything he had fought for, and by all too many evidences that those in charge of the destinies of the new nation, mostly his own disciples, were making compromises and following policies of which he could not wholly approve. Gandhi is still one of the most alive forces in India today, but the Gandhian image is fading, and one may ask whether contemporary India, in its political, economic, social, or spiritual life, is being true to his high principles and example.

## The Integration of the Indian States

When Gandhi died, not only were the leaders of the new Government engrossed in the problems created by partition, such as the rehabilitation of refugees, but also in the many tasks of consolidating independence. Foremost among these were the integration of the Indian States and the work of constitution-making.

The Indian Independence Act of 1947 did not propose a solution for the problem of the Indian States, but it did terminate the paramountcy of the British crown over these political units and granted their independence. But it was obviously absurd to think of the subcontinent peppered with scores of other "independent states," ranging in size from Hyderabad and Jammu and Kashmir, each having an area of more than 80,000 square miles, to States comprising a few score acres.

The position of the British Government and the Indian National Congress on this issue was clear enough. In his speech introducing the Indian Independence Bill in the House of Commons, on July 5, 1947, Prime Minister Attlee said: "It is the hope of His Majesty's Government that all the States will in due course find their appropriate place with one or the other Dominion within the British Commonwealth." On July 15, 1947, the All-India Congress Committee categorically rejected the claims of some of the States to independence. Speaking at this meeting of the A.I.C.C. Nehru declared that the States had only two alternatives: they could join the Indian Union either individually or in groups. "There is no third way out of the situation — third way meaning independence or special relation to a foreign power."

Immediately after the plan to partition the subcontinent and to grant independence on August 15, 1947 was announced by the British Government, the Interim Government decided to set up a States Ministry to handle the problem of the integration of the Indian States. Sardar Vallabhbhai Patel was placed in charge of the States Ministry, and in the next two years or so this determined and influential man, who also served as Deputy Prime Minister until his death in 1950, by a combination of cajolery and firmness not only secured the accession of most of the Indian States to the Union of India but also merged many of these States and laid the foundations for their full integration into the new Indian nation. "The work accomplished by him at the States' Ministry amounts to a silent revolution. The accession of the States to the Indian Union was secured by peaceful negotiations before August 15, 1947, and in a little over two years after independence the political geography of India was rationalised by the *merger or the consolidation and integration* of the States. . . . India was unified as never before in her history. . . . Sardar Patel may be truly described as the architect of Indian unity."[6] His top lieutenant at the States Ministry, V. P. Menon, many years later wrote a detailed account of *The Story of the Integration of the Indian States,* a book which depicts something of the magnitude, the difficulties, and the brilliant diplomacy of Sardar Patel's great work.[7]

Patel's first act as States Minister was to appeal to all the princely rulers of Indian States in territories contiguous to the India-Union-to-be to accede to the Union in three subjects: foreign relations, defense, and communications. Lord Mountbatten, in an address to the Chamber of Princes on July 25, 1947, made the same appeal. In a remarkable display of cooperation, whatever their misgivings, the Indian Princes responded to these appeals. By August 15, 1947, all but three of the Indian States whose territories were geographically contiguous to the new State of India had acceded to the Indian Union. The three exceptions were significant, particularly since they imposed further strains on the already unhappy relations with Pakistan.

The Muslim ruler of Junagadh, a small state in Kathiawar, near the southeastern frontier of West Pakistan, acceded to Pakistan, and Pakistan accepted the accession even though the population of the State was predominantly Hindu. Encouraged no doubt by outside forces, the people of the State forced the ruler to flee, and in November 1947 the Muslim Diwan (Finance Minister) was compelled to invite the Government of India to intervene. Junagadh became associated with the Indian Union after a plebiscite in February 1948 showed that this was the wish of the overwhelming majority of its people.

Hyderabad, the largest of the Indian States, with a Muslim ruler and a Hindu majority, and entirely surrounded by Indian territory, presented an even more difficult problem. Apparently the Nizam of Hyderabad, then regarded as one of the world's richest men, desired to maintain an independent status. In November 1947, he signed a standstill agreement with the Government of India, but prolonged negotiations failed to persuade him to accede to India. In the meantime disorders broke out inside the State, encouraged by Communists and by

[6] N. Srinivasan, *Democratic Government in India* (Calcutta, 1954), p. 108.
[7] V. P. Menon, *The Story of the Integration of the Indian States* (New York, 1956). See also Government of India, Ministry of States, *White Paper on Indian States* (Delhi, 1950); and Urmila Phadnis, *Towards the Integration of Indian States, 1919–1947* (New York, 1968).

members of a militant Muslim group known as Razakars, and raiders from Hyderabad made incursions into Indian territory. In September 1948, Indian troops were ordered into Hyderabad, and after three days of spasmodic fighting the Nizam capitulated. In November 1948, he agreed to accede to the Indian Union. Eight years later, with the re-organization of the Indian States, Hyderabad officially ceased to exist. It was distributed among four States, with the largest part going to Andhra Pradesh.

Prior to August 15, 1947, the Maharaja of Kashmir, a Hindu who ruled despotically over a Muslim majority, refused to accede either to Pakistan or to India, contrary to the advice of Lord Mountbatten. On October 26 he acceded to India, but only because tribal invaders, en-couraged by Pakistan, had pushed to within a few miles of Srinagar, the capital of the State, and because the Government of India, to which he appealed for aid, refused to send help unless he acceded to India. The next day the Governor-General of India, Lord Mountbatten, an-nounced that "as soon as law and order have been restored in Kashmir and her soil cleared of the invader, the question of the accession should be settled by a reference to the people." This referendum has never been held, much to Pakistan's chagrin. India and Pakistan nearly be-came involved in a war over Kashmir in 1948. Since January 1, 1949, a cease-fire has prevailed in Jammu and Kashmir and the State has been divided along the cease-fire line between India and Pakistan. Re-peated efforts by representatives of the United Nations and by the U.N. Security Council to work out a plan for the steps leading to a plebiscite which would be acceptable to both India and Pakistan have failed. India now regards the accession of Kashmir as final and irrevocable, and the State is one of the constituent units of the Indian Republic. Pakistan, of course, has refused to accept this claim and still insists that the future of all of Jammu and Kashmir should be determined by a vote of the people.

The peaceful accession before independence of all of the Indian States in the territories embraced in the Indian Union, except Junagadh, Hyderabad, and Kashmir, averted what could easily have been a major political crisis. After accession came the equally difficult problem of integration, democratization, and modernization of political units which,  save for a few enlightened States such as Mysore, were notoriously backward and even feudal. This task was also tackled vigorously by Sardar Patel and his associates in the States Ministry, but even today it is far from satisfactory fulfillment.

Out of former British India and the India of the princely States a new map of India emerged. Only three Indian States, Hyderabad, Jammu and Kashmir, and Mysore, retained their original form. These large States, plus 275 smaller States which were merged into five State Unions, became the eight Part B States of the Indian Union. Two hundred and sixteen States were merged with the Part A States. Sixty-one others were merged with Part C States. After the reorganization of the States in November 1956, Hyderabad disappeared as a separate unit, and only Mysore and Jammu and Kashmir remained. The boundaries of Mysore were substantially changed, and, of course, a large part of Jammu and Kashmir remained on the Pakistan side of the cease-fire line.

## Basic Objectives and Decisions

What was to be the nature of the new Indian state? To what extent would it incorporate some of the ideas and institutions of the ancient past, and to what extent would it be patterned after British and Western models? To what extent would it embody Gandhian ideas and ideals? What type of government would be created? Would it be a democratic state? If so, what form of democracy would be adopted? What would be its orientation in foreign policy? What would be its ideology? These and other questions basic to the very nature of the state were answered either before independence or within a short time thereafter. Although they raised fundamental problems of government, most of them were resolved quickly, with very little opposition. This remarkable fact reflects no lack of attention to fundamentals but instead a widespread agreement regarding them. Out of the varied experience of the past came a political consensus which was most impressive, and rather unexpected.

The basic aims and objectives of the new state had been clearly and positively stated many times prior to independence, and they have been reaffirmed on countless occasions since 1947. Jawaharal Nehru, one of the most eloquent and loquacious of world leaders, with a great capacity to voice the sentiments of his people and to enunciate basic principles, often spoke in terms of fundamentals. Two of the most significant statements were the so-called Objectives Resolution, approved by the Constituent Assembly on January 22, 1947, and the Preamble to the Constitution of 1950.

At the first meeting of the Constituent Assembly, on December 9, 1946, Nehru, then head of the Interim Government, moved the Objectives Resolution. It was especially significant because of its timing, its mover, and its contents. Introduced in the very first session of the Constituent Assembly, it seemed to mark the successful conclusion of the struggle for freedom from British rule and the beginning of an independent existence. The fact that it was moved by Nehru, the political spokesman of the New India, was also of great practical and symbolic significance. The document was a statement of the bases on which the new Indian state would be established. It contained these declarations:

> This Constituent Assembly declares its firm and solemn resolve to proclaim India as an Independent Sovereign Republic and to draw up for her future governance a Constitution,
>
> Wherein all power and authority of the Sovereign Independent India, its constituent parts and organs of government are derived from the people;
>
> Wherein shall be guaranteed and secured to all the people of India justice, social, economic, and political; equality of status, of opportunity, and before the law; freedom of thought, expression, belief, faith, worship, vocation, association, and action, subject to law and public morality; and
>
> Wherein adequate safeguards shall be provided for minorities, backward and tribal areas, and depressed and other backward classes, and
>
> Whereby this ancient land shall attain its rightful and honoured place in the world and make its full and willing contribution to the promotion of world peace and the welfare of mankind.

The Preamble to the Indian Constitution of 1950 is patterned along the lines of the Objectives Resolution of 1947.

Seven of the basic decisions regarding the nature of the new state which were made with due consideration but without significant opposition were: (1) India should be a parliamentary democracy; (2) it should be a federal state; (3) it should be a republic; (4) it should have a written constitution; (5) it should be a member of the Commonwealth; (6) it should be a secular state; and (7) it should be a welfare state.

## Parliamentary Democracy in India

As the time of independence approached there was no doubt that the new Indian state would be a democracy, in form if not in spirit. Most of the leaders of India, for more than a century, had been steeped in the principles of nineteenth-century liberal democracy and of twentieth-century socialist democracy. To a certain extent some of these leaders — such as Subhas Chandra Bose and even Gandhi himself — looked for other principles on which to found the future Indian state, but they could not fashion alternatives which gained widespread acceptance or even understanding. Undoubtedly, too, Indian leaders were conditioned to favor parliamentary democracy because of their close associations with the British, who over the centuries had evolved the most successful example of this form of democracy.

From the British, educated Indians learned the principles of parliamentary democracy, even though in India the British seldom practiced this or any other form of democracy. In fact, almost to the last, a few prominent Englishmen denied that they considered a parliamentary system either suited to or desirable for India. This was, however, not the prevailing opinion. As the date for independence approached, it was generally assumed, by both Indians and Englishmen, that India. would adopt the parliamentary system. The Congress Experts Committee in the Constituent Assembly, from its first meetings in July 1946, seriously considered only the parliamentary system of democracy, and gave little attention to other alternatives, even the Gandhian approach. In debates in the Constituent Assembly in the following years, a few Gandhian principles and institutions were introduced into the Draft Constitution, but most of the Assembly members were firmly committed to the principles of parliamentary democracy.[8]

While parliamentary democracy has been increasingly under attack in many quarters and has failed in several Asian countries, including the neighboring states of Burma and Pakistan, the leaders of India have repeatedly reaffirmed their dedication to it. Speaking in the Lok Sabha on March 28, 1957, Prime Minister Nehru said:

> We chose this system of parliamentary democracy deliberately; we chose it not only because to some extent, we had always thought on those lines previously, but because we thought it was in keeping with our own old traditions, not the old traditions as they were, but adjusted to the new conditions and new surroundings. We chose it — let us give credit where credit is due — because we approved of its functioning in other countries, more especially in the United Kingdom.

### Federalism in India

For understandable reasons there is a tremendous interest in the subject of federalism among students and practitioners of the art of government in India. A large new state such as India, faced with the problem of establishing a central authority strong enough to govern a vast area inhabited by millions of people with different historical and linguistic backgrounds and interests, almost inevitably has to establish some form of federal structure. The Republic of India is a federation, although it has many distinctive features which seem to modify the essentially federal nature of the state.

[8] See Granville Austin, *The Indian Constitution: Cornerstone of a Nation* (London, 1966), pp. 32–49.

Some students of government, Indian and foreign, describe India as a quasi-federal state, and some even regard it as more unitary than federal. G. N. Joshi, a leading authority on the Indian Constitution, holds that "the Union is not strictly a federal polity but a quasi-federal polity with some vital and important elements of unitariness. . . . It is designed to work as a federal government in normal times, but as a unitary government in times of emergency."[9] "It must be remembered," states Professor Suda, "that though India is a federation, her constitution departs from the ideal of a true federation in several vital and significant ways. She is not a genuine federation, but a quasi-federation having several features of a unitary state."[10] Professor Kenneth Wheare, a well-known British authority on federalism, classified India as "a unitary state with subsidiary federal principles rather than a federal state with subsidiary unitary principles."[11] However, as Professor Charles Alexandrowicz, former Research Professor of Law at Madras University, pointed out, the application of such "a rigid definition of the federal principle to various types of existing federations may deprive it of any practical meaning."[12] He argued that India is a true federation — although, like all other federations, it has distinctive characteristics — and that it is misleading to refer to India as a quasi-federation. It is difficult to determine to what extent these differences are merely semantic ones and to what extent they are based on fundamentally different interpretations of the nature of the Indian state.

In any federation the key questions center around the relative roles and powers of the central government and the constituent units. Centralizing tendencies are manifest in all federations under modern conditions. In India the central government was deliberately given rather extraordinary powers, and since independence these powers have been rather freely exercised in a state dedicated to a planned economy and beset by regional and linguistic divisions.

India is an example of an administrative rather than a contractual federation. It was imposed from above, not from below. The Indian Constitution of 1950 was modeled in large part on the Government of India Act of 1935, as amended to fit the needs of an independent state. The Act of 1935 was designed to establish a highly centralized federation with a fair measure of provincial autonomy, always subject to

[9] G. N. Joshi, *The Constitution of India* (3rd ed., London, 1954), p. 32.
[10] J. P. Suda, *Indian Constitutional Development and National Movement* (Meerut, 1951), p. 523.
[11] "India's New Constitution Analyzed," *A.L.J.,* XLVIII, 21.
[12] C. H. Alexandrowicz, "Is India a Federation?", *The International and Comparative Law Quarterly,* III (July, 1954), 402.

the ultimate control of the paramount powers. Its federal features were never implemented, but their influence on the character of the government of independent India is manifest.

This Constitution contains a number of provisions which seem to give the Centre such extraordinary powers as to raise questions regarding the federal nature of the Indian state. Article 3 authorizes the central Parliament, presumably by a simple majority, to form new States or to alter the boundaries of any State, without necessarily obtaining the consent of the State or States affected. Under this authority the new State of Andhra was carved out of the States of Madras and Hyderabad in 1953, and the political map of India, especially in the South, was drastically changed by the States Reorganization Act of 1956. Article 248 vests residuary powers in the Indian federation in the Centre, unlike the arrangement in most federations. Article 249 provides that if two-thirds of the members of the Council of States approve, Parliament may "make laws with respect to any matter enumerated in the State List," and specified in a resolution of the Council. Article 254 provides that if any law passed by a State Legislative Assembly is repugnant to a statute of the federal Parliament, the latter shall prevail. Articles 352 to 360 contain the emergency provisions which empower the President in effect to suspend the Constitution and to take over the administration of a State or States of the Indian Union if he is satisfied that there is a threat to the security of the nation, or a breakdown in the constitutional machinery of a State or States, or a financial emergency. Some commentators maintain that these emergency provisions, stronger than those to be found in any other federal constitution, would transform India from a federal to a unitary state during periods of emergency. It is doubtful, however, whether the basic character of any state can be changed so easily. The essential tests relate to the precise relationships between the Centre and the Indian States.

Many other provisions of the Constitution could be cited to support the view that the Central Government has in fact such extraordinary authority that India is no more than a quasi-federation at best, or that if it is a federation at all, it has many unitary features. When Nehru was the unquestioned leader of the country, and when the Congress Party was in a virtually unchallenged position at the Centre, if less so in some of the States, the powers of the Central Government were augmented by the extraordinary role of a single leader and a single party. The power and prestige of the Centre have been further enhanced by its assumption of the overall initiative and control in the fields of economic planning and development, social reform, and fiscal administration, not to mention the usual dominance of the Centre in foreign policy, defense, and communications, in a state dedicated to "the socialist pattern of society." In India there has been, and still is, a tendency to look to government for most things, and this usually means the Central Government.

The Constitution of 1950 itemizes the powers of the Centre and the States in three lists, a Union List, a State List, and a Concurrent List. Subject to certain qualifications, which give the Central Government a fairly wide area of discretionary authority, the State Legislatures have power to make laws respecting any item on the State List and to share with the central Parliament in the supervision and control of subjects on the Concurrent List.

In spite of the many evidences of extreme concentration of authority in the Centre — a tendency accentuated by the needs of the welfare state and by the general Indian attitude toward government — there are also many decentralizing tendencies in the Indian state. Dr. Paul Appleby, in his studies of the Indian administrative system, was astounded to discover how much the Centre was dependent on the States for the actual implementation of major national programs and how little real authority the Centre seemed to have in vital areas of policy and administration. "In both the Centre and the States," he wrote in his report on public administration in India, "prevailing structures, except in a few fields . . . provide chiefly for 'co-ordination' rather than for administration." His conclusion in this area of mutual responsibility and power was a rather startling one:

> It is not too unfair, I think, to say that except for the character of its leadership, the new national government of India is given less basic resource in power than any other large and important nation, while at the same time having rather more sense of need and determination to establish programs dealing with matters important to the national interest. The administrative trend is evidently to go still further, to give over to the states some financial resource now in the province of the Centre, to minimize in practice some of the marginal or interpretative zones of power, and to retreat before an opposition state minister's charges of "interference" with the states.[13]

During the debates on the draft Constitution in the Constituent Assembly, Dr. Ambedkar, chairman of the drafting committee, declared that the States of the Union of India "are as sovereign in their field which is left to them by the Constitution as the Centre in the field which is assigned to it."[14] This statement seems rather misleading, in view of the extraordinary powers given to the Centre in the Consti-

[13] Paul H. Appleby, *Public Administration in India: Report of a Survey* (Delhi, 1953), pp. 16–17.
[14] *Constituent Assembly Debates*, X, 339.

tution and the dominant role of the Centre in the years since the Constitution went into effect; but, as Dr. Appleby noted, the Centre is dependent to an extraordinary degree on the States for the implementation of many basic decisions and policies, and talk of "decentralization" is in the air. Moreover, the States are the strongholds of the growing opposition to the dominant Congress Party and of the tendencies toward provincialism, regionalism, and lingualism, strengthened by the reorganization of the State boundaries along essentially linguistic lines, which constitute major threats to the unity and even to the survival of the nation. As Benjamin Schoenfeld has pointed out, "The problems which Indian federalism faces stem from the needs of her people to have a central government armed with sufficient powers needed to solve modern economic and political problems on one hand, and the strong sentiments of regionalism found throughout the land."[15] This is a problem with which almost all federal states are necessarily concerned, but it seems to be an unusually critical one in the case of India.

In actual practice the balance of power in the Indian federation seems to be constantly changing. Since 1967, for example, when non-Congress governments were formed in several States following the fourth general elections, and since the break-up of the Congress Party in 1969, there has been an apparent increase in the relative importance and role of the States and of State Chief Ministers, Congress and non-Congress. And although the impact of a decade of experience with *Panchayati Raj*, or government by local councils, is still not clear, in theory and to some extent in practice, it is one of the most exciting experiments in "democratic decentralization" in any developing country.[16]

## The Republic of India

The Preamble to the Constitution declares that India is a "sovereign democratic republic." It did not become a republic until January 26, 1950, when the Constitution went into effect. From August 15, 1947, until that date it functioned under the Government of India Act of 1935, the Indian Independence Act, and other basic statutes, most of which were originally enacted by the British Parliament and then after independence adapted to the needs of independent India. During this interval the Head of the Union of India, as the federal state was officially known, was a Governor-General, appointed by the British Sovereign on the advice of the Indian Prime Minister. Free India had two Governors-General — Lord Mountbatten, who was also the last of the British Governors-General, and C. Rajagopalachari, a veteran leader of

[15] Benjamin N. Schoenfeld, *Federalism in India* (Washington, D.C., 1960), p. 21.
[16] See below, Chap. 7.

the Congress Party, who later became a critic of the Congress and the super-chief of the Swatantra Party. Lord Mountbatten continued as Governor-General after India became independent, at the urgent request of Nehru and his associates. It is a significant commentary on the attitudes of the leaders of the new state toward Britain that Lord Mountbatten should have been asked to serve in this capacity. For a time there seemed to be a possibility that Pakistan too would ask him to serve as its Governor-General, but the leaders of Pakistan became rather embittered at Lord Mountbatten, and Mohammed Ali Jinnah decided that he wanted to be Pakistan's first Governor-General, instead of Prime Minister. Lord Mountbatten's services to independent India until his resignation in June 1948 were great, and were generally recognized and appreciated.

Rajagopalachari, one of Gandhi's closest and most distinguished associates, was the logical choice to be the first Indian Governor-General of the Indian Dominion. He held this office until January 26, 1950, when Dr. Rajendra Prasad, another old Gandhian, who had been President of the Constituent Assembly, was inaugurated as the first President of the Republic of India.

While there was little opposition in India in the weeks prior to independence to the British proposal that free India should be a Dominion, with a Governor-General as Head of State and representative of the British Crown, the constitution-makers decided soon after independence, that the new Constitution should make India a republic, with an indirectly elected President as Head of State in no way responsible to the British Crown. The position and powers of the President of the Republic of India are very different from those of the American President, who is the effective as well as the nominal head of the executive branch of the government; they are in fact more similar to those of the British sovereign.

## A Written Constitution

While it is true that "the British Constitution is by no means wholly unwritten," there is no single written document which has the status of organic law and "no marked or clear distinction between laws which are not fundamental or constitution and laws which are fundamental or constitutional."[17] If India had followed the British precedent, it too would have had no written constitution. A different decision, however, was made, for reasons which seemed to be compelling. The British, departing from their own practice, had given India a kind of consti-

[17] Sydney D. Bailey, *British Parliamentary Democracy* (3rd ed., Boston, 1971), p. 7.

tution in the Government of India Act of 1935, one of the longest and most involved pieces of legislation ever enacted by the British Parliament. This Act, supplemented by the Indian Independence Act of 1947, another elaborate legislative measure of the British Parliament, as amended by the interim Parliament, gave the Indian Union a kind of constitution from independence until the Constitution went into effect on January 26, 1950.

The leaders of the Congress Party, and the members of the Constitution drafting committee, were in substantial agreement on India's need for a single written Constitution, which should be the organic law of the Indian Republic and which would spell out clearly the nature of the Republic, the organization and powers and mutual relations of the Centre and the States, the fundamental rights of the citizen, the directive principles of State policy, and many matters which in more established and less divided republics might be left to ordinary law or to custom and convention. In a vast country with little tradition of unity, with people of different historical, racial, cultural, and religious backgrounds, with special problems of communalism, regionalism, lingualism, and casteism, and differing social customs and differing concepts of law and society, it was deemed necessary to spell out the basic principles of the new state in elaborate detail.

The story of the framing of the Indian Constitution is truly impressive and should be of interest to all students of governance.[18] It has been described as "by far the most massive and ambitious enterprise in the world-wide history of constitution-making."[19] It was carried out by the Constituent Assembly of India, and especially by its Drafting Committee between December 9, 1946, and November 26, 1949. Key participants besides Dr. B. R. Ambedkar, the Chairman, included B. N. Rau, the Constitutional Adviser, Acharya Kripalani, T. T. Krishnamachari, K. M. Munshi, Pandit G. B. Pant, and above all, the four leaders who "constituted an oligarchy within the Assembly"[20] — Jawaharlal Nehru, Vallabhbhai Patel, Dr. Rajendra Prasad, and Maulana Abul Kalam Azad.

India's Constitution-makers prepared themselves well for their heavy

[18] Fortunately, the story has been told well and often. On Nov. 26, 1968, the ninth anniversary of the adoption of the Constitution by the Constituent Assembly, the President of India officially released a five-volume work, entitled *Framing of the Constitution*, edited by B. Shiva Rao. See also B. N. Rau, ed., *India's Constitution in the Making* (Madras, 1960); Panchanand Misra, *The Making of the Indian Republic* (Calcutta, 1966); and Austin, *The Indian Constitution*, the best single volume on the subject.

[19] L. M. Singhvi, "Constitution-Making in India," *India News*, VIII (Aug. 15, 1969), 3.

[20] Austin, *The Indian Constitution*, p. 21.

responsibility. They examined most of the world's constitutions, past and present, borrowed ideas and practices from many, discussed the fundamental principles of democratic government and India's special traditions and needs, and debated and scrutinized every draft and every provision with great care. The resulting Constitution, which went through several drafts and was amended many times, reflected its mixed parentage and the meticulous processes that were followed in framing it. In particular, it showed the influence of the Government of India Act of 1935. It was, in fact, the longest constitutional document in the world[21] and has served India well during the formative years of the Republic.

## India in the Commonwealth

The decision of the leaders of the Congress Party to join the Commonwealth was a surprise, in India and abroad. Many persons in India felt that India should sever all ties with the former ruling power. Nehru and other Congress spokesmen had often indicated that an independent India would break away completely from the nation which had governed it for so long; but the happier relations between the Indian leaders and the British Government after the end of World War II, and some sober second thoughts of the Indian leaders as they faced the imminent problem of India's emergence as an independent state, led to the decision to become a Dominion in the Commonwealth, at least for the time being.

In deciding to make India a republic the leaders of the new state were confronted with the problem of India's continued relationship, if any, with the Commonwealth — or the British Commonwealth of Nations, as it was then generally called — whose members, all having Dominion status, professed loyalty to the British Crown. No precedent existed for a republic within the Commonwealth constellation. Some of the older Dominions seemed to feel that the Commonwealth should remain a smaller and more homogeneous association, and they looked askance at the inclusion of peoples of very different racial and cultural backgrounds, especially those with antimonarchist views.

There was also some criticism inside India of the decision that the Republic of India should remain within the Commonwealth. "Britain's past relations with India, her imperialism and power politics and the racial discrimination practised in the Dominions were urged against India's association with the Commonwealth. It was pointed out that there were no affinities of race or religion or of language and culture between India and the white members of the Commonwealth to make

---

[21] The official edition of the Indian Constitution runs to more than 250 pages, with another 64 pages of Contents and Index.

such association natural and that the decision showed a lack of faith on the part of India in her strength and destiny."[22] In October 1947, when it was already apparent that India woud become a republic, the question of continued association with the Commonwealth was discussed at a Commonwealth Prime Ministers meeting in London, and the formula which seemed to be most seriously considered called for multiple citizenship with the King of England as "first citizen" in each Dominion. Since both India and the other members of the Commonwealth wished to find some way to continue the Commonwealth tie after the Indian Republic was established, a formula was agreed upon at a special meeting of the Commonwealth Prime Ministers, held in London in late April, 1949. This formula was announced in an historic declaration:

> The Government of India have informed the other Governments of the Commonwealth of the intention of the Indian people that under the new constitution which is about to be adopted India shall become a sovereign independent Republic. The Government of India have, however, declared and affirmed India's desire to continue her full membership of the Commonwealth of Nations and her acceptance of the King as the symbol of the free association of its independent member nations and as such the Head of the Commonwealth.
>
> The Governments of the other countries of the Commonwealth, the basis of whose membership of the Commonwealth is not hereby changed, accept and recognize India's continuing membership in accordance with the terms of this Declaration.

Thus by a simple declaration India's continued membership in the Commonwealth was assured. The formula worked out at the Commonwealth Prime Ministers Conference in 1949 is an important step in the evolution of this unique and successful international association. It has since been invoked by other Commonwealth members.

### India as a Secular State

In a country inhabited by people with such diverse religious backgrounds and beliefs, in which religious factors were interwoven with historical experience to a degree hardly equalled in any other part of the world, it was necessary for the framers of the Constitution to face squarely the question of the role of religion in the new republic. The answer was unequivocal: India should be a secular state, in which every

---

[22] N. Srinivasan, *Democratic Government in India* (Calcutta, 1954), p. 154. For the ups and downs of India's association with the Commonwealth, see below, pp. 296–298.

citizen has the right to practice his own faith and has the same political and social rights as every other citizen, a state neutral in matters of religion and not organized along religious lines.

While the word "secular" does not appear in the Constitution, the principles of secularism are embodied in it, especially in Part III, dealing with fundamental rights, and in Article 325, which provides for "one general electoral roll for every territorial constituency," thus abolishing the separate communal electorates which had existed ever since the Morley-Minto Reforms of 1909.

Nehru was a leading champion of the concept of a noncommunal, secular state. Indeed, the creation of India as a secular state may in time come to be accepted as one of his greatest achievements. Nehru boasted of the fact that "Our Constitution is based on this secular conception and gives freedom to all religions." [23] He had a great aversion to the intrusion of religious factors into politics, and he was especially concerned with transforming his country from "a caste-ridden society" in which communalism constituted a major threat to all the values that he cherished to "a national State which includes people of all religions and shades of opinion and is essentially secular as a State."[24] "Religion is all right," he said, "when applied to ethics and morals, but it is not good mixed up with politics."[25]

This statement seems to be in direct contrast to the views of Mahatma Gandhi, whom Nehru himself once described as "essentially a man of religion, a Hindu to the innermost depths of his being."[26] In a famous passage in his *Autobiography* Gandhi wrote: "I can say without the slightest hesitation, and yet in all humility, that those who say that religion has nothing to do with politics do not know what religion means."[27] Gandhi and Nehru, the master and the disciple, approached the problem of the relation between religion and politics  from very different angles, but essentially their positions concerning the nature of the Indian state were not so far apart. Gandhi, a deeply religious man, saw merit and truth in all religions, and he "felt that any form of political association based exclusively on adherence to a par-

[23] Nehru, *Circular to the Pradesh Congress Committees*, August, 1954. "The Government of a country like India," Nehru declared on another occasion, "with many religions that have secured great and devoted followings for generations, can never function satisfactorily in the modern age except on a secular basis." *The Hindu*, Sept. 13, 1950, p. 9.

[24] Speech at Aligarh in 1948; quoted in Donald E. Smith, *Nehru and Democracy* (Calcutta, 1958), p. 147.

[25] Speech in the Lok Sabha, Sept. 17, 1953.

[26] Jawaharlal Nehru, *The Discovery of India* (New York, 1946), p. 365.

[27] M. K. Gandhi, *An Autobiography, or The Story of My Experiments with Truth* (2nd ed., Ahmedabad, 1948), p. 615.

ticular religion was worse than undemocratic."[28] Nehru, who professed to be an agnostic, said that "I have no desire to interfere with any person's belief"; but he objected strongly to any efforts to perpetuate "a complete structure of society . . . by giving it religious sanction and authority," and he desired a State which "protects all religions, but does not favour one at the expense of others and does not itself adopt any religion as the State religion." Hence it is easy to understand why both Gandhi and Nehru were so strongly opposed to the whole idea of partition, and why Nehru referred to the decision of the Constituent Assembly in Karachi, in November 1953, to make Pakistan an Islamic Republic as "a medieval conception, . . . totally opposed to any democratic conception."[29]

In various ways the Government of India has been attempting to implement the goal of a secular state. It has sponsored various acts of legislation designed to lay a firmer base for secularism, in both a political and social sense. Some of these, like the Hindu Code Bill (a series of acts passed by Parliament between 1954 and 1956, designed to "codify Hindu law and at the same time introduce drastic changes that reflected the influence of Western thought"),[30] have had a profound effect on many areas of Indian life and society.

It is difficult to determine to what extent the people of India have truly accepted the idea of a secular state. Can the political order be secularized while the society remains fundamentally nonsecular? As Dr. B. R. Ambedkar, India's most famous "untouchable," declared in the debates on the draft Constitution in the Constituent Assembly: "The religious conceptions in this country are so vast that they cover every aspect from birth to death. There is nothing which is not religious."[31]

Communalism, particularly in its most virulent form of Hindu-Muslim antagonism, is deeply rooted in Indian soil. After the excesses of partition, the long-standing Hindu-Muslim tensions seemed to abate; but more recent events, notably the communal riots and bloodshed in Ahmedabad and other parts of Gujarat — the very part of India from which Gandhi, the apostle of nonviolence and Hindu-Muslim unity,

---

28 Smith, *Nehru and Democracy*, p. 155.
29 These four statements may be found in the following sources, respectively: (1) Nehru, *Circular to the Pradesh Congress Committees*, August, 1954; (2) Jawaharlal Nehru, *Glimpses of World History* (New York, 1942), p. 736; (3) *The Hindu* (Madras), July 17, 1951, p. 4; and (4) *The Hindu*, Nov. 16, 1953, p. 1.
30 Beatrice Pitney Lamb, *India: A World in Transition* (3rd ed., New York, 1968), p. 157.
31 Constituent Assembly Debates, VII, 781. For a thorough treatment of this whole subject, see Donald E. Smith, *India as a Secular State* (Princeton, 1963).

came, and in the centenary year of his birth (1969) — have been grim reminders that Hindu-Muslim tensions are still strong, lying just beneath the surface and occasionally erupting in tragic ways.

The main concern of many Hindus, however, seems to be not so much the danger from the Muslims, but rather "a preoccupation with the threat of a secular assault upon the traditional institutions that have sustained the status and the security of many Indians."[32] The many communal parties, which have had little electoral success, except occasionally in limited areas, but which have deep roots in traditional Hindu society, appeal to persons who share this preoccupation. "As managers of protest, the communal parties play up the solidarities, the securities, the privileged access to scarce resources which social structures like caste, religion and ethnolinguistic community have always afforded Indians and whose survival depends upon the retention of salient features of the traditional culture pattern."[33]

Officially, India is as fully dedicated to the concept of a secular state as it was when it was led by the great champion of secularism, Jawaharlal Nehru; but this dedication is constantly being threatened by some of the most deeply-rooted forces in Indian society.

## India as a Welfare State: The Socialist Pattern

Reflecting the basic orientation and desires of most of the leaders of modern India and mindful of the Preamble to the Objectives Resolution of December 1946, the framers of the Indian Constitution incorporated many provisions designed to make India a welfare state. The basic aims of a welfare state were clearly foreshadowed in the Preamble to the Constitution and in virtually all of Part IV of the Constitution, containing the Directive Principles of State Policy. Article 38 states: "The State shall strive to promote the welfare of the people by securing and protecting as effectively as it may be a social order in

---

[32] Harold A. Gould, "Religion and Politics in a U. P. Constituency," in Donald E. Smith, ed., *South Asian Politics and Religion* (Princeton, 1966), p. 53. Professor J. P. Suda expressed a point of view which is quite widespread among the Hindus of India: "By making India a *secular* state it is not meant that the government or the state becomes anti-religious or irreligious or that it cannot promote the higher or spiritual values of life. All that the phrase means is that the state is absolutely neutral in religious matters. . . . There is . . . one great danger lurking in the idea of a secular Indian state. The genius of our race has been spiritual . . . ancient India struck the note of spiritual greatness and placed before mankind deep and eternal spiritual truths. These truths are preserved in the great epics, the *Ramayan* and the *Mahabharata*, and the *Bhagwad Gita*. If the secular Indian Republic ignores these great treasure-houses of spiritual knowledge, it would do itself great and irreparable injury." Suda, *Indian Constitutional Development and National Movement*, pp. 520, 521–522.

[33] Gould, "Religion and Politics in a U. P. Constituency," p. 53.

which justice, social, economic and political, shall inform all the institutions of the national life." Most of India's prominent political leaders
have been and are professed socialists, although it is often difficult to
determine exactly what socialism means to them. Gandhi's economic
and social views could hardly be subsumed under the term "socialism,"
although there were undoubtedly many socialist elements in his creed.
Nehru regarded himself as a socialist. He was obviously influenced by
Marxist views, but at the same time he did not identify himself as a
Marxist, and he often attacked communism and the Communists.

Even most of the so-called conservative parties and leaders, except
the Swatantra Party and its spokesmen, profess support for socialism
in one form or another. A common statement in almost all circles in
India — sometimes, it is true, made with tongue in cheek — is: "We
are all socialists now." Dominant Indian opinion is opposed to capitalism and the "acquisitive society" and is unabashedly in favor of a
socialist welfare state. One of the best known statements of this goal
was made in a resolution adopted by the Congress Party at its annual
session at Avadi in January 1955:

> In order to realise the object of the Congress . . . and to further
> the objectives stated in the Preamble and Directive Principles of
> State Policy of the Constitution of India, planning should take
> place with a view to the establishment of a socialistic pattern of
> society, where the principal means of production are under social
> ownership or control, production is progressively speeded up and
> there is equitable distribution of the national wealth.

In subsequent years the Congress reaffirmed the Avadi resolution
and endorsed specific suggestions for implementing it. At its annual
session at Indore in January 1957, the Congress amended its Constitution to read that the object of the Congress is the "establishment in
India by peaceful and legitimate means of a Socialist Co-operative
Commonwealth."

The Second Five Year Plan contained a noteworthy explanation of
the meaning of the "socialist pattern of society" (the word socialist is
usually used instead of socialistic), and this statement was quoted in
both the Third and the Fourth Plans. Presumably, therefore, it may
be regarded as the official interpretation. It included the following
sentences:

> Essentially, this [the phrase "socialist pattern of society"]
> means that the basic criterion for determining lines of advance
> must not be private profit, but social gain, and that the pattern
> of development and the structure of socio-economic relations
> should be so planned that they result not only in appreciable in-

creases in national income and employment but also in greater equality in incomes and wealth. Major decisions regarding production, distribution, consumption and investment — and in fact all significant socio-economic relationships — must be made by agencies informed by social purpose. . . .

The socialist pattern of society is apt to be regarded as some fixed or rigid pattern. It is not rooted in any doctrine or dogma. . . . The accent . . . is on the attainment of positive goals, the raising of living standards, the enlargement of opportunities for all, the promotion of enterprise among the disadvantaged classes and the creation of a sense of partnership among all sections of the community. . . . The directive principles of State policy in the Constitution have indicated the approach in broad form: the socialist pattern of society is a more concretised expression of this approach.

Democracy, it has been said, is a way of life rather than a particular set of institutional arrangements. The same could well be said of the socialist pattern.

Statements of this kind may be somewhat more illuminating than the more general pronouncements of the Congress Party, but they still indicate direction rather than spell out concrete programs. India is clearly dedicated to the principle of the welfare state under a "socialist pattern of society"; but is it in fact such a state? When the Congress Party split in 1969, each of the contending factions vied with the other in endorsing the ten-point socialist program which the united Party had adopted some time before, in embracing more radical policies, and in implementing these policies more effectively. In these exchanges the gap between policy and performance was starkly revealed.

These, then, were seven vital decisions regarding the basic nature of the Indian state: that India should be a "sovereign democratic republic," to use the language of the Preamble to the Constitution, with a parliamentary system, a federal structure, a written Constitution, associated with the Commonwealth, and dedicated to the objectives of secularism and the welfare state. These decisions were made with so little debate and discussion that they may almost be regarded as assumptions rather than decisions. It is nevertheless remarkable that there should have been so marked a political consensus on questions which are inherently so controversial and which affected sensitive areas of India's political and social anatomy.

## Universal, Direct Suffrage

Two other major decisions required extensive debate and considerable soul-searching, and even today many people, for various reasons, doubt their wisdom. The first of these decisions was embodied in Article 326 of the Indian Constitution, as follows: "The elections to the House of the People and to the Legislative Assembly of every State shall be on the basis of adult suffrage." These innocuous sounding words reflected a bold gamble and a radical departure from previous practice. Even in the elections for the provincial assemblies which were held in 1937 under the Government of India Act of 1935 only some 35 million Indians, all but 6 million being males, were eligible to vote. Prior to that time the electorate had been only about one-fifth as large. Most of the people of India, therefore, had had no previous experience in voting. Moreover, all but a small proportion — certainly less than 20 per cent — were illiterate. What would be the consequences of giving the vote to every adult person over the age of twenty-one, male or female, literate or illiterate?

The decision to base the Indian democracy on unrestricted, universal, direct adult suffrage was a momentous one, perhaps the boldest decision the framers of the Constitution made. Direct election, it was argued, would give the fledgling Indian democracy a broad sense of popular support, would promote feelings of political participation and national identification, and would be "the pillar of the social revolution."[34]

It is still too early to determine whether the gamble in genuine democracy will pay off, but it may be that the future of democracy in India depends on the results of this gamble. The experience since independence has, on the whole, been encouraging. In the first two decades four mammoth general elections, plus several State elections and many by-elections and local and municipal elections, were conducted with impressive success; and in February 1969, a small general election was held in five States. Elections have become a normal and central part of the Indian political process.

The Indian experiment in adult suffrage contrasts favorably with the limitations on the franchise, including an increasing resort to indirect elections, which have been imposed in many other Asian countries which profess to be democratic, including the system of "basic democracies" in Pakistan and of "guided democracy" in Indonesia. It remains to be seen which approach to democracy will prevail in the Asian scene.

## States Reorganization Along Linguistic Lines

The second decision, which was taken with grave misgivings and against the known opposition of Nehru and many other leaders of the Congress Party, was to organize the Republic of India essentially along linguistic lines. Ironically, this decision was wholly in keeping with

[34] See Austin, *The Indian Constitution,* pp. 46–49.

demands of the Indian National Congress, dating back to 1921: "In stimulating linguistic agitation the Congress Party before independence helped to create a monster which now challenges India's existence as a single nation and taxes her Government's ability to maintain law and order."[35] For six years the Government of India resisted mounting demands for the reorganization of the State boundaries to conform more closely to linguistic considerations. Actually, in at least fifteen of the twenty-eight States of India after independence more than 75 per cent of the people spoke a single dominant language, and in Bombay State, with two dominant languages, 76 per cent listed either Marathi or Gujarati as their mother tongue.[36]

But this did not satisfy the champions of linguistic regionalism, especially in the South of India. In 1953 the floodgates of lingualism were opened. In December 1952, Potti Sriramulu, in a gesture of self-sacrifice which aroused the Telegu-speaking people of north Madras State, fasted unto death in Madras on the issue of a separate state for his people, and shortly afterward the Government of India reluctantly promised to create a separate State of Andhra. This new State came into existence in the fall of 1953.

A few weeks later, still under the pressure of linguistic agitation and tensions, the Government appointed a three-man States Reorganization Commission. The Commission took two years to make its report, thus giving time for passions to die down, on the one hand, and for advocates of the linguistic principle to state their case and organize for later activity, on the other. Bearing in mind that its first task was the "preservation and strengthening of the unity and security of India," the Commission warned against excessive deference to linguistic feelings, for "further emphasis on narrow loyalties by equating linguistic regions with political and administrative frontiers must diminish the broader sense of the unity of the country." Nevertheless, the Commission recommended new linguistic states for the South, and it warned that "further deferment of a general reorganization will cause dissatisfaction and disappointment."[37] It recommended some changes in the boundaries of Bombay State, but it did not favor the division of Bombay State into two states, in which Marathi and Gujarati were generally spoken. This decision was received with satisfaction by the Gujaratis, but was

[35] Marshall Windmiller, "The Politics of States Reorganization in India: The Case of Bombay," *Far Eastern Survey,* XXV (September, 1956), 129.

[36] See "The Effect of the Territorial Reorganization of India in 1956 on Linguistic Homogeneity and Concentration," *Intelligence Report* (issued by the Office of Intelligence Research, Department of State), No. 7579, Sept. 17, 1957. Table 1.

[37] See *Report of the States Reorganization Commission* (New Delhi, 1955), pp. 45, 229–237.

strongly objected to by many Marathi-speaking people. A Samyukta Maharashtra Samiti (United Maharashtra Committee) was formed to press for a separate State of Maharashtra — including Vidarbha, a predominantly Marathi-speaking section which the Commission proposed to create as a separate State.

After heated debates the Working Committee of the Congress Party endorsed most of the SRC Report, but it proposed an entirely different arrangement in Bombay State. It recommended that this State should be divided into three States — Maharashtra, Gujarat, and Bombay (chiefly the city of Bombay). This recommendation was especially unsatisfactory to Maharashtrians and embarrassed Congress members from the Maharashtra area, while giving further impetus to the Samyukta Maharashtra Samiti and an excellent opportunity for the Communists to exploit the anti-Congress feeling in this part of India.

In the next few months the Working Committee changed its mind, and when the States Reorganization Bill was introduced into the Parliament, it called for the reorganization of India into fourteen States, with a clearly dominant language in each, with the exception of Bombay, which was to be enlarged instead of divided, and the Punjab, where the main prevailing languages were associated with Hindi. Hindi was the dominant language in Uttar Pradesh, Bihar, and Madhya Pradesh, and languages related to Hindi, namely Rajasthani and Punjabi, were dominant in Rajasthan and the Punjab, respectively. Kashmiri prevailed in the Valley of Kashmir, although other languages were spoken by large numbers of Kashmiris. Each of the other languages officially recognized in the Eighth Schedule of the Indian Constitution, except Sanskrit, the classical language of Aryan India, Marathi and Gujarati, which shared linguistic importance in different parts of Bombay, and Urdu, closely related to Hindi, was the dominant language in one State, and in only one State. Listed in order of numbers of persons speaking each language as a mother tongue, the coincidence of language and State was as follows: Telegu — Andhra Pradesh; Tamil — Madras; Bengali — West Bengal; Kannada — Mysore; Malayalam — Kerala; Oriya — Orissa; Assamese — Assam.

Having in effect conceded the essentially linguistic basis of States reorganization, the Indian Government found that its decision was generally welcomed in most of the country, but definitely unpopular in linguistically frustrated Bombay and the Punjab. The demands for separate States of Gujarat and Maharashtra would not die down, and at length, on May 1, 1960, the Government of India, reflecting the surrender of the Congress Party on this issue, officially divided Bombay State into these two States, to bring the number of Indian States to fifteen. This action in effect signified as complete a concession to the linguistic principle as seemed possible, except perhaps in the Punjab, where the linguistic issue was complicated by the fact that the two main languages, Hindi and Punjabi, were linguistically similar, and by the added fact that the members of the militant Sikh organization, the Akali Dal, were demanding a separate Sikh State (some even demanded an independent Sikhistan). This demand was met, at least to some extent, on November 1, 1966, with the division of the Punjab into two states, known as the Punjab (with the majority of the Sikhs and Punjabi-speaking people) and Haryana (with a Hindu and Hindi-speaking majority), each with its capital in Chandigarh, the former capital of the larger Punjab State, which became a Union Territory, administered by the President of India through an administrator. Since a separate State of Nagaland had been officially inaugurated on December 1, 1963, the division of the Punjab in 1966 gave India seventeen States.

The agitation over linguistic States demonstrated that the Congress had opened a Pandora's box indeed when it championed the principle of the reorganization of India on a linguistic basis, and it stimulated the divisive forces in India to such an extent as to raise doubts about the capacity of free India to survive as a unified state dedicated to the democratic way. Whereas most of the other basic decisions regarding the nature of the Indian state have tended to give meaning and reality to the concept of a viable Indian nation, the reluctant concessions to linguistic demands have revealed the strength of regional as against national loyalties.

# * 6 *

# The Central Government

New Delhi, the capital of India since the early 1920's, is a British-built city next to historic old Delhi, and it contains many reminders of the days of British rule. Some of the buildings which house the ministries and other units of government, notably the Secretariat buildings, the domed Rashtrapati Bhavan, once the residence of the Governor-General and now of the President of India, and the vast circular Parliament building nearby, are very British and, as some think, rather un-Indian. But with the expansion of the governmental apparatus of independent India, many contemporary buildings are appearing in New Delhi. Notable among these are the imposing new Supreme Court building and the modernistic structures rising in the spacious diplomatic enclave, including the new United States Embassy, perhaps the most discussed diplomatic structure in the world. Many more functionally designed new buildings provide quarters for governmental agencies and personnel.

The Government of India today is a vast, sprawling bureaucracy, centered in New Delhi but reaching out to the remotest village. Most of the people on the government rolls are lesser government servants, who do routine work for very low salaries, and peons, who run errands, do odd jobs, sit outside of office doors, and presumably enhance the prestige of the persons for whom they work. At the apex of the structure are the senior civil servants, mostly members of the Indian Administrative Service, with a few active members of the old Indian Civil Service in key positions of central or State administration or in the diplomatic service, and at the very top the Ministers, the members of the Parliament, and the judges of the Supreme Court. The official head of the Indian Union is the President, but the real executive head is the Prime Minister.

## The President and Vice President

The Executive Branch of the Indian Government is headed by the President, the Vice President, the Prime Minister and the members of the Council of Ministers. Article 53 (1) of the Indian Constitution states: "The Executive power of the Union shall be vested in the President and shall be exercised by him either directly or through officers subordinate to him in accordance with this Constitution." The President is chosen by an electoral college composed of the elected members of both Houses of the Indian Parliament and of the Legislative Assemblies of the States, by a complicated system of weighted voting. He is elected for a term of five years and may be removed only by impeachment. He is eligible for re-election.

The Constitution was deliberately vague in defining the constitutional position of the President in relation to his Council of Ministers. On the one hand, it contains some provisions which seem definitely to assume, as was stated in the debates on the proposed Constitution in the Constituent Assembly, that "the President means the Central Cabinet responsible to the whole Parliament."[1] This would be the normal situation in a parliamentary system of responsible government, which presumably was the system which the framers of the Indian Constitution intended to establish. In practice the President has been the head of what Bagehot called "the dignified parts of the Constitution" and has largely governed through and with the advice of his Ministers, who have been responsible to the Parliament. On the other hand, the Constitution seems to leave a remarkably wide area of discretion to the President and to give him emergency powers which could in fact make him far more than a nominal executive head.

Opinions on the role and powers of the President vary greatly. Udaya Narayan Shukla concluded that "the President has very wide powers, more than those possessed by either [the] English monarch or the American President," and she held that "the Indian Executive . . . is perhaps [the] most powerful of all the democratic executives of the world."[2] R. Ramaswamy, a senior advocate of Bangalore, reflected the more widely accepted interpretation when he stated: "The Constitution does not define in specific terms the nature of the relationship between the President and the Council of Ministers. But there are clear indications available in the provisions of the Constitution as to what the framers of it intended that relationship to be. And if we

[1] *Constituent Assembly Debates,* IX (Aug. 3, 1949), 150.
[2] Udaya Narayan Shukla, "Federal Executives with Special Reference to India" (unpublished Ph.D. dissertation, Lucknow University, 1956), pp. 296, 332.

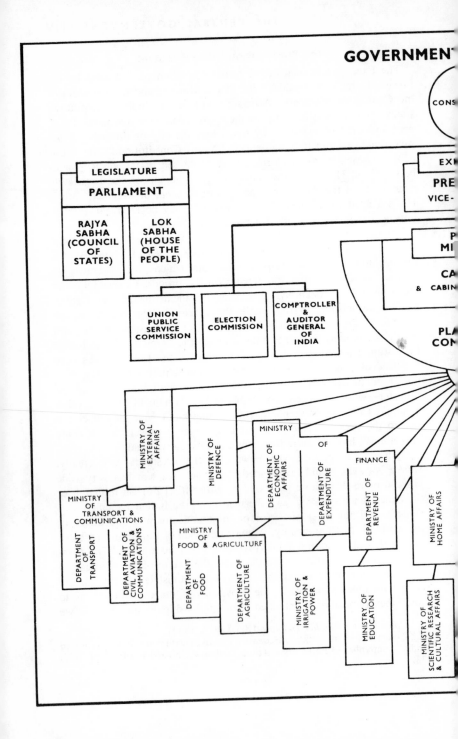

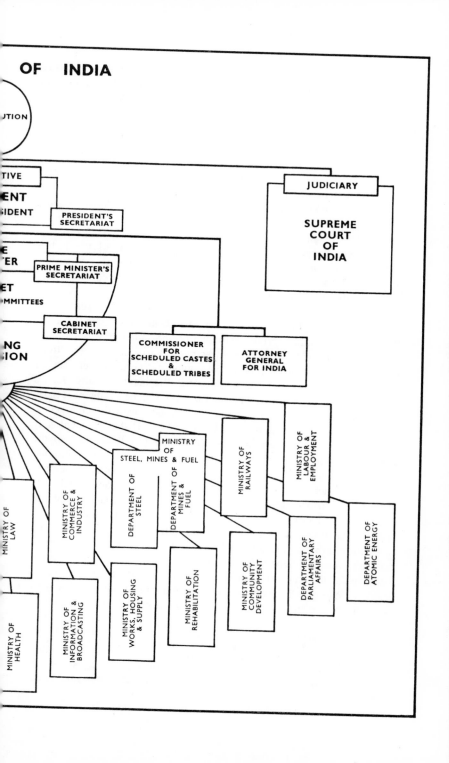

consider all the relevant provisions as an integral whole, the conclusion, I think, seems clear that the constitutional relationship created by the new constitution between the President and the Council of Ministers will be substantially analogous to the position the King of Great Britain occupies *vis-à-vis* the British Cabinet. In other words, the President of India will be a constitutional head who has only the right to be kept informed of and to express his views upon the many questions which arise within the Union orbit of activity but who cannot override the advice tendered to him by his ministers relative to any action he has to take as executive head of the Union."[3] Professor D. N. Banerjee concurs. The President of India, he argues, "occupies in the Indian constitutional system the same position as the Crown does in the English Constitution."[4] A peculiar feature of the Indian political system is that the President is a part of the Indian Parliament, although he is not a member of either House. According to Article 79 of the Constitution, "Parliament in the Union . . . shall consist of the President and two Houses. . . ."

In addition to the normal executive powers, which he exercises on the advice of the Prime Minister and the Council of Ministers, the President of India has certain legislative powers, such as various kinds of veto, the power to issue ordinances while Parliament is not sitting, some important financial powers, and some extraordinary emergency powers. In cases of grave emergency the President is authorized to issue a proclamation and to take such measures as he deems necessary, within the provisions of the Constitution, to deal with the emergency. According to the Constitution (Articles 352–360), the President may assume emergency powers in three situations: (1) if a threat to the security of India, "whether by war or external aggression or internal disturbance," has arisen (Article 352); (2) if a situation has developed in a State which makes it impossible for the constitutional machinery in that State to operate (Article 356); or (3) if the financial stability or credit of India or any part of it is threatened (Article 360). In each instance the President is nominally sole judge of the existence of an emergency, although presumably he will act as an agent of the Government and not on his own discretion. He must lay each proclamation issued under the emergency provisions of the Constitution before Parliament. Without the approval of the Parliament no proclamation may remain in effect for more than two months; with the approval of

[3] M. Ramaswamy, "The Constitutional Position of the President of the Indian Republic," *The Canadian Bar Review,* June–July, 1950, p. 649.
[4] D. N. Banerjee, "The Growth of Parliamentary Government in India, 1919–1950," *Parliamentary Affairs,* IX (Spring, 1956), 172. See also D. N. Banerjee, "The Indian Presidency," *The Political Quarterly,* January–March, 1955.

the Parliament, no Proclamation of Emergency under Article 356 may be maintained for more than six months at a time; and in no event may it be extended beyond a period of three years.

Article 352 has been invoked only once, but this led to a long period of emergency rule and to much controversy and opposition. Almost immediately after the Chinese attack in late October 1962, India was placed under emergency rule, and this condition was maintained for more than five years, until January 10, 1968. Since the emergency powers were used sparingly and were little publicized, most Indians were probably unaware that for a long time they were living under what could be described as constitutional dictatorship.

Article 360 has never been invoked, although the financial condition of several states has been most precarious. Article 356, however, has been invoked many times. There were five instances in the first decade of the Indian Republic: in the Punjab in 1951–52 for a period of ten months, in PEPSU (Patiala and East Punjab States Union) in 1953–54 for approximately one year, in Andhra in 1954 for four months, in Travancore-Cochin for eleven months in 1956–57, and in Kerala (comprising substantially the same territorial area as the former State of Travancore-Cochin) in 1959–60 for about six months.[5] For the next six years President's rule was imposed only twice, but after the fourth general elections in 1967, which resulted in political instability, shifting coalitions, and mass defections and "floor-crossing," Article 356 was invoked so often as to raise the question whether emergency rule in some States had not become a way of life and "normal" constitutional government the exception. Emergency rule was in effect in Rajasthan in March–April 1967, in Haryana from November 1967 to May 1968, in West Bengal from February 1968 to February 1969, in Uttar Pradesh from April 1968 to February 1969, in Bihar from June 1968 to February 1969, and in the Punjab from August 1968 to February 1969. Bihar was again placed under President's Rule in 1969, Uttar Pradesh and West Bengal in 1970, and Orissa in January 1971.

A detailed study of each of these cases would show that the President's emergency powers are extensive, that they have been exercised with firmness but with discretion, that they provide real safeguards against the collapse of State administration, that they have not thus far been abused, although the danger of abuse is always present, and that in accordance with the intent of the framers of the Constitution, the President has used his emergency powers only at the request of the Prime Minister.

[5] See Kishore K. Koticha, "Presidential Intervention under Article 356 of the Constitution of India," *Journal of the Indian Law Institute,* II (October–December, 1959), 125–133; especially the chart on p. 126.

Grave reservations have been expressed regarding the emergency provisions of the Constitution. During the debates in the Constituent Assembly H. V. Kamath declared: "I have ransacked most of the constitutions of the democratic countries of the World . . . and I can find no parallel to this chapter of emergency provisions in any of the other constitutions of democratic countries in the world. The closest approximation to my mind is reached in the Weimar Constitution of the Third Reich which was destroyed by Hitler taking advantage of this very provision contained in that constitution."[6] C. V. H. Rao has expressed the opinion that the "peculiar constitutional provisions relating to the President" can be used as "a convenient stepping stone for [the] establishment of dictatorship" and that "the combination of an adventurous Prime Minister and a complacent or unscrupulous President" (or vice versa) "could certainly subvert parliamentary democracy."[7] Professor Suda has asserted flatly that "by declaring an emergency the President can transform the federal constitution into unitary. Such a power of converting a federal into a unitary state is not to be found in any other federal constitution."[8]

The reasons for including the emergency provisions in the Constitution are clear. The framers of the Constitution, for all their doubts and reservations, felt that the central government of the new and weak state had to be given sufficient authority to deal with emergency situations arising from internal disorders and divisions or from external dangers. The riots and murders and general dislocation which accompanied partition, the strained relations with Pakistan arising from the tension over Kashmir, and a variety of other unresolved issues, convinced them that such emergencies might indeed arise.

As G. N. Joshi suggested, "the actual part which a President may play in the decisions" of the Indian Government "will largely depend upon the personal equation."[9] India was very fortunate to have as its first President Dr. Rajendra Prasad, a beloved elder statesman and old Gandhian, a former President of the Indian National Congress and President of the Constituent Assembly from its inception in late 1947 until he assumed the office of President of the Indian Republic in January 1950. Dr. Prasad conceived of his role as a unifying and symbolic one. He did not attempt to take advantage of the emergency powers he possessed under the Constitution. He acted only upon the advice of

[6] *Constituent Assembly Debates,* IX (Aug. 2, 1949), 104.
[7] Mohan Lal, "The President and Parliament," in A. B. Lal, ed., *The Indian Parliament* (Allahabad, 1956), p. 226.
[8] J. P. Suda, *Indian Constitutional Development and National Movement* (Meerut, 1951), p. 575.
[9] G. N. Joshi, *The Constitution of India* (3rd ed., London, 1954), p. 123.

the Prime Minister, Jawaharlal Nehru, who was the real head of the Indian executive.[10]

Dr. Prasad's successors — Dr. Sarvepalli Radhakrishnan (1962–67), Dr. Zakir Husain (1967–69), and Varahagiri Venkata Giri (1969– ) — carried on in the same tradition. Thus a good precedent has been set, although there is still a danger of a reversion of roles if a strong-minded President and a weak Prime Minister happen to occupy the two top offices.

The Vice President of the Republic of India is elected for a term of five years by the members of both Houses of Parliament. In the event of a vacancy in the office of President as a result of death, resignation, or removal from office, the Vice President shall act as President, but only until a new President is elected, which must be within a period of six months following the vacancy in that office. The Vice President is also ex officio Chairman of the Council of States.

Obviously the Vice President of India has rather limited functions and almost no real powers, unless he is called upon to act as President; but again much depends on the personal equation. India has had distinguished Vice Presidents — Dr. Radhakrishnan (1950–62), Dr. Husain (1962–67), V. V. Giri (1967–69), and Gopal Swarup Pathak (1969– ). The first three succeeded to the Presidency, Dr. Radhakrishnan with little opposition, Dr. Husain in a spirited contest with K. Subba Rao, a former Chief Justice who was supported by most opposition parties, and V. V. Giri, who was denied the Congress nomination, only after a close and exciting contest with the Congress candidate, N. Sanjiva Reddy.

## The Prime Minister and the Council of Ministers

Consecutive paragraphs of Article 75 of the Indian Constitution contain the following provisions regarding the Council of Ministers:

> The Ministers shall hold office during the pleasure of the President. The Council of Ministers shall be collectively responsible to the House of the People.

These and other provisions of the Constitution, plus certain ambiguities and omissions, have led some students of Indian government and politics to suggest that there is some confusion as to the precise role of the

[10] On one famous occasion, however, Dr. Prasad provoked a great deal of surprise and controversy simply by calling upon the Indian Law Institute to examine how far the powers and functions of the President under the Constitution were identical with those of the British monarch. His remarks aroused fears that later Presidents might take undue advantage of the emergency powers of the Constitution. See *The Hindu* (Madras), Nov. 29, 1960.

Council of Ministers and as to the relation of its head, the Prime Minister, and its members to the President. There is the further question of the real degree of responsibility of the Council to the Parliament. Given Indian political experience under the British and the intent of the framers of the Constitution, however, there can be little doubt that the Constitution was designed to provide India with a genuine system of parliamentary democracy, in which the Council of Ministers would be responsible to the Parliament and in which the Prime Minister would be the *de facto* head of the executive.

In the actual operations of the Government of India under the Constitution, the Council of Ministers has functioned with relation to the symbolic head of the State, the President, in a manner which has encouraged respect for the high office of the presidency without detracting from the real powers of the responsible executive. However, Parliament has not had the control over the executive which would seem desirable in a healthy parliamentary system.

From the Interim Government of 1946 until his death in 1964, the Prime Minister of India was Jawaharlal Nehru. Nehru was much more than Prime Minister of India, important as that role was; he was a leader of the Indian "revolution," which he interpreted in economic and social as well as in political terms, the political heir of Gandhi, the leader of the dominant political organization, a charismatic leader par excellence, the very symbol of the new India. Important and able men held ministerial posts, but with the exception of Vallabhbhai Patel, who served as Deputy Prime Minister until his death in 1950, no one really shared Nehru's authority. Nehru's successors — Lal Bahadur Shastri and Indira Gandhi — lacked his charisma and authority, but they soon learned how to use the office to assert their primacy over apparently stronger figures in the Cabinet or the Congress Party.

The Council of Ministers is composed of Ministers who are members of the Cabinet, and Ministers who are not members of the Cabinet, known as Ministers of State. The Council of Ministers which was sworn in on March 13, 1967, for example, following the fourth general elections, consisted of 19 Cabinet Ministers and 14 Ministers of State. In addition to the Prime Minister, the Deputy Prime Minister (who was also Finance Minister), and a Minister without Portfolio, the remaining 16 Cabinet Ministers were in charge of the following major departments of the Government: External Affairs; Defense; Home Affairs; Law; Food and Agriculture; Industrial Development; Steel, Mines and Metals; Planning, Petroleum, Chemicals, and Social Welfare; Railways; Transport and Shipping; Commerce; Tourism and Civil Aviation; Labor and Rehabilitation; Parliamentary Affairs; Information and Broadcasting; and Education. Special mention should also be made of the

Planning Commission, which is concerned with one of the most vital aspects of Indian policy, the work of economic planning and development.[11]

## The Indian Parliament

In the vast circular Parliament House in New Delhi, with its scores of marble columns, the Parliament of India sits. This central law-making body consists of the President and two Houses. The Upper House is known as the Rajya Sabha, or the Council of States, while the Lower House is called the Lok Sabha, or the House of the People. The relations between the two Houses are roughly comparable to those between the British House of Lords and House of Commons. The procedures followed in the Indian Parliament are based on those in the British Parliament.

On the other hand, the Indian Parliament has not achieved in its political system a position of such central importance as has the British Parliament in its parliamentary system. This is due to many factors, including the relative lack of experience of the Indian Parliament and of most of its members, the absence of deeply rooted conventions, the limitations placed upon it under the Constitution, and, in the Nehru era, its actual subordination to the strong personality of the Prime Minister and to the central organs of the Congress Party, which has a top-heavy representation in the legislative body.

The Indian Parliament normally holds three sessions a year. According to the Constitution not more than six months may elapse between sittings.

**Council of States (Rajya Sabha).** The Council of States is limited in size to 250 members. Twelve of the members are nominated by the President to represent the arts and professions — the Constitution specifically mentions "literature, science, art, and social service," and 238 members represent the States. These members are elected by the elected members of the State Legislative Assemblies, with the representation of each State determined roughly in accordance with population. The Council is not subject to dissolution, but the terms of approximately one third of its members expire every second year. The presiding officer of the Council, acting in an ex officio capacity, is the Vice President of India. When this office is vacant, or when the Vice

[11] For a detailed description of the organization and functions of the ministries, departments, and other branches of the Government of India, see The Indian Institute of Public Administration, *The Organisation of the Government of India* (Bombay, 1958). The chart on pp. 120–121 above represents the typical breakdown of the Government of India. With changes in Governments, there may be minor changes in ministries.

President is absent, a Deputy Chairman, chosen from among the members of the Council, presides.

Presumably the Council of States is a coordinate branch of the Indian Parliament, but it is in fact much less influential than the House of the People. Professor J. P. Suda calls it "one of the weakest second chambers in the world, weaker than even the House of Lords."[12] As in the British Parliament, all money bills must originate in the House of the People, and in case of doubt whether a measure is a money bill or not the Speaker of the House alone decides. If the two Houses differ on any bill, the differences are resolved in a joint sitting, in which each member of each House has one vote. This obviously gives the advantage to the House of the People, which is more than twice the size of the Council of States. Practically all the members of the Cabinet sit in the House of the People, although occasionally they may meet with the Council of States. Although its members are chosen on a different basis from the members of the Lower House, and although presumably these members represent the States of the Indian Union, there is little difference in age, experience, background, and outlook between members of the two Houses. As Morris-Jones has noted, "Composed of men similar to those who sit in the House of the People, the Council has, not surprisingly, failed to evolve a distinct role for itself."[13]

Most democratic states of the world have bicameral legislatures, but in many of these states there is growing criticism of the upper chamber. In India doubts about the value of the Council of States were voiced even during the debates on the draft Constitution in the Constituent Assembly. On one occasion Dr. Ambedkar, the chairman of the committee which drafted the Constitution, stated: "I cannot say that I am very strongly prepossessed in favour of a second chamber. To me it is like the curate's egg — good only in parts."[14] In the opinion of Professor M. P. Sharma "the Council of States does not seem to have been created with any particular purpose beyond bringing the Constitution in line with the prevailing fashion of bicameralism. In our country, the credit of second chambers has at no time been high, and it will not be surprising if the Council of States lives simply to serve as one of the ornamental parts of the Constitution."[15] Many members of the Council have expressed impatience over the limitations imposed

[12] Suda, *Indian Constitutional Development and National Movement*, p. 604.
[13] W. H. Morris-Jones, *Parliament in India* (Philadelphia, 1957), p. 257. This is by far the most thorough and objective study of the Indian Parliament.
[14] *Constituent Assembly Debates,* VII, 1317.
[15] M. P. Sharma, *The Government of the Indian Republic* (Allahabad, 1951), p. 147.

upon them, and criticism of the Council seems to be growing. It seems unlikely, however, that it will be abolished.

While it is undoubtedly a weak upper chamber, as are most upper chambers, the Indian Council of States does serve a number of useful functions, although perhaps not as effectively as its advocates expected. It has not functioned well as a delaying and revising chamber, which presumably should be one of its major contributions, but it has been an active body. In the lifetime of India's first Parliament, from 1952 to 1956, the Council of States, in fifteen sessions, dealt with 363 bills. One hundred and one bills — 69 Government bills and 32 private members' bills — originated in the Council. Among these were four important social measures — the Hindu Marriage Act, the Hindu Minority and Guardianship Act, the Hindu Succession Act, and the Hindu Adoptions and Maintenance Act — which formed vital parts of the so-called Hindu Code Bill. "The Council of States thus took credit for enacting what might perhaps rightly be claimed to be the most important social reform measures affecting the vast majority of the people of India."[16] During the same fifteen sessions of the Council no less than 12,733 questions were admitted; 6,572 were answered orally, together with 34,839 supplementary questions. Twenty-one Governmental resolutions were adopted in the Council. Forty-one private members' resolutions were discussed, and four were adopted.

The level of discussion and debate in the Council of States has been consistently high. It is a more orderly but no less interesting assembly than the House of the People. Some of the speeches of its members, such as those of Pandit H. H. Kunzru on the Preventive Detention Act in 1952, are worthy of comparison with the best efforts in the House of the People and really probe to fundamentals. Debates on foreign affairs are frequently held in the Council, and are usually of a high order.

**House of the People (Lok Sabha).** According to the Representation of the People Act of 1950, membership in the House of the People was fixed at no more than 496 members, with all members except nine, at most, to be elected by universal, direct suffrage, and with each member to represent at least 75,000 and no more than 500,000 people. The President was authorized to nominate one member for the Andaman and Nicobar Islands, six members for Jammu and Kashmir (until a regularly constituted Legislative Assembly was set up), and two members for the Anglo-Indian community, if this community received no

---

[16] P. Vijayaraghavan, "Second Chamber of the Indian Legislature" (unpublished Ph.D. thesis, University of Saugar, 1960), p. 187. For a more recent doctoral thesis on the Rajya Sabha, see Bimla Nangia, "Rajya Sabha at Work Since 1950" (unpublished Ph.D. thesis, University of Delhi, 1970).

representation in the regular voting. While the principle of separate electorates was not recognized, certain seats were reserved for a period of ten years for Scheduled Castes, Scheduled Tribes, and the Anglo-Indian community.

Membership in the House of the People, which officially became known as the Lok Sabha in 1954, is now limited to 525. The fourth Lok Sabha, elected in 1967, consisted of 523 members — 520 directly elected, one nominated by the President of India to represent the North East Frontier Agency and two to represent the Anglo-Indian community.

The normal life of the House is five years, although it may be dissolved by the President at any time, in accordance with the usual practice in a parliamentary system, and its life may be extended for no more than one year at a time if the President proclaims a national emergency. The presiding officer of the Lok Sabha is the Speaker. This important office has been held by able men, G. V. Mavalankar, M. Ananthasayanam Ayyangar, Hukam Singh, N. Sanjiva Reddy, and G. S. Dhillon.

*1. Committees of the House.* Much of the work of the Lok Sabha is done through various committees. From the time of their introduction into the Central Legislative Assembly in 1922, until March 1952, the various central legislative bodies which functioned under British rule or after independence had a well-developed system of advisory standing committees. After the first general elections in 1951–52 the Nehru government decided that standing committees should be abolished. In reply to criticism of this decision the Prime Minister "explained that these committees had been formed in quite different conditions and that they would now have 'no meaning.' They belonged to a different system of institutions from those now in existence, and in any case they had proved of little use in recent years."[17]

As might have been expected, the Government and the members of the Lok Sabha soon discovered that the Lok Sabha could not function effectively without committees to discharge much of its day-to-day work. Broadly speaking, committees of the Lok Sabha can be classified as standing committees and *ad hoc* committees. These committees fall into three categories: (1) general committees concerned primarily with the organization and powers of the House, such as the Committee on Rules, the Business Advisory Committee, and the Committee on

[17] Morris-Jones, *Parliament in India,* p. 310. See also Norman D. Palmer and Irene Tinker, "Decision Making in the Indian Parliament," in Richard L. Park and Irene Tinker, eds., *Leadership and Political Institutions in India* (Princeton, N.J., 1959), pp. 122–123.

Government Assurances; (2) legislative committees, chiefly select committees appointed for the consideration of particular bills and committees on petitions, resolutions, and subordinate legislation; and (3) the finance committees, notably the powerful Committees on Public Accounts and on Estimates.

The most detailed study of committees of the Lok Sabha that has yet been made used a five-fold division for standing committees, namely (1) committees to inquire (Committee on Petitions and Committee of Privileges), (2) committees to scrutinize (Committee on Government Assurances), (3) committees to control (Committee on Subordinate Legislation, Estimates Committee, Public Accounts Committee), (4) committees to advise (Business Advisory Committee, Committee on Private Members' Bills and Resolutions, Rules Committee, Committee on Absence of Members from the Sittings of the House), and (5) housekeeping committees. *Ad hoc* committees were classified under two heads: regular (including select committees and joint committees) and incidental.[18]

The Committee on Government Assurances, established in December, 1953, appears to be "a wholly Indian invention." Its terms of reference are sweeping ones: "The functions of the Committee are to scrutinise the assurances, promises and undertakings, etc., given by Ministers from time to time on the floor of the House and to report on (a) the extent to which such assurances have been implemented; and (b) where implemented, whether such implementations have taken place in the minimum time necessary for the purpose." The rationale of this unique committee is explained by Professor N. Srinivasan:

> It is common experience that when criticised Governments are profuse in their assurances that mistakes pointed out will not be repeated, that reparation would be made for any injuries and wrongs complained of and that steps would be taken to implement some particular policy. But no means or machinery exist in democratic countries to enforce the fulfilment of such assurances other than the continued interest of private members. The Committee on Government Assurances . . . is an attempt to provide such machinery.[19]

Because there is a considerable body of delegated legislation in India, the work of the Committee on Subordinate Legislation, also established in December 1953, is particularly important. The main function of

[18] B. B. Jena, *Parliamentary Committees in India* (Calcutta, 1966), pp. 11–12.

[19] N. Srinivasan, *Democratic Government in India* (Calcutta, 1954), pp. 260–261. See also Jena, *Parliamentary Committees in India,* Chap. V.

the Committee is to study all such delegated legislation and to report to the Lok Sabha "whether the authority delegated by Parliament . . . has been properly exercised to the extent permissible and in the manner envisaged."[20]

The Public Accounts Committee not only checks the audit reports of the Comptroller and Auditor General and other records and operations for technical irregularities, but it also is interested in any evidences of waste, corruption, inefficiency, or operational deficiencies in the conduct of the nation's financial affairs. It is thus "Parliament's watchdog and guardian of the people against official negligence or corruption."[21] Since 1954 it has included members from both Houses — 15 from the Lok Sabha and 7 from the Rajya Sabha. But "it is not a Joint Committee. It is a Committee of the Lok Sabha with which some members from Rajya Sabha are 'associated.' "[22]

According to the Rules of Procedure of the Lok Sabha the function of the Estimates Committee is to "examine such of the estimates as may seem fit to the Committee and to report what, if any, economies consistent with the policy underlying these estimates may be effected therein, and to suggest the form in which the estimates shall be presented to Parliament." It is a large and prestigious committee, with 30 members. Normally it works through a number of subcommittees. It takes a broad view of its functions and does not hesitate to make studies and recommendations affecting the whole field of administrative organization and policy. For this reason its many substantial reports have been more than technical studies. Some of these reports, such as the ninth report on "Administrative, Financial and Other Reforms," have been major contributions to public administration in India. As W. H. Morris-Jones points out:

> . . . this type of committee, inspired as it is by the idea not simply of economy nor even of efficiency alone but also of acting as a check against an oppressive or arbitrary executive, achieves a special significance as a substitute for a real Opposition. Indeed, it may well be that in an underdeveloped country — in which there is a wide measure of agreement not only on goals but also on methods — this kind of arrangement may be more suitable. . . . Finally, it must be noted that the Estimates Committee, perhaps more than the Public Accounts Committee, performs two tasks of quite special importance in India. In the

[20] Address by Deputy Speaker to the Committee, July 16, 1957, in *Journal of Parliamentary Information,* II, 140. See also Jena, *Parliamentary Committees in India,* Chap. VI.

[21] Morris-Jones, *Parliament in India,* p. 286.

[22] Jena, *Parliamentary Committees in India,* p. 178. See also Chap. VIII.

first place, it is a most valuable training-ground for members of the House. . . . In the second place, the reports of the Committee have a great educative value inside the House and also outside. They can help greatly to build up that layer of informed public opinion which is so urgently needed if the gap between rulers and ruled is to be closed.[23]

*2. Procedure in the House.* Within the broad framework of powers and responsibilities specified in the Constitution, the Parliament of India functions according to rules of procedure which are similar to those in the British Parliament. A bill is introduced in the House of the People through the usual British procedure of three readings, with the first reading largely by title only, the second the stage of debate and detailed consideration, and the third a general discussion usually leading to a vote, by viva voce or by division. Between the first and second readings a bill may be referred to a select committee, although in India this practice is usually followed on important bills only. In the British Parliament more bills are referred to select committees, and consideration by these committees comes after and not before the second reading.

Question time is an important part of the work of both Houses of the Indian Parliament. It takes place every day during a session in the Lok Sabha and four days a week in the Rajya Sabha. The procedure of the question period is patterned after that followed in the British House of Commons. Hundreds, even thousands, of written questions are filed with the Speaker at every session, and many oral supplementary questions are entertained. The question period is usually the most interesting and lively part of the meetings of the Parliament. It puts the Ministers and other governmental spokesmen on the stand by giving the opposition members of the Parliament their best opportunity to force the Government to pay some attention to them and to defend itself against criticisms. Twice a week in the House, whenever time permits, a half hour is allotted late in the afternoon for discussions of topics of national importance which have been the subjects of questions.

A "unique Indian innovation in modern parliamentary procedure" is the calling attention notice, a kind of "half-way house between the short-notice question and the adjournment motion." "The innovation combines the asking of a question with supplementaries and short comments, in which different points of view are expressed. Sometimes it develops into an impromptu discussion, with the Government on the

---

[23] Morris-Jones, *Parliament in India,* pp. 307–308; see also Jena, *Parliamentary Committees in India,* Chap. VII.

mat for an act of commission or omission. The activity cuts across party loyalties, with Congress M.P.'s vying with the others in tabling calling attention notices."[24] Usually the Government is expected to respond to such notices within 24 hours.

Most of the bills that are introduced are, of course, Government bills. Very little time is allowed for the introduction of private members' bills, and very few of the private bills that are considered are approved. Opposition members may influence legislation by putting questions in the question period, by calling attention notices, by participating in debates on Government bills, and by membership on select committees, finance committees, and other committees of the House, but they have little chance of pushing through any legislation of their own.

To be officially recognized by the Speaker as an opposition group, a party or coalition of parties must have at least fifty members in the Lok Sabha. No opposition party came even close to this figure until 1967, whereas membership in the Congress Party ranged between 350 and 400 members in a House of approximately 500. When Dr. Shyama Prasad Mookerjee, one of the most powerful parliamentarians India has seen, was a member of the Lok Sabha as leader of the Jan Sangh, he was recognized as leader of a rightist coalition known as the Democratic Nationalist Party, but even this coalition was unable to command fifty seats. After the fourth general elections in 1967, the Congress membership in the Lok Sabha declined to 281, but the next largest party (Swatantra) had only 44 seats. In November 1969, the Lok Sabha got its first officially recognized opposition party. The Congress Party split, and the faction opposed to Mrs. Gandhi, led by the so-called Syndicate and which came to be known as the Congress Party (Organization), was recognized by the Speaker as the official opposition, since it had slightly more than 50 members in the Lok Sabha.

**Powers and Functions of Parliament.** The Parliament of India has rather extensive powers and performs a variety of important functions. Its main function, that of India's chief lawmaking body, is limited legally by the federal nature of the Indian Republic and by the power of the Supreme Court to declare Parliamentary legislation of most types unconstitutional.[25] It is limited in an extra-legal way by the degree of

---

[24] G. S. Bhargava, "Parliament: View from the Press Gallery," *Indian and Foreign Review,* June 15, 1967, p. 8.

[25] In the famous case of *Golaknath* v. *the Punjab,* the Supreme Court of India, in February 1967, ruled in a 6 to 5 judgment that the Parliament had no right to amend the chapter in the Constitution on Fundamental Rights. "These rights are given a transcendent position and kept beyond the reach of parliamentary legislation."

real control over it which is exercised by the Prime Minister and the chief organs of the Congress Party. It has some constituent powers. It is authorized by the Constitution, for example, to alter the boundaries of a State, and it has reorganized some Indian States in a major way by ordinary legislation. A majority of the total membership in each House may amend the Constitution, with the President's assent, except in certain vital matters specified in Article 368, in which case amendments proposed by the Parliament must receive the assent of at least half of the State legislatures. Since the Council of Ministers, i.e., the *de facto* executive of the Indian Republic, is "collectively responsible to the House of the People," "we can say that it is the character of the House of the People which will determine the character of the government of the day."[26] As we have seen, the House has control over the nation's finances, and in this vital area the Government must therefore obtain the cooperation and approval of the House.

The Indian Parliament is the country's major deliberative body. It is here that important problems of domestic and foreign policy are debated and passed upon. In spite of the widespread illiteracy and concentration on matters of local concern, increasing interest has been shown in the deliberations of the Parliament. When any important measure is being discussed, crowds of people try to get into the few seats in the gallery of the House of the People or the Council of States, and the parliamentary discussions are printed almost verbatim in leading newspapers. Parliament also serves as a means of ventilating the grievances of the public. Even though the opposition is weak and divided, the value of this function should not be minimized. As Morris-Jones observed, "opposition groups are able to be far more effective in Parliament than their proportion of seats might suggest."[27] On some occasions, when public opinion seemed to be well ahead of the Government, this fact has been most effectively dramatized by the Opposition and has eventually had some bearing on Government policy. Generally speaking, however, the Opposition has had little success in changing Government policy. As Dr. Lanka Sunderam, a leading Independent M.P., has remarked, "in the Lok Sabha there are few recorded instances when Government has acceded to the demands of the Opposition, and each such measure is something to be cherished."[28]

Undoubtedly Parliament serves a most important function by pro-

[26] Suda, *Indian Constitutional Development and National Movement,* p. 602.

[27] W. H. Morris-Jones, *The Government and Politics of India* (Garden City, N.Y., 1967), p. 186.

[28] Lanka Sunderam, "The Role of An Independent Member," in Lal, ed., *The Indian Parliament,* p. 67.

viding a training ground for national leaders, and by giving such people practical experience in the workings of parliamentary democracy. This is especially important in India, where democracy is not deeply rooted, where the responsibilities of government are imperfectly understood, and where relatively inexperienced people are charged with vast responsibilities.[29]

Language is an added problem in the Parliament. Article 120 of the Constitution states that the business of the Parliament shall be conducted in Hindi or in English, but it also provided that the Speaker could "permit any member who cannot adequately express himself in Hindi or in English to address the House in his mother tongue." This makes for a babel of tongues and for mutual incomprehensibility in the proceedings of the Parliament. Most of the M.P.'s can speak English or Hindi or both, but many of those from the South and from tribal areas and other parts of the country cannot, and many of those who can refuse to do so for reasons of local pride or aversion to the idea of using a foreign language or a North Indian tongue.[30] The introduction of simultaneous translation facilities has aided the process of comprehension, but many M.P.'s dislike them and their use causes considerable delay.

The conditions under which the Indian M.P.'s have to work impose further handicaps. "They are not only inexperienced; they are also poorly educated, poorly paid, and usually in straitened circumstances. They lack adequate staff assistance, and they receive little help in research and preparation of speeches and reports. Moreover, many M.P.'s do not even make good use of the facilities at their disposal. It is difficult for them to find the time or the opportunity for serious reflection or study; their ways of life as well as their living arrangements make them easy prey for hordes of people who may flock about them at all hours. Often they are out of touch with their constituents, who in any event, if they have any interest in politics at all, are probably more

[29] The number of M.P.'s with previous legislative service has been increasing. In the first regular Indian Parliament, from 1952 to 1956, more than 55 per cent of the members had no previous legislative experience. In the third Parliament, from 1962 to 1967, 88 per cent had some previous experience — 182 in State legislatures and 202 in the second Lok Sabha. The increase in the number of former State legislators in the Lok Sabha should be particularly noted. "The accumulation of legislative experience is the most significant factor in the strengthening of parliamentary democracy." Surinder Suri, "Pattern of Membership," *Seminar*, No. 66 (February, 1965), p. 19.

[30] The distinguished Muslim, Maulana Azad, who was Minister of Education until his death in 1958, always spoke in Urdu in the House, although he also spoke English fluently. See Morris-Jones, *Parliament in India*, pp. 144–146.

interested in their representatives to local bodies and the state assemblies than in their representatives in far-off New Delhi."[31]

It is difficult to assess the precise role of the Parliament of India in the Indian political system. It is the chief lawmaking agency, but it does not really make the basic decisions. Certainly it does not yet play the central role which would be expected in a parliamentary system.

With all of its limitations, the Parliament of India, especially the Lok Sabha, has functioned with remarkable effectiveness, and it has established itself as an indispensable part of the governmental machinery. Nehru was an active participant in its proceedings, and he paid great deference to it. He helped to establish strong foundations for the continuance of parliamentary rule in India. His successors, with lesser stature and influence, inevitably have paid even greater attention to the Parliament. "There are abundant reasons to believe that, even in the Congress Party, the support that the Prime Minister enjoys will be subject to the overall consent of Parliament. A major political revolution has thus appeared almost as a convention."[32]

## The Supreme Court of India

Unlike the United States with its system of dual courts, India has a single judicial system, with the Supreme Court at the head of the judicial hierarchy, with High Courts for each of the States,[33] and with district courts and other subordinate courts in the local areas of government. In framing the judicial provisions of the Constitution, special attention was paid to the practice in the United States as well as in Great Britain and other countries, and decisions of the Indian Supreme Court frequently cite decisions of the Supreme Court of the United States.[34] After considerable discussion the framers of the Constitution did not adopt a due process of law clause, along the lines of the American model, but at least two articles of the Constitution use words suggestive of due process. Article 21 declares that "No person shall be deprived of his life or personal liberty except according to procedure established by law," and Article 31 (1) states that "No person shall be

[31] Palmer and Tinker, in Park and Tinker, eds., *Leadership and Political Institutions in India,* pp. 135–136.

[32] "The Stature of Parliament," *The Eastern Economist,* XXXI (Dec. 5, 1958), 849.

[33] There are 15 High Courts for the 17 Indian States. The High Court of Assam also serves as the High Court for Nagaland, and the Punjab and Haryana have the same High Court.

[34] "In recent times, the influence of American Constitutional Law and of American political thought is making itself felt increasingly." K. Lipstein, "The Reception of Western Law in India," *International Social Science Bulletin,* IX (1957), 95.

deprived of his property save by authority of law." In the famous case of *Gopalan* v. *Madras,* the Supreme Court of India rejected a contention that Article 21 was the equivalent of the American due process clause, but Justice William O. Douglas of the United States Supreme Court, in a brilliant comparative analysis of the legal systems of India and the United States, observed: "I discern in Indian judicial decisions a flavor of due process when it comes to questions of substantive law."[35] A preliminary draft of the Constitution contained a provision specifically providing for judicial review, but this was omitted in the final text. There can be no question, however, that judicial review is a significant prerogative of the Indian judiciary, and that the Supreme Court exercises a wide jurisdiction in this area.

The Court has three areas of jurisdiction: original, appellate, and advisory. Its original jurisdiction extends to (1) disputes between the Government of India and one or more States, between the Government of India and a State or States, on one side, and one or more States on the other, or between two or more States, and (2) claims of infringement of constitutionally guaranteed "fundamental rights." Hundreds of petitions invoking this jurisdiction have been filed. The Court's appellate jurisdiction extends to four types of cases, namely constitutional, civil, criminal and "special leave." In these types of cases, under certain conditions, appeals may be made from any State High Court to the Supreme Court. The President may refer a question of public importance to the Court for its consideration, and the Court, if it so chooses, may submit an advisory opinion.

According to the Constitution the Supreme Court of India was to consist of a Chief Justice and not more than seven other judges. Parliament was authorized to change the number of judges and has done so. The present number is fourteen, in addition to the Chief Justice. The Chief Justice and other judges are appointed by the President of India, "after consultation with such of the Judges of the Supreme Court and of the High Courts in the States as the President may deem necessary," and the Chief Justice "shall always be consulted" in the case of appointments of other members of the highest court.

Although the Constitution provides that a judge of the Supreme Court must be a "distinguished jurist," or a High Court advocate of at least ten years' practice, or a High Court judge of at least five years' service, in practice every appointee to the Supreme Court has been a High Court judge, with ten years' experience or more on a High Court. Appointments to the Supreme Court, and to the position of Chief Jus-

---

[35] William O. Douglas, *We the Judges: Studies in American and Indian Constitutional Law from Marshall to Mukherjea* (Garden City, N.Y., 1956), p. 28.

tice, have ~~invariably~~ been based on seniority. Since the Chief Justice and all the Supreme Court judges must retire at the age of 65, there have been frequent changes of personnel on the Supreme Court.

"The composite picture of the typical judge of the Supreme Court of India includes being a Hindu, birth in a socially prominent and economically comfortable family, legal education at a prominent Indian University or at one of the Inns of Court in London, more than two decades of private law practice before the High Court of the State of his birthplace, non-involvement in active politics, and ten years of experience with consequent seniority as a member of a High Court."[36] This profile suggests that judges of the Supreme Court are highly qualified, but are drawn from rather narrow and unrepresentative sectors of Indian Society.

Muslims are very much underrepresented on the Supreme Court, but the Court has always included at least one. The first Muslim Chief Justice was M. Hidayatullah, in 1968. The prevailing tradition of non-involvement in politics has occasionally been broken, especially after resignation or retirement. K. Subba Rao, who became Chief Justice in 1966, resigned in April 1967 to become the candidate of the United Opposition for President of India, losing to Dr. Zakir Husain, the Congress candidate, by a relatively narrow margin.

Located in the splendid new Supreme Court building in New Delhi, which also houses a magnificent legal library and the Indian Law Institute, an important legal research agency, the Supreme Court of India has won an enviable place for itself in the Indian constitutional system. It has invariably been composed of able judges, and its decisions have been of real importance. This is true in spite of the fact that its sphere of competence can be, and has been, limited by the Indian Parliament and is restricted in certain other ways under the Constitution. Many of its most important judgments on constitutional issues have related to the interpretation of Article 14, guaranteeing equality before the law, Article 19, guaranteeing important freedoms to the individual, and Article 31, regarding property rights. The Preventive Detention Act, first enacted in 1950 and renewed subsequently, has given rise to a number of cases which have come before the Supreme Court. The best known of these cases was that of *Gopalan* v. *Madras*.[37] A. K. Gopalan, then the leader of the Communists in the House of the People,

---

[36] George H. Gadbois, Jr., "Selection, Background Characteristics, and Voting Behavior of Indian Supreme Court Judges, 1950–1959," in Glendon Schubert and David Danelski, eds., *Comparative Judicial Behavior: Cross-Cultural Studies of Political Decision-Making in the East and West* (New York, 1969), p. 237.

[37] 1950 *Supreme Court Journal* 174–311.

was arrested and confined under this Act, and he brought legal action for release on the ground that he had been deprived of his rights as a citizen under Articles 14 and 19. The Supreme Court, in a historic decision, which Professor Alexandrowicz has called "the first great pronouncement of the Supreme Court of India on the Constitution generally,"[38] denied Gopalan's claim and upheld the Government's action.

Article 31 of the Constitution provided for compensation for any property "acquired for public purposes," but it apparently gave the Parliament full authority to fix the amount of the compensation. Soon after the Constitution went into effect, various questions arose regarding the propriety and legal authority for land reform programs enacted by some of the States, with the strong encouragement of the federal Government. The Constitution (First Amendment) Act of 1951 modified and clarified Article 31 by stating clearly that no law for the acquisition of property by any State should be declared void on the ground that it was inconsistent with Article 31. A number of Supreme Court cases upheld the claims of former land-holders that their property had been taken from them without just compensation. Nehru maintained that the Supreme Court should not attempt to act as a "third House of Parliament," and the Government pushed through the Constitution (Fourth Amendment) Act in 1955, providing that the question of the reasonableness of the compensation was no longer justiciable. Many Indian and foreign students of Indian constitutional law have criticized this amendment, but others have argued that the amendment was necessary to clarify the intent of the framers of Article 31 and to insure that important measures of social reform are not blocked by judicial decisions.[39]

This whole area is a delicate one, involving issues of ideological ori-

---

[38] Alexandrowicz, *Constitutional Developments in India* (London, 1957), p. 5.

[39] In his Tagore Law Lectures at the University of Calcutta in July 1955, Justice Douglas said: "Whatever the cause, the 1955 amendment casts a shadow over every private factory, plant, or other individual enterprise in India. The legislature may now appropriate it at any price it desires — substantial or nominal. There is no review of the reasonableness of the amount of compensation. The result can be just compensation or confiscation — dependent wholly on the mood of the Parliament." Douglas, *We the Judges*, p. 296. Professor Alexandrowicz holds a different view: "It is difficult for the reader of the Fourth Constitutional Amendment Act to escape the conclusion that it simply aims at restoring to some extent what was laid down by the Constituent Assembly but changed by judicial interpretation. . . . The Constitution has in fact not been changed much but rather redrafted in order to reflect better the original intentions of the constitution-makers." Alexandrowicz, *Constitutional Developments in India*, p. 94.

entation, broad public policy, and the respective roles of the Government and the Supreme Court. The issues raised are more political than judicial, but inevitably the Supreme Court, a nonpolitical body of non-political judges, is directly involved. "Indeed, the most important single category of cases decided by the Supreme Court of India since 1950 has been those in which the Court had to mediate and reconcile the competing claims of individual freedom and the needs of an aspiring welfare state. The decisions of the Court in this area were clearly of great political significance, and yet they were made by men who were not drawn from community affairs — men who in the course of their careers had generally maintained a posture of aloofness from what went on about them."[40]

## The Public Services

In one respect, at least, India was probably more fortunate than any other formerly dependent territory which has achieved independence. It inherited from the British an elaborate and well-organized administrative structure and a variety of Imperial Services, manned by well-trained men. At the head of these services was the Indian Civil Service, the "steel frame" of the British Indian administrative system. Even today, although their ranks, never numerous, have been decimated by death, resignation, and assignment to other duties, and although all of the British I.C.S. Officers have gone, former Indian I.C.S. Officers hold many of the administrative posts of highest responsibility and prestige, both in the Centre and in the States.

The successor to the I.C.S. is the Indian Administrative Service, which has more members and far less prestige than the old Indian Civil Service. Its members are recruited from among the most promising young Indians holding university degrees, through a system of examinations; they are carefully trained at an in-service training school in Mussoorie; they serve an apprenticeship at the Centre and in the States, including at least one assignment with a District Officer and, with increasing frequency, with officials of the Community Development Program. After their probationary period they receive more responsible assignments. By their sixth or seventh years they may become District Officers.

The Public Services of India consist of two broad groups, the Defense Forces and the Civil Services. The Constitution says nothing about the recruitment, training, or conditions of service of members of the armed forces; but many of the officers appointed to the National

[40] Gadbois, "Selection, Background Characteristics, and Voting Behavior of Indian Supreme Court Judges, 1950–1959," p. 251.

Defense Academy, the Military College, the Indian Air Force Flying College, and to the commissioned ranks of the Indian Navy are appointed in consultation with the Union Public Service Commission, after examinations conducted by the Commission.

The Civil Services may be divided into three main categories: the All-India Services, the Central Public Services, and the State Public Services. Although the Parliament is authorized by the Constitution to create other All-India Services, provided at least two-thirds of the members of the Council of States approve a resolution to this effect, the only All-India Services which were created prior to 1963 were those specified in Article 312 of the Constitution, namely the Indian Administrative Service and the Indian Police Service. In 1963 three additional All-India Services — the Indian Forest Service, the Indian Service of Engineers, and the Indian Medical and Health Service — were established, and the Rajya Sabha passed a resolution in favor of the creation of two more — an Indian Education Service and an Indian Agricultural Service. Members of the All-India Services may be assigned to the States or to the Centre; the I.A.S., in fact, is divided into State cadres. The Central Public Services include services in various administrative departments of the Government of India, such as the Foreign Service, the Audits and Accounts Service, the Customs and Excise Service, the Defence Accounts Service, the Railway Accounts Service, the Income Tax Service, and the Postal Service. There are also several engineering and ministerial services. These services are grouped into four main classes, with Class I and II employees having the highest status. Class III encompasses personnel in clerical jobs, and Class IV, the largest class, includes persons doing mostly menial jobs.

Members of the State Public Services are usually appointed by the Governor on the recommendation of the State Public Service Commission. Some of the highest posts in State administration, such as Divisional Commissioners, District Magistrates, Inspectors General of Police, and Superintendents of Police may be filled by officers of the I.A.S. or the Indian Police Service. The Chief Secretary, "the nervous center of the State," who is head of the State Civil Services, head of the General Administrative Department, the principal adviser to the Chief Minister, and the Secretary to the Cabinet, is usually an I.A.S. Officer, and usually, but not always, the senior civil servant in a State.[41] State Public Services are also divided into four classes; Classes I and II constitute the officer classes.

Some local governments in India have their own public services, and a few States have a separate Panchayati Raj service. Another large

41 Shriram Maheshwari, *Indian Administration* (Bombay, 1968), p. 208.

group of public employees consists of the employees of public enterprises (usually referred to in India as public undertakings).

In addition to the Armed Services, some 10 million persons are employed by national, State, and local governments in India. In 1965–66 the approximate number of employees of all governmental units was as follows:

| | |
|---|---|
| Centre | 2.4 million |
| States | 3.7 " |
| Local Governments | 1.7 " |
| Public Undertakings | 2.0 " |

Responsible for the main task of recruiting, training, and maintaining high standards in the Indian Civil Services is the Union Public Service Commission. This body is the direct successor to the Public Service Commission which was established in 1926. It is not surprising that the Union Public Service Commission of independent India should follow procedures similar to those which had been developed in the British period under the supervision of similar bodies.

The Constitution of India provided for the establishment of a Union Public Service Commission, consisting of an unspecified number of members to be appointed by the President, and of a Public Service Commission in each State, whose members were to be named by the Governor. There are now eight members of the Union Public Service Commission, including the Chairman. Each member is appointed for a six-year term or until he reaches the age of 65, the compulsory retirement age. He is not eligible for reappointment. To maintain the complete integrity of the Commission, the Constitution states that when he ceases to hold office the Chairman of the Union Public Service Commission "shall be ineligible for further employment either under the Government of India or under the Government of a State," and that other members of the Union Commission shall be similarly ineligible for any office except that of Chairman of the Union or of a State Public Service Commission.

The Commission is an independent statutory body. Its relations with the Government of India are coordinated through the Ministry of Home Affairs, but it deals directly with other ministries and departments. It has a Secretariat of over 500 members, and its office is organized into five branches.[42]

Article 320 of the Constitution specifies a wide variety of duties and functions for the Union Public Service Commission. It is charged with

[42] See Indian Institute of Public Administration, *The Organisation of the Government of India,* pp. 357–367.

the conduct of examinations for appointment to the All-India and Central Public Services; if requested by two or more States, it shall assist those States "in framing and operating schemes for joint recruitment for any services for which candidates possessing special qualifications are required"; it shall be consulted "on all matters relating to methods of recruitment to civil services and for civil posts," on principles to be followed in making appointments, promotions and transfers from one service to another, and on all disciplinary matters and claims affecting members of the civil services; it shall advise on any matter which the President may refer to it; it may be, and in fact has been, given additional functions by the Parliament; and it shall submit an annual report to the President, who shall present it to the Parliament, together with a statement of his reasons for not accepting the advice of the Commission, if such cases have arisen. Almost invariably the advice and recommendations of the Commission have been accepted.

India was fortunate indeed to inherit an administrative system which was characterized by high standards of integrity and efficiency and which gave an increasing number of Indians experience in the conduct of administrative affairs; but, as Dr. Paul Appleby observed, this system was "designed to serve the relatively simple interests of an occupying power,"[43] and it was not adequate, either in structure or in spirit, for the administration of a vast new country in the interests of the people of that country and not of a foreign power. The major weaknesses of the Indian administrative system are rather generally recognized. They have been pointed out repeatedly by Indian students and practitioners of administration, notably A. D. Gorwala,[44] and by foreign observers, including Dr. Paul Appleby, an American specialist in administration who, at the request of the Government of India, made two detailed surveys of public administration in India and submitted two much-discussed reports. These weaknesses are those of structure and of orientation.

Dr. Appleby, a friendly critic who rated the Government of India "among the dozen or so most advanced governments of the world," stated that his "major over-all concerns" related to constitutional structure, which provides "chiefly for 'co-ordination' rather than for administration," to "the related but more extended diffusion of administrative responsibility," a very major and pervasive weakness, and to "flexibility and future adequacy in administrative conceptions, terminology, structure and practices.[45] He found that "administration" in

[43] Paul H. Appleby, *Public Administration in India: Report of a Survey* (Delhi, 1953), p. 40.

[44] A. D. Gorwala, *Report on Public Administration* (Delhi, 1951), a report prepared for the Planning Commission.

[45] Appleby, *Public Administration in India,* pp. 8–9.

India was conceived much too narrowly and formally and was "largely negative." He concluded that for all its merits the Indian administrative system was not adequate for the tasks ahead, and he recommended many fundamental changes. "The great achievements of recent years," he stated in his second report in 1956, "have been beyond the capacity of the Indian administrative system. By working key personnel very excessive hours, by giving special attention to a very disproportionate number of transactions, by stubborn persistence of programmatic officials in the face of frustration, great results have been achieved. There is an early limit, however, to what may be done in this fashion. It puts too much reliance on a very small number of individuals, whereas for a much larger achievement reliance must be on a greatly improved organizational performance of systematic character."[46]

One of the features of the Indian civil services which is constantly baffling to foreigners who are not familiar with the traditions and practices of these services is the remarkably limited number of personnel in the top ranks. One would think that a nation of over half a billion people, engaged in the major work of nation-building and development, would require the services of hundreds of thousands of highly trained administrative personnel in its higher services. Instead, the really top civil servants can be numbered in the hundreds.

The total strength of the I.A.S., for example, is less than 3,000. Many university graduates in India aspire to careers in these top services, which have great prestige and which offer positions of relative security and at least a comparatively good standard of living in a country where other positions are hard to obtain; but few of the university-trained people who try to get into the higher civil services are successful. Each year only about 125 persons are taken into the Indian Administrative Service. The result is a great deal of frustration among the educated young Indians and a dearth of top administrative talent in the services. While "big government" suggests the evils of an inflated and entrenched bureaucracy, the fact is that the Government of India is a big government and must become even bigger if it is to discharge the many tasks imposed upon it in the crucial years ahead. For this reason Dr. Appleby warned in his second report:

> It is of the highest importance here that all leaders, in party, parliament, and private life understand that the government must grow rapidly in size — in numbers employed and in annual costs — and that this growth will be greater than, not less than, the estimate it is thought acceptable to publish. . . . The needs will be

[46] Paul H. Appleby, *Re-examination of India's Administrative System with Special Reference to Administration of Government's Industrial and Commercial Enterprises* (Delhi, 1956), p. 2.

great in both the private and the public sectors, but the public need will be central and primary. . . . In such a condition anything pretending to be precise forward planning is futile and unnecessary except as such planning is done in terms of enlarging the capacity to produce such personnel to an expanding maximum.[47]

In view of the legacy of the past and the tremendous demands that are now placed upon it, it is hardly surprising that, as Dr. Appleby pointed out, "the great achievements of recent years have been beyond the capacity of the Indian administrative system." This same observation could be made about the Government of India generally, including the Parliament, the Ministers, and the top leadership everywhere. The Government has significant achievements to its credit, but it has yet to prove that it can gear itself adequately to the tremendous tasks of nation-building.

[47] *Ibid.*, p. 10.

# 7

# State and Local Government

As the capital of a vast nation of more than 500 million people, the city of New Delhi occupies a uniquely conspicuous and important place in Indian political life. But New Delhi is not India. Like the capitals of most states, it is quite unrepresentative of the country as a whole. It is the seat of administration and government, but it is not the "real India."

That "real India" is to be found in the more than 550,000 villages where some 80 per cent of the people live. It is to be found in the districts, the major administrative units of rural India. It is to be found in the great cities — the old Presidential municipalities of Bombay, Madras, and Calcutta; the capitals of the former princely States such as Hyderabad and Mysore and Jaipur; industrial centers such as Kanpur and Ahmedabad and Jamshedpur; the capitals of contemporary States, such as Lucknow and Patna; the holy cities of the Hindus, such as Benares (Varanasi), Allahabad, Hardwar, Nasik, and Puri, and of other faiths, such as Amritsar, the holy city of the Sikhs.

Except for a cosmopolitan city like Bombay, this "real India" is less modern, less affected by Western ways, but more influenced by caste and tradition, than is New Delhi. To the masses of the Indian people New Delhi is far away, and they are inclined to be suspicious of what goes on in this British-built, "un-Indian" city. The limits of their political worlds are often the boundaries of their village, their subdistrict, their district, or at most their State. Yet, whether the people realize it or not, the long arm of the Centre extends into every village and district in the country. It is extended not just to perform the ordinary functions of government, such as taxes, police administration, and law and order, but also to help provide the more positive services of a welfare

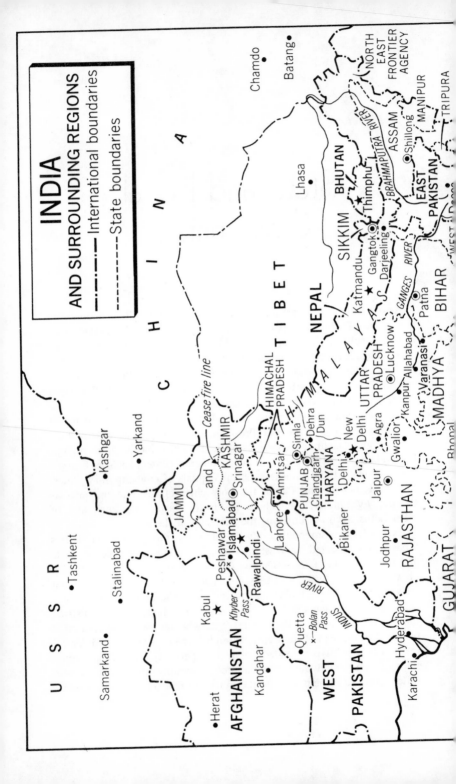

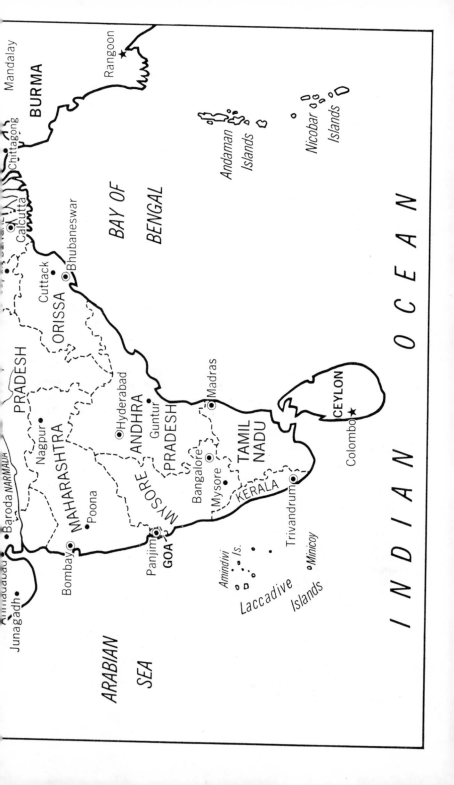

state to people whose standards of life must be revolutionized to be tolerable. Much of the responsibility for the latter task falls upon new post-independence institutions, such as the Community Development Program and the National Extension Service, and especially the comprehensive pattern of district and subdistrict government, administration, and development known as Panchayati Raj, based on revitalized institutions of ancient origin, the village *panchayats*.

However much New Delhi may dominate the country, administratively and politically, it must work in large measure with and through the various units of State and local government, which have more direct contacts with the masses of people. As Dr. Paul Appleby and other astute observers have noted, the central government is extraordinarily dependent on the States and on units of local government and often appears to function more as a coordinating body than as a central authority.[1]

## The States

**The States in the Indian Political System.** With the ending of the "Congress system" trends toward the regionalization of Indian politics have become more manifest, and the States have become increasingly important and powerful units of the Indian political system; some students have considered them as separate political systems.[2] They should be the objects of more serious scholarly study and systemic analysis than they have thus far received.[3]

In a sense the State governments play an unusual middle role. They are in touch with both the central government and the district and subdistrict governmental units and officials. "In the Indian political system, . . . the States have responsibility for most matters that directly affect the lives of the people."[4] Much of the politics of India takes place at State, district, and subdistrict levels. For the majority of Indians this is where the action — or inaction — is.

[1] In his famous report on *Public Administration in India* (New Delhi, 1953), p. 21, Dr. Paul Appleby wrote: "No other large and important national government, I believe, is so dependent as India on theoretically subordinate but actually rather distinct units responsible to a different political control, for so much of the administration of what are recognized as national programs of great importance to the nation."

[2] See, for example, Myron Weiner, "Political Development in the Indian States," in Myron Weiner, ed., *State Politics in India* (Princeton, 1968), pp. 4–5.

[3] The first comprehensive studies of State politics in India, incorporating theoretical and comparative analysis as well as detailed case studies of individual States, were not published until 1968. See Iqbal Narain, ed., *State Politics in India* (Meerut, 1968); and Weiner, ed., *State Politics in India*.

[4] Gunnar Myrdal, *Asian Drama: An Inquiry into the Poverty of Nations* (New York, 1968), I, 295.

**The Structure of State and Local Government.** The major subdivisions of the Republic of India today are the eighteen States: Assam (including the "autonomous State" of Meghalaya), Andhra Pradesh, Bihar, Gujarat, Haryana, Himachal Pradesh, Jammu and Kashmir, Kerala, Madhya Pradesh, Maharashtra, Mysore, Nagaland, Orissa, the Punjab, Rajasthan, Tamil Nadu (formerly Madras), Uttar Pradesh, and West Bengal. Outside of the State boundaries are the Protectorate of Sikkim, the North East Frontier Agency, and nine centrally administered territories: the Andaman and Nicobar Islands; Chandigarh (soon to be incorporated into the Punjab); Dadra and Nagar Heveli; Delhi; Goa, Daman and Diu; the Laccadive, Minicoy, and Amindivi Islands; Manipur; Pondicherry; and Tripura. Geographically, and to some extent politically and culturally, the States of India may be grouped into the Northern, Eastern, Western, Southern, and Central regions; but there are no intermediate political divisions between the Centre and the States. The Zonal Councils, one for each of the five regions listed above, are merely weak coordinating bodies and are thus not considered political divisions.

The States of India vary greatly in size, population, and levels of development, as well as in language, culture, social patterns, and ways of life. The largest in area are Madhya Pradesh (171,217 sq. mi.) and Rajasthan (132,152 sq. mi.), and the smallest are Kerala (15,000 sq. mi.), Himachal Pradesh (10,885 sq. mi.), and Nagaland (6,366 sq. mi.). The largest in population are Uttar Pradesh (73,750,000 in 1961), with more people than all but eight or nine of the nations of the world, and Bihar (46,500,000 in 1961), and the smallest Jammu and Kashmir (hardly more than 4 million, even if the population in the Pakistan-held part is included), Himachal Pradesh (1,351,000 in 1961), and Nagaland (less than half a million). The Punjab, Maharashtra, Gujarat, West Bengal, and Tamil Nadu are relatively well-developed States, whereas Orissa, Jammu and Kashmir, Himachal Pradesh, and Bihar are relatively underdeveloped.

The major subdivisions of the States are the divisions (not all States have them), the districts (the most important administrative units in India below the State level), *talukas* or *tahsils* (subdivisions of districts), and villages. The cities and urban areas are under separate administration.

In practice, governmental and administrative organization varies greatly from State to State, but three patterns can usually be discerned. First there is the conventional pattern of State, district, *taluka* or *tahsil*, and village government. The key officials in this hierarchy are department heads and members of the State secretariat in the capital, headed by the Chief Secretary, the commissioners in the divisions, the district officers (sometimes called deputy commissioners or collectors) in the

# STATE AND LOCAL GOVERNMENT

**LEGISLATURE**

LEGISLATIVE ASSEMBLY (VIDHAN SABHA)   LEGISLATIVE COUNCIL (VIDHAN PARISHAD*)

**EXECUTIVE**

GOVERNOR — CHIEF MINISTER — CABINET

**JUDICIARY**

HIGH COURT — SUBORDINATE COURTS

| LEVELS OF GOVERNMENT | STATE DEPARTMENTS AND THEIR REPRESENTATIVES | REGULAR ADMINISTRATIVE OFFICERS | COMMUNITY DEVELOPMENT PROGRAM | PANCHAYATI RAJ |
|---|---|---|---|---|
| STATE CAPITOL | DEPARTMENT HEADS | CHIEF SECRETARY | | |
| DIVISION | DIVISIONAL CHIEFS | DIVISIONAL COMMISSIONER | | |
| DISTRICT | DISTRICT HEADS | DISTRICT OFFICER (COLLECTOR) | | ZILA PARISHAD |
| TALUKA OR TAHSIL | SUBDIVISIONAL OR CIRCLE OFFICERS | SUBDIVISIONAL OFFICER, CIRCLE OFFICER, TALUKADARS, OR TAHSILDARS | BLOCK DEVELOPMENT OFFICER (BDO) | PANCHAYAT SAMITI |
| VILLAGE | EXTENSION OFFICIALS | PATIL, PATWARI, ETC. | VILLAGE LEVEL WORKER (GRAM SEVAK) | VILLAGE PANCHAYAT GRAM SABHA |

*LESS THAN HALF OF THE INDIAN STATES HAVE LEGISLATIVE COUNCILS.

districts, the subdivisional officers supervising a group of *tahsils,* or *talukas,* circle officers in groups of villages, and local officials in villages. Even here there is a dual pattern, for officials of various State departments and agencies, responsible to key local officials as well as to their own departments, abound at almost every level. A second pattern was introduced after 1951–52 in the Community Development Program and the National Extension Service. Development blocks, often corresponding in area to *talukas* and *tahsils,* became important new units of local administration, and the BDO's — the block development officers — and the Gram Sevaks — the village level workers — became important new agents in the Indian countryside. The Community Development pattern still remains, but it has to some extent been absorbed, or at least overshadowed, by the Panchayati Raj system, inaugurated in a few States in 1959 and now officially in existence in all States.[5]

**Federal-State Relations.** As in any federal state, special attention should be given to the relations between the Central Government in India and the States. In dealing with the items on the Concurrent List in the Constitution, a high degree of cooperation between the Centre and the States is obviously essential. An equally high degree of cooperation is required in financial administration, in joint federal-State planning and in the coordination and execution of programming, in governmental services, and in many other fields of activity including joint federal-State projects. Various kinds of relationships between the Centre and the States should be examined, particularly political, administrative, financial, legal, and constitutional relationships. This is an important field of study, which has not been sufficiently explored.

The Ministry for Home Affairs in the Central Government is charged with direct responsibility for administrative, financial, and economic problems of States, and the Minister for Home Affairs is chairman of each of the five Zonal Councils which were provided for in the States Reorganization Act of 1956; but every other Ministry and branch of the Central Government has some responsibilities relating to the States. Their responsibilities extend even to matters which are on the State List, such as the vital one of education, and their activities are often far more than advisory and coordinating.

One of the major assignments of the Administrative Reforms Commission, set up in January 1966, was to consider Centre-State relations and to make recommendations which would help to make these relations harmonious and cooperative. In a comprehensive report on Centre-State relations, submitted to the Prime Minister in June 1969, the Commission recommended the formation of an Interstate Council for discussion and resolution of Centre-State differences. It suggested

[5] For the Panchayti Raj system, see pp. 164–166 below.

that the members should be the Prime Minister, the Finance and Home Ministers, the Leader of the Opposition in the Lok Sabha, and one representative from each of the Zonal Councils.

**State-State Relations.** Many of the problems in the Indian federal system arise from differences not between the Centre and the States but between the States themselves. These arise as a result of historic, cultural, linguistic, or economic differences, and often create such issues as boundary and water disputes. In such disputes the central government usually tries to play a mediatory role and to bring the contending States together to resolve their differences directly, or through third parties. Often such disputes are referred to a commission, normally consisting of one or more retired members of the Indian Supreme Court. Some disputes, such as the boundary dispute between Mysore and Maharashtra, fester for a long time and lead to a great deal of inter-State hostility and tension.

**Zonal Councils.** The States Reorganization Act of 1956 grouped the States into five Zonal Councils. The Punjab, Rajasthan, Jammu and Kashmir, and the Union Territories of Delhi and Himachal Pradesh formed the Northern Zone; Uttar Pradesh and Madhya Pradesh were associated in the Central Zone; Bihar, West Bengal, Orissa, Assam, and the Union Territories of Manipur and Tripura comprised the Eastern Zone; Bombay and Mysore formed the Western Zone; and Andhra Pradesh, Madras, and Kerala were grouped together in the Southern Zone. New States and Union Territories created since 1956 are associated with appropriate Zones.

The Zonal Councils do not constitute a layer of government between the Centre and the States. They are advisory bodies; they "discuss and make recommendations to the Centre with regard to matters of common interest in the field of economic and social planning, border disputes, linguistic minorities, inter-State transport and any matter arising out of the reorganization of States."[6] The central Minister for Home Affairs is chairman of each Zonal Council, whose other members are the Chief Ministers and two other Ministers of the member States. Each Union Territory associated with the Councils is represented by not more than two members. A member of the Planning Commission, the Chief Secretaries of the States, and the Development Commissioners or other officers deputed by the States act as advisers to the Councils.

Zonal Councils could be a means of developing a healthy type of regionalism in the Indian Republic, and could be important agencies of coordination between the Centre and the States, but as yet they have not played a conspicuous role. They are useful agencies, chiefly for

[6] "The New Map of India," *The Hindu Weekly,* Nov. 5, 1956.

implementing national plans and objectives, but they do not make much of an impact on the government of the country.[7]

**The Executive in the States.** In structure, if not in power, the government of each State is very similar to the Central Government of India. Parliamentary government exists in the States as well as in the Centre. Executive power is vested nominally in the Governor, appointed for a five-year term by the President of India. The Governor has a considerable amount of discretionary and other power, but he exercises this largely as an agent either of the Central Government or of the Ministry in power in the State. Not all of the Governors are or have been Hindus; among the persons who have given distinguished service in the post of Governor are Professor Gurmukh Nihal Singh, a Sikh, as Governor of Rajasthan, Dr. Zakir Husain, one of India's leading Muslims (later Vice President and President of India), as Governor of Bihar, and Dr. H. C. Mookerjee, a Christian, who was Governor of West Bengal.

Frequently Governors have shown how useful a permanent, nonpartisan executive can be in times of political instability and crisis. This role may become increasingly important if, as seems likely, the political situation in various States becomes more chaotic. During periods of President's Rule, which have been fairly frequent in the past and will probably be even more frequent in the future, Governors exercise supreme power, in the name of the President of India, although a senior civil servant is usually appointed to handle the day-to-day administration. Some students of Indian politics have recommended the abolition of the office of Governor on the ground that such an official serves no useful purpose and is merely a drain on the treasury; but the predominant opinion, reinforced by the experience in the States since independence, is that there is a need for such a dignitary in each of the Indian States.[8]

The real executive in the States is the Chief Minister, corresponding to the Prime Minister at the Centre. He is appointed by the Governor but is responsible to the State Legislative Assembly. Some of the most influential of Indian political leaders have served as Chief Ministers, and some promising younger men first gained national recognition in this position. Shortly after independence five of the best known political leaders of India held the post of Chief Minister: Pandit Pant

[7] See Shriram Maheshwari, "Zonal Councils in the Indian Federal System — a Case Study," *The Economic Weekly,* XVII (July 11, 1965).

[8] See J. P. Suda, *Indian Constitutional Development and National Movement* (Meerut, 1951), pp. 624–628; and five articles on "Office of the Governor," in the *Journal of Constitutional and Parliamentary Studies,* II (October–December, 1968), 67–131.

in Uttar Pradesh, C. Rajagopalachari in Madras, Dr. B. C. Roy in West Bengal, Ravi Shankar Shukla in Madhya Pradesh, and Morarji Desai in Bombay. They were often referred to as "Nehru's five war lords." In some States Chief Ministers have remained in office for long periods; others have witnessed a procession of Chief Ministers.

In the years following independence, strong Chief Ministers, including "Nehru's five war lords," were very influential in the Congress Party, and they ran their States with little supervision or direction from the central government or the Congress high command. This was particularly true of Dr. B. C. Roy in West Bengal, who was a power unto himself and did not hesitate to challenge even Jawaharlal Nehru on some issues. For some time thereafter the Chief Ministers, with occasional exceptions, played a lesser role in Congress politics, but since Nehru's death in 1964 the Chief Ministers have become a major national political force. In the second and third successions to the Prime Ministership, and to some extent in the first, they played an important, and perhaps a decisive, role.[9] All the Presidents of the Congress since Nehru gave up that post in 1954, with the exception of his daughter, Mrs. Indira Gandhi, were former Chief Ministers.[10] After the Congress split in 1969, a former Chief Minister remained as President of the "organization" Congress while Jagjivan Ram, a veteran Congress leader, a long-time member of the Cabinet, and an untouchable, but not a former Chief Minister, became President of Mrs. Gandhi's wing of the Congress.

Before 1967 non-Congress Chief Ministers were a rarity; but after the 1967 elections more than half of the States of India, at one time or another, have had Chief Ministers from an opposition party or dissident Congress group. Some have gained a widespread following and a considerable reputation. If, as seems likely, the position of the Congress, now divided, in some States, and indeed in the country as a whole, continues to deteriorate, the role of non-Congress Chief Ministers in Indian politics will become increasingly significant. As yet no non-Congress Chief Minister — except perhaps E. M. S. Namboodiripad of Kerala, who had been for years a leader of the Indian Communists — has emerged as a national political leader.

Each State has a cabinet and a Council of Ministers, headed by the Chief Minister. Members are appointed by the Governor on the advice

[9] See Michael Brecher, *Nehru's Mantle: The Politics of Succession in India* (New York, 1966), and Michael Brecher, "Succession in India: the Routinization of Political Change," *Asian Survey*, VII (July, 1967).
[10] U. N. Dhebar (Saurashtra), N. Sanjiva Reddy (Andhra Pradesh), Sanjivayya (Andhra Pradesh), K. Kamaraj Nadar (Madras), S. Nijalingappa (Mysore).

of the Chief Minister. Article 164 (2) of the Indian Constitution provides: "The Council of Ministers shall be collectively responsible to the Legislative Assembly of the State." In most States the size of the Council ranges from ten to twelve members, but there is no constitutional limitation in this respect. The members head the most important departments of the State government, but as in the Central Government some department heads may not have cabinet rank. "Finance, general administration, home, food, civil supplies, education, agriculture, forests, medical, health and sanitation, local self-government, public works, legislative, justice, industries and labour, police, jails, excise, registration, information, co-operation, development, are the more important departments found in every State."[11]

**The Chief Secretary and the State Public Services.** A key figure in State administration is the Chief Secretary, who is invariably a senior civil servant and usually a member of the Indian Administrative Service. In every State except two — the Punjab and Uttar Pradesh — he is the senior civil servant in the State. He heads the General Administrative Department (under a Minister, of course) and the State civil service. He is principal adviser to the Chief Minister and Secretary to the Cabinet. More than anyone else, he directs the day-to-day administration of State affairs. "In times of emergency or crisis he constitutes the nervous center of the State."[12] Some senior civil servants have remained in the same State as Chief Secretaries for many years, and have become real powers there. They deserve much more credit and more attention than they usually receive.

As head of the State's civil service a Chief Secretary has direct charge of several thousand public employees, who number some 3.7 million in all the Indian States. Aside from a number of central government employees, some of whom occupy key positions in the States (as has been noted, the Chief Secretary is usually an official of the central government), the most influential public employees in the States are the members of the State public services. In some States there are other services, such as local public services and Panchayati Raj services, but these are not statewide.

**State Legislatures.** The Constitution of India provided that in each State there should be a Legislative Assembly (Vidhan Sabha), chosen by direct election and consisting of not less than sixty nor more than five hundred members, and that in the States of Bihar, Bombay, Madras, Punjab, Uttar Pradesh, and West Bengal there should also be an Upper House, known as the Legislative Council (Vidhan Parishad),

[11] Suda, *Indian Constitutional Development and National Movement,* p. 629.

[12] Shriram Maheshwari, *Indian Administration* (Bombay, 1968), p. 208.

chosen by a complicated system of indirect nomination and election,[13] and not exceeding one-fourth of the total number of members of the Legislative Assembly in each of these States, but in no event having less than forty members. Like the Central Government, those States which have a bicameral legislature have a weak second chamber. "The Legislative Councils are not intended to be a check upon the Lower Houses but are merely revising and ventilating chambers representative of a variety of interests and experience."[14]

The number of members in the Legislative Assemblies of the States, the source of real authority on most matters on the State level, is prescribed in the Representation of the People Act of 1951, with certain later amendments. Since there is one electoral roll for elections to the Lok Sabha and to the State Legislative Assemblies, each Assembly constituency is an equal unit of a Lok Sabha constituency. Each member of an Assembly represents no more than 75,000 voters, and some seats are reserved in most States for Scheduled Castes and Scheduled Tribes. The size of the Legislative Assemblies varies greatly, from 41 in Himachal Pradesh and 46 in Nagaland to 318 in Bihar and 430 in Uttar Pradesh.

The Constitution contains fairly detailed provisions regarding the powers and duties of State Legislatures, the officers (a Speaker and Deputy Speaker preside over a Legislative Assembly, and a Chairman and Deputy Chairman over a Legislative Council), the conduct of business, the disqualification of members, privileges of members, legislative procedure, procedure in financial matters, and general rules of procedure. The procedures laid down in the Constitution are similar to those for the Union Parliament. Article 210 specifies that "business in the Legislature of a State shall be transacted in the official language or languages of the State or in Hindi or in English." In practice, most of the proceedings in State legislative bodies are now conducted in the prevailing language of the area.

In the State Legislative Assemblies many of the future leaders of the Indian nation are receiving valuable training and experience. Many of these men are different politicians from the Western-educated elite which thus far has dominated the political life of the country.[15] In Indian terms the Members of the Legislative Assemblies (MLAs) are both "traditional" and "modern," speaking in traditional idioms as

---

[13] Ten States now have Legislative Councils. In 1969 the Legislative Council in West Bengal was abolished.

[14] N. Srinivasan, *Democratic Government in India* (Calcutta, 1954), p. 306.

[15] See W. H. Morris-Jones, "The Exploration of Indian Political Life," *Pacific Affairs*, XXXII (December, 1959), 419.

representatives of those people who live mainly in "traditional India," and also in the more modern idioms as participants in state and national politics. "The MLA is thus another critical point in the drama of Indian politics: which language of politics does he speak? . . . The MLA is one of the great 'gap-closers' in Indian politics, but we do not yet know whether he is achieving this in ways favourable to the modern or to the traditional style."[16] It remains to be seen how many of these men who move from the States to the Centre will be able to keep their ties and roots in their home constituencies, and how many of them will keep their heads and measure up to the needs of the nation as a whole as they embark warily on the national, and perhaps even the international, scene.

**The Judiciary in the States.** The highest court in each State is a High Court, consisting of a Chief Justice and "such other Judges as the President may from time to time deem it necessary to appoint." The Chief Justice and the other judges are appointed by the President of India. "The jurisdiction of the High Court extends to all cases under State or federal laws. The extent of its jurisdiction is determined by Parliament in relation to matters in the Union and Concurrent Lists and by the State Legislatures in respect of matters in the State and Concurrent Lists, subject to the provisions of the Constitution. . . . Its jurisdiction extends to civil, criminal and revenue cases and is both original and appellate."[17] Article 227 of the Constitution stipulates that "Every High Court shall have superintendence over all courts and tribunals throughout the territories in relation to which it exercises jurisdiction." District judges are appointed by the Governor of the State in consultation with the High Court.

The High Courts of the Indian States are second in importance only to the Supreme Court of India in the unified judicial system that exists throughout the country. They set the tone of judicial practice in the States, since they constitute the highest courts of record and since they exercise supervision over all lower courts and other judicial agencies and representatives. Some of the outstanding legal minds of India have been or are Chief Justices or Judges of High Courts, and many more have been celebrated Advocates of the High Courts.

## The Divisions

While there is no uniform pattern of State administration between the State government and the districts, most States are divided into divisions, headed by divisional commissioners. "The Divisional Commis-

[16] W. H. Morris-Jones, *The Government and Politics of India* (New York, 1967), pp. 57, 60.

[17] Srinivasan, *Democratic Government in India*, p. 316.

sioner is, broadly speaking, the coordinator, at the Divisional level, of all activities connected with general administration including law and order, revenue administration, and development administration."[18] In the early post-independence years the divisional commissioners were criticized as costly and unnecessary links between the district and State governments — "kings whose subjects are unconscious of their existence." More recently, however, although the divisional commissioners have continued to be relatively inconspicuous senior officials, their utility has been increasingly recognized.

In 1952 the Planning Commission recommended the appointment of regional officers, not necessarily divisional commissioners, to coordinate and supervise the work of district administration, and in 1957 it cited an "increase in district work and some decline in the quality of district administration" as a justification for "strengthening administration at the regional level."[19]

At least fourteen States have Boards of Revenue (sometimes under different names) at the regional level as well as divisional commissioners, and three have special Boards of Revenue and no divisional commissioners.

## The Districts

As in British days, the district is the most important unit of administration in India, at least below the State level. In 1969 there were 319 districts in the seventeen Indian States. In the British period, largely because of the cosmopolitan character of most district officers and the close liaison between the districts and the British administration in India, the district could properly be called the lowest "modern" political unit. It still retains much of this character, but because of the changing types and roles of district officers, the multiplication of officials and activities at district and subdistrict levels (including a host of appointed and elected officials), the emergence of the Panchayati Raj system, more detailed concentration on local issues and politics, and wider popular participation on the part of people deeply rooted in traditional India, the districts have become less "modern," but more representative.

**District Officers.** In the days of British rule the district officer — variously called the collector or deputy commissioner or district magistrate — was the kingpin of the administrative system. He is still the most important governmental official in rural India, and his functions have in fact increased; but he is a very different person from the district officer of British days, who was constantly on the move in his district, in

18 Maheshwari, *Indian Administration*, p. 221.
19 See *First Five Year Plan* (New Delhi, 1952), p. 142; and *Review of the First Five Year Plan* (New Delhi, 1957), p. 310.

direct touch with the people, the symbol of the kind of benevolent paternalism which existed rather generally in much of the subcontinent in the latter years of British rule. Most of the I.C.S. officers, British or Indian, served much of their apprenticeship in government and administration as district officers.[20]

Today most of the district officers, except in Jammu and Kashmir and Mysore, are members of the Indian Administrative Service, less qualified, on the whole, than the old I.C.S. group, less experienced, less closely in touch with the people, and much less respected.[21] Their changing role in the changing Indian political scene is one of the most fascinating aspects of Indian politics and administration.[22] Their functions and responsibilities are in some respects even greater than those of the district officers in the British period.[23] Studies of the incredible work load of a district officer have documented the countless hours which he has to devote to correspondence and reports, attendance at various meetings and committees (in many cases as chairman), inspections, field trips and other travel, hearing cases, supervising the work of scores of officials, looking after VIP's and almost daily visitors.[24] "The Deputy Commissioner is a man with many masters, answerable and responsible to all, expected to serve them all with equal impartiality and courtesy."[25] Many new functions have been added to the old ones of administrator, collector, and magistrate. Since independence district administration in India has undergone a series of changes, arising largely from three major developments which may be summarized under the terms democratization, development, and decentralization.

As citizens of an independent and democratic state, the people of India have been given new opportunities to shape and control their own

[20] See Sir Percival Griffiths, *The British Impact on India* (London, 1952); Philip Woodruff (pseud. for Philip Mason), *The Guardians,* Vol. II of *The Men Who Ruled India* (New York, 1954); R. Carstairs, *The Little World of an Indian District Officer* (London, 1912); and Hugh Tinker, "Authority and Community in Village India," *Pacific Affairs,* XXXII (December, 1959), 370.

[21] See Tinker, "Authority and Community in Village India," pp. 369–371.

[22] See "The Collector in the Nineteen Sixties," a special issue of *The Indian Journal of Public Administration,* XI (July–Sept., 1965); Hardiwar Rai, "The Changing Role of the District Officer," *The Indian Journal of Public Administration,* IX (April–June, 1963); and Henry Maddick, "The Present and Future Role of the Collector in India," *Journal of Local Administration Overseas,* II (1963).

[23] Maheshwari, *Indian Administration,* pp. 229–234.

[24] See *Report on the Reorganization of District Revenue Officers* (Bombay, 1959); and Satish Kumar Sharma, "Deputy Commissioner in the Punjab" (unpublished Ph.D. thesis, Punjab University, 1969), Chap. XII.

[25] E. N. Mangat Rai, *Civil Administration in the Punjab* (Cambridge, Mass, 1963), p. 45.

destinies and to voice their grievances and demands. A new relationship has developed between government, at all levels, and the citizenry, who evidence traditional deep-seated suspicions of government as well as some awareness that it is now their government. The district officer is a key link between government and people and is personally responsive and responsible to each. "As chief agent of the government in the district he has today, as compared to his predecessors, a more difficult and complex job to perform, particularly with mounting pressures of local politics, interest groups, and citizens."[26] He is supposed to remain aloof from politics, but he must deal almost daily with very politically minded local leaders and citizens.

Since 1955, district officers, with some exceptions, have been given general responsibility for the development efforts in their districts. In 1957 the Balvantray Mehta Study Team recommended: "At the district level the Collector or Deputy Commissioner should be the captain of the team of officers of all development departments and should be made fully responsible for securing the necessary coordination and co-operation in the preparation and execution of the district plans for community development."[27] This formidable addition to the duties of the district officers makes sense administratively, for it provides the needed coordination between the usual functions of administration and justice and the new efforts in economic development and social welfare; but it calls for skill and imagination beyond that which most district officers can reasonably be expected to possess, especially in the light of their backgrounds and orientations, and it saddles them with such a variety of duties that they can hardly be expected to discharge any of them adequately. There is much truth in the observation of Hugh Tinker: "The District Officer is the bottleneck of the government process: loaded with new duties, compelled to fill a quasi-political role (like the French prefect) yet still burdened with all his former responsibilities, he is now expected to coordinate and inspire development. . . . The District Officers remains the keystone of the development structure but has been unable to make this his principal concern."[28]

The introduction of the Panchayati Raj system, a coordinated institutionalized program at the district and subdistrict levels, led to a reassessment of the role of district officers in such areas as development which were also of primary concern to the new PR institutions and officials, and it raised the new question of the proper relationship of the district officer, the administrative head of the district, to the elected offi-

[26] Sharma, "Deputy Commissioner in the Punjab," p. 477.

[27] *Report of the Team for the Study of Community Projects and National Extension Service* (New Delhi, 1957), I, 39–40.

[28] *Ibid.*, p. 364.

cials of PR institutions, especially to the chairman of the *zila parishad,* the new district council. What is the role of the district officer, once the virtual czar of the district, in the era of "democratic decentralization" which PR purports to introduce? It is understandable that district officers and elected PR officials are still feeling their way and that formal and informal relationships differ greatly. In some States the district officer is clearly identified with PR, whereas in others he is virtually outside this system.[29]

What will be the future role of the district officer in the Indian political system? He is often criticized as an undemocratic bureaucrat, not qualified by temperament or training to be the main administrator in an Indian district in an age when so much emphasis is being placed on development, decentralization, and democratization. In 1960 Richard L. Park stated that "the signs are strong that the Collectorate (a task of the District Officer) is fading away in its power as the people try their hands at the coordinating tasks."[30] Some States have abolished the post of district officer, although most of them have reinstated it after a trial period. In all probability, however, the district officer will be around for a long time, even though his character and functions may be quite different. His future role "seems to be in co-ordination, not in administration *per se.*"[31]

**District Boards.** In 1951 there were 186 District Boards in the 267 Districts of India. These Boards, like the District Officers, were an inheritance from the British, but, unlike the District Officers, they seldom played the role in rural administration that was expected by their creators. They were composed of members elected on the basis of adult franchise, and also of nominated nonofficial and official members. They had elected chairmen and vice-chairmen. Their constitution, powers, and functions were laid down in a series of local self-government acts, often dating back to the nineteenth century. Their main functions were in education and communications (meaning chiefly roads). They had very limited financial resources. It was hoped, as the Governor of a province of British India said in 1922, that "these bodies . . . will be an admirable school to give the people that training in administration

[29] Sharma, "Deputy Commissioner in the Punjab," p. 345.

[30] Richard L. Park, "Administrative Coordination and Economic Development in the Districts of India," a paper prepared for a seminar at the Commonwealth Studies Center, Duke University, February, 1960, p. 25.

[31] Harold Alderfer, *Local Government in Developing Countries* (New York, 1964), p. 183. See also Hardiwar Rai, "The District Officer in India Today," *Journal of Administration Overseas* (January, 1967), and "Local Government, Local Administration and Development: Role Adaptation of the District Officer in India," *Indian Journal of Public Administration,* XIV (January–March, 1968).

and in business methods and in responsibility which they need to fit them for eventual complete Self-Government."[32]

When "complete Self-Government" came the Boards were continued, but they did not fit in well with the new patterns of administration. The Balvantray Mehta Report, issued in late 1957, referred to "the gradual eclipse of district boards from the social polity."[33]

Most of the States have adopted the recommendations of the Mehta Report for a three-tier system of *panchayats* and the former district boards have been abolished, or have survived only as supervisory bodies. Many of their former functions have been taken over by the States, while others have been transferred to the village *panchayats* or to other new agencies, such as *panchayat samitis* or development blocks.

## Panchayati Raj

In 1956 the Committee on Plan Projects of the Planning Commission appointed a Study Team, headed by Balvantray G. Mehta, to investigate the reasons for the faltering operations of the Community Development Program and the National Extension Service, and to recommend measures to improve development efforts. The Committee interpreted its mandate broadly, and after a comprehensive study of local government in rural areas, it strongly recommended the "democratic decentralization" of Indian administration. It proposed a system of local government, with extensive responsibilities for community development to be vested in three locally-elected bodies: a directly elected *panchayat* at the village level, with a *gram sabha* (village assembly) sometimes playing a supervisory or even controlling role, a *panchayat samiti* (assembly) within each development block, and a *zila parishad* (district committee) at the district level. This system is generally referred to as Panchayati Raj (government by panchayats).[34] It provides a new framework of "democratic decentralization" in rural India, at the district level and below, and it is perhaps the most significant and most comprehensive pattern of local government, administration, and development that has been introduced in any developing country.

The Balvantray Mehta report has had a profound impact on Indian thinking about rural administration and democratic reorganization. In 1959 Rajasthan and Andhra Pradesh pioneered in the actual introduc-

[32] Quoted in Chetkar Jha, *Indian Local Self-Government* (Patna, 1953), p. 146.

[33] *Report of the Team for the Study of Community Projects and National Extension Service* (Balvantray G. Mehta, Leader) (New Delhi, 1957), II, 12. This report, in three volumes, was prepared for the Committee on Plan Projects, Government of India, after months of investigation. Hereafter referred to as the *Balvantray Mehta Report*.

[34] For the traditional *panchayat*, see below, pp. 167–169.

tion and implementation of Panchayati Raj legislation. By 1964 eleven States had implemented the program. PR legislation has been introduced in all the Indian States, and in most the program is a working reality, with varying degrees of support and implementation. By 1968 there were 253 *zila parishads,* 3,494 *panchayat samitis,* and 212,424 village *panchayats* "covering 93 per cent of the villages and 97.5 per cent of the rural population."[35]

Panchayati Raj patterns vary widely in different States. With the exception of Maharastra and Gujarat, all the States have accepted the recommendation of the Mehta Study Team that the *panchayati samiti* be made the pivot of the entire PR system, with the village *panchayat* functionting as its agent and the *zila parishad* as a coordinating and supervisory body. Maharashtra and Gujarat have made the *zila parishad* the main operating institution, with the *panchayati samiti* and the village *panchayat* as its agents. In these States members of *zila parishads* are directly elected, whereas in most States members of *panchayats* are directly elected, but members of the higher bodies are indirectly elected, or, in some cases, appointed.[36]

It is still too early to evaluate the actual workings of this experiment in "democratic decentralization." Potentially, it is of the greatest significance. If, by happy chance, it should prove to be generally successful, it might go far toward rooting democracy firmly in India. Opinions regarding it vary widely,[37] but there is considerable evidence to show that it is having a profound, if uneven, impact on Indian rural life, as well as administration.[38] "In the context of universal adult franchise, the political setup of *panchayati raj* is bound to play a vital role in the emerging pattern of [the] political process in India, especially

[35] U. C. Ghildyal, "Urbanization and Rural Government," *The Indian Journal of Public Administration,*" XIV (July–September, 1968), 523.

[36] See *Report of Committee on Democratic Decentralisation* (Bombay, 1960); and *Report of the Democratic Decentralisation Committee* (Ahmedabad, 1960). These are official reports on the workings of Panchayati Raj in Maharashtra and Gujarat.

[37] See Iqbal Narain, "Democratic Decentralisation: The Idea, the Image, and the Reality," *The Indian Journal of Public Administration,* IX (January–March, 1963).

[38] The Planning Commission and nearly every State Government have issued many reports on Panchayati Raj. The subject is featured in many Indian journals, especially *Kurukshetra,* the organ of the central Ministry of Community Development, Panchayati Raj, and Cooperation, and *The Indian Journal of Public Administration.* Among the many volumes on PR are the following: B. L. Maheshwari, *Studies in Panchayati Raj* (New Delhi, 1963); R. V. Jathar, *Evolution of Panchayati Raj in India* (Dharwar, 1964); and S. C. Jain, *Community Development and Panchayati Raj in India* (New Delhi, 1967).

in terms of weakening sectional loyalties at the *panchayati raj* level."[39] Extensive survey research has shown that "although a large number of village people do not comprehend the implications of panchayati raj, they are not unfavorably disposed toward it."[40] "Given time," Professor A. H. Hanson has predicted, *"panchayati raj* may make an important, and even decisive, contribution toward the creation of a useful democratic political culture."[41] It deserves the special attention of students of political development and mobilization, as well as of economic development and administration, in developing countries.

### Subdivisions of Districts

The famous Resolution on Local Self-Government, issued with the approval of Lord Ripon in 1882, stated: "The Governor-General in Council considers it is very important that the area of jurisdiction allotted to each Board should in no case be too large. If the plan is to succeed at all, it will be necessary to secure among the members both local interest and local knowledge." The Resolution, then, envisaged local boards having jurisdiction over areas much smaller than districts. Such boards were set up in many parts of British India, in subdivisions of districts which were usually called *tahsils* or *talukas*. Some districts are still subdivided into such subdivisions, but today they are declining in numbers and in importance. Some of the *tahsil* officials are assigned responsibilities in administering development blocks, in addition to their regular duties, but it is difficult to associate officials in a dying pattern of administration with new patterns of development.

The community development block has proved to be a major new unit in rural government.[42] It is often, but not always, coterminous with a *taluka* or *tahsil*. The key official in CD blocks is the BDO (the

[39] Iltija H. Khan, "Consequences of Democratic Decentralization in India," *Canadian Journal of Public Administration,* X (March, 1967), 191.

[40] See Lalit K. Sen, V. P. Gaikwad, and G. L. Verma, *People's Image of Community Development and Panchayati Raj* (Hyderabad, 1967), based on interviews with 7,224 respondents in 365 villages in 16 States. A very interesting and rather surprising finding of one intensive survey was that the elected officials of PR institutions do not lag behind the appointed officials in the districts in initiative or in "modernizing" interests. See Marshall M. Bouton, "Role and Politics in India: A Study of Elected and Appointed Officials in Panchayat-I-Raj" (unpublished M. A. thesis, University of Pennsylvania, 1968), Chapter VIII. This study is based on data collected by Indian interviewers in selected development blocks in Uttar Pradesh, Gujarat, and Maharashtra for the International Studies of Values in Politics project.

[41] Hanson, *The Politics of Planning,* p. 441.

[42] See Howard W. Beers and Douglas Ensminger, "The Development Block as a Social System?," *The Indian Journal of Public Administration,* V (1959).

block development officer), who is responsible to the regular local officials as well as to the State and national development officials. In a sense he is also responsible to the people in his block, especially to the members and officers of the *panchayat samiti.* In several States he serves as secretary of the *panchayat samiti,* and hence is the official who is closest to the workings of the key agency in the PR system. Much depends on his relationship with the chairman of the *panchayat samiti.*

### The Villages

Thus we come to the village, the hope and despair of India today. Because, as Gandhi often pointed out, India lives in its villages, national vigor depends on the revitalization of the village. The average Indian village is still a most depressing place, particularly for any one who has lived anywhere else. "In a sense each village in India is its own private world, connected in many cases only in an ephemeral way to neighboring villages, the state, and the nation."[43]

One of the major objectives of the Five Year Plans, the Community Development Program, and Panchayati Raj is to enlist the cooperation of the Indian villager in the work of national development and to improve the quality of his life as well as his living conditions. Only limited progress is being made in either direction, although in time a revolution may indeed sweep the Indian countryside. If this is to come, the villagers themselves must develop a greater sense of participation in the development efforts. Thus far they have been more or less passive recipients of efforts from on high. They need a more vigorous and enlightened leadership. This leadership, as Hugh Tinker has perceived, "would be strengthened if the flight of the educated to the towns could be reversed. . . . But nothing about the village of today makes it any more attractive to the educated; it is still a place to get away from."[44]

In the past the affairs of the village were supervised in a general way by the district officers and various other officials of the District, and also of the *tahsil* or *taluka,* such as the *tahsildar* or *mamlatdar,* as well as by police officials. Almost every village was in direct charge of a headman or *patil,* usually a person whose authority was derived more from hereditary sources than from legal position. Other officials usually included a village accountant, often known as the *patwari,* and a village policeman, sometime hardly more than a glorified *chowkidar* or watchman.

**The Panchayat.** The most discussed institution in the Indian village, or groups of villages, at the present time is the *panchayat.*

[43] Richard L. Park, "Administrative Coordination and Economic Development in the Districts of India," p. 6.

[44] Tinker, "Authority and Community in Village India," p. 374.

"The word *panchayat* describes form, not purpose — a technique of seeking agreement through consultation, hallowed, according to tradition by divine sanction."[45] *Panchayat* means a council of five, and it usually refers to a village council — which may or may not have five members — which has a great deal to say about the life of the people of the village, in social and religious as well as in economic and political matters. Officially speaking, the *panchayat* is today the lowest — and in a sense the most basic — unit of self-government in India. Many different kinds of *panchayats* have existed, and many still exist, in India.

The *panchayat* is an institution which existed and which apparently played a rather significant role in many parts of ancient India. Some Indian writers are inclined to glorify this role, and to speak of the ancient *panchayats* as "little village republics" — consciously or unconsciously parroting a much-quoted statement of Sir Charles Metcalfe in 1832 — and as the seedbeds for a democratic tradition in India. Such writers are inclined to see an organic link between the *panchayats* of centuries ago, and the *panchayats* which exist in a growing number of villages today. Actually the link is a tenuous one, for the *panchayat* almost died out as an institution in Indian village life. Hugh Tinker insists that "while the *panchayat* is an ancient institution of unique prestige, it provides no precedent for the village council of today."[46] There is a vast literature on *panchayats,* much of which would partially substantiate and partially refute the validity of Professor Tinker's conclusion.[47]

The British made some efforts to revive the *panchayat,* but with indifferent success. Gandhi attached great importance to the *panchayats:* "The greater the power of the panchayats," he said, "the better for the people." "To Gandhi perfect panchayat democracy was synonymous with Ram Rajya,"[48] the kind of India to which he aspired. Although this was one matter on which the British authorities and the leaders of the Indian National Congress seemed to agree, the Simon Commission in 1930 was compelled to report that the *panchayat* movement had not made much progress.

When India became independent in 1947, perhaps one third of the villages of India had *panchayats,* and many of these were in far from

---

[45] *Ibid.,* p. 357.

[46] *Ibid.,* p. 358.

[47] See, for example, D. Malaviya, *Village Panchayats in India* (New Delhi, 1956); R. L. Khanna, *Panchayat Raj in India* (Chandigarh, 1956); A. V. Raman Rao, *Structure and Working of Village Panchayats: A Survey Based on Case Studies in Bombay and Madras* (Poona, 1954).

[48] Khanna, *Panchayat Raj in India,* p. 9.

flourishing condition. The Congress Government made a determined effort to promote the creation of *panchayats* and to make them effective units of local government. Article 40 of the Constitution of 1950 declared: "The State shall take steps to organise village *panchayats* and to endow them with such powers and authority as may be necessary to enable them to function as units of self-government." All the States have enacted legislation in the spirit of this constitutional provision, giving legal status to *panchayats,* and the central Parliament has passed a number of acts designed to promote the *panchayat* system. The plan is not only to spread *panchayats* throughout the villages of India but to make these bodies the main agencies for village administration and cooperation in the Community Development and Panchayati Raj programs.

At the beginning of the First Five Year Plan, some 83,000 *panchayats* existed in Indian villages. Today nearly all of the over 550,000 villages of India are in the *panchayat* system. Thus an ancient institution, which centuries ago served different needs in a different society, is being revived and remodeled to serve the needs of a modern welfare state.

The revival of the *panchayats,* their extension to most of the villages of India, their legal recognition as basic administrative units of government, and their association with the Community Development Program and Panchayati Raj are significant new departures in Indian politics and administration, and they may indeed mark the revitalization of rural India and the beginnings of a true popular awakening. If the Panchayati Raj system proves to be successful, the village *panchayat,* linked with the *panchayat samiti* and the *zila parishad,* which are in a sense larger *panchayats,* may still play the administrative and social role envisioned for it by those who are planning the new India.

### The Cities

Between one fifth and one sixth of the people of India live in urban areas. In 1961 there were 112 cities of over 100,000 population. More than 5,500,000 people now live in the metropolitan area of Calcutta and over 4,600,000 in Bombay; Delhi-New Delhi has around 2,500,000, and Madras around 2,000,000. The population of both Ahmedabad and Bangalore is about 1,200,000, and Kanpur is around the 1,000,000 mark. Thus, while over 80 per cent of the Indian people still live in rural areas, urbanization is becoming an increasingly important factor, especially since it affects the lives and attitudes of people in rural as well as in urban areas. Moreover, gradually the distinction between rural and urban areas will become less sharp. As a report of the Rural-Urban Relationship Committee pointed out in 1966, urbanization today must be considered as a "continuous process of transition from rural to urban, treating the present differences as only a stage in the continuum."[49]

As the great cities of India expand in area and population, their government will have to be carried on on an increasingly more integrated basis, embracing large regional urban administrative units. Such a plan has already been proposed for problem-ridden Calcutta. Some years ago the Calcutta Metropolitan Planning Organization, set up with the financial and technical assistance of the Ford Foundation, drafted a comprehensive plan for the entire metropolitan region, the Calcutta Metropolitan District, which encompasses an area of over 400 square miles.[50] This plan attracted worldwide attention. It was approved by the governments of West Bengal and India, and by the Calcutta Corporation; but the necessary political and financial support have not been forthcoming, and the plan is being implemented with agonizing slowness. In the meantime Calcutta's population increases rapidly, and its problems mount.

There is a considerable similarity in the pattern of municipal government throughout India. Large cities are corporations, smaller cities of 10,000 population or more are municipalities, and smaller and less developed urban areas are either Notified Areas or Town Areas. The cities of India are generally under the supervision and control of the State Governments, although under the State Municipality Acts and under the charters granted by the States they have a considerable measure of autonomy.

In a special category are the old Presidency municipalities of Calcutta, Bombay, and Madras. These cities have been Corporations for many years.[51] After independence this status was redefined by special legislation in the States in which they are located, and they were associated more closely with the evolving pattern of municipal government

---

[49] *Report of the Rural-Urban Relationship Committee* (New Delhi, 1966), I, 17. See also Ali Ashraf, "Report of the Rural-Urban Relationship Committee 1966 — A Critical Review," *The Indian Journal of Public Administration,* XIV (July–September, 1968), 816–829.

[50] "Within the Calcutta Metropolitan District, which sprawls over an area of 400 square miles covering as many as four districts there are 2 municipal corporations, 33 municipal councils, and one cantonment board." Maheshwari, *Indian Administration,* pp. 269–270. See also M. M. Singh, *Municipal Government in the Calcutta Metropolitan District: A Preliminary Survey* (Bombay, 1964). This is second of a series of 13 volumes in the Calcutta Research Series, which are being published by the Asia Publishing House (Bombay) for the Institute of Public Administration, New York.

[51] Madras since 1688, and Calcutta and Bombay since 1726. See Hugh Tinker, *The Foundations of Local Self-Government in India, Pakistan and Burma* (London, 1954), pp. 25–26.

under general State supervision. All three great Corporations are governed by a Municipal Council, ranging in size from slightly more than 80 members in the cases of Calcutta and Madras to nearly 125 members in the case of Bombay City. These members are elected by adult franchise. They in turn choose a President or Mayor. Each Corporation also has a Municipal Commissioner, appointed by the State government, who is the chief executive officer. Most of the other Corporations in India are governed along similar lines.

Municipalities are the most common form of urban government. They are usually divided into classes, in accordance with their size and importance. The main governing body is a municipal council, with membership ranging in most cases between 20 and 100. In some States a few council members are appointed or co-opted or otherwise nominated, but the trend is toward councils made up only of elected members. Smaller municipalities are also usually governed by municipal councils, with less autonomy and fewer financial resources.

The functions of Indian municipalities are spelled out in State municipality acts and other measures. Some are obligatory, while others are optional. "Important obligatory functions relate to the construction and maintenance of roads, conservancy, lighting, abatement of public nuisances, regulation of dangerous and offensive trades, water supply, drainage, hospitals and dispensaries, vaccination, public markets, sanitation, education and fire protection, etc." Optional functions "generally relate to laying out new streets, reclamation of unhealthy localities, acquisition of land, public parks, gardens, museums, lunatic asylums, rest-houses, poor houses, dairies, baths, public utilities like water, electricity and transport, fairs and exhibitions."[52] Many additional functions may also be given to municipalities, although some authorities advise against this.

It is clear that Indian municipalities are overburdened with functions and poorly equipped to undertake even essential duties. The reasons for this state of affairs are many, but for the most part they revolve around inadequacy of funds and problems of personnel. Taxation is by far the chief source of income, but the total amount of money available to municipalities is very small in relation to the functions and services they are expected to perform. An even more serious problem is the low standard of performance and even of integrity in municipal administration. Chetkar Jha has suggested that four factors are primarily responsible for this unfortunate state of affairs: (1) "the absorption of the elected personnel in administrative details"; (2) the "absence of a proper division of responsibility between the whole council

---

[52] Jha, *Indian Local Self-Government*, pp. 40–41.

and committees"; (3) the "absence of an honest and competent staff"; and (4) the "absence of a right system of financial administration."[53]

Substantial parts of the area covered by some Indian cities and some of the functions normally devolving on municipal authorities may be vested in the control of semi-autonomous bodies, usually created by special State legislation or under the supervision of a Central Government agency. Among these semi-autonomous bodies are improvement trusts, for city planning and development, and port trusts in the port cities. Cantonments (permanent military stations) may cover large areas within city limits, and these areas, so important in British days, are under the control of the defense authorities, with only limited responsibility to the municipal administrations.

## Is the Machinery of State and Local Government Adequate?

Even a brief survey of State and local government in India suggests some of the anomalies that arise from what Selig Harrison has called the peculiar "imbalance of the Union."[54] The Central Government speaks for India as a whole in world affairs and in many respects dominates the country in an administrative and political sense. On the other hand, as we have seen, there are many signs that the Centre is dependent, to a degree almost unprecedented in other federations, upon the State and local authorities, and upon the people generally, for the implementation of its basic plans and policies and in some respects seems to function more in a coordinating than in a governing capacity.

Administratively speaking, State governments are functioning quite effectively. Politically, the record is more spotty. Now that the fight for essentially linguistic States has been fought and won — an outstanding and rare instance of the victory of regional and local pressures over the wishes of the top leaders of the Government and the Congress Party — it is hoped that within their new boundaries the Indian States can prove to be effective units; but many scars remain from this historic battle, which was in a sense a victory of emotion over reason, of regional and local pressures over administrative stability.

Since the 1967 general elections political instability in many key Indian States has increased. The Congress Party has weakened while opposition parties and groups, except in Tamil Nadu, have lacked the strength and cohesion to govern, even ineffectively, except through shaky coalitions of diverse hues. Can the administrative apparatus function effectively, or even adequately, under conditions of political

---

[53] *Ibid.*, p. 66.
[54] Selig S. Harrison, *India: The Most Dangerous Decades* (Princeton, N.J., 1960), p. 303.

instability and ideological, factional, and personal rivalries in political circles?

Some kind of incipient revolution seems to be going on in the Indian countryside, as the impact of the twentieth century and of the "revolution of rising expectations" meets the barriers of social conservatism and localism, and as the efforts at national planning and development gradually penetrate the areas where the masses of the Indian people live. This incipient revolution raises questions of the suitability of old patterns of administration, such as those in the district, in the *talukas* and *tahsils,* and in the villages. Moreover, new agencies are being introduced into rural India, and old ones are being revived and adapted to new needs. Many of the new agencies are basic ingredients of the Community Development Program and especially of the Panchayati Raj system. They have introduced new units, such as development blocks, and new types of government servants, notably the *gram sevaks* (the village level workers) and the block development officers, and new types of local leaders, especially the chairmen of the *panchayats,* the *panchayat samitis,* and the *zila parishads* of the Panchayati Raj system, into the districts, the *talukas,* and the villages.

In the villages the old customs and patterns endure, along with the old prejudices and superstitions; but the villagers are inevitably affected by such direct onslaughts on their time-honored ways as the attacks on untouchability and the caste system and by the efforts to associate them with larger units of government and administration and to give them a feeling of participation in a nationwide effort at development and change. Unhappily, many of these changes are not working well, and one wonders whether, even if they do in time "catch fire," the results will be as revolutionary as the times seem to demand.

In the Indian municipalities, which are more immediately responsive to social and political changes — and which in fact do much to bring about these changes — the agencies of government and administration are fairly well established, although they are subject to many kinds of criticism and do not seem to be functioning very effectively. The great cities of India are centers of life and movement; however unrepresentative they may be of the "real India," they have an almost fatal attraction for the more enterprising villagers. In a sense, almost every Indian, whether he lives in Calcutta or Bombay or Delhi or Lucknow, or in a remote and tiny village, is a villager at heart; almost certainly he has roots in a village and thinks of this village as his home. Thus there are special, and often not fully perceived, links between rural and urban India. This condition may be one of the factors which gives India a greater basic unity than those who are so disturbed by the obvious divisions and diversities can see.

While much depends on greater vitality in local and municipal administration than now exists, the general patterns of administration and the special powers of the States and the Central Government tend to stifle these basic units of local government. "District boards, urban municipalities and village *panchayats* are not subject to the jurisdiction of each other, but are rather independent units, each directly controlled by the state government through a hierarchy of civil servants headed by a state official called a director or inspector who reports to the secretary of the Local Government Ministry" in the State. "The tradition of centralism in the country makes the local body more a kind of administrative agent of the state government, subject to the same conditions of discipline as its paid employees, rather than a governmental authority with some exclusive jurisdiction or initiative of its own." This administrative dominance is accentuated by the financial limitations under which almost all local bodies have to operate. "All local bodies have only one-third of the income of the state governments and all state governments together have less than three-fourths of the resources of the central government."[55]

The great changes that are occurring in India today impose new demands on the instrumentalities and officials of State and local administration. Old agencies are being forced to take on additional duties and responsibilities, and new agencies are being created. All kinds of problems of coordination and overlapping jurisdiction arise from this evolving situation. Can the organs of State and local government, which have not been functioning very well in discharging their regular duties and responsibilites, be adapted to meet the new needs and opportunities? Certainly if a new India is to be created, it will have to have its roots in the villages and districts and cities, and here the local bodies and State governments will either be agencies of change or bottlenecks too narrow to permit the entrance of vitalizing forces into those areas where most of the people of India dwell.

[55] Harold Zink, Arne Wåhlstrand, F. Benvenuti, and R. Bhaskaran, *Rural Local Government in Sweden, Italy and India: A Comparative Study* (London, 1957), pp. 80, 81, 95.

# *  *8*  *

# The Politics of Planning

Since 1950–51 India has been engaged in the world's largest and most comprehensive experiment in democratic planning. The stakes in India's great experiment are much more than economic stakes; they are the stakes of national and human survival.

## Approaches to Planning

**Political Aspects of Planning.**   Planning on such a gigantic scale is obviously more than an economic process. It is a total national effort and commitment, which includes political leaders at all levels, the administration, and the people of the country, as well as those specifically entrusted with the tasks of economic planning and development. The broader problems of economic development, as Professor A. H. Hanson has pointed out, "are the *economic* problems which, for their solution, demand *social* changes triggered off by *political* action. In this sense, planning is a total process."[1]

One does not have to be a believer in the primacy of politics over economics to subscribe to the view that the political aspects of planning are of very special significance. "All planning," Gunnar Myrdal has observed, "implies political choices. . . . A plan for development is thus in essence a political program. . . . Plan-making . . . is itself a part of the political process in a country."[2] Large-scale planning involves the top policy-makers of a country, as well as an extensive central planning apparatus. Indeed, as Edward S. Mason has noted, "Planning implies centralized decision making. There is no such thing as

[1] A. H. Hanson, *The Process of Planning: A Study of India's Five Year Plans* 1950–1964 (London, 1966), p. 24. Italics in original.
[2] Gunnar Myrdal, *Asian Drama: An Inquiry into the Poverty of Nations* (New York, 1968), III, 1888, 1889.

decentralized planning."[3] Planning has to be carried on within the framework of the political system, and it has to rely for implementation on State and local leaders and administrators and ultimately on the cooperation of the people. It is thus related in a very significant way to the political system and the political culture of the country.[4]

These observations are particularly relevant in India, where the existing political system cannot possibly survive if a significant degree of economic development is not achieved. Successful economic development, in turn, depends to a large degree on effective political leadership and support and a considerable degree of political stability. In a typology of political systems developed by David E. Apter and other political scientists, India is primarily a "reconciliation" system, and it is by no means certain that such a system can achieve the degree of national and individual self-discipline and participation or can mobilize the human and physical resources that national planning in a very underdeveloped country requires.

Even among those who support the broad planning policies laid down by the leaders of the Government of India, there are many political differences regarding major aspects of national planning. Some concern the relative merits of small-scale and large-scale industries, the relative emphasis on agriculture and industrial development, the relative value of public and private investment, the relative role of the public and private sectors, the role of foreign capital, the desirability or undesirability of foreign aid. Some of the differences are even more fundamental, reflecting divergencies in political, economic, and social values and goals.

Any political scientist who seeks to understand the mainsprings of actions and the major trends and developments in post-independence India must give special attention to the politics of planning; and he will have to turn to specialists in other disciplines for interpretation of matters of fundamental importance in national planning. Some important problems — such as financing, foreign exchange, foreign assistance, savings, investment, and tax policies, food production, unemployment and underemployment, the most effective means of mobilizing scarce resources — can best be treated by the economist. Others — such as planning and social change, population problems, questions of status and structure, problems of communalism, caste, and factions — belong more in the domains of the anthropologist and the sociologist. All of these problems are of interest to the political scientist, for they all have

[3] Edward S. Mason, "Planning for Economic and Agricultural Development," in *Development and Change in Traditional Agriculture: Focus on South Asia* (East Lansing, Mich., 1968), p. 9.

[4] *Ibid.*, p. 10.

political implications and can be dealt with satisfactorily only with the right kind of political policies and leadership.

Before considering the nature of India's development efforts and some political problems relating to them, we should examine briefly the economic philosophy which motivates India's leaders.

**The "Socialist Pattern of Society."**  The proclaimed objective of the Government of India is the establishment of a "socialist pattern of society." This objective has been proclaimed in one way or another for many years; it has been incorporated in all the Five Year Plans. It was stated specifically in a famous resolution adopted at the Annual Session of the Congress Party at Avadi in January 1955, which declared that "planning should take place with the view to the establishment of a socialistic pattern of society, where the principal means of production are under social ownership and control, production is progressively speeded up and there is equitable distribution of the national wealth."

The term "socialist pattern of society" (the word "socialistic" in the Avadi resolution was soon replaced by "socialist") expresses India's concept of the welfare state. It is a rather nebulous concept, which has never been rigidly defined. It seems to embrace a mild degree of Marxism, a considerable amount of Gandhism, including emphasis on nonviolent means and peaceful change, and ideas of social and economic equalitarianism.[5] "What do we mean when we say 'socialist pattern' of life?", asked Nehru when he presented the Second Five Year Plan to the Indian Parliament. "Surely we mean a society in which there is social cohesion without classes, equality of opportunity and the possibility for everyone to have a good life." The text of the Second Plan itself was hardly more specific: "The accent of the socialist pattern is on the attainment of positive goals; the raising of living standards; the enlargements of opportunities for all, the promotion of enterprise among the disadvantaged classes and the creation of a sense of partnership among all sections of the community."[6]

The Third Plan, in a section on "Progress Towards Socialism," laid stress on "the development of a large public sector and a cooperative sector," equality of opportunity, the provision of "basic necessities" and "tolerable living standards" for all, the reduction of economic and social disparities, and the fostering of "social values and incentives." According to the Plan, "development along socialist lines will require rapid economic growth and expansion of employment, reduction of disparities in income and wealth, prevention of concentration of eco-

[5] See "Indian Approaches to a Socialist Society," *Indian Press Digests,* Monograph Series No. 2 (Berkeley, Calif., 1956).

[6] Planning Commission, Government of India, *Second Five Year Plan* (New Delhi, 1956), p. 24.

nomic power, and creation of the values and attitudes of a free and equal society."[7]

There has always been an irritating and baffling vagueness about most varieties of socialism that have flourished in the Indian scene. No socialist party has been able to formulate a specific statement of its ideological and economic views, and the ideas which are subsumed under the term, "socialist pattern of society," would surely be accepted by many who do not regard themselves as socialists at all. In India almost everyone thinks of himself as a socialist, and believes that the path of democratic socialism is the only path to true democracy. Yet it is certainly true, as Professor William Lockwood observed, that India "preaches more socialism than it practices," and that many critics of the "socialist pattern of society" are alienated by the term and not by the goals which it embraces.[8]

In some respects India is one of the least socialist of countries. "India has, in fact," states Professor J. K. Galbraith, "superimposed a smallish socialized sector atop what, no doubt, is the world's greatest example of functioning anarchy."[9] Most of the instruments of production are still in private hands, and most of the income is produced by the private sector. "It is not often realised," wrote Professor D. R. Gadgil, Deputy Chairman of the Planning Commission, in mid-1969, "that the . . . public sector in India is, in some cases, even smaller than . . . in some of the industrially advanced European capitalistic countries."[10] In an interview with a representative of *U.S. News & World Report* in 1970 Mrs. Gandhi said: "Our plans do not call for socializing the entire economy, or even the greater part of it. We do want the commanding heights of the economy to be in state hands — the basic industries, the defense industries and, to a large extent, the import trade. . . . We are a people in a hurry for progress, but we have chosen a mixed economy, with plenty of room and a real need for the private sector's initiative."[11] "A mixed economy," wrote Professor Gadgil, "necessarily postulates operation of various types of organisations side by side in mutual cooperation. The public sector,

[7] Planning Commission, Government of India, *Third Five Year Plan* (New Delhi, 1961), pp. 9–10.

[8] William W. Lockwood, " 'The Socialistic Society': India and Japan," *Foreign Affairs*, XXXVII (October, 1958), 130.

[9] J. K. Galbraith, "Rival Economic Theories in India," *Foreign Affairs*, XXXVI (July, 1958), 590.

[10] D. R. Gadgil, "Industrial Growth and Total Development Process," *Indian & Foreign Review*, VI (July 15, 1969), 10.

[11] "We Are a Poor People in a Hurry for Progress," *U.S. News & World Report* (Interview of Charles S. Foltz, Jr. with Prime Minister Indira Gandhi), May 25, 1970, p. 67.

the private sector, and the cooperative sector have each its own merits and defects. The essence of planning is to see that they expand in directions and occupy fields in which their advantages are predominant."[12]

A summary of the First Five Year Plan, issued by the Planning Commission in December 1952, contained the following statement: "In a planned economy, the distinction between the public and the private sector is one of emphasis. The two sectors are and must function as parts of a single organism." The summary also stated: "Private enterprise functions largely within the conditions created by the State."[13] According to spokesmen of the Government of India these conditions are favorable to the "private sector," and to foreign private investment. In support of their claim they point to the Industrial Policy Resolutions, issued by the Government in 1948 and again in 1956, and to the major role which is assigned to the private sector in the Five Year Plans.

During the course of the First Five Year Plan (1951–56) about as much was invested in the private sector as in the public sector, including contributions of both federal and state governments and foreign grants and loans. The total in each case was approximately four billion dollars. The Second Five Year Plan (1956–61), as revised, called for an expenditure of somewhat over ten billion dollars in the public sector and of half that amount in the private sector. Actually, the amounts expended in each sector fell short of planned objectives by some 20 per cent. The Third Five Year Plan (1961–66) envisaged an investment in the public sector of over $15 billion and in the private section of $8.4 billion. Actual public sector expenditures were around $18 billion, but the increase was more than neutralized by a rise in prices. The final version of the Fourth Plan, presented to the Indian Parliament on May 18, 1970, by Prime Minister Indira Gandhi, provided for an outlay of $21.2 billion in the public sector and nearly $12 billion in the private sector.

While it is still true that well over 85 per cent of the total gross national product is contributed by the private sector, this percentage is bound to decrease as the steel mills, the multi-purpose river valley projects, and other major projects in the public sector begin to operate. In any event, the private sector will continue to be circumscribed by Government orientation and policies, and it will be expected to develop in ways which will contribute most directly to the overall development program.

The Government is placing a great deal of emphasis on various kinds

[12] Gadgil, "Industrial Growth and Total Development Process," p. 11.
[13] Planning Commission, Government of India, *The First Five Year Plan* (New Delhi, 1952), p. 9.

of cooperatives. In a famous resolution adopted at the Nagpur session of the Congress Party in January 1959, the Congress went on record in favor of service cooperatives and village cooperatives. At a public meeting in Bhopal in November 1960, Nehru declared that he hoped to see a cooperative society, as well as a *panchayat* and a school, in every Indian village.

The exact kinds of cooperatives that are envisioned have not been made clear, and the Congress Party and the Government have been notably slow in pushing this new departure, partly because of inertia and a lack of real dedication to the goal. This is particularly true of such large-scale cooperatives as village and farming cooperatives. "In India," Dr. Gadgil drily observed in 1969, "cooperative farming has been favored, though not much progress has been registered in regard to it."[14]

Many of the leaders of India hold rather doctrinaire socialist views, are distrustful of the profit motive, suspect private businessmen, and favor the growing intervention of the state in the economic life of the country. As Prime Minister, Mrs. Gandhi has been making a conscious effort to emphasize socialist goals and to keep her branch of the Congress Party well to the left of center. The decision to nationalize the major private banks of the country, approved by Parliament in late July 1969 in spite of opposition by leading conservatives in the Party, seemed to be consistent with her basic economic orientation. In the same *U.S. News & World Report* interview, Mrs. Gandhi said: "Our concern . . . for the masses, not just for the more fortunate few in big business . . . is one reason for our action in nationalizing the banks."

**Democratic Planning.**   "The central objective of planning in India," stated the Planning Commission at the beginning of the First Five Year Plan, "is to raise the standard of living of the people and to open out to them opportunities for a richer and more varied life." Nehru believed that this "central objective" could only be achieved in the democratic way. "We have definitely accepted the democratic process," he told delegates to the annual session of the Congress Party in 1957, "because we think that in the final analysis it promotes the growth of human beings and of society." All those who have thus far guided the destinies of independent India have been just as strongly committed to promote economic development and a "socialist pattern of society" through democratic means.

At a time when various patterns of authoritarianism seem to be the prevailing political forms in most of the underdeveloped countries, the

[14] Gadgil, "Industrial Growth and Total Development Process," p. 10.

conscious and strong dedication of India to the democratic way is a source of inspiration and hope. If India can show not only that democracy is compatible with planning on a large scale but that democratic planning can provide masses of people with a richer and more varied life without the appalling human costs of totalitarianism, the prospects for democracy in the world as a whole will be vastly brighter. If India fails in its great experiment in democratic planning, its failure will be a blow to hopes for freedom everywhere.

### The Five Year Plans

Planning on a national scale, within the framework of comprehensive plans, dates from 1950. The Planning Commission was appointed in 1950 and the First Five Year Plan was inaugurated in 1951 and "finalised" in December 1952. But even before independence was achieved, a series of economic plans and proposals had been drawn up by the British Government, the Indian National Congress, and private business organizations.[15] As early as 1938 the Indian National Congress appointed a National Planning Committee with Jawaharlal Nehru as chairman. Although he had few qualifications as an economist, he played a central role in India's planning for a quarter of a century. Indeed, "Up to 1964, India's plans were Nehru's plans."[16]

In an effort to achieve tolerable standards of living for a vast and rapidly growing population in one of the world's most underdeveloped economies, within the desired framework of a "socialist pattern of society," the political leaders of India, beginning in 1950, launched a nationwide program of economic development through a series of annual and five year plans. There was general acceptance of the assumption that "planned economic development in a poor country aiming at increasing the pace of development necessarily requires the imposition of a regulatory frame."[17]

The broad objective of the First Five Year Plan, which was really not a coordinated plan at all, was "to lay the foundations on which a more progressive and diversified economy could be built up." More than 66 per cent of the total expenditure in the public sector of somewhat over $4 billion was devoted to agriculture and community development, irrigation and power projects, and transport and communications; less than 10 per cent went for industrial development.

The official verdict on the First Five Year Plan was that it was a great success, that for the most part its goals had been reached and

---

[15] For a good summary of the "prehistory" of Indian planning, see Hanson, *The Process of Planning,* pp. 27–49.

[16] *Ibid.,* p. 49.

[17] Gadgil, "Industrial Growth and Total Development Process," p. 11.

often substantially exceeded. A more realistic verdict would be that it was "good in parts." In the private sector the investment target was fulfilled and production was substantially increased; but "in the public sector the performance was very patchy."[18] Whether because of the Plan or the good luck of favorable monsoons and economic climate "the economic situation on the eve of the second plan," as reported by the Planning Commission in the introductory chapter of the Second Five Year Plan, was "distinctly better than it was on the eve of the first plan; there is more confidence and greater readiness for a larger effort."[19]

Reflecting the optimistic assessment of economic possibilities, the Second Five Year Plan called for a public expenditure more than double that of the First Plan period (about $9.2 billion) and for an increase of about 75 per cent in investment in the private sector. A marked reorientation was indicated by the emphasis on industrial development in the public sector.

The principal objective of the Second Plan was "to secure a more rapid growth of the national economy and to increase the country's productive potential in a way that will make possible accelerated development in succeeding plan periods." Four objectives were enunciated as of prime importance: (1) a "sizeable increase" in national income; (2) "rapid industrialisation with particular emphasis on the development of basic and heavy industries"; (3) "a large expansion of employment opportunities"; and (4) "reduction of inequalities in income and wealth and a more even distribution of economic power."

The Second Plan ran into serious difficulties, and midway in the Plan period the targets had to be reduced. It is estimated that when the Second Plan was completed in late March 1961, it fell short of its targets by about 30 per cent. The unemployment picture was darker at the end of the Plan than at the beginning, and not much progress had been made in reducing "inequalities in income and wealth." Because of a series of unforeseen circumstances, India's need for foreign exchange during the Second Plan period was greater than was anticipated — for example, serious droughts forced India to use precious foreign exchange to import far more food than was planned — and greater reliance than was intended had to be placed on international financial assistance and deficit financing. The expenditures in the public sector during the period of the Second Plan were nevertheless more than twice those of the First Plan.

While the targets set in the Third Plan were about 50 per cent higher than those of the Second, they did not provide for the "accelerated

[18] Hanson, *The Process of Planning*, p. 111.
[19] Planning Commission, *Second Five Year Plan*, p. 5.

development" that was apparently contemplated when India embarked on "the difficult and tremendous journey" of planned economic growth. The total outlay contemplated under the Third Plan was $24.35 billion, of which $15.75 billion would be expended in the public sector and $8.6 billion in the private sector. Actually, the financial outlay during the Plan period (1961–66) was 15 per cent higher than contemplated; but this increase was largely offset by a sharp rise in prices. In general, the performance of the Third Plan was not at all satisfactory. The national income increased by less than half the 5 per cent per year which was the goal; except in one year agricultural production did not increase at all; larger amounts of food grains had to be imported; and industrial production was lower than had been expected.

In many respects the Third Plan period was abnormal. Weather conditions were adverse during three of the five years, with a serious drought in 1965–66. India was engaged in major hostilities with China in the second year of the Plan and with Pakistan in the last year. These hostilities upset the economy in many respects and led to a sharp and unplanned increase in defense expenditures and, after the September 1965 war with Pakistan, to the temporary suspension of economic aid from the United States and the United Kingdom.

By the end of the Third Plan everything seemed to be going wrong, and many Indian and foreign observers were referring to "the crisis in Indian planning" and were insisting that a drastic reorientation was needed in both planning procedures and national policies to give a fresh boost to the flagging development effort. One of the casualties of the planning crisis was the scheduled continuation of the Plans themselves. Although the Fourth Plan was scheduled to begin on April 1, 1966, immediately on the expiration of the Third Plan, and although a draft outline was published in August of that year, for three years annual plans replaced the more elaborate framework of the Five Year Plans.

In 1967, due largely to better weather, the economic situation began to improve, and in September a reorganized Planning Commission turned first to the task of preparing some realistic annual plans and then of re-thinking and re-drafting the Fourth Five Year Plan. The new Draft Fourth Plan finally went into effect in April 1969. The final document of the Fourth Plan was not presented to Parliament until May 18, 1970.

Although they had been scaled down considerably from the figures released in the draft outline of 1966, the targets suggested in the Fourth Plan were 33 per cent larger than the unrealized targets of the Third Plan for the public sector and 50 per cent larger for the private sector. "The Plan . . . has equality with social justice and the care of the common man, weak and underprivileged, as its dominant theme. It aims at achieving 5.5 per cent growth rate and refashioning socio-economic institutions to accelerate the tempo of development 'in conditions of stability and reduced uncertainties.' . . . [It] aims at growth with social justice and progressive self-reliance — doing away with concessional food imports by 1971, halving the foreign aid net of debt servicing by 1973–74 and dispensing with aid after 1980–81."[20]

In 1958, the Planning Commission, drew up the planned progress for the two decades 1956–76 as follows:[21]

### Twenty Years of Growth: 1956–76

| | AT THE END OF | | |
| --- | --- | --- | --- |
| | 1st Plan 1955–56 | 2nd Plan 1960–61 | 3rd Plan 1965–66 |
| National Income (in millions of dollars) | 22,680 | 28,308 | 36,246 |
| Total Net Investment (in millions of dollars) (Total for entire Plan period) | 6,510 | 13,020 | 20,790 |
| Rate of Investment (as percentage of national income) | 7.3 | 10.7 | 13.7 |
| Population (millions) | 384 | 408 | 434 |
| Capital-output Ratio (over the Plan period) | 1.8:1 | 2.3:1 | 2.6:1 |
| Per Capita Income (in dollars) | 59.01 | 69.51 | 83.16 |

| | AT THE END OF | | |
| --- | --- | --- | --- |
| | 4th Plan 1970–71 | 5th Plan 1975–76 | % Increase 1956 to 1976 |
| National Income (in millions of dollars) | 45,528 | 57,267 | 152.5 |
| Total Net Investment in (millions of dollars) (Total for entire Plan period) | 31,080 | 43,470 | 576.7 |
| Rate of Investment (as percentage of national income) | 16.0 | 17.0 | 132.9 |
| Population (millions) | 465 | 500 | 30.2 |
| Capital-output Ratio (over the Plan period) | 3.4:1 | 3.7:1 | —— |
| Per Capita Income (in dollars) | 97.88 | 114.66 | 93.9 |

(All at 1952–53 Prices)

[20] "Final Document of Fourth Five Year Plan Presented to Parliament," *India News,* IX (May 29, 1970), 1.
[21] This table is taken from *India News,* Jan. 26, 1959, p. 5. It is adapted from a table in Planning Commission, Government of India, *The New India: Progress Through Democracy* (New York, 1958), p. 29.

These figures suggest an impressive planning effort; but even if they are translated into reality, India will still be a very poor and very underdeveloped country. The per capita income will be only about $115 by 1975–76, an amount now exceeded by more than thirty underdeveloped countries. It is quite apparent, moreover, that these estimates were overly optimistic. By 1970–71, during what was supposed to be the last year, but which turned out to be the second year of the Fourth Plan, the population of India was nearly 100 million more than had been envisaged in 1958 (a tremendous underestimate that could wreck the entire plan), and the rate of investment and the per capita income were far below the estimated figures. India is obviously still a long way from the much-discussed "take-off to self sustaining growth."[22]

## Political Problems in Planning

Three major clusters of problems with major political aspects in relation to the development efforts may be singled out for special attention. These are problems arising from the inadequacies of the Indian administrative system, from the nature of the Indian political system, and from the difficulties of enlisting the cooperation of the people in the work of economic development and national revitalization. Here we shall confine our discussion to these three major clusters of political problems, although obviously many other basic problems facing India today have major political aspects and directly affect the development program, such as unemployment and underemployment, food production, population growth, divisive tendencies in Indian life — regional, linguistic, caste — and pressures impinging upon India from the outside.

**Problems of Administrative Reorganization and Reform.** After a searching examination of the Indian administrative system, Dr. Paul Appleby rated the Government of India as one of the most advanced governments, perhaps the most advanced, in any underdeveloped nation. Yet he pointed out that "the very system that justified classifying the Indian government among the few that are most advanced was conceived in pre-revolutionary terms" and indicated that the administrative structure which had been developed impressively in British days has grave defects for a large developing nation. The administrative system, he found, was too rigid and too authoritarian; instead of being geared for action responsibilities, it put a premium on excessive attention to detail and unwillingness to make decisions or to accept responsibility. "There are too many forms of class, rank and prerogative conscious-

[22] In the opinion of Walt W. Rostow, whose concept of "the stages of economic growth" attracted worldwide attention, India entered its "take-off" period in 1952; but, as he noted in 1960, "it is still too soon to judge whether the Indian take-off will be successful." See Walt W. Rostow, *The Stages of Economic Growth* (Cambridge, England, 1960), p. 38.

ness, too much insistence on too-uniform concentration of communication in formal channels, too much cross-reference including too many reviews of administrative papers by legal officers, too much control of detail, too much preoccupation with 'saving' rupees and too little with larger effectiveness."[23] "Perhaps nowhere else," he asserted, "have so many systematic barriers been erected to prevent the accomplishment of that which it has been determined should be done." At the outset of the Second Five Year Plan he warned that "full success of the Plan . . . turns rather exclusively on administrative reform to make the government as an organism equal to its identified goals." If India wished to realize broad goals it must have an administrative structure and outlook adequate for the task. "Will the people and the Parliament," he asked, "be sufficiently willing to pay enough and to give through delegation sufficient scope for the discretion and wisdom providing the kind of public service of performance necessary for administrative effectiveness?"[24]

The First Five Year Plan contained a long section on "Administration and Public Cooperation," which included a brief chapter on "Reform of Public Administration." Subsequent plans have given even fuller treatment to problems of administration and cooperation. Large numbers of reports and papers stressing the need for administrative reorganization and improvement have been issued under the auspices of the Planning Commission,[25] and the subject has also been given special consideration by the Estimates Committee of the Lok Sabha and the Administrative Reforms Commission. The Indian Institute of Public Administration has given extensive consideration to this problem, and its *Journal* has carried numerous articles and reports on the same theme. Almost every book on Indian administration and planning, whether written by Indian or foreign specialists, has struck the same note.[26]

[23] Paul H. Appleby, *Public Administration in India: Report of a Survey* (New Delhi, 1953), pp. 8, 9, 21. This report was issued by the Cabinet Secretariat, Government of India.

[24] Appleby, *Re-examination of India's Administrative System,* pp. 17, 49.

[25] See, for example, Cabinet Secretariat, *Papers on Measures for the Strengthening of Administration* (Planning Commission, Government of India, 1961), and V. T. Krishnamachari, *Report on Indian and State Administrative Services and Problems of District Administration* (Planning Commission, Government of India, 1962).

[26] In his fascinating book on the Etawah project in India, Albert Mayer states: "But by far the most doubtful and maybe baffling problem is this: that while within our project we have developed something which works within itself, unlocking some new strengths, it exists within an over-all administrative system where its direct methods and unlocked action are still unknown. Our system is basically alien to theirs, which is very much a sys-

Many of the proposals for administrative improvements call for organizational and financial reforms and for improvements in recruitment and training procedures. These are undoubtedly badly needed, but even more important are changes in what Professor Hanson called "the motivations and social relationships of the bureaucracy,"[27] from the topmost ranks of the Indian administration down to the officials working at block and village levels.

If a favorable administrative climate is to be developed, special attention must be given to the planning process and the organization of planning, to the organization of local government and its adaptation to development activities, to the administration of the Community Development Program and the National Extension Service, to the relationship of administrative officials to the new institutions and new leaders that are emerging in rural India, especially through the Panchayati Raj system, and to the efforts to revive the *panchayats* as basic units of local government and administration and to develop a system of village cooperatives. All of these involve fundamental problems of administrative reorganization and reform, and require, as the First Five Year Plan emphasized, "a reorientation of outlook on the part of officials as well as non-official representatives."[28]

## The Planning Process

**The Planning Commission.** The central agency for planning in India is the Planning Commission. Established early in 1950 by a Cabinet resolution, shortly after the Constitution of India entered into effect, and working under the general guidance of the provision in the Constitution for promoting the general welfare by securing political, economic, and social justice, the tasks of the Planning Commission are "to assess the nation's resources, draw up a plan to use them with proper priorities and allocation, determine the conditions, machinery and adjustments needed to make the plan succeed; appraise the progress of the plan from time to time and make any recommendations necessary to facilitate it."[29]

The Planning Commission has neither constitutional nor statutory

---

tem of checks and balances, delays, refinements, and decisions passing through many hands. In the routine administrative system, a sense of problem and urgency are second-hand. We hitherto existed within it by dint of strenuous special effort and high-level attention to pry things open — efforts and attention which cannot be expected to continue when such enterprises multiply." Albert Mayer and Associates, with McKim Marriott and Richard L. Park, *Pilot Project, India* (Berkeley, Calif., 1958), p. 92.

[27] Hanson, *The Process of Planning*, p. 309.

[28] *First Five Year Plan*, pp. 113, 114.

[29] *The New India*, p. 66. See Chap. V, "How India Plans," pp. 64–75.

status; it is an advisory body, not a line agency. Although it has changed greatly in membership, organization, and to some extent in functions since it was established, it has had an extraordinary influence in India. Until it was thoroughly reorganized in 1967 it had an elaborate organization, a very large staff, many affiliated committees and agencies, and it carried on many activities that were far more than advisory in nature.

From its inception the Prime Minister has been the Chairman of the Planning Commission. Until its reorganization in 1967 the Deputy Chairman was usually a minister; sometimes the post was combined with that of Minister of Planning. The number of full-time members has varied from three to seven. Although it started out with a mainly nonofficial membership, it soon had at least three ministerial members, usually the Finance Minister and the Minister of Planning, as well as the Prime Minister. Other ministers have from time to time also been members. The staff of the Commission, headed by a Secretary, increased from fewer than 300 in 1952–53 to nearly 2,000 by 1967. Organizationally the Commission, located in an impressive building — Yojana Bhavan — in New Delhi, became a labyrinthian structure, with many Divisions and Associated Agencies.[30] It had advisers on program administration in the States, who helped in the evaluation of the progress of the plans and in making recommendations for more effective implementation. Through its Research Programmes Committee the Commission benefited from, and occasionally sponsored, studies and reports by a large number of private and public, domestic and foreign, organizations and institutes.

Within the Planning Commission's framework the Programme Evaluation Organization issued frequent reports on the progress of the rural development programs. To associate officials and nonofficials of the country with the work of national planning, and to enlist the cooperation of the people generally, a Co-ordination Committee for Public Co-operation was established in 1952, with the Chairman and Deputy Chairman of the Planning Commission as the chief officers.

While there was widespread agreement that the Commission functioned in an impressive way, it was criticized for exceeding its functions and for failure to enlist the cooperation of local governmental units and officials and of the people generally. K. M. Munshi, a veteran Indian political leader, stated flatly at a public meeting in New Delhi in 1959: "Parliament, in fact, does not govern the country. . . . The

[30] For detailed descriptions of the organization of the Planning Commission and its affiliated agencies see the Indian Institute of Public Administration, *The Organisation of the Government of India* (Bombay, 1958), pp. 342–353, and H. K. Paranjape, *The Planning Commission: A Descriptive Account* (New Delhi, 1964).

nominated super-cabinet, the Planning Commission, does the supervision, control and direction of the Government of India, and owes no responsibility to Parliament."[31] Nearly a decade later, in 1967, the Administrative Reforms Commission reported: "Unfortunately over the past seventeen years, the Planning Commission has, in some measure, earned the reputation of being a parallel Cabinet and sometimes a super-Cabinet."[32] One of the sharpest criticisms of the Planning Commission was voiced by an eminent Indian economist, Professor D. R. Gadgil, who at the time was Director of the Gokhale Institute of Economics and Politics at Poona. In a lecture at the Harold Laski Institute of Political Science in Ahmedabad in 1958 Professor Gadgil stated:

> Examination of events since 1955 shows that barring the theoretical formulation, the Planning Commission has failed in almost every respect. . . . The root of the failure lies in the process by which the Planning Commission, essentially only an Advisory body, has come to mix itself with the actual process of the formation of public policies even in matters other than development. . . . It is the power complex of the Planning Commission or its members, their natural desire to exercise power and patronage like Ministers that are chiefly responsible for the neglect by the Commission of its main functions and for a needless extension of its activities over many irrelevant fields. The misdirection has been helped largely by membership of the Prime Minister and the Finance Minister of the Planning Commission which appears to have invested the Planning Commission and its decisions with an unnatural kind of prestige and importance.[33]

In its influential *Interim Report on the Machinery for Planning*, issued in 1967, the Administrative Reforms Commission, crystallizing the dissatisfaction with the leviathan growth and manifold activities of the Planning Commission, recommended that the Commission should be reorganized and reduced substantially in functions, personnel, and expenditures, and changed in composition, mainly by eliminating ministerial members. "Its role should be confined to the formulation of the plans . . . and the evaluation of plan performance. It should cease to

[31] Quoted in "The Super Cabinet," *The Radical Humanist*, XXIII (Dec. 6, 1959), 571.

[32] Administrative Reforms Commission, *Interim Report on the Machinery of Planning* (New Delhi, 1967), para. 15.

[33] D. R. Gadgil, *Indian Planning and the Planning Commission* (Ahmedabad, 1958). For a more favorable commentary on the role and work of the Planning Commission, see Appleby, *Re-examination of India's Administrative System*, pp. 31–32.

involve itself in executive functions and decisions." The Government of India agreed with the general tenor of the ARC's report and with most of its specific recommendations, although it decided that the Prime Minister would continue as Chairman and that one other Cabinet member, the Finance Minister, would be an *ex officio* member.

In September 1967, the reconstituted Planning Commission, with the Prime Minister as Chairman, Dr. D. R. Gadgil, a prominent Indian economist and leading critic of the Commission in previous years, as Deputy Chairman, and four nonofficial members, began its operations. Among the first actions were the coordination of steps to streamline the organization of the Commission and reduce its staff, the abolition of all advisory committees and panels, the shelving of the draft outline of the Fourth Five Year Plan, issued in August, 1966, and the postponement of a new draft outline in favor of the preparation of annual plans until the whole planning effort and the economic situation could be reassessed. It was hoped that the reconstituted Planning Commission would be more efficient as an advisory body, would discharge more effectively its main functions of the preparation and evaluation of the plans, and would avoid too close identification with officialdom and the evils of leviathanitis. It can no longer fairly be accused of being a "super-cabinet."

**The National Development Council.** In 1952 the National Development Council was established by a resolution of the Cabinet. It was a high-powered body consisting of the Prime Minister as Chairman, the Chief Ministers of all the States, and the members of the Planning Commission.[34] In 1967 the Administrative Reforms Commission recommended that the NDC should be reorganized to include all Union Cabinet ministers, as well as all previous members.

The main functions of the NDC are to supervise the work of national planning, to recommend measures for the achievement of plan targets, and to consider important questions of social and economic policy affecting national development.[35] Formally it is an advisory body to the Planning Commission, where it gets most of its administrative support. But its actual role has been quite different, as would be expected in view of its membership. As H. M. Patel observed in 1959, "The N.D.C. is a body obviously superior to the Planning Commission."[36] In the same year Michael Brecher wrote in his biography of

[34] See Shriram Maheshwari, *Indian Administration* (Bombay, 1968), pp. 96–101.

[35] Cabinet Secretariat, Government of India, Resolution No. 62/CF/50, dated Aug. 6, 1952.

[36] H. M. Patel, review of *The Organisation of the Government of India*, in *The Indian Journal of Public Administration*, V (October–December, 1959), 460.

Nehru: "Since its inception the N.D.C. . . . [has] virtually relegated the Planning Commission to the status of a research arm."[37] In 1960 K. Santhanam maintained that "The position of the N.D.C. has come to approximate that of a super-cabinet of the entire Indian Federation, a Cabinet functioning for the Government of India and the Governments of all the States."[38] There is some basis for Shriram Maheshwari's claim that "The NDC is . . . the apex policy-making organ of the country."[39] With the streamlining of the Planning Commission in 1967 and the enlargement of the NDC, the latter body has become even more important in its planning role; and its position as a central organ in Union-State relations, assured from the outset by its composition, has been enhanced since the death of Nehru and especially since the advent of non-Congress governments in several States following the general election in 1967.

**Planning in the States and Districts.** Although the States have a major role in the implementation, and to some extent the formulation, of the national plans, most States, so far, have tended to regard planning as a slightly peripheral function, to be discharged by an official who has no special qualifications for it, possesses no special status, and sometimes combines planning responsibilities with other extremely onerous duties. Moreover, the State administrative machines are not designed for the coordination of development programs, which is the essence of planning. Planning organization and procedures, and interest in the planning process, vary greatly from State to State. No State has a Planning Commission; several, however, have a Planning Board, usually headed by the Chief Minister, a Planning Committee, usually with the Chief Secretary as Chairman, and a Minister for Planning. The latter official, however, is seldom an important one, and in some cases the main responsibility for planning rests elsewhere, often in the Ministry of Finance. The Chief Secretary usually has a major role in coordinating State planning efforts, sometimes assisted by a senior official designated as Additional Joint Secretary, Development Commissioner, or some other title.

At the district level and below, the machinery for planning and its coordination is even more rudimentary. Usually the district officer or deputy commissioner plays the central coordinating role, assisted by district development and *panchayat* officers, subdivisional officers, a district statistics officer, district heads of State development departments, block development officers, *gram sevaks,* (village level workers)

[37] Michael Brecher, *Nehru: A Political Biography* (London, 1959), p. 521.
[38] K. Santhanam, *Union-State Relations in India* (Bombay, 1960), p. 47.
[39] Maheshwari, *Indian Administration,* p. 102.

and other officials connected with the Community Development Program, the National Extension Service, and Panchayati Raj. Much of the responsibility for planning activities at the district level and below has now been assigned to the three tiers of Panchayati Raj, and especially to the chairmen of the PR bodies at each level. At the village level little real planning can be done, and both elected and appointed officials working in villages have difficulty in convincing the villagers that they have a stake in the overall national effort and in eliciting their cooperation in the tasks of development. The role of the Community Development Program, the National Extension Service, and Panchayati Raj in planning and development implementation is supposed to be of crucial importance, but in fact it has been limited.

## Community Development, Panchayati Raj, and Cooperatives

**The Community Development Program and National Extension Service.** On October 2, 1952, the anniversary of Mahatma Gandhi's birthday, the Community Development Program was officially launched in India. This Program has been one of the most publicized features of India's development efforts. Less public attention was attracted by the inauguration of the National Extension Service in 1953,[40] but this came to be "regarded as one of the most significant achievements of the First Plan years."[41]

Under the general supervision of a Central Committee and a Ministry for Community Development, and similar committees and ministries in each of the States, the community projects are multi-purpose efforts in rural areas. Groups of roughly a hundred villages are associated in "development blocks," the basic units of development. By the end of the First Five Year Plan 1200 blocks — about one-fourth of which were intensive Community Development blocks, with the larger number being less intensive National Extension Service blocks — had been established, reaching about one-fourth of the people of rural India. The goal was to cover all of India by the end of the Second Plan, but because of unforeseen difficulties this goal was repeatedly postponed. It was reportedly achieved by the end of the Third Plan in 1966, when all of rural India was divided into 5,268 development blocks.

The Community Development Program is at once the most exciting and one of the most discouraging features of economic and social planning in India. It has attracted worldwide attention and comment, and

[40] NES blocks were less intensively developed than CD blocks, but "the organization and purpose of both are identical." *The New India*, p. 173. During the Second and subsequent Five Year Plans many NES blocks were converted into more intensive CD blocks.

[41] *The New India*, p. 170.

it has many ardent champions. One of the most enthusiastic proponents, S. K. Dey, long-time Minister for Community Development, has recalled that "the slogan which was inscribed on the banner of the pioneers" of the Community Development Program was "Destination Man." "The implications were never clearly analysed, . . . but it was generally understood that the focus was on human growth and not on material development." For all the shortcomings of the Community Development Program, Dey believes that the fundamental approach is sound, and that there are grounds for hope: "Happily, there are some still in India whose faith in community development remains undimmed. They are to be found in all walks of life. . . . They have been privileged to see the first faint stirrings of the human spirit which can be evoked under sensitive ministration. . . . The human factor will still remain crucial. . . . There can be sustained response only when people feel the urge within themselves. Community development is the only way in which that urge can be awakened."[42]

In spite of glowing reports of substantial and indeed revolutionary progress, the Community Development Program has bogged down badly, and its entire future is in· jeopardy. It has been very difficult to enlist the participation of the people in the program, or to give them a sense of real identity with it, and these have been the basic objectives of the entire effort. It has been difficult to recruit and train properly qualified persons to serve in the key positions of block development officers and village level works. It has been difficult to provide the proper coordination and direction for the program, whether on the national and State levels or in the districts. The Balvantray Mehta Study Team, which was appointed because the Community Development Program was lagging, made devastating criticisms of the program, and its recommendations for democratic decentralization of administration in India in effect proposed a different structure of organization and popular participation in rural India. Subsequent reports on the program have been quite critical and discouraging. The seventh evaluation report of the Programme Evaluation Organization of the Planning Commission, issued in the summer of 1960, stated that there were "lights and shades in the picture of the C. D. Programme in actual operation. The shades, however, predominate and one gathers the impression of an inadequately co-ordinated endeavour, governmental rather than popular in character and sustained more by hope than achievement."[43]

[42] S. K. Dey, "The Crisis in Community Development," *The Radical Humanist,* XXIV (Jan. 10, 1960), 17–18, 24.

[43] Quoted in "Crucial Factors in Community Development," *The Radical Humanist,* XXIV (July 24, 1960), 355.

The introduction of Panchayati Raj, beginning in 1959, interposed new institutions at district, block, and village levels, and to some extent pushed the Community Development Program and National Extension Service into the background. Panchayati Raj institutions were given extensive development functions, and key officials of the Community Development Program were closely associated with Panchayati Raj. Surveys have shown that rural people feel closer to the PR institutions, especially the revived village panchayats, than to the Community Development activities. Moreover, they feel that the latter activities have been more effectively implemented since the introduction of Panchayati Raj, and "they seem to comprehend the practical aspects of the community development programme in a much better fashion."[44]

**Panchayats and Cooperatives.** In addition to its efforts to spread the Community Development Program, the National Extension Service, and Panchayati Raj all over India, the Government is also placing a great deal of emphasis on the widespread organization of village *panchayats* and village cooperatives, with extensive responsibilities for development work. Speaking at Ernakulam in Kerala on January 18, 1960, Prime Minister Nehru said that the steps which the Government of India was taking all over the country to give powers to *panchayats* and to establish village cooperatives were of revolutionary importance as a means of bringing masses of people into the administrative structure in rural areas and thereby of laying the bases of real democratic self-government.

The efforts of the Government of India to implement Article 40 of the Constitution, which called for the creation of village *panchayats* "as units of self-government," have already been described. These efforts have been impressive. They have led all the States to pass *panchayat* acts, and *panchayats* have been established for more than half of the villages of India; but there are ample grounds for Hugh Tinker's conclusion that "in general, the *panchayat* experiment has shown the same discouraging refusal to 'get off the ground' as before independence." Professor Tinker is doubtless justified in believing that "their poor performance stems directly from the circumstances of rural life."[45] Indian villages are still relatively static social groups, riddled by factional and caste divisions, tradition-bound and resistant to change,

[44] Lalik K. Sen, V. P. Gaikwad, and G. L. Verma, *People's Image of Community Development and Panchayati Raj* (Hyderabad, 1967), p. 30. This study reports the findings of a survey of "Awareness of Community Development in Village India," embracing 7,224 respondents in 765 villages in 16 Indian States.

[45] High Tinker, "Authority and Community in Village India," *Pacific Affairs,* XXXII (December, 1959), 361.

suspicious of government in any form, desirous of resisting all alien influences. It is possible, nevertheless, that *panchayats* may be the vehicles for associating villagers with national development, and people with government.

The cooperative movement has been strong in India for more than half a century, especially since the passage of the Cooperative Credit Society Act of 1904. "In 1919 cooperation became a subject for action by the States, under the control of an elected Minister. . . . By 1950–51, the eve of the First Plan, there were 181,000 cooperative societies," mostly rural credit societies.[46] The First Five Year Plan called the cooperative form of organization "an indispensable instrument of planned economic activity in a democracy." Thousands of cooperatives have been formed since the First Plan was inaugurated. By mid-1964 about 83 per cent of the villages had cooperative societies, with a membership of 24 million people.[47] Another official source gave the number of cooperative societies in 1963–64 as 350,000, and the membership as 47 million.[48] All the Plans have stressed the importance of cooperatives and have provided for the development of many different kinds.[49]

At its sixty-fourth annual meeting, held at Nagpur in January 1959, the Indian National Congress endorsed a far-reaching resolution regarding cooperatives, which referred specifically to cooperative joint farming and to service cooperatives. Nehru himself attached great importance to this resolution, and he envisaged village cooperatives as a means of economic organization of village India, comparable in importance to the *panchayats* as the main units of political organization. "We should cover every village as a co-operative," he said. "We are launching out, in this way, in new directions outside the scope of our old administrative apparatus and we want to give far greater power to panchayats and to the village co-operatives than they have today, knowing that they may misuse it, make mistakes, and the like."[50] "My outlook," he said in 1960, "is to convulse India with the Cooperative Movement, or rather with Cooperation; to make it, broadly speaking, the

---

[46] *The New India,* pp. 202–203.

[47] Planning Commission, Government of India, *Fourth Five Year Plan: A Draft Outline* (New Delhi, 1966), p. 136.

[48] Ministry of Food, Agriculture, Community Development and Co-operation, Government of India, *Pocket Book of Information on Community Development* (New Delhi, n.d.), p. 67.

[49] An excellent bibliography on cooperation and cooperatives is given in the *Indian Cooperative Review,* III (October 1965–July 1966), Part VII.

[50] "Towards a Dynamic Administration," address at the Indian Institute of Public Administration, New Delhi, April 25, 1959; in *The Indian Journal of Public Administration,* V (April–June, 1959), 131–132.

basic activity of India, in every village as well as elsewhere, and finally, indeed, to make the cooperative approach the common thinking of India."[51]

The Nagpur Resolution of 1959 for greater emphasis on village cooperatives provoked a great deal of criticism and opposition within India. The Swatantra Party was formed largely to fight the tendencies toward the abolition of private property and collectivism. Nehru indignantly denied the sweeping charges of the leaders of the Swatantra Party and of others who opposed the Nagpur Resolution approach, and he undertook a campaign of national education regarding the real objectives of the Resolution and the role of village cooperatives in the New India which he was trying to create; but while he had some success in arousing popular interest and in counteracting some of the extreme charges against the program, the objectives of the Nagpur Resolution remain largely unfulfilled. It is significant that the resolutions of the annual sessions of the Congress and of the A.I.C.C. (All-India Congress Committee) since 1959 have contained only passing references to these objectives.

**Panchayati Raj and Planned Development.** Panchayati Raj is designed mainly to provide a more effective institutional base for and to give impetus to programs of economic development in rural India. The *panchayats, panchayat samitis,* and *zila parishads* are entrusted with a wide variety of powers and responsibilities in connection with the development efforts. Fully one half of the ten "main tests by which the success of Panchayati Raj will need to be measured," as itemized in the Fourth Five Year Plan, are essentially economic tests, and most of the others, which emphasize the political, administrative, and social functions of Panchayati Raj, have significant economic aspects.

In its actual operations Panchayati Raj has proved to be, in A. H. Hanson's words, "a very feeble and halting vehicle for policies of economic development," although the record hardly justifies Professor Hanson's views that the "main contribution of *panchayati raj* has been a negative one," or that it is, "for the present, . . . irrelevant if not positively hostile to the purposes of community development."[52]

These observations raise the larger questions of the prospects for India's development — political and social as well as economic — within a democratic framework, without far-reaching political, economic, and social changes that have not yet occurred, and that in fact seem unlikely to occur unless present policies and directions are radically reversed. It may be true, as Professor Hanson seems to believe

---

[51] *Cooperative Leadership in South-East Asia* (London, 1963), p. 1.
[52] Hanson, *The Process of Planning,* pp. 436, 440.

and as Gunnar Myrdal has specifically stated, that "in the short run democratic decentralization, like general suffrage at all levels, works mostly for reaction and stagnation;"[53] but there is already evidence that Panchayati Raj, which is a comprehensive program of democratic decentralization, is, in many States of the Indian Union, serving as an agency for decision-making at local levels and for enlisting more general popular support for and cooperation in the tasks of nation-building, including the vital task of economic development.

## Planning and the Political System

In implementing economic planning in India the political system itself presents a number of serious problems. Among these are the tendencies toward centralization, on the one hand, and toward decentralization, on the other; the problem of leadership at all levels; and problems of political participation and identification.

**Problems of Centralization and Decentralization.** In all democratic countries the increasing concentration of power, authority, and functions is a matter of deep concern. In India the concentration of authority seems to be particularly obvious. There is today a strong and pervasive tendency to look to the Central Government whenever difficulties arise in the "private sector" or in the States or in local units of government. The dominant position of the Congress Party until 1967, and of Nehru until his death in 1964, reinforced this tendency. Moreover, there is widespread acceptance of the view that without strong direction from the Centre India cannot hope to deal effectively with its vast problems, carry out its comprehensive experiment in national planning, and establish a "socialist pattern of society."

National planning, by definition, implies strong central direction, but in a multi-national state as vast as India much of the responsibility for the implementation of the plans devolves upon the States. As has been noted, Dr. Paul Appleby was concerned not so much with the growing power of the Central Government in India as with what he regarded as "its extraordinary national dependence upon the States for a large part of its administration."[54] Few observers would go as far as Appleby in this regard, but the experience to date with the implementation of the development programs has indicated that his concern was justified. Generally speaking, the States have not provided the resources or carried out the tasks assigned to them in the Five Year Plans, and the Central Government has been unable to hold them to greater accountability.

[53] Myrdal, *Asian Drama,* I, 300.
[54] Appleby, *Re-examination of India's Administrative System,* p. 47; and Appleby, *Public Administration in India,* p. 21.

Some States have incurred a very heavy indebtedness to the Centre. Most have requested, or demanded, larger amounts of money from the Centre for development purposes, and some, especially those which have been controlled by non-Congress governments, have sought greater autonomy and have publicly objected to the nature and course of the whole planning effort.

Authority is also concentrated in the States at the expense of local units of government and at the expense of individual initiative and autonomy. This may be due to reluctance to take responsibility at the lower levels, or to inadequacies of leadership and organization in the districts and their subdivisions, or to limited financial resources, or to inadequate popular response; but, whatever the cause, it calls attention to one of the most serious failings in India's development efforts. The Balvantray Mehta Report, as has been indicated, recommended a reversal of the tendency to centralization, and the adoption, as a deliberate policy of the Government, of a program of decentralization, designed to give real substance and vitality to local units of government and to enlist the cooperation of the people more effectively, in ways that are meaningful to them.

**Leadership and National Development.** In the development field, as in all other areas of national endeavor, India has benefited greatly from the quality and orientation of its top leaders. Here as elsewhere Nehru played the leading role. Although he was in no sense an economist, he assumed direct supervision and control over India's whole development effort. The economic philosophy motivating the development planning, the priorities assigned in the Five Year Plans, and many of the unique features of the Plans were determined in large measures by him. He was an active chairman of the Planning Commission and of the National Development Council. He did far more than any one else to explain the Plans to the people and to mobilize popular support, to the extent that it has been mobilized, for the great experiment on nation-building.

India has no dearth of trained and competent economists, and many of the best of them have had a major share in the development of the Five Year Plans.[55] However, all too often the leadership at State and local levels has been lacking in understanding, initiative, and imagination. This has greatly handicapped the development efforts. Although some of the ablest of the Congress Party leaders have devoted most of their time to the affairs of their States, and although the Chief Ministers

[55] The role of Professor P. C. Mahalanobis, former Director of the Indian Statistical Institute in Calcutta, is noteworthy. As chief adviser on planning to the Prime Minister and as a member of the Planning Commission, he had a great influence on planning goals and methodology.

of all the States are members of the National Development Council and the Zonal Councils and participate in the work of planning and development in many other ways, the States have in fact been bottlenecks in the implementation of the Five Year Plans.

At district levels and below, developmentally-minded leaders have been even fewer. New types of rural leaders are needed for the implementation of the experiments in the regeneration of the country which are the warp and the woof of the development programs. One of the main problems in implementing the Community Development and National Extension Service programs has been that of finding the right kind of leaders to serve as block development officers and village level workers. Some of the chairmen and members of the Panchayati Raj institutions have proved to be village leaders who can and will respond to the challenge of the new programs and who can enlist the participation of the people in them, but such leaders are still all too rare.

**Problems of Popular Participation and Identification.** Underlying all the problems of implementing economic planning in India is how to secure the active cooperation of the people and identify them with the great effort in "the building up of India, taking this country and its millions of people forward." The eventual success or failure of India's total national effort may revolve around this problem. It is at once the most challenging and the most discouraging aspect of the entire development effort.

All the Five Year Plans have emphasized the point that "Public cooperation has been recognized as an essential condition for the success of our Plans."[56] The Plans have specifically referred to the effectiveness of voluntary organizations, socio-economic programs, and, since 1959, the institutions of Panchayati Raj. "The participation of the people is of the very essence of the programme," stated the Planning Commission in a summary of the First Five Year Plan. "Unless people feel that the program is theirs and value it as a practical contribution to their own welfare, no substantial results will be gained."[57]

To what extent have popular participation and identification been achieved? Optimistic observers, including most Government spokesmen, have often referred to the great revolution that is under way throughout India as the "awakening of the countryside." "The revolutionary character" of the development program, according to a popular work, *The New India,* issued under the aegis of the Planning Commission, "lies precisely in that it has succeeded in awakening this participation and organizing it on a national scale."[58]

[56] *Third Five Year Plan,* p. 291.
[57] *First Five Year Plan,* p. 223.
[58] *The New India,* p. 171.

Few candid observers of the Indian scene, however, can find evidence of a widespread awakening or mass identification. Even some official reports have acknowledged the magnitude of the problem of enlisting genuine and widespread public cooperation,[59] and the draft outline of the Fourth Plan, released in August 1966 (and later shelved), admitted frankly "that in the implementation of the Plans, it has not been possible to enlist the support of the people in the requisite measure. The difficulties encountered are due partly to defective administrative arrangements and partly to other factors inherent in our present social set-up which tend to make the process of involvement relatively slow."[60] Most unofficial observers would probably agree with the following assessment of A. H. Hanson: "The Indian government's attempts to give the plans 'grass roots' have . . . achieved little success. There has been some, but not much, decentralization of plan formulation to the district and block levels, but hardly any effective popular participation in the process, while the involvement of the people in plan implementation, through the Community Projects and *panchayati raj,* has been patchy and generally disappointing in its results."[61]

Popular participation and cooperation are obviously necessary for the successful implementation of the program of family planning, which many observers feel is absolutely central to India's entire development effort. "India is one of the few countries which has taken up family planning as a national program. The objective . . . is to bring down the birth rate from the existing 41 per thousand to 25 per thousand in the shortest possible time by ensuring the direct and indirect participation in the program of 90 million couples in the reproductive age group."[62] During the Third Plan period (1961–66) only $57 million was spent on family planning, but the Fourth Plan contemplated an expenditure nearly six times larger. The Plan warned that the assumed population growth rate of 2.5 per cent would have "crippling" effects on development, and it called for a major program backed by adequate funds to check this trend. Main reliance has been placed on the establishment of family planning centers, contraceptive programs, compensation for sterilizations, the insertion of inter-uterine devices, and widespread education. India's population experts claim that these efforts are bearing fruit; but as yet they have

[59] The seventh report of the Programme Evaluation Organisation of the Planning Commission contained the following observation: "Peoples' attitudes and reactions in most of the Community Development Blocks are not yet generally favourable to the success and growth of the Community Development Programme. The majority of the villages . . . seem to rely mainly on the Government for effecting the development of rural areas."

[60] *Fourth Five Year Plan: A Draft Outline,* p. 404.

[61] Hanson, *The Process of Planning,* pp. 442–443.

[62] "Family Planning in India," *India News,* July 19, 1969.

reached only a small percentage of the people in rural areas, and they have not been able to overcome the social, economic, and psychological barriers that stand in the way of adequate popular cooperation.[63]

It is probably too much to expect that the people of India, living in mental and geographical isolation in a stratified society, accustomed to having decisions imposed on them from above, without any experience in effective cooperation in national efforts, would respond to another and greater program which has come to them from the far-away centers of power in New Delhi. With the possible exception of the mass response to Gandhi's appeals and teachings, and to a more limited degree to Vinoba Bhave's Bhoodan Yagna movement, no movement has "succeeded in awakening" widespread popular participation and "organizing it on a national scale." Thus India's planners today are confronted with an inescapable dilemma: they have almost no prospects of securing effective popular initiative and participation in national development programs, yet their programs cannot possibly succeed without such initiative and participation.

## Planning for What?

How is India's "experiment in democratic planning" progressing? The sober answer is that it is not progressing well — at least not well enough. As India's planners settle down to a more realistic basis for the formulation and implementation of the development programs, the gap between needs and fulfillment grows ever larger. Because of the low living conditions of its people and the pressure of a growing population, it has, to paraphrase the words of the Red Queen, to run so fast in order to stay where it is, and staying where it is is not enough.

"There seems to be general agreement," noted a team of American agricultural specialists who visited India in early 1959 at the request of the Union Ministries of Food and Agriculture and Community Development and Co-operation, under the sponsorship of the Ford Foundation, "that the major problems in India lie not so much in basic idea or philosophy of the programmes but in implementation."[64] "In a society as divided and tradition-bound as India," Professor Hanson observed, "effective planning may be impossible so long as the planners have to operate within the framework of the present political system."[65]

One should not forget that there is as yet no basic agreement in India,

[63] See Joseph Lelyveld, "It's God's Will. Why Interfere?," *The New York Times Magazine,* Jan. 14, 1968.

[64] *Report on India's Food Crisis and Steps to Meet It,* by the Agricultural Production Team sponsored by the Ford Foundation (New Delhi, April, 1959). This report was issued by the Ministry of Food and Agriculture of the Government of India.

[65] Hanson, *The Politics of Planning,* p. 526.

even on ideas, objectives, and philosophy. What kind of India do the people of India want? What are the objectives of Indian society? India, it may be said, has not yet made peace with the twentieth century. It is not even certain that Indians wish to do so. Do they want to modernize? Do they really want fundamental changes? How real is the Indian "revolution"? There is clearly what may be called an "inner struggle" in India, at various levels, involving conflicting viewpoints, often in the same minds, on fundamentals. Many Indians do not accept the basic approach of those who are governing India today. They may favor other ways of social and political organization and polity. Some favor the Gandhian way, from which, they insist, Nehru and his associates in the Government of India departed. This would involve a conscious effort to resist many of the consequences of modernization, to create a simple *sarvodaya* society with a maximum of decentralization and an emphasis on satisfying basic human wants, not on creating new wants. Others favor some kind of communal approach, with a return to traditional ways, perhaps seeking the establishment of a kind of Hindu Raj in more or less modern dress. Still others favor the Communist way, perhaps on the China model, with such adaptations as would be necessary to fit the Indian scene. Others speak vaguely of a partyless democracy, quite different from any Western form. A few openly advocate military rule.

In spite of diverse views, growing doubts, and failures in performance and in spirit, India seems to be fully committed to the goal of economic development through national planning, with an emphasis on social welfare and justice, within a democratic framework. The modest successes of the Indian experiment to date raise questions in many minds, in India and elsewhere, whether totalitarianism is the only path to economic progress in underdeveloped lands. Much depends on the eventual success or failure of India's efforts to demonstrate that domestic development is not an unrealizable goal, and that even under conditions of instability, transition, and underdevelopment the existing political system is a viable one.

# 9

# The Party System

## Experience with Political Parties in Asia

With the possible exceptions of Japan, the Philippines, and Israel (some would add India, Ceylon, and Malaysia), no effective democratic party system has emerged anywhere in Asia. Indeed, "Asia has had pathetically little experience with working party systems" of any kind.[1] "In several Asian countries individual parties are or have been extremely important in making policy, but in doing so they have acted more as administrative hierarchies in the tradition of imperial monopolistic polities than as aggregating political parties functional to a political system."[2]

The very idea of parties is strange and even unacceptable to many Asians; it conforms neither with their traditions nor with their concepts of how political life in their countries should be organized to meet the needs of a changing, yet basically static, society. As they look at the present state and activities of political parties in most Western countries, they are not impressed; and they reason that if parties are functioning so unsatisfactorily in the countries of the West, where the tradition of parties is deeply rooted and where literate and economically fortunate peoples have had long experience with party systems, it would be folly to expect that parties could be successfully grafted onto the institutions of Asian peoples.

Thus it is not surprising that Asia has few, if any, developed party systems, and that Asian attitudes toward political parties have been ambivalent. "Asian politics are caught in a profound dilemma: they

[1] Lucian Pye, "Party Systems and National Development in Asia," in Joseph LaPalombara and Myron Weiner, eds., *Political Parties and Political Development* (Princeton, 1966), p. 369.
[2] *Ibid.,* pp. 388–389.

can neither get along well without political parties nor work well with them."[3]

Only a few Asian political parties date back to the nineteenth century. Most of them arose as "umbrella" organizations in the latter days of the struggle for independence from the ruling colonial powers and then carried on as the dominant parties for a few years after independence. "An independence movement," as Richard L. Park observed, "is not the best breeding ground for political parties in the Western sense. In the search for unity in opposition to the ruling imperial power, the Asian nationalist movements exerted every effort to bring all factions together into one independence-bound organization. . . . After independence, as was natural, these movements tended to break down, with groups of minority views leaving the parent body to form new political groupings."[4] Generally speaking, these dominant political groupings, which were both more and less than political parties, performed a useful service, not only in the independence struggle but in the years of trial and difficulty which followed its success.

In some respects new countries with a dominant national political organization fared better than those in which the pattern of political activity was more diffuse. There may be considerable merit in Professor Park's contention that "a well-organized political party system might have hindered the relative stability. . . . Much of the success of the legislative and planning programs in these countries can be traced to the large, disciplined majorities held by the party in power in the respective parliaments. The hard test of parliamentary government, of course, will come when this situation no longer prevails."[5]

In most Asian countries which adopted the parliamentary system, at least in form, the hard test has already come, and few of these systems have been able to meet it. Most of the umbrella organizations that directed the independence movements have either disappeared or have fallen on evil days. Almost all the charismatic leaders have gone. Only in India does the party of independence still dominate the political life of the country, and this party is split. It is a far cry from the Indian National Congress of the Gandhian era, or even of the Nehru era, and its future is very much in doubt.

## The Nature of Political Parties in India

Since the Congress Party has fared better than any other Asian nationalist-movement-turned-political-party, the hard test of parliamen-

[3] *Ibid.*, p. 369.
[4] Richard L. Park, "Problems of Political Development," in Philip W. Thayer, ed., *Nationalism and Progress in Free Asia* (Baltimore, 1956), p. 103.
[5] *Ibid.*, p. 104.

tary government has been postponed. There are manifold signs, how-ever, that the "hard test" is at hand; they are to be found in growing criticisms of the Congress; in the marked decline in its strength in the Lok Sabha and in most of the States; in the internal divisions that, while not new, have led to a formal split in the Congress; in the ad-mitted failings of its leadership, especially on State and local levels; in the growing political opposition to it in the States and municipalities and local areas; in the dissatisfaction with its economic and social achievements; in the rise of regional and linguistic and communal pres-sures which challenge the basic tenets of national unity and the secular state; in the failure of the Congress to train a new generation of leaders to replace the "tall leaders" who have passed from the scene; and in the recurrent crises that have beset the party in the post-Nehru era.

From independence to 1967 the Congress dominated the Indian polit-ical scene to such an extent that India was often described as a one dominant party system. This typology was a commonly accepted one, and it had considerable utility; but, even at the height of Congress dominance, it was only partially accurate. It suggested an even greater imbalance in the party system than in fact existed. While the Congress had, even after the 1969 mid-term elections in five States, an over-whelming preponderance in the Lok Sabha, it never won a majority of the popular votes in any national election, and the many opposition parties, while weak in number of candidates elected to the Lok Sabha, reflected many facets of Indian political life that were not always em-braced in the Congress and exercised an influence out of proportion to their electoral successes.

In the States the description of one party dominance was even more misleading, and after the 1967 general elections and the 1969 mid-term elections in four key States (and Nagaland), it was obviously invalid. Hence, in spite of the frequent use of the terms "one dominant party system" or "one party dominant system" by some of the most astute students of Indian politics, including Professors W. H. Morris-Jones and Rajni Kothari,[6] they should in fact be used cautiously and with qualifications even for the period prior to 1967. After 1967 they no longer characterize the political situation in many States and are of

[6] See, for example, the following publications of W. H. Morris-Jones: "Dominance and Dissent," *Government and Opposition,* I (July–September, 1958); "The Indian Congress Party: A Dilemma of Dominance," *Modern Asian Studies,* I (April, 1967); and *The Government and Politics of India* (Garden City, N.Y., 1967). For a sample of Rajni Kothari's views, see: "The Congress 'System' in India," *Asian Survey,* IV (December, 1964); "India: The Congress System on Trial," *Asian Survey,* VII (February, 1967); and *Politics in India,* especially Chap. V. See also Gopal Krishna, "One Party Dominance — Development and Trends," *Perspectives,* Supplement to *The Indian Journal of Public Administration,* XII (January–March, 1966).

limited utility even with reference to the Centre. Rajni Kothari has pointed out, "India has been for some time now moving from a dominant party system to a system of *competitive dominance.*"[7] Rajni Kothari's reference to the change from a dominant party system to one of "competitive dominance" is suggestive and useful, but it does no more than suggest the new and more complex pattern of party politics that seems to have developed in India.

Even more basic objections can be raised to the concept of one party dominance. As Stanley Kochanek pointed out in his study of the Congress Party, "to classify India as a dominant one-party system during the first two decades of independence tells very little about the nature of the dominant party or about the Indian political system. An alternate approach . . . would be to focus more attention on the nature of the dominant party. The study of such factors as the locus of power within the dominant party, party-government relations, inner party structures, and the social base from which the party derives its leadership and support could provide a more comprehensive understanding of the particular one-party regime under investigation and of the nature of the political system itself."[8]

If these deeper considerations are borne in mind, there is some justification and value in using the term "one dominant party system" to describe the kind of party system — if indeed it was a "system" — that prevailed in India on the national level during the first two decades of independence. With caution it may be used to characterize the national political scene even after 1967 — at least until the split in the Congress in November 1969.

The lopsided dominance of the Congress Party may have provided the kind of political stability which India needed in the early years of independence, as Professor Park suggested, but it has thus far prevented a healthy party system from emerging. The situation is made even worse by the weakness of the Praja Socialist Party and other socialist parties which presumably could provide the nucleus of an effective democratic opposition; by the challenge of the Communist Party (which in 1964 split into two parties), which would use the ballot box and its representation in the Parliament to destroy the institutions of democracy; by communal groups with political representation,

---

[7] Rajni Kothari, *Politics in India* (Boston, 1970), p. 200. Italics in original.

[8] Stanley A. Kochanek, *The Congress Party of India: The Dynamics of One-Party Democracy* (Princeton, 1968), p. xix. It is interesting to note that although Dr. Kochanek believes that "the concept of dominant one-party systems" is "far too simple, if not meaningless," he gave his book the subtitle: "The Dynamics of One-Party Democracy."

which in their own way are equally determined enemies of secular democracy; and by regional and State parties, which promote local rather than national interests.

Another major barrier to the development of a healthy party system in India is posed by those who do not believe in parties at all. This group includes many people who are influential in Indian political life and many more who are influential in Indian society. Many of these people look upon parties as undesirable organizations, and they would substitute for them other means for permitting popular expression and for implementing the peoples' will. Often they derive their ideas from Gandhi and from his ideal of the *sarvodaya* society. Such ideas are being propagated today by two of the most influential people on the Indian scene, both long-time followers of Gandhi, Acharya Vinoba Bhave, in his Bhoodan Yagna movement (a crusade of sacrificial land-giving), and Jayaprakash Nayayan, through his support of the Bhoodan movement and through his frequent writings and advocacy of a "party-less democracy" — although he has never been able to formulate a specific statement of precisely what a system of "partyless democracy" would involve.[9]

From time to time other eminent Indians have expressed their disillusionment with political parties. In July 1968, C. Rajagopalachari, a veteran former Congress leader, the only Indian Governor-General of India, and one of the few surviving "elder statesmen" of India, wrote: "We have had enough of political parties. Wherever else this system may have done well, it is not doing well in India, and will not do better as time goes on but will get worse and worse."[10]  Many Indians feel, as did M. N. Roy and as do his followers, the Radical Humanists, that the people are too backward to become politically conscious and discriminating members of any party; hence, a different approach to the participation of the individual in social and political life is held to be necessary.[11]

Although many Indians profess to believe in "partyless democracy," parties have mushroomed in great profusion in the years since independence. Most of the major parties originated within the Indian National Congress; among them the Congress Socialist Party, which

[9] See Jayaprakash Narayan, "Towards a Fuller Democracy," *The Radical Humanist*, XXII (June 15 and 22, 1958), 281–282, 288, 295–296.

[10] See *Swarajya*, July 19, 1968.

[11] The pages of *The Radical Humanist*, the organ of the Radical movement, frequently contain articles on this theme. See, for example, M. N. Roy, "Opening of a New Chapter in Indian History," *The Radical Humanist*, May 25, 1958, and Ellen Roy, "Indian Party Politics," *The Radical Humanist*, July 24, 1955. See also M. N. Roy, *Power, Parties and Politics* (Calcutta, 1960).

became the nucleus of the Praja Socialist Party (PSP) and the Communist Party, which was not expelled from the Congress until 1945. Prominent leaders of many of the major opposition parties were once active workers in the Congress ranks. Most parties are really local or at most regional groupings, often hardly more than the followers of some leader. Such groupings spring up, put up their candidates in a general election, and disappear quickly, or merge with similar groups, or move in and out of "electoral arrangements," sometimes of a weird character. In India, as elsewhere, politics makes strange bedfellows.

India's experience with political parties has not been an altogether happy one, but parties have been and are prominent features of Indian political life. Parties in India, imperfectly but discernibly, have been significant in performing such functions as political aggregation, articulation, socialization, and participation, and thus they have been important components of the Indian political system. It may be preferable, however, as Rajni Kothari suggests, to "look at the party system in India not so much in terms of discrete organizational entities known as parties in the fashion of the interest aggregation theory, but rather as part of an interacting process of governmental penetration, performance at various levels, and society's response to such penetration and performance."[12]

In a statement issued on March 18, 1953, in connection with his talks with Jayaprakash Narayan regarding the bases of closer cooperation between the Congress and the PSP, Prime Minister Nehru made an interesting comment on the party situation in India:

> The parties, as they exist in India today, apart from the Congress, may be divided into four groups. There are certain political parties with an economic ideology. There is the Communist Party with the allied organizations. There are the various communal parties under different names but essentially following a narrow communal ideology, and there are a number of local parties and groups having only a provincial or even narrower appeal.[13]

Various typologies of political parties in India could be suggested, but basically they consist of the Congress Party and all the rest. Another possible division is between national and regional, state, or local parties.[14] Although the Congress has been the only truly national

[12] Kothari, *Politics in India*, p. 160.
[13] *The Hindustan Times*, March 19, 1953.
[14] "One dimension of the system is articulated along the federal axis, between the Congress dominant center and the multi-party states with different parties and coalitions wielding governmental power in different states: it is the dimension of non-aggregation. A second dimension is found at the

party, several others — presently the two main Communist parties, the Jana Sangh, Swatantra, the Praja Socialist Party (PSP), and the Samyukta Socialist Party (SSP) — are often referred to as national parties and are so recognized by the Election Commission, even though most of them have significant strength only in one or a few States — for example, Swatantra in Gujarat, Rajasthan, and Orissa, and the CPI(M) in West Bengal, Kerala, and Andhra Pradesh.[15]

The most important of the State parties is the Dravida Munnetra Kazhagam (DMK), which, as a result of the 1967 general elections won control of the government of Madras (which it renamed Tamil Nadu) and elected 25 members to the Lok Sabha. Another important State party is the Akali Dal, essentially a Sikh party, which is a major political force in the Punjab.

Other common divisions are between secular and nonsecular parties, between "left" and "right" parties, between communal and noncommunal parties, and between democratic socialist parties, such as the Congress (both branches), the PSP, and the SSP, and nondemocratic socialist parties to the left (notably the Communist parties).

Indian politics seems to have entered an era of coalitions, defections and "floor-crossing," united fronts, and general instability. A common practice has been for dissident Congressmen to form their own parties or coalitions. Current examples are the Bharatiya Kranti Dal (BKD), which is particularly strong in Uttar Pradesh, the Bangla Congress in West Bengal, and the Kerala Congress in Kerala. More comprehensive coalitions, often involving parties or groupings of very divergent views united mainly in their opposition to the Congress, have sometimes been formed. Examples are the United Fronts in West Bengal and Kerala, both of which were dominated by the Communists, and the Samyukta Maharashtra Samiti, a coalition of many parties from the

state level where either the Congress is still the dominant party . . . or some other party is dominant. . . . A third dimension operates at the level of the electoral constituency where it is found that 'the number of constituencies where one party enjoys a virtual monopoly over its competitors is on the decline . . . the modal constituency in India remains the dominant party constituency — typically, a constituency in which the winner gets a little over 45 per cent of the vote and the next-best trails about 12 to 16 percentage points behind.' " Kothari, *Politics in India*, p. 200, quoting Peter McDonough on the measurement of party systems (University of Michigan dissertation, 1969).

[15] "Some national parties are acquiring a regional character by emerging as powerful in one or two states, and virtually disappearing from the rest of the country." "End of National Parties?," *The Times* (London), quoted in *The Mirror* (Singapore), March 3, 1969.

right to the left, which gave the Congress Party formidable opposition in the Marathi-speaking areas of undivided Bombay State in 1957.

For convenience, the Indian parties will be discussed under the following headings: (1) the Congress Party; (2) other socialist parties; (3) the Swatantra Party; (4) the Jana Sangh and communal parties; (5) Communist parties; and (6) regional, state, and local parties.

### The Congress Party

To the extent that it can be considered a political party prior to 1947, the Indian National Congress is probably the oldest party in Asia. Three main periods in the history of the Congress prior to 1947 may be discerned. During the first period, from 1885 to about 1907, the objective of the Congress was not independence for India but cooperation with the British and mild pressure on the foreign rulers to give greater political representation to Indians. In these years the Congress was under the control of Western-educated moderates, men like Dadabhai Naoroji, Surendranath Banerjea, Pherozeshah Mehta, and especially G. K. Gokhale. From about 1907 until the end of World War I the Congress was split between the moderates and the more extreme and militant elements, led by Bal Gangadhar Tilak, Aurobindo Ghose (until he retired from politics), Bepin Chandra Pal, and Lala Lajpat Rai. Tilak and his associates raised the cry of *swaraj* and *swadeshi,* advocated resistance to the British, and harked back to the ancient Hindu past for their ideology and inspiration. The extremists introduced new vigor into the nationalist movement and attracted a larger following than the moderates ever could.

With the deaths of Gokhale in 1915 and of Tilak in 1920, with new forces entering the Indian scene, and above all with the entry of Gandhi into the political life of the country, the Gandhian period of the nationalist movement began. Under the influence of Gandhi the Congress adopted new techniques of nonviolent noncooperation or civil disobedience which gave a new militancy to the national movement and brought it nearer to the masses. The new militancy was reflected in various civil disobedience campaigns and in the noncooperation of the Congress with the British during World War II, because the British would not grant immediately the demands for *swaraj,* which by the late thirties had come to mean complete independence.

With better organization, more widespread popular support, and the magic influence of Mahatma Gandhi, the Congress became a truly national movement. As long as it was the main organization for independence, it could include in its ranks people of very diverse backgrounds and interests, and it could function as an umbrella organization without serious political indigestion. There were, however, marked divergencies within its top leadership. In the Gandhian era a kind of right wing and left wing split developed. The right wing was led by more conservatively inclined Congressmen, such as Motilal Nehru and Vallabhbhai Patel, while the left wing was led by younger spokesmen of such diverse viewpoints as Subhas Chandra Bose (who later left the Congress to form his own party, the Forward Bloc, and then collaborated with the Nazis and the Japanese during World War II), Jawaharlal Nehru, more radically minded than his father, especially before he assumed the responsibilities of political office, and Jayaprakash Narayan, a founder of the Congress Socialist Party and still one of the most influential "unconventional" leaders in India. Over all of these divergent groupings and individuals was Gandhi, a kind of super-leader who was at times not even officially a member of the Congress, whose views were *sui generis,* not easily categorized as either left or right wing. In some respects Gandhi was more conservative than most conservatives, and in others he was more radical than most radicals. Thus it was not surprising that, as Robert Crane has written, "From the time of the first civil disobedience campaign the internal history of the Congress was the reconciliation of a multitude of special interests and different points of view."[16]

After independence the Congress had to play a very different role. It ceased to be a national movement, a unifying omnibus organization which could embrace almost any Indian who wanted his country to be free, and became instead a political party, which at the same time directed the government of independent India and functioned as a social and propaganda agency. This inevitably meant that it could no longer command the support of many of its former followers, and that its internal divisions and factions could no longer be sublimated in the interests of the national struggle. Even after August 1947, however, it retained some of its former mystique and influence. It was still the party of Gandhi and of Nehru, the organization that had led India to freedom, and it still tried to be all things to all men. Gandhi suggested that since its main objective had been achieved the Congress should disband and should be reformed as a Lok Sevak Sangh, a kind of social service organization. He did not think that it should continue "as a propaganda vehicle and parliamentary machine." His advice, of course, was not followed, and his assassination so soon after independence removed from the scene the most unifying influence of all. Many

[16] Robert I. Crane, "Leadership of the Congress Party," in Richard L. Park and Irene Tinker, eds., *Leadership and Political Institutions in India* (Princeton, N.J., 1959), p. 181.

former members of the Congress left the party, either individually or in groups; others were expelled or were forced out by changes in Congress policy.

With Gandhi's death, Nehru emerged as the dominant figure on the Indian stage. Only Vallabhbhai Patel, much more conservatively inclined, could hold his own with Nehru. As long as Patel was alive, Nehru had a co-worker with great administrative ability and iron will. Although the two men disagreed on many points, the Nehru-Patel duumvirate was a most effective one.[17] After Patel's death in 1950 no one of equal stature emerged, either to challenge or to buttress Nehru's role.

> The present distribution of power in the Congress evolved through three major phases, each distinguished by the way in which the Congress President and his Working Committee interacted with the Prime Minister and his Cabinet. The first phase, extending from 1946 to 1951, was a period of conflict and transition. . . . The second phase, which may be characterized as the period of centralization and convergence, can be subdivided into two stages: the years from 1951 to 1954 during which Nehru attempted to achieve harmony by merging the roles of Congress President and Prime Minister and the years from 1954 to 1963 during which the Congress organization was headed by a series of young leaders who presided over the day-to-day affairs of the Congress organization under the supervision of their senior colleagues in the government. The third phase, from 1963 to 1967, was a period of divergence which marked the restoration of a new equilibrium between the Prime Minister and the Congress President.[18]

In 1967 the position of the Congress was weakened both at the Centre and in most of the States, and in 1969 the party, after existing as a unified organization for 84 years, openly and formally split.

The most serious challenge to Nehru's control of the Congress came in 1950, when Purshottamdas Tandon, a representative of the conservative wing in the Congress, with more than a marked flavor of communalism, was elected President of the Congress, with the support of Patel, over Acharya Kripalani, who was backed by Nehru. Nehru made this a test of his position in the party. By resigning from the Congress Working Committee Nehru forced Tandon to resign the Con-

[17] See Michael Brecher, *Nehru: A Political Biography* (London, 1959), Chap. XV, "The Duumvirate."

[18] Kochanek, *The Congress Party of India*, pp. 3–4.

gress presidency. After 1951 Nehru's position in the party remained supreme, although from time to time some of his associates complained publicly of his policies, or his dictatorial methods, or his failure to groom a successor, or the stifling effect of his overall dominance of the party.

After the Tandon crisis Nehru himself assumed the post of President of the Congress, a position which he had held more than twenty years before (in succession to his father, Motilal Nehru). He held this position for some four years, although he repeatedly stated that in his judgment the offices of Congress President and Prime Minister should not be held by the same man. When he finally yielded the party presidency, it was to a hand-picked successor, U. N. Dhebar, who was not at all prominent in the higher circles of the party or of the Government. In 1959 Dhebar was succeeded by Indira Gandhi, Nehru's daughter, hostess, and inseparable companion. Although her father stated that he was not happy with this arrangement, he obviously did little to prevent it.

Mrs. Gandhi, however, soon tired of the job. Her successors, except for K. Kamaraj Nadar, who was elected Congress President in 1963, were not particularly distinguished men.[19]

In 1967, largely because of the withdrawal of Mrs. Gandhi's support, Kamaraj was succeeded by S. Nijalingappa, Chief Minister of Mysore, who remained at the head of the "organization" wing of the Congress when the party split in November 1969. C. Subramaniam became interim President of the "requisionist" wing of the Congress, which controlled the Government of India, with Mrs. Gandhi as Prime Minister, and Jagjivan Ram, a veteran Congress leader and an untouchable, became the first regular Congress(R) President.

The Congress Party is the only political group in the nation with a truly all-India organization. Its lowest organizational unit is the local committee in a village or town or city ward. There are over 5,000 block/ward committees, nearly 450 district or city Congress committees, 20 Pradesh (State) and 6 territorial Congress committees. The line of organization extends from the local committee to other committees in larger subdivisions of the States, to the Pradesh Committees, and from the Pradesh Committees to the central party apparatus, headed by the All-India Congress Committee (A.I.C.C.) and the Working Committee. Theoretically the annual sessions of the Congress, usually held in January, are the supreme policy-making bodies, but in practice, while they are highly publicized and bring together the top

---

[19] See Michael Brecher, *Nehru's Mantle: The Politics of Succession in India* (New York, 1966).

leaders of the party and thousands of party representatives, they are something in the nature of party rallies. The delegates and others who attend listen to interminable speeches by party leaders and to numerous reports from party committees, and they endorse, usually without much debate, large numbers of resolutions, formulated or at least approved by the party's high command.

Another important central agency of the party is the Congress Parliamentary Party, which has its own offices and organization. Since the Congress is so dominant in the Parliament, many of the major decisions are taken not so much on the floor of the Lok Sabha as in the closed meetings of the members of the Congress Parliamentary Party; but the decisions invariably reflect the more basic decisions that have been made by the top leaders of the party (most of whom are members of the Congress Parliamentary Party), with the support of the Working Committee and/or the A.I.C.C. The whole question of the relationship between the Congress Parliamentary Party and the regular agencies of the party machinery deserves more detailed investigation. It is in a sense a phase of the larger question of the relationship between the Government of India and the Congress Party, a relationship which is in a constant state of flux.[20]

The A.I.C.C. is a fairly sizable body, elected by the Pradesh Congress Committees, and consisting of one-eighth of the members of each of these Committees, plus a few other State and some national party leaders. It meets irregularly, usually more than once a year. The Working Committee, a smaller body which meets more frequently, is the most important agency in the Congress structure.[21] Most of the top leaders of the party are members of the Working Committee. A roster of long-term members would include virtually all of the front-rank leaders of the Indian independence movement and of the Congress Party and the government since independence.

The Working Committee is composed of the President of the Congress and 20 members of the A.I.C.C., 7 elected and 13 appointed by the President. Very often it includes members of the Congress Parliamentary Party and members of the Cabinet. Nehru, who of course was always a member, relied heavily upon this Committee for advice and support. The basic policies of the Congress, and therefore of the coun-

---

[20] See W. H. Morris-Jones, *Parliament in India* (Philadelphia, 1957), pp. 185–199; Norman D. Palmer and Irene Tinker, "Decision Making in the Indian Parliament," in Park and Tinker, eds., *Leadership and Political Institutions in India*, pp. 129–134; and Kochanek, *The Congress Party of India*, pp. 157–187.

[21] For a detailed description and analysis of the role of the Committee, see Kochanek, *The Congress Party of India*, Chaps. V–XII.

try, are usually formulated or approved in the Working Committee before they are placed before the agencies of the Party which technically have a larger policy-making authority, the A.I.C.C. and the annual session. Thus the Working Committee is not only the executive of the Congress but is a kind of shadow cabinet, often with more real power and influence than the regular Cabinet. In recent years, however, as factionalism has increased in the party and has extended to the highest levels, and as the party organization has become more decentralized, the role of the Working Committee has noticeably lessened. Since the split in the party each wing has its own organizational apparatus, including an A.I.C.C. and a Working Committee.

Two important subcommittees of the Working Committee are the Parliamentary Board, which is primarily concerned with coordinating party-government relations at the State level, and the Central Election Committee, which has a major role in the selection and final approval of party candidates in all elections and in the conduct of elections.[22]

For a political organization which has dominated the political life of the country, the Congress has a rather small membership — only about 6,000,000 "primary" members and fewer than 100,000 "active" members. An active member, according to the Party Constitution, must be 21 years of age or over, be "a habitual wearer of khadi (homespun cotton cloth)," abstain from alcoholic drinks, oppose untouchability, believe in communal unity and have "respect for the faith of others," perform constructive activity, pay one rupee annually, and enroll at least 5 primary members each year. Anyone who is 18 years of age or over, who accepts the objectives of the Congress, who is not a member of any other political party, and who pays an annual subscription of 25 paise, may become a primary member.

Considering the heterogeneous character of the Congress from its inception, it is hardly surprising that its stated objectives are rather nebulous and comprehensive. Undoubtedly the Congress as a party has tried, consciously or unconsciously, to preserve a good deal of the national character and catholicity of views which it possessed when it was a national movement for independence. Economically, its ideology is rather clear, but this reflects the prevailing orientation in Indian thinking and practice generally toward a high degree of state initiative and control. Even here, however, the Congress reflects its mixed heritage and the varied strands of thought which are subsumed under the Indian varieties of socialism. The economic ideology of the Congress has been evolved from three or four main currents of modern Indian thought. These include the Gandhian ideal of the *sarvodaya* society,

---

[22] See *ibid.,* Chaps. X and XI.

with emphasis on service, social welfare, decentralization, cottage industries, and village self-sufficiency; the continuance of a system of free enterprise, even in a "socialist" state, which is reflected in the fact that well over 85 per cent of the productivity of the country is contributed by the "private sector"; socialist ideas of state ownership and control of the instruments of production; and a variety of other socialist views, Marxist or non-Marxist in character. The main trend, however, with certain lip service to Gandhian ideals, has been toward the welfare state, with a strong socialist flavor. Long before the Avadi resolution of 1955 the Congress was in favor of "the socialist pattern of society," although there was never complete agreement on the precise outlines and prerequisites for the "socialist pattern." Under the leadership of Nehru and later of his daughter, Mrs. Indira Gandhi, the Congress has followed a markedly left-of-center course, with considerable concessions to the "private sector."

This socialist bent of the Congress has tended to undermine the other parties calling themselves socialist, such as the PSP, the SSP, and the Communists. To the consternation of both the Socialist and Communist parties, the Congress is as closely identified with "socialism" as they are. *"The* socialist party of India is not the Communist Party or the Socialist Party but the Congress Party; it cornered socialism decades ago. The great socialist efforts in India since independence — the Five-Year Plans and the development programs — were conceived and carried out, or are being carried out, by the Congress."[23]

Like India itself, the Congress passed through one crisis after another in the 1960's. Like India, it showed a remarkable vitality and survival capability in crisis situations; but in late 1969 it split, giving a wholly new complexion to its future prospects and to the Indian political scene. Unless the two wings of the party come together again, the Congress Party has come to the end of its long existence. Even if it is revived, it seems highly unlikely that it will be able to regain its former influence and prestige.

In place of a united Congress, two parties, each claiming to be the real Congress Party, have come into existence. One, called the organization Congress, has the support of most of the former leaders of the Congress, especially the more conservative leaders represented by the so-called "Syndicate"; but it is the weaker of the two wings, with far fewer members in the national and State legislatures and with the support of only a few Chief Ministers and State governments. The other, known as the "requisionist" Congress, headed by Mrs. Indira Gandhi,

[23] George Bailey, "Pandit Nehru's One-Party Democracy," *The Reporter*, Nov. 13, 1958, p. 31.

has many more members in the Lok Sabha and most State Assemblies, commands the support of most of the Congress Chief Ministers and the regular party organization in most States, and controls the Government of India. Although the Congress Party(R) has far more members of the Lok Sabha than any other party, it is well short of a majority. If it is to remain in power after the next general elections, it will probably have to enter into election alliances with other parties and in the post-election period head a coalition government, which has never yet existed at the Centre.

There is a great deal of basis for the following observation of Rajni Kothari: "A cohesive political center presiding over a diverse structure of political affiliations is vital to the efficient performance of the Indian political system, including performance in the economic sphere. There is little doubt that at least for the next decade only the Congress Party can provide such a center." These words were written shortly before the Congress Party split. It is doubtful that either of its successors, the two wings which emerged from the split, or a reunited Congress, can remain in power for anything like a decade, or provide a "cohesive political center."[24] Therefore the future of democracy may not necessarily depend upon the continuance in power of the Congress Party, or one branch of it. Indeed, some would argue that the prospects for democracy would improve without a dominant single party.

## Other Socialist Parties

Between the Congress Party, which has proclaimed its dedication to "the socialist pattern of society," and the Communist parties, which espouse their own brands of socialism, the Praja Socialist Party, the major Socialist party outside of the Congress, is trying to find a more influential place in the Indian political arena. In these efforts it is experiencing serious difficulties. "Inconsistencies and the indecisiveness are still apparent among the leaders over certain matters of ideology, parliamentary strategy, and program. They are unable to agree on whether or not the party needs an ideology, what constitutes an ideology, and whether it should be Marxian, Gandhian, some synthesis of both, or a pragmatic search for a new doctrine of democratic socialism relevant to India. . . . The party's crises have been those of the national leadership: the party's inability to communicate effectively with the secondary echelons and the membership concerning the changes desired in ideology, organization, and strategy; its failure to assess correctly and adhere consistently to a given role in Indian politics; and its

[24] Kothari, *Politics in India*, p. 190.

failure to maintain its own cohesion in the face of public adversity and party rebellion."[25]

Five stages in the history of organized Socialist parties in India may be distinguished: (1) from 1934 to 1948, when the Congress Socialist Party functioned within the Congress organization; (2) from 1948 to 1952, when the independent Socialist Party, composed largely of former members of the Congress Socialist Party, tried unsuccessfully to develop the basis of an effective democratic opposition to the Congress; (3) from 1952, when, after a disappointing showing in the first general elections, the Socialist Party merged with the Kisan Mazdoor Praja Party to form the Praja Socialist Party, until 1955, when Dr. Ram Manohar Lohia broke away from the PSP to form the Socialist Party of India; (4) from 1955 to 1964, when Asoka Mehta led a number of his supporters in the PSP back to the Congress fold, and the main body of the PSP merged with the Socialist Party of India to form the Samyukta Socialist Party (SSP); and (5) from 1965, which witnessed the break-up of the short-lived PSP-Socialist Party of India merger, until the present, a period of declining fortunes for both the PSP and the SSP.

Ideologically speaking, the leaders of Indian socialism were from the beginning, as Thomas A. Rusch has observed, "divided by three amorphous and overlapping tendencies: Marxism, social democracy of the British Labor Party type, and a democratic socialism tempered by Gandhian concepts and the use of nonviolent civil disobedience techniques for nationalist and class struggle." In 1934 a small group of young Congress members, mostly from North India, organized the Congress Socialist Party within the Congress.[26] "Though a majority . . . were non-Marxists, the most influential were the Marxists."[27] Neither Gandhi nor Nehru was identified with this group, but both of them showed a great deal of sympathy with its aims and objectives. Gandhi, in particular, tried to act as a moderator between the members of the Congress Socialist Party and the more conservatively-inclined Congressmen, led by Vallabhbhai Patel. The Socialist leaders refused to participate in Congress ministries which functioned in most of the Provinces of British India in 1937–39, and in the Constituent Assembly which was elected in 1946. In 1947 the word "Congress" was dropped

[25] Thomas A. Rusch, "Dynamics of Socialist Leadership in India," in Park and Tinker, eds., *Leadership and Political Institutions in India,* pp. 204, 208.
[26] R. C. Gupta, "An Analysis of Political Parties in India. Part Two: Praja Socialist Party," *The Radical Humanist,* March 24, 1963. See also L. P. Sinha, *Left Wing in India, 1919–47* (Muzaffarpur, 1965).
[27] Rusch, "Dynamics of Socialist Leadership in India," p. 189.

from the name of the party-within-a-party, and the decision was made to recruit non-Congressmen as members.

In 1948, after Gandhi's assassination, the Patel group in the Congress was instrumental in securing a resolution of the A.I.C.C. which outlawed political parties within the Congress ranks. This action forced the Socialists to choose between giving up their organized status within the Congress or to leave the parent organization. The latter course was decided upon at the Nasik congress in March 1948, and for the first time a significant independent Socialist party came into being. Some former supporters stayed within the Congress, while others went over to the Communists.

The Socialist Party proclaimed the ideological goal of a "democratic socialist" society. "The organizational goal was to fashion a democratically structured, mass membership party controlled and financed by its members." A stern test of the success of its popular appeal came in the first general elections, and the results were disappointing. "In place of the expected second-rank status in India's legislative bodies, the socialists achieved only third place in terms of seats won, though they were second in terms of popular votes. They were forced to accept the defeat of all their national leaders and the election of only one fourth of the seats anticipated."[28]

One of the results of the post-mortems that followed the elections of 1951–52 was the merger of the Socialist Party with the Kisan Mazdoor Praja Party, which had been formed by dissatisfied Congressmen led by Acharya Kripalani just before the elections and which had fared even worse than the Socialists in the voting. "The KMPP was interested in practical parliamentary activity and Gandhian village constructive work, thereby complementing the Socialist Party leadership's interest in urban trade union, intellectual and agitational activities."[29] The new party was called the Praja Socialist Party. In the spring of 1953 its best-known member, Jayaprakash Narayan, held a series of talks and exchanged some correspondence with Nehru, at the Prime Minister's request, with the object of exploring possible bases of cooperation between the Congress and the PSP. These exchanges did not lead to any specific agreement, but they aroused widespread interest and speculation.

The PSP experienced the same difficulties and differences as had all previous Socialist parties. It suffered two serious blows in 1954, when Acharya Narendra Deva, a highly respected elder statesman who as chairman helped to hold the party together, died and when its best-

[28] *Ibid.*, pp. 200, 202.
[29] *Ibid.*, p. 203.

known leader, Jayaprakash Narayan, announced his retirement from active politics. The remaining top leaders differed publicly over ideology, strategy, and tactics.

One prominent PSP leader, Dr. Ram Manohar Lohia, deviated so emphatically from the position of the majority of the PSP leaders that in 1955 he was expelled, and he proceeded to form his own Socialist Party of India. Both socialist parties suffered from the split and the confusion in their high commands. At about the same time the Congress adopted the Avadi resolution, declaring its goal to be a "socialist pattern of society." Some PSP members thereupon rejoined the Congress. In the third general elections, in 1962, the PSP representation in the Lok Sabha fell from 19 to 12, and in the State Assemblies it also lost heavily, while the Lohia socialists won only 6 Lok Sabha seats and 59 Assembly seats.

In 1959 Asoka Mehta, under increasing attack from more militant members of his party, resigned as chairman, and in June 1964, he and several hundred of his followers joined the Congress. In the same month the leaders of the PSP and the Socialist Party of India agreed to unite to form the SSP. The union was short-lived. Early in February 1965, many members of the PSP wing withdrew and revived the PSP as a separate party.

Since then the PSP has barely managed to survive, and it has ceased in effect to be a national party. It has some able leaders, but they do not work well together, and they have little popular following or appeal. It is essentially a party of urban intellectuals who have no rural base. "Opportunism, indiscipline, electoral setbacks, pessimism over the Party's future electoral prospects and the ambivalent attitude of the leadership towards the struggle for socialism have been the causes of continuous defections and deteriorating morale of the socialist workers."[30]

After the break-away of most of the former PSP members, the SSP continued to function under the leadership of Dr. Lohia, with whom few other leaders could co-exist. Dr. Lohia had some success in appealing for support on the basis of unity against the Congress, and his strong advocacy of Hindi and his championing of the "backward classes" were vote-getting programs in the north of India. In the fourth general elections in 1967 the SSP won 23 seats in the Lok Sabha and nearly tripled its representation in State Assemblies. Its significant strength, however, was and is concentrated in two huge northern States, Bihar and Uttar Pradesh. In each of these States it lost more than ten seats in the mid-term elections of 1969.

[30] L. P. Singh, "Indian Socialists in Disarray" (unpublished manuscript), p. 4.

The death of its supreme leader, Dr. Lohia, in 1968 was a major blow to the SSP. Some of his successors, notably S. M. Joshi, Raj Narain, and Madhu Limaye, are tough and experienced leaders, and at least one relatively new leader, George Fernandes, a young labor leader of Bombay who unseated S. K. Patil, a top Congress leader, in 1967, is also tough and dynamic, with considerable mass appeal. But the prospects of the SSP, like those of the PSP, are not bright. "The politics of irresponsibility which the SSP has made its hallmark reflect the tortuous search the party has been making to carve out a *niche* for itself in the Indian political scene."[31]

The experience of the KMPP, PSP, Socialist Party of India, and SSP seems to indicate that all socialist parties in India have had a difficult time and that no effective democratic socialist alternative to the Congress is possible, unless the left wing of the Congress joins with the PSP and SSP to form a new democratic socialist party.

## The Swatantra Party

In 1959 the first democratically oriented conservative party of any importance in India came into being. The Swatantra (Freedom) Party was formally inaugurated at a convention in Bombay in August. The formation of the new party, it was reported, was hastened because of the opposition to the resolution in favor of farming cooperatives adopted by the Congress Party at its annual meeting in Nagpur in the previous January. A report of the June meeting in Madras contained the following statement of the new party's aims and beliefs:

> We are of the opinion that social justice and welfare can be reached more certainly and properly in other ways than through techniques of so-called Socialism. . . . Social justice and welfare should not be brought about by violence or State compulsion . . . but must be brought into being by the spread of the doctrine of trusteeship as suggested by Gandhiji. . . . The educational activities of government, direct and indirect, should be such as to emphasize the moral obligations of those who possess wealth to hold it in trust for society, and a doctrine of life based on that moral obligation as distinguished from seeking to establish a socialistic structure based on legislative sanctions involving expropriation and loss of incentive for the individual to work and increasing dependence on the State and its officials in every walk of life.[32]

[31] Dilip Mukerjee, "Militancy for Its Own Sake Has Hardly Helped SSP," *The Statesman Weekly,* June 22, 1968.

[32] Quoted in Ellen Roy, "A Closer Look at the Swatantra Party," *The Radical Humanist,* Feb. 14, 1960, pp. 77–78.

The Swatantra Party is conservative in its economic and social views, very anti-Communist, and opposed to many of the policies and to the socialist orientation of the Congress. It emphasizes the freedom of the individual, the importance of private enterprise, the ancient concept of *dharma,* and the principle of trusteeship, in the Gandhian sense. It is opposed to socialism (but it insists that it is not an advocate of laissez faire) and to the kind of planning that the socialist government of India has been undertaking (but not to all planning), and it advocates the minimum interference of the state in all spheres. It stands for "farm, family, and freedom" and is opposed to what C. Rajagopalachari has called the "license-permit-control raj." In foreign affairs it favors cooperation with Pakistan in the defense of the subcontinent, a tough policy toward Communist China, and closer cooperation with the Western powers.[33]

One of the main promoters of the Swatantra Party was M. R. Masani, once a prominent founder-member of the Congress Socialist Party who had been critical of Congress and Socialist policies for many years. At the time of the founding of the Swatantra Party Masani had an important public relations position with the Tata industrial enterprises, the best known of all private concerns in India. A smooth, polished, Western-educated man of the world, he was elected to the Lok Sabha in the general elections of 1957. Masani has continued to be one of the inner circle of the Swatantra Party, having served both as General Secretary and President, and is one of its most effective and articulate spokesmen, although he has sometimes disagreed with his colleagues in the top leadership of the party.[34]

Two other prominent members were Professor N. G. Ranga and Dr. K. M. Munshi. Ranga, long-time President of Swatantra, was a peasant leader from Andhra Pradesh, with close associations. Oxford-educated, he was a former professor of economics. Munshi, a distinguished scholar-politician, was at one time a leading figure in the Congress Party, a chief architect of the Indian Constitution, and a former Governor of Uttar Pradesh.[35]

But the stellar attraction in the Swatantra Party was Chakravarti Rajagopalachari — fortunately known as just C. R. or Rajaji — who was an intimate associate of Gandhi and the first — and last — Indian Governor-General of the Dominion of India. In 1959 he was a wizened

---

[33] See Howard L. Erdman, *The Swatantra Party and Indian Conservatism* (Cambridge, England, 1967), Chap. 8; and Motilal A. Jhangiani, *Jana Sangh and Swatantra: A Profile of the Rightist Parties in India* (Bombay, 1967), Chap. 5.

[34] Erdman, *The Swatantra Party and Indian Conservatism,* pp. 103–104.

[35] See *ibid.,* Chap. 5.

old man in his early eighties, but there was still magic in his name. "C. R. is acutely aware of his messianic role. He speaks to people as a biblical leader come to *his* people."[36] "After Gandhi is dead," he said, "we have socialism. Socialism is now preached boldly because there is no Gandhi to answer it. I say the same things as Gandhi said. . . . If Gandhi had been alive or Vallabhbhai Patel had been alive I would not have had to do all this work."[37] He charged that the Congress had "in effect accepted communistic principles." In particular he regarded the experiment in cooperative farming announced in the Nagpur resolution of the Congress in 1959 as "the royal road to communism." The Swatantra Party, he proclaimed, was "dedicated to saving India from the dangers of totalitarianism."[38] Week after week, in the pages of the party magazine, *Swarajya,* Rajaji expounded his views, which were often at variance with those of other Swatantra leaders. No party could possibly confine this grand old man, almost the last of the giants of the Gandhian era.[39]

The party to which Rajaji gave his blessing and which brought him out of retirement into active political life once more attracted a great deal of attention, and it gained the support of influential businessmen and others who had little taste for socialism or who welcomed the appearance of a non-communal conservative opposition and alternative to the Congress. It was also, paradoxically, welcomed by many who were more liberally inclined, who were attracted by the appeals of the new party to the Gandhian tradition or to ancient Indian ideals, or who for any other reason were not satisfied with existing Indian political parties. Even Nehru professed to be happy over the formation of the Swatantra Party, but he also denounced Swatantra as "a reactionary party, drawing into its fold various types of vested interests," and he declared that if India "follows the policies of the Swatantra Party, India will be doomed."

Until 1969, at least, the Swatantra Party fared better than most political observers had predicted. In the 1962 general elections it won 22 seats in the Lok Sabha, thus becoming the second largest opposition party, and 166 seats in the State Assemblies. In the 1967 elections it did even better, gaining 44 Lok Sabha seats, the largest number of any opposition party, and 255 Assembly seats. Heavy losses in Bihar were

[36] Suyash Chander Malik, "The Mixed Potion of Swatantra, *The Radical Humanist,* May 22, 1960, p. 251.

[37] Address at Kakinda, Feb. 28, 1960; quoted in *ibid.,* pp. 251–252.

[38] Quoted in Ashwini Kumari, "Indian Statesman, Friend of Gandhi, Forms Party to Challenge Congress," *The Washington Post,* Aug. 29, 1960.

[39] See Erdman, *The Swatantra Party and Indian Conservatism,* pp. 87–95 ("Rajaji and Indian Conservatism").

more than offset by substantial gains in Gujarat, Madras, Mysore, Orissa, and Rajasthan. In 1962 it won 50 seats in Bihar, but in 1967 and again in the mid-term elections of 1969 it could get only 3. This phenomenal drop is explained by defections and divisions in the Swatantra Party in Bihar, and particularly by the loss of the support of the Raja of Ramgarh. In several States, notably Rajasthan and Orissa, where it has fared well, Swatantra's main support has come from princely rulers and other large landowners, who in the more "feudal" States are still excellent "vote banks."[40]

Swatantra is often criticized as a party of "vested interests," particularly as a party of former princely rulers, big businessmen, and retired civil servants; a party of the past, economically and politically out of touch with the interests and needs of the second half of the twentieth century; with no positive program; with a strangely assorted group of leaders, mostly elder statesmen, with high caste Hindus, businessmen, and princes predominating; with no mass base and with only spotty following in the rural areas. There is some basis for these charges. Since 1969 divisions within the party and the narrowness of its support base have become more evident. However, as it is the only important non-communal conservative party in India, it may win the support of many conservative Congressmen, or it may merge with this group to form a really effective conservative party. It may serve as a catalytic agent, presaging a realignment of Indian political groupings.

There have been recurrent rumors of a possible merger with the Jana Sangh. In 1969 the question of a merger was discussed by top leaders of the two parties. But Swatantra and Jana Sangh are still separated by the communal divide, and by differences on language, Pakistan, and other issues. As the main representatives of two different types of Indian conservatism, the prospects of either party acting alone or in concert are not very bright. And in view of the growing radicalization of Indian politics, it is doubtful that any political organization openly opposed to socialism in any form will gather much momentum.

### The Jana Sangh and Communal Parties

"Communalism" is a term that is frequently used in descriptions of Indian politics and society. It refers to the strong ethnocentrism which characterizes many Indian social, religious, caste, ethnic, racial, linguistic, and other groups, and to the frictions which often develop within and between these groups. The greatest of all communal problems over the years has been the Hindu-Muslim problem, and the term is often used with reference to this main problem.

[40] Jhangiani, *Jana Sangh and Swatantra,* p. 188.

A great variety of communal organizations exists in India. These "represent homogeneous political units only in the sense that each is concerned with the prerogatives of a single segment of Indian society — they are pressure groups seeking to secure for the cultural unit they represent a larger measure of prestige, power, wealth, and predominance of cultural patterns."[41]

The most important of the many Hindu communal organizations is the Rashtriya Swayamsevak Sangh (RSS). The RSS has great political influence, but it is not a political party. Rather it "is a tightly knit, disciplined, hierarchical organization seeking to incorporate larger and larger segments of the public within its ranks. Its primary aim is to establish within its own group a model of a revitalized Hindu society and eventually to secure the adoption of this cultural form in the whole country."[42] It is organized along semi-military and hierarchical lines. The basic units are the cells. Deliberative councils composed of elected and appointed members exist on State levels and at the Centre. The inner core consists of a group of Organizers who devote their lives to the service of the RSS. At the apex is the leader, known as the Sar Sanghchalak, a lifetime post which is passed along from one Sar Sanghchalak to another. Only two men have held this post, the founder of the RSS, Dr. Keshav B. Hedgewar, and his successor, Madhav Rao Golwalkar.

The RSS is a militant Hindu organization that is much more influential and much better disciplined than any Hindu communal political party. It has given various kinds of encouragement and support to Hindu parties, especially to the Hindu Mahasabha and the Jana Sangh. Only three of these parties, the Hindu Mahasabha, the Ram Rajya Parishad, and the Bharatiya Jana Sangh, have had any political importance, and of these only the Jana Sangh has polled enough votes to be recognized as a national party. The Hindu Mahasabha and the RSS, under the leaderhip of Dr. Shyama Prasad Mookerjee and Golwalkar, respectively, prospered in the mid-1940's, when the Congress

[41] Richard D. Lambert, "Hindu Communal Groups in Indian Politics," in Park and Tinker, eds., *Leadership and Political Institutions in India*, p. 211. To paraphrase a statement of Myron Weiner, in *Party Politics in India* (Princeton, N.J., 1957), p. 164, the terms "communal" and "communalism" are used only because they are "used by Indians in common parlance" and because they are useful in referring to certain parties and organizations. Their use does not imply any normative judgment.

[42] *Ibid.*, p. 215. See also J. A. Curran, Jr., *Militant Hinduism in Indian Politics — A Study of the R.S.S.* (New York, 1951); Jhangiani, *Jana Sangh and Swatantra;* Craig Baxter, *Jana Sangh: A Biography of an Indian Political Party* (Philadelphia, 1969); and Inder Malhotra, "Banning Communalism: Vain Search for a Short Cut, "*The Statesman,* June 25, 1970.

leaders were in jail and when the Muslim League, supported by various more militant Muslim organizations, was also gaining strength. After Gandhi's assassination in January 1948 by a Maharashtrian Brahman who had had some affiliation with both Hindu communal organizations, the RSS was outlawed for several months, and the Mahasabha, still under Mookerjee's leadership, suspended political activity until the furor had died down. The Ram Rajya Parishad has some strength in Rajasthan, Madhya Pradesh and a few North Indian States. It is the most reactionary of the Hindu communal parties. Its goal is "an Indian India." After the 1967 general elections neither the Hindu Mahasabha nor the Ram Rajya Parishad had a single seat in the Lok Sabha. The RRP had only two Assembly seats, in Madhya Pradesh, and the Hindu Mahasabha had none at all. (It did capture one seat in the Uttar Pradesh Assembly in the mid-term elections of 1969). For all practical purposes these two communal parties have ceased to exist.

The Bharatiya Jana Sangh was formed in 1951 by Dr. Shyama Prasad Mookerjee, who left the Hindu Mahasabha after Gandhi's murder and who for a time held a post in the Cabinet of the Central Government. Dr. Mookerjee insisted that the Jana Sangh was not a communal party at all, and this has been the position of almost all of the leaders of the party. It "drew its support from refugees, remnants of former princely power, others favoring a stronger policy toward Pakistan, and various groups with conservative economic interests,"[43] and it was also associated with the RSS. Dr. Mookerjee seemed to be working for a coalition of conservatively-oriented parties in the Indian Parliament, with the Jana Sangh at the center. As long as he was alive, he exerted a powerful influence on Indian politics, far beyond the electoral strength of the Jana Sangh. He was one of the ablest parliamentarians and orators of modern India. After he died in Srinagar in 1953, the prospects of an anti-Congress rightist coalition faded, and the Jana Sangh became almost leaderless.

An intriguing question in Indian political life is the exact relationship between the Jana Sangh and the RSS. In an interview in May 1960, Deendayal Upadhyaya, one of the most prominent leaders of the Jana Sangh, declared: "Constitutionally there is no relationship. The only relationship is that many of the members of the Party are also Swayam Sevaks of the Rashtriya Swayam Sevak Sangh. . . . The RSS is a cultural organization, taking no part in politics."[44] Yet there can be little doubt that the relationship is a close if not a "constitutional" one. Upadhyaya and many other top leaders of the Jana Sangh, as well as

[43] Lambert, "Hindu Communal Groups in Indian Politics," p. 222.
[44] Interview quoted in Jhangiani, *Jana Sangh and Swatantra*, p. 189.

some of its strongest supporters, are or have been members of the RSS. Perhaps this accounts for the fact that the Jana Sangh has been the most tightly organized and disciplined political party in India. Occasionally a Jana Sangh leader will protest against the influence of the RSS on the party, or will differ with some pronouncement of the RSS Sar Sanghchalak; but the RSS has been called the Jana Sangh's "inner core," and its influence is obvious, if indeterminate.

Ideologically the Jana Sangh is "socially more conservative and economically more progressive than the Swatantra Party. . . . One unique claim of the Jana Sangh is that it is the only party rooted in Bharatiya culture and thought; all the others draw their inspiration from abroad." It "does not recognize the concepts of majority and minority in India. It has faith in one nationhood, with a single culture." It claims to ignore communal and caste considerations, but many of its leaders are high-caste Hindus, it has had little support from non-Hindus, and the culture it seeks to promote is obviously "Bharatiya culture." It advocates a synthesis of ancient and modern systems of education, the speedy "introduction of Hindi and the regional languages as official languages in the place of English," the preservation of "Bharatiya culture," traditions, and social values, small-scale and cottage industries, a greater emphasis on agriculture, a unitary rather than a federal form of government. Because it believes in "Akhand Bharat" (undivided India) it takes a hard line toward Pakistan and toward the Kashmir question. It has been critical of the Government of India's "soft" policy toward Communist China. It advocates a strong defense establishment, and it wants India to "go nuclear." It favors a "policy of 'non-involvement' in such international affairs as do not directly affect India." At the same time it encourages foreign aid and foreign investment, and it wants India to have closer associations with the non-Communist countries of the West.[45]

In the first general elections (1951–52) the Jana Sangh, then a new party, got slightly more than 3 per cent of the total popular vote, and thereby won 3 Lok Sabha seats and gained recognition, for election purposes, as a national party, a position it has been able to maintain ever since. By 1967 it had 35 seats, becoming the second largest opposition party in the Lok Sabha. In the State Assemblies its membership rose steadily, from 34 to 267. Its strength is concentrated almost wholly in the Hindi heartland; except for one seat from Nagaland, it has never won a Lok Sabha seat from any State other than a northern, usually Hindi-speaking, State. In 1967, for the first time, it made

[45] Jhangiani, *Jana Sangh and Swatantara,* Chap. 4; see also Baxter, *Jana Sangh;* and Mohammed Ali Kishore, *Jana Sangh and India's Foreign Policy* (New Delhi, 1969).

some small inroads in a few non-Hindi speaking States, but its real strength is concentrated in Madhya Pradesh and Uttar Pradesh, where in 1967 it won 22 of its 35 Lok Sabha seats and 175 of its 267 Assembly seats. In the mid-term elections of 1969 in Uttar Pradesh, however, its representation in the State Assembly fell from 97 to 48 seats. It has lost some of its ablest leaders, notably Dr. Shyama Prasad Mookerjee in 1953, and Deendayal Upadhyaya, who served as both General Secretary and President, in 1968. Upadhyaya's successor as President is Atal Behari Vajpayee, another very able leader.

The Jana Sangh has had little appeal to non-Hindus, or even to Hindus outside the Hindi-speaking States of north India, as it championed Hindi and appealed to the kind of Hindu orthodoxy particularly prevalent in north India. "Being a political party with a purpose, it has kept on modifying its earlier heavier emphasis on things Bharatiya,"[46] in order to gain more widespread support, but it has had little success in these efforts. As B. G. Verghese noted in 1962, "Unless the Jana Sangh can cast itself in a new image it will remain a Hindi regional party and no more."[47] It seems, however, to be deeply rooted in the Hindi heartland, and since regionalism seems to be becoming an increasingly important factor in Indian politics and since communalism seems to be losing none of its pervasive appeal, the Jana Sangh may benefit from both persistent and new trends.

None of the Hindu communal parties has fared well on the national scene, or even, with some exceptions, on the State level. "The strength of the Hindu communal organizations, however, lies outside the elective assemblies. . . . Their importance comes from the catalytic function that they play in exacerbating tensions and divisive forces already present in the society."[48] As such they are major threats to the unity of India, for they operate largely beneath the surface and they have roots deep in traditional Indian society.

Many non-Hindu communal groups have some political influence in India, usually in opposition to Hindu communalism; but since they are largely concentrated in certain local, State, or at most regional areas of the country, they will be considered under the heading of local and regional parties.

### The Communist Parties

Before independence the Communist Party of India (CPI) made little headway in its efforts to infiltrate the nationalist movement or to appeal to the masses of the people. Since 1947 it has passed through a

[46] Jhangiani, *Jana Sangh and Swatantra,* p. 91.
[47] B. G. Verghese, "Two Cheers for Democracy," *The Times of India,* April 4, 1962.
[48] Lambert, "Hindu Communal Groups in Indian Politics," p. 224.

number of tactical phases, usually in delayed response to shifts in the international Communist line.[49] By following essentially neo-Maoist tactics since the early 1950's, by emphasizing the policy of collaboration with socialist and even with "bourgeois" groups, and by professing a policy of constitutionalism and relying on the ballot box to gain political strength, the CPI has won numerous electoral victories. It has also suffered some serious electoral reverses due to internal dissension, notably in Andhra in 1955 and 1967, and it suffered a serious blow in 1964, when the left wing seceded to form another more radical and pro-Chinese Communist party — the Communist Party of India (Marxist).

In Kerala the CPI formed a government between 1957 and 1959, and it was a major, but not the main, component of the United Front governments which were formed in West Bengal and Kerala after the 1967 general elections. The CPI(M), within a few years, emerged as more important than the CPI in some States, and in West Bengal and Kerala it became the dominant member of the United Front governments. However, in 1969 a CPI leader became the Chief Minister of Kerala, at the head of a coalition of "non-Marxist" parties.

Communists now sit in nearly all of the State Legislative Assemblies. They are particularly strong in Kerala and West Bengal, and to a lesser extent in Andhra Pradesh and Bihar. While the CPI and CPI(M) have appreciable strength at the Centre, their roots are in the States and local areas of the country, where they usually play down international and ideological issues and base their appeal on local and regional interests and grievances.

Of all the Communist parties of the world the CPI has been one of the most undisciplined. The Indian Communists, in the opinion of Ellen Roy, wife of the most famous of all Indian Communists, M. N. Roy, "are no different from other Communists, except that they have to their credit probably more mistakes, more turnabouts and somersaults than Communists elsewhere."[50] The CPI has had a number of able leaders, but it has been weakened by personal and ideological differences, and no single leader has emerged, unless S. A. Dange could be given this distinction after the defection of the more extreme leaders in 1964.

Generally speaking, the major shifts in the position of the CPI prior to 1962 were from a leftist to a rightist to a leftist and then to a Maoist or neo-Maoist strategy, and were occasioned largely by directives from Moscow. The rightist strategy regarded imperialism and feudalism as

[49] For the history of the Communist Party of India and its relations with the international Communist movement and with the Soviet Union, see the Selected Bibliography, Political Parties and Elections, pp. 316–317 below.

[50] Ellen Roy, "Indian Party Politics," *The Radical Humanist*, July 24, 1955, p. 356.

the main enemies, and favored a "united front from above," that is, alliance with labor and bourgeois groups and anti-imperialist parties. The leftist strategy regarded capitalism and the bourgeoisie as the main enemies and favored a "united front from below," by alliances with workers, peasants, and petty bourgeoisie. The Maoist or neo-Maoist strategy combined both "right" and "left" strategies by directing its attack against imperialism and feudalism and also by seeking to form a "united front from below."[51]

The major problems of strategy confronting the CPI were to decide who was the principal enemy, what classes should be accepted as allies, what kinds of alliances should be formed with those classes, what should be their attitude toward the Congress Party and toward Nehru himself, and what position should be taken toward Communist China. The latter question caused considerable soul-searching and bitter intra-party debates after the Chinese Communist suppression of the revolt in Tibet and the moves along India's Himalayan frontiers in 1959, and especially after the Chinese attack on India in the North East Frontier Agency and Ladakh in late 1962. The Chinese issue, and the changes within the Communist world which this symbolized, was perhaps the major — but not the sole — factor leading to the split in the CPI in 1964

The CPI entered the 1960's in the same confused state that had characterized it from the beginning, with the handicaps of divided leadership, the absence of a single dominant leader, the stigma of the "failure" of the Communist government in Kerala, the dilemmas created by the Chinese moves, and what seemed to be a growing recognition in the country as a whole that the Communist tactics of working within the democratic system were "Trojan horse" tactics at best. It was still following a policy of apparent cooperation with the Congress at the Centre and strong opposition to the Congress at State and local levels, where questions of national and international moment were of less importance than more immediate issues. As Marshall Windmiller pointed out in 1956, the CPI believed, perhaps quite rightly, "that real power exists primarily at the state level and that control of a mass following either in a particular region or in a trade union organization is more important than holding national office."[52]

In the early 1960's the growing rift between the right and left wings of the CPI, generally identified as being pro-Soviet and pro-Chinese,

[51] For a brilliant analysis of the strategies followed by the international Communist movement at different periods, see John H. Kautsky, *Moscow and the Communist Party of India: A Study in Postwar Evolution of Communist Strategy* (Cambridge, Mass. and New York, 1956), Chaps. 1 and 7.
[52] Marshall Windmiller, "Indian Communism and the New Soviet Line," *Pacific Affairs*, XXIX (December, 1956), p. 361.

broke out into the open, like the Sino-Soviet dispute, and led to a split in the party. After the death, in January 1962, of Ajoy Ghosh, who had been General Secretary of the CPI since 1951 and who had exercised a mollifying and restraining influence in the top circles of the party, a bifurcation of the leadership was created by the appointment of S. A. Dange, leader of the pro-Soviet wing, as Party Chairman, and E. M. S. Namboodiripad, former Chief Minister of Kerala, identified with the pro-Chinese wing, as General Secretary. Namboodiripad was forced to resign in May 1963, "in a bitter factional showdown provoked by the Chinese invasion of India."[53]

In July 1964, the left faction decided to break away from the CPI and form a new Communist party, to be known as the Communist Party of India (Marxist).[54] Since then there have been two major Communist parties, not one, and since the spring of 1969 there have been three. The third was formed by extremists who broke away from the CPI(M), and who called themselves the Communist Party of India (Marxist-Leninist). It consisted mainly of Naxalites, who took their name from Naxalbari, in the Darjeeling District of West Bengal, where in the spring of 1967 major tribal and local disturbances were exploited by Communist extremists and hailed by the Chinese Communists as the "prelude to a violent revolution by hundreds of millions of people throughout India."[55] This third Communist group, however, has been mainly a group of agitators and has not yet attempted to function as a political party. Although it is the best organized political expression of the Maoist "stream" of Indian communism, it does not command the support of the majority of Indian Maoists.

Generally speaking, the CPI has been identified with the Soviet Union, and the CPI(M) with Communist China, but neither has given complete support to its alleged "Big Brother." This is especially true of the CPI(M), which has frequently taken issue with China, especially on China's policies toward India and some of the more violent phases of the "Cultural Revolution" in China, and whose leadership, notably E. M. S. Namboodiripad, former Chief Minister of Kerala, and Jyoti Basu, former Deputy Chief Minister of West Bengal, have been publicly denounced by the Chinese. Actually the difference between the CPI and the CPI(M) are too complex to be explained in terms of a pro-Soviet and pro-Chinese orientation.

[53] Selig S. Harrison, "Indian Reds Oust Party Secretary as Pro-Peking," *The Washington Post*, Feb. 13, 1963.
[54] See John B. Wood, "Observations on the Indian Communist Party Split," *Pacific Affairs*, XXXVIII (Spring, 1965); and J. M. Kaul, "The Split in the C.P.I.," *India Quarterly*, XX (October–December, 1964), 372–390.
[55] "The Darjeeling Peasant Armed Struggle," *Peking Review*, July 14, 1967. See also Bhabani Sen Gupta, "Moscow, Peking, and the Indian Political Scene after Nehru," *Orbis*, XII (Summer, 1968), 549–552.

In each general election the Communists have managed to get about 10 per cent of the total popular vote and to elect representatives to the Lok Sabha and to nearly all of the State Assemblies. In 1962 the CPI won 29 seats in the Lok Sabha, making it the largest opposition party, and 153 seats in State Assemblies. In 1967 the two Communist parties got about 9 per cent of the popular vote, but they substantially increased their representation in the Lok Sabha (23 seats for the CPI and 19 for the CPI(M)) and in the State Assemblies (122 seats for the CPI and 127 for the CPI(M)). In the mid-term elections in 1969 they held their own in Bihar, lost slightly in the Punjab, and scored heavily in West Bengal (the CPI(M) increased its seats from 43 to 80 and the CPI from 16 to 30). The representation of the CPI in Uttar Pradesh was reduced from 14 to 4, while that of the CPI(M) remained at one.

In a challenging and provocative study published in 1969 Mohan Ram, an Indian journalist who has been a long-time student of Indian communism, wrote:

> The Indian communist movement now comprises four segments: two non-Maoist parties — the Communist Party of India and the Communist Party of India (Marxist), a Maoist party — the Communist Party of India (Marxist-Leninist), and a potential Maoist party which can consolidate the numerous Maoist groups which have chosen to keep out of the Communist Party of India (Marxist-Leninist). But whatever the number [of] communist parties India is likely to have in the future, it is certain that it will have two distinct streams — a Maoist stream and a non-Maoist stream and the contradiction between them will be an antagonistic one barring unification.[56]

Ram regards the differences between the CPI and the CPI(M) as less serious than they seem, and he feels that a merger of the two non-Maoist Communist parties might eventuate. The Maoist "stream", although smaller than the non-Maoist "stream", is more dynamic and potentially more challenging to the Indian political system. The non-Maoist Communist parties are willing to work within the system, without abandoning the objective of destroying it, while the Maoists insist on functioning outside of the system and are dedicated to armed struggle.

The general picture that emerges is that the Communist parties in India have obtained a conspicuous but still minor position in the national political scene, that the CPI is not a really important force in

[56] Mohan Ram, *Indian Communism: Split Within a Split* (Delhi, 1969), p. 267.

any State, except in West Bengal and Kerala, where it is clearly over-shadowed by the CPI(M), and that the CPI(M) is even weaker in most States than the CPI, with the conspicuous exceptions of Kerala and West Bengal. The strength of the Maoist party and other Maoist groups is still indeterminate, but due regard should be given to Mohan Ram's warning that "the Maoist challenge in India will be real."[57]

Since the split in 1964, the intensification of the Sino-Soviet dispute, and the formation of a Maoist party in 1969, the positions of the Indian Communist parties have been even more uncertain than previously, and their internal divisions more apparent. They stand ready, however, to exploit local grievances and dissatisfactions and to capitalize on the continued weaknesses of the other opposition parties and the growing weakness of the divided Congress Party. The CPI and CPI(M) are supporting Mrs. Gandhi against the organization Congress, and she may be forced to enter into some kind of election understanding with them and may even have to include some members of one or both in a coalition government. Thus if the position of the divided Congress party at national, State, and local levels, as well as the political situation generally, continues to deteriorate, the future prospects for communism in India may be much brighter than they presently appear.

## Regional and Local Parties

A study of the composition of the Lok Sabha would give the casual observer the impression that the political parties of India consist of the two Congress parties, and the six other parties that have been given special attention in this chapter, plus, as a result of the 1967 elections, a strong State party — the DMK — in Tamil Nadu. On regional, State, and local levels, however, a very different picture emerges. In addition to the eight national parties — all of which, except the two Congress parties, are really regional or State parties — a plethora of other so-called parties exists. Some of these are of great significance in their localities; some, indeed, can give the Congress stiff competition in these areas. They usually are built around a few leading personalities and emphasize communal, caste, or sectional interests and loyalties. Special mention may be made of other communal parties, other left-wing socialist parties, tribal parties, certain electoral coalitions, and a major conservative party in Orissa.

**Communal Parties.** The Jana Sangh, the RSS, the Hindu Maha-sabha, and the Ram Rajya Parishad are orthodox Hindu groupings, with a strong Brahman influence. There are many other communal groupings, some representing or largely supported by lower-caste Hin-

[57] *Ibid.*, p. 271.

dus or by untouchables and others which are non-Hindu in character.

The leading party of India's untouchables is the Republican Party of India, formerly the Scheduled Castes Federation. This party has been in existence for many years. Its leader, until his death in 1957, was Dr. B. R. Ambedkar, the most famous of India's untouchables. Its main strength has been among the Mahar untouchables of Maharashtra. It has had a small representation in both the Lok Sabha and the Rajya Sabha, but it has never been a truly national party. In 1967 it won 2 seats in the Andhra Pradesh Assembly, one in Bihar, 2 in Haryana, 2 in Mysore, 3 in the Punjab, and 9 in Uttar Pradesh. Its aim is to gain for India's untouchables a status equal to or at least approaching that of the caste Hindus, socially, economically, and politically. Obviously, however, it will be a long time before the nearly 60 million untouchables of India will be able to emerge from the lowly position to which their ancestors were confined for centuries by the rigidities of the Hindu caste system.

In the Tamil-speaking areas of South India — chiefly in the State of Madras — the Dravidian movement has won considerable popular support. This movement "is essentially a social protest of the Tamil masses against Brahmans and even elite non-Brahmans at the top of the caste hierarchy" and "a channel for protest against alleged north Indian economic imperialism. Indeed, as an alliance of aggrieved Tamil castes, the movement typifies the political potential of regional caste groups united behind a catch-all slogan against a 'foreign' scapegoat." It has taken political expression in the "Blackshirt" movement, "composed of two kindred groups, the Dravida Kazhagam or Dravidian Federation, and the Dravida Munnetra Kazhagam or Dravidian Progressive Federation."[58]

Major credit — or blame — for "the Tamilization of politics" in Madras must be given to two of the most fascinating political leaders to emerge in South India in the twentieth century: E. V. Ramaswami Naicker, whom his followers knew as "Periyar" or "Great Sage," and C. N. Annadurai, whom his countless admirers affectionately called "Anna." In 1938 Periyar became President of the Justice Party (the South Indian Liberal Federation), founded in 1917 and dedicated to the cause of the non-Brahmans of South India. Under the leadership of Periyar the party demanded the creation of Dravidasthan, a separate state in Tamilnad. In 1944 Periyar reorganized the party as the Dravida Kazhagam and proclaimed its goal to be an independent Dravidasthan. It also had a strong anti-Brahman, anti-British, and anti-religious character. It emphasized the necessity of preserving the "Dra-

[58] Harrison, *India: The Most Dangerous Decades*, pp. 122, 124, 188.

vidian tradition and Tamil culture," and it "encouraged the [Tamil] community to raise its status as a whole through political activity."[59]

C. N. Annadurai, 29 years younger than Periyar, was an active member of the Justice Party and one of Periyar's chief lieutenants in the DK. He was gradually alienated from his political *guru* by the latter's autocratic and anti-democratic ways. Periyar's marriage in 1949, when he was 72 years of age, to a girl of 28 was apparently the last straw for Annadurai, who seceded from the DMK and founded the Dravida Munnetra Kazhagam (DMK), which soon overshadowed the DK. "Using the symbols of common culture within Tamilnad, harking back to the glories of the Dravidian past, and dwelling upon the social oppression suffered by the non-Brahmin at the hands of the Brahmin, the Bania, and the Aryan North, the party attempted to mold the masses into a self-conscious community."[60] In Annadurai it had a spell-binding orator and a popular mass leader.

In the 1957 elections — the first that it contested — the DMK got about 15 per cent of the popular vote, 15 seats in the Madras Legislative Assembly, and 2 in the Lok Sabha. Thereafter its political rise was rapid. In the fourth general elections in 1967 it scored perhaps the most surprising and the most decisive victory over the Congress in any Indian State. It won 138 of the 234 seats in the Assembly, and returned all 25 of its candidates for the Lok Sabha (making it the third largest opposition party in the national Parliament). The comparable figures for the once-dominant Congress were 139 and 31. Annadurai formed a wholly DMK government in Madras. As Chief Minister he worked effectively with the Government of India, while at the same time he asserted the rights of the States and the special linguistic, regional, and cultural claims of his State, which was renamed Tamil Nadu.

The death of its great leader in February 1969 and growing personal rivalries and difficulties within the party have confronted the DMK with fresh problems. In all probability it will not be able to regain the strength and enthusiastic support that it enjoyed in 1967, but it will continue to be a major force — perhaps the major force — in Madras State. It has been by far the most successful of the many State parties that have emerged in post-independence India.

The most important of the non-Hindu communal parties is the Shiromani Akali Dal, the major Sikh political — and social — organization.

---

[59] Robert L. Hardgrave, Jr., "Religion, Politics, and the DMK," in Donald E. Smith, ed., *South Asian Politics and Religion* (Princeton, 1966), pp. 213, 216, 222. See also Robert Hardgrave, Jr., *The Dravidian Movement* (Bombay, 1965).

[60] Hardgrave, "Religion, Politics, and the DMK," p. 224.

Founded in the early 1930's, with headquarters in the precincts of the Golden Temple in Amritsar, the holy city of the Sikhs, it controlled the Shiromani Gurdwara Parbandhak Committee (SGPC), a committee for the management of the gurdwaras (Sikh shrines or temples), and also was active in political affairs. Religiously it stood for "the protection of the Panth" (the Sikh religion, group, or community). Politically, according to its Constitution, it stood for "the creation of an environment in which the Sikh national expression finds its full satisfaction." Its political objective led it to demand a Punjabi Suba, or Punjabi-speaking State. In pursuance of its objective it followed what Baldev Raj Nayar has described as three strategies: constitutional, infiltrational, and agitational.[61]

For a third of a century the leader of the Akali Dal, Master Tara Singh, one of the most colorful personalities in twentieth-century India, bestrode "the Sikh political world like a colossus." From 1930 to 1962 the President of the Akali Dal "was either Master Tara Singh himself, one of his protégés, or a party leader loyal to him."[62] In 1962, however, his chief lieutenant, Sant Fateh Singh, established a rival branch of the Akali Dal, which gradually became more influential than the Master's group.

Although the Akali Dal took part in the general elections, it was overwhelmed by the Congress until 1967. In October 1966, however, its long-standing and hard-pressed demand for a Punjabi Suba was finally granted, with the splitting up of the Punjab into two States: (1) the Punjab, where most of the Sikhs lived, and (2) Haryana, largely Hindi-speaking. Master Tara Singh died in 1968. Before the midterm elections in 1969 the two wings of the Akali Dal merged, under the leadership of Sant Fateh Singh. The reunited party elected more members to the Assembly than did the Congress, and, in a strange coalition with the Jana Sangh, formed a government in the Punjab. Thus the Akali Dal, long a religious, social, and cultural force in the Punjab, has become a powerful political force as well.

After partition most of the Muslims who remained in the Union of India, including most of those who had supported the Muslim League for many years, left the League and entered into other political groupings. In Pakistan the League was the dominant party for some years, occupying a position comparable to the Congress Party in India; but in India it ceased to have any great political significance. There is, however, an all-Indian Muslim League, and it has some strength in

[61] Baldev Raj Nayar, *Minority Politics in the Punjab* (Princeton, 1966), Chap. VI.
[62] Baldev Raj Nayar, "Sikh Separatism in the Punjab," in Smith, ed., *South Asian Politics and Religion,* p. 170.

the South. In Kerala it has been an important political force, joining with the Congress in anti-Communist coalitions, with both the left and right Communists in a United Front against the Congress, and with the right Communists in a United Front against the left Communists. In 1967 it elected 2 members to the Lok Sabha and 14 to the Kerala State Assembly (where the Congress representation was reduced to 9!).

Many extreme left-wing socialist parties exist in India. Some of these are hardly distinguishable from Communist-front and fellow-traveler organizations, but others are able to preserve a distinction between their socialism and the Communist variety. Foremost among these groups is the Peasants' and Workers' Party, which has some strength in the West and South of India, mainly in Maharashtra. Others are the Forward Bloc, with some strength in West Bengal and Tamil Nadu, and the Revolutionary Socialist Party, with some following in Kerala and West Bengal.

**Tribal Parties.** Best known of the many tribal parties is the Jharkhand Party, which draws its main support from tribal groups in the State of Bihar. Founded in 1945 by Jaipal Singh, a tribal who held an M.A. degree with honors from Oxford, where he won an Oxford blue, and a long-time member of the Lok Sabha, the Jharkhand Party has had its ups and downs in Bihar. In 1962 it elected 3 members to the Lok Sabha and 20 to the Bihar Assembly. In 1967 it did not contest the elections as a separate party, having presumably merged with the Congress, but it re-emerged as the Hul Jharkhand and won 10 Assembly seats in the 1969 mid-term elections.

Other tribal parties of some significance are the All-Party Hill Leaders' Conference (APHLC), which was mainly responsible for the creation in 1970 of an "autonomous" tribal state of Meghalaya within the State of Assam, and the Nata National Organization in Nagaland.

**Electoral Coalitions.** Many electoral coalitions and arrangements were entered into by minor parties — and sometimes even by major parties as well — in each of the general elections, and in almost all of the other elections that have been held in India. Most of these are arrangements of convenience and do not survive long after the voting occurs. The most common form is an election arrangement among parties to the left or right of the Congress for the purpose of defeating Congress candidates and electing agreed-upon candidates instead. Occasionally the Congress itself has entered into such agreements, as in the Andhra elections in 1955 and in the Kerala elections in 1960, in each case to defeat a strong challenge by the Communists.

Two unusually important and durable coalitions came into existence in what was then Bombay State shortly before the general elections in 1957, to support the demands for separate linguistic states in Maharashtra and Gujarat and to defeat the Congress candidates by opposing them with a single slate. In Maharashtra the coalition was known as the Samyukta Maharashtra Samiti, and in Gujarat as the Mahagujarat Janata Parishad. These were strange coalitions, uniting political parties and groups as widely divergent as Hindu communal parties, the PSP, the Peasants' and Workers' Party, and the CPI. Each elected some members of the Lok Sabha and each scored striking successes in elections to the Bombay Legislative Assembly. Needless to say, the CPI benefited particularly from these electoral arrangements. Thanks to the coalition support, and to astute bargaining and pressures in selecting and placing its candidates, it elected several members to the Lok Sabha — one, the well-known veteran Communist, S. A. Dange, from a constituency in Bombay City by the largest plurality of any candidate for the Lok Sabha in all of India — and it increased its representation in the State Assembly from 1 to 18. Both coalitions refused to accept the decision of the Congress Party not to divide Bombay State, and by their successful tactics and unremitting agitation they were undoubtedly instrumental in forcing Nehru, the Congress high command, and the Indian Government to reverse their decision and to create, in May 1960, the separate states of Maharashtra and Gujarat.

Once this major piece of political surgery had been accomplished, the *raison d'être* of the two highly successful electoral arrangements in former Bombay State disappeared. The Samyukhta Maharashtra Samiti, without the support of some of the parties that had been responsible for its formation, has lingered on in Maharashtra, but it has been hardly more than a weak front for the Communists.

Two of the most successful, and most bizarre, electoral coalitions were the two United Fronts that came into existence in West Bengal and Kerala prior to the fourth general elections in 1967. They were both dominated by the left Communists, and both included many parties, very different in character and aims. Both were anti-Congress coalitions. The United Front in Kerala was composed of the two Communist parties, the Muslim League, the SSP, the Revolutionary Socialist Party, the Kerala Socialist Party, and the Karshaka Thozhalali Party. In Bengal the Front consisted of no fewer than fourteen parties and groups, of which the most important were the two Communist parties and the Bangla Congress. For a time after the 1967 elections these two United Fronts were in power in Kerala and West Bengal.

The Bangla Congress in West Bengal and the Kerala Congress in Kerala were outstanding examples of political groups that were formed almost exclusively by dissident Congressmen. Each was confined to one State, but some groupings of Congress dissidents cut across State lines. An outstanding example was the Bharatiya Kranti Dal, which won 98 seats in the Uttar Pradesh Assembly in the mid-term elections of 1969 and which for a time was a key group in both an anti-Congress coalition government and a Congress(R)-dominated government. The BKD also won six seats in the Bihar Assembly in 1969. It attempted to take the lead in organizing a national party, in association with the Bangla Congress, the Kerala Congress, the Janta Congress in Madhya Pradesh and Orissa, and other groups of dissident Congressmen, but these attempts met with little success.

# *  *10*  *

# Elections and
# Electoral Procedures

Since most of the people of India not only had had no experience in the electoral process, but also were illiterate and in other respects seemingly unprepared to play a responsible role as free citizens in a democratic society, the decision of the Constituent Assembly and the Government of India to give every adult Indian, male or female, the privilege of the franchise, under a system of universal and direct suffrage, was truly momentous. It was, as the Election Commission later characterized it, "an act of faith — faith in the common man of India and in his practical common sense."[1]

### India's "Act of Faith"

Part XV (Articles 324–329) of the Indian Constitution dealt with elections. It gave the vote to every citizen of India who was not less than 21 years of age, except those who were mentally unsound or who had been found guilty of criminal or corrupt practices; it decreed that there should be "one general electoral roll for every territorial constituency for election to either House of Parliament or to . . . the Legislature of a State"; it created an Election Commission charged with "the superintendence, direction and control of the preparation of the electoral rolls" and with the conduct of all elections to Parliament, to the State Legislatures, and to the offices of President and Vice-President of the Indian Union; and it empowered the central Parliament and the State Legislatures, within their respective spheres, to make provi-

[1] Government of India, Election Commission, *Report on the First General Elections in India, 1951–52* (New Delhi, 1955), I, 10.

sion "with respect to all matters relating to . . . elections to either House of Parliament or to . . . the Legislature of a State including preparation of electoral rolls, the delimitation of constituencies and all other matters necessary for securing the due constitution of such House or Houses."

Under the Government of India Act of 1935, separate electorates or reserved legislative seats were provided for no fewer than fifteen different categories of voters. The question of separate electorates had been highly controversial for many years, especially after the British granted the Muslim requests for a separate status in elections as early as 1909. Gandhi and the leaders of the Indian National Congress generally were opposed to separate electorates, in principle and in practice. The framers of the Indian Constitution would have none of them. Article 325 of the Constitution stated that "no person shall be eligible for inclusion . . . in any special electoral roll . . . on grounds only of religion, race, caste, sex or any of them." Articles 330 and 332, however, provided for reserved seats in the House of the People and in every State Assembly in Part A and Part B States for "Scheduled Castes," meaning untouchables, and "Scheduled Tribes." These seats were to be filled by representatives of these "backward" groups, but not by a system of separate electorates. Instead, all voters in the constituencies affected were to vote for these representatives. Hence, in such constituencies two, or sometimes three, members were elected by all the eligible voters who exercise their franchise.

The only other special arrangement for particular groups in the Constitution related to the Anglo-Indian community. Article 331 empowered the President of the Union of India, if he decided that this community was not adequately represented in the House of the People, to nominate not more than two members to the House.

According to the Constitution, both the provisions for reserved seats for scheduled castes and tribes and for the nomination of representatives of the Anglo-Indian community were to "cease to have effect" after ten years. These provisions were renewed in 1960 and again in late 1969.

Because of its "act of faith" India became the great testing ground of the adaptability and workability of universal adult suffrage in free and secret elections in underdeveloped countries. In most of the newly independent countries universal suffrage has not been given a fair test, if it has been tried at all, and even in cases where reasonably free elections have been held, the results have seldom been encouraging.[2]

In India the principle of giving every adult Indian the ballot was

[2] See T. E. Smith, *Elections in Developing Countries* (New York, 1960).

accepted in the Constituent Assembly with remarkably little opposition. Second thoughts on the wisdom of the decision in favor of direct, secret elections have doubtless been occasioned by the unhappy experience with such elections in neighboring Asian countries and, above all, by the considerable success of the Indian Communists in their efforts to use the ballot box for their own ends, which are clearly not in consanance with the basic goals of democratic India. There has, however, been relatively little open objection in India to the principle of direct elections, and the Indian experience with elections in the years following the adoption of the Constitution has on the whole been encouraging.

Five nationwide general elections — the world's largest democratic elections — have been held, in 1951–52, 1957, 1962, 1967, and 1971; and in 1969 "mid-term" elections were held in five Indian States — West Bengal, Uttar Pradesh, Bihar, the Punjab, and Nagaland — with about two-fifths of the total population of India.

While there have been many examples of minor violations and a great deal of evidence of a lack of understanding of the purposes and procedures of voting, these elections have been impressive demonstrations of the ability of a largely illiterate people to exercise the franchise wisely. The conduct and results of the several State elections and many by-elections that have been held since 1950 have not always been so satisfactory or encouraging, but these too have usually been carried out without major incidents or acts of violence.

## Preparations for First General Elections

In April 1950, the Constituent Assembly, still functioning as the Indian Parliament, passed the first electoral law, which dealt with the registration and qualifications of voters. Even before that date the Election Commission, headed by the able Sukumar Sen as Chief Election Commissioner, began to prepare for the first general elections. This was in itself a tremendous task, and there was considerable urgency about it since the elections were originally scheduled for the spring of 1950. They were actually held in the winter of 1951–52. By that time over 173 million voters had been registered by more than 1,600 registrars, mainly on the basis of a house-to-house canvass throughout the country. There were special problems arising from linguistic complications, the difficulty of obtaining accurate names in a country where varying practices are followed in this respect and where many people are known by the same designation, the ambiguous status of hundreds of thousands of refugees from Pakistan, and the virtual impossibility of obtaining reliable information in "backward" areas. In the preliminary rolls some 4 million women were registered simply as the "wife of — " or "daughter of — ." When the registration officials, upon instructions from Sukumar Sen, tried to get the proper names of these women, 2,800,000 of them refused to give such information, and were accordingly struck off the rolls.

Another difficult task was the delimitation of the constituencies. This was accomplished only after lengthy deliberation and debate. Eventually 3,772 constituencies were demarcated, 489 for the Lok Sabha and 3,283 for the State Assemblies. In the Part A and Part B States each M.P. would therefore represent some 720,000 persons. In addition to the general seats, 477 seats were assigned to scheduled castes and 192 to scheduled tribes, on the basis of population. Since the third general elections, all constituencies have been single member constituencies, with some reserved for candidates from scheduled castes and scheduled tribes (77 and 37, respectively, in 1967).

To make the procedures of voting as simple as possible and to instruct the voters in these procedures, a great deal of advance preparation was obviously necessary. Because of the shortage of election officials and some special problems of geography and climate, the voting was scheduled at different times in different places, extending over a period of some four months, from October 25, 1951 to February 21, 1952, although most of the voters went to the polls in January 1952. Some 900,000 government employees, including thousands of teachers, were used as election officials.

To obviate some of the problems created by the illiteracy of perhaps 80 per cent of the voters, symbols and the multiple ballot box scheme were employed. Each of the many parties was assigned a symbol, either by the national Election Commission or by a State Election Commission. Fourteen of the larger parties were recognized as national parties, and each was assigned a symbol for its exclusive use throughout the country. The symbols could not have special political or religious significance; thus no party was allowed to use a picture of Gandhi, or a cow, or the charka wheel (which appears on the Indian flag), or a hammer and sickle. Some of the parties, however, benefited greatly from the symbols assigned to them. The Congress Party, for example, obtained approval for a pair of bullocks as its symbol, and this suggested all kinds of favorable connotations. Many Indians could be persuaded that they should certainly not vote against bullocks, which symbolized the source of their livelihood, their main source of power and transportation, and perhaps even their religious faith as well. While the Communists could not use the hammer and sickle, they did obtain approval for a sickle and an ear of corn, a very appealing symbol to the Indian farmer.

In the first two general elections the balloting system of voting was used, since it was felt that this system was the simplest possible one and would be most suitable for a vast, inexperienced, and largely illiterate electorate. Under this system a voter received a ballot paper marked with only a serial number, and he put the ballot, without marking it in any way, inside a ballot box bearing the symbol of the party of his choice. A voter cast two ballots in two booths, for his choices for the Lok Sabha and the State Legislative Assembly.

This system worked reasonably well; at least, most voters seemed to understand it. But it was slow, cumbersome, and expensive, and it gave rise to many difficulties and allegations of fraudulent practices, such as tampering with the ballot boxes, the failure of some voters to insert their ballot papers in the boxes, carrying away ballot papers instead of putting them in the boxes, and other practices arising out of deliberate fraud or ignorance. After the second general elections the Election Commission abandoned this system — except for a few more backward or isolated constituencies — and adopted a marking system.

Since at least 80 parties contested the elections (including individually oriented groups the figure was over 190) in 1951–52, since each polling booth had to contain as many ballot boxes as there were candidates of different parties, some 2,600,000 ballot boxes were required, and 620,000,000 ballot papers were printed, using 170 tons of paper. More than 200,000 polling booths and stations were set up in every part of the country. This large number was necessary because of the decisions that each polling station could effectively accommodate a relatively small number of voters — approximately 1,000 — and that, where possible, there should be a polling station or booth within walking distance of virtually every eligible voter. This latter decision posed major problems of logistics, especially in areas where distances were great and voters were few. Voters came to the polls on foot, by bullock carts, on bicycles, by public conveyance, and by almost every conceivable means of transportation. Parties and candidates were forbidden to provide any form of transportation to the voters, for obvious reasons.

## The First General Elections, 1951–52

India's first general elections were held for 489 seats in the House of the People (for twelve of these seats Congress candidates ran unopposed) and for approximately 3,300 seats in State Legislative Assemblies.[3] Nearly 17,500 candidates ran — or perhaps one should say stood — for these seats. More than one-third of these ran as Independents; only 240 were women. The Congress contested every constituency, but it was the only party to do so. The Socialists entered candidates in some 1,500 constituencies, which proved to be unwise

[3] For details regarding India's first general elections, see "The Indian Experience with Democratic Elections: Results and Procedures (1951–1956)," *Indian Press Digests* Monograph Series, No. 3 (December, 1956); Election Commission, Government of India, *Report on the First General Elections in*

in view of their relatively limited resources and their lack of support in many of the constituencies which they contested. The Communist Party concentrated its efforts in some 500 constituencies where its strength was greatest, and as a result it was more successful in electing its candidates than were the Socialists, even though its popular vote was well below the total votes cast for Socialist Party candidates.

The campaign was conducted by a variety of familiar techniques, such as speeches and meetings, ceaseless travel by the candidates, more or less effective party organization for campaign purposes, handshaking and house-to-house canvassing, extensive use of placards and posters, partisan appeals, and profuse promises. Certain techniques of campaigning extensively employed in Western countries were either not available or were used quite sparingly. Of course India had no television, and parties were not allowed to use the facilities of All-India Radio, the only radio network in the country. The radio was used to instruct voters in voting procedures and to urge them to exercise their privilege and right of the franchise. The election manifestoes of the parties were read over the radio from time to time. Some of the parties and candidates were quite ingenious in developing novel election techniques, and in reaching voters in remote areas. In cities, towns, and even in many villages, placards and posters were everywhere, and loudspeakers mounted on jeeps blared forth the messages of particular parties and candidates in an almost unceasing babel of sound. Truckloads of shouting young people, most of whom were obviously well below the voting age, cruised through the streets and along the highways. Mobs followed candidates through the streets or massed outside of party headquarters. Even elephants and camels were used in electioneering.

It is difficult to isolate the real issues in the election. In a sense there were no real national issues, except those arising from differences in party allegiance or support of different personalities. Broadly speak-

India, 1951–52 (2 vols., Delhi, 1955); S. V. Kogekar and Richard L. Park, eds., *Reports on the Indian General Elections, 1951–52* (Bombay, 1956); Edward R. O'Connor, *India and Democracy — A Study of the 1951–52 General Elections and Their Political Impact* (unpublished doctoral dissertation, Notre Dame University, 1954); Irene Tinker and Mil Walker, "The First General Elections in India and Indonesia," *Far Eastern Survey,* XXV (July, 1956), 97–110; Richard L. Park, "Indian Election Results," *Far Eastern Survey,* XXI (May 7, 1952), 61–70; Taya Zinkin, "The Indian General Elections," *The World Today,* VIII (May, 1952), pp. 181–192, and Ela Sen, "The Indian General Election and After," *The Asiatic Review,* XLVIII (April, 1952), 115–125. Many of the comments on all of the general elections are based on first-hand investigations and impressions of the author, who was in India in 1952–53, shortly after the first general elections and in 1956–57, 1961, 62, and 1966–67, before, during, and after the second, third, and fourth general elections.

ing, in the voting for members of the House of the People, the voters were either voting for or against the Congress. Naturally the magic of Nehru's name, and the memories of Gandhi, were great sources of strength for the Congress; whereas the Congress was vulnerable because over the years it had alienated many people for one reason or another, or because, as the party in power, it could be blamed by almost anyone who was frustrated or unhappy with his lot in life. In the elections for members of the State Assemblies local issues and grievances were predominant. These varied from State to State, and indeed from constituency to constituency.

On the whole, India's first nationwide elections went off well, and were an encouraging demonstration that masses of voters, mostly illiterate, could act with dignity and with a fair measure of judgment in selecting those who would represent them in the central Parliament and the State Assemblies. The actual process of voting, though simplified, was a new and strange experience for most of the voters — an experience at once frightening and exhilarating. Very often long lines queued in front of the polling places, usually divided into two lines, one for men, the other for women. This division was almost invariably the case in rural areas. In the cities, however, single lines were common, and in almost every instance people of many different religions and castes, including even the lowly untouchables, stood in the same line together. After having his name checked on the election roll and receiving a ballot, and after an official placed a drop of indelible ink on his hand, to ensure against anyone's voting more than once, the voter normally cast a ballot in a curtained area for a candidate for the State Assembly, and then received another ballot, which he thereupon cast for his choice for the House of the People. In double-member constituencies the voter cast two votes in each instance instead of one. This was a source of some confusion, and accounted for many of the 1,635,000 votes which were invalidated. Many other voters left their ballots on top of the ballot boxes, or on the floor in the booth, instead of dropping them into the ballot boxes, and hence their votes too were thrown out as invalid.

Most of the people took their electoral responsibilities seriously. The turnout of voters was impressive, except in a few parts of the country, as in most of Rajasthan. Of the 176,000,000 eligible voters, 88,600,000, or slightly more than 50 per cent, actually voted, and nearly 106,000,000 valid votes were cast.

It is of course impossible to determine what considerations motivated the Indian people in their exercise of their new democratic privilege of the franchise. Undoubtedly bloc voting, on a village, caste, association, or sectional basis, was fairly widespread. Apparently many villagers, in particular, voted as the headman or the village elders instructed them to do, and many women voted in accordance with their husbands' instructions. Doubtless many voted for the symbols rather than for the parties. This often led to invalid practices, such as the extreme example of a man who wanted to vote for the tree — the symbol of the Socialist Party — and who took his ballot out of the polling place and deposited it atop a tree. Some voters, especially women, appeared to regard the process of voting as a ritual or as a religious ceremony. Occasionally they worshipped the ballot box and left some kind of offering beside it, or on top of it, or even in it. On the whole, however, the people, with some diffidence and hesitation, followed the proper procedures, and seemed to vote with discretion. The numerous cases of invalid voting, and the few cases of attempted use of fraudulent methods, such as impersonation or voting more than once, were exceptions to the generally efficient conduct of the election. For this considerable credit must go to the Election Commission for the careful preparations which it made for the elections, and to the army of nearly a million election officials and police who supervised the actual voting, but the main credit must go to the people themselves, who rose to the occasion in a truly impressive way.

The Congress Party, while polling less than half (about 45 per cent) of the votes cast for members of the House of the People, won nearly 75 per cent of the seats and continued to be dominant at the Centre. The next largest group consisted of the 27 Communists and their allies. While the Socialist Party polled about twice as many votes as the Communists, it won only 12 seats. The reasons for this have already been suggested: the Socialists spread themselves too thin, whereas the Communists concentrated on fewer constituencies where they had appreciable strength. No other party got enough members to be of any real significance, although two others, the KMPP (which shortly after the elections merged with the Socialists to form the Praja Socialist Party) and the Jana Sangh, received more than 3 per cent of the total vote and therefore retained their status as recognized national parties. Large numbers of Independents contested the election, and while many of these were among the nearly 9,200 candidates for Parliament and the State Assemblies who forfeited their deposits because they did not receive one-sixth of the total votes cast in their constituencies, 37 Independents were elected to the House of the People.

For the State Assemblies the results were not markedly different, except in a few States. In total votes cast the Congress fared almost as well in the States as on the national level, gaining nearly 45 per cent of the total votes and about 2,250 of the approximately 3,300 seats. The Socialists and KMPP together won 205 seats. No other party had much success on an all-India level, although the CPI won 62 seats in the Madras Assembly, 34 seats in the Assembly of Travancore-Cochin, 28 in the West Bengal Assembly, and a few seats in other State Assemblies. The Congress won a clear majority of seats in all of the States except Orissa, where the Ganatantra Parishad scored some successes, in PEPSU (Patiala and East Punjab States Union), where Sikh political groups were strong, in Travancore-Cochin, where the Communists scored heavily, and in Madras, where Communists in the Andhra area and pro-Dravidian groups in Tamilnad represented a formidable opposition. In Rajasthan the Congress had a bare majority, and in West Bengal the Congress majority was achieved largely by solid support in the rural areas, against the strong Communist opposition in the city of Calcutta.

Despite many gloomy predictions, the prospects for democracy in India seemed brighter after the general elections than they had before. Leaders of the Congress Party were alarmed because, in spite of their overwhelming successes in electing candidates to both the House of the People and the State Assemblies, less than half of the voters had cast their ballots for Congress candidates, and there were disturbing signs of a trend away from the Congress in many parts of the country. Particularly disturbing, also, were the signs that the CPI had considerable support, and that on local levels many political groups or alliances which championed ideas inimical to the unity of the nation had attracted so many votes. An encouraging result was that the Hindu communalist parties had on the whole fared so badly. The large number of Independents who were successful in their campaigns indicated that many thousands of Indian voters were unwilling to throw their support to any party.

## State Elections and States Reorganization, 1954–56

Between 1952 and 1955 by-elections were held in many parts of India for seats in both the House of the People and State Assemblies which had been vacated because of death or resignation or other reasons. Important elections were held in three of the States — in PEPSU and Travancore-Cochin in 1954, and in Andhra in 1955. All three State elections were necessitated by the failure of the Congress Party to maintain a working majority in the State Assembly. In PEPSU and Andhra the situation had become so unstable that President's rule, under the emergency provisions of the Constitution of India, had been imposed.

In PEPSU the State-wide elections held early in 1954 helped to clarify the atmosphere, for the Congress won a clear majority of seats in the State Assembly, and the new Congress Ministry proved to be both more efficient and more honest than the Congress Government that had ruled uneasily before President's rule was proclaimed.

Unlike the outcome in PEPSU, the elections of 1954 in Travancore-Cochin did nothing to clear the political atmosphere. Even though top Congress leaders toured the State — Nehru himself spent six days there and was well received — the Congress was unable to increase its membership in the State Assembly. The opposition leftist parties agreed to run only one candidate in each constituency against the Congress candidate, so that straight contests were fought in all of the constituencies. Of the 117 legislative seats the Congress won 45, the Communists 29, and the PSP 18. Since the Congress Party could not carry on by itself, and since the last thing it wanted was a Communist government in the State, it reluctantly threw its support to the PSP, which thereupon organized a government under its leader, P. T. Pillai. The minority government of the PSP continued in office, if not in power, until the spring of 1956, when President's rule was again imposed. This was the situation in Kerala — as the former State of Travancore-Cochin, with slightly different boundaries, was called after the States' reorganization went into effect in November 1956 — at the time of the second general elections a year later, which brought into office the first Communist government in any Indian State.

When the new State of Andhra Pradesh was created in October 1953, a Congress government was installed, even though the Congress did not have a majority in the State Assembly. In November 1954, the Communists, who held almost as many seats in the Assembly as did the Congress, were able to bring down the Congress Ministry, but they were not given a chance to form a government themselves. Instead, the Central Government assumed direct control, under President's rule, until new elections could be held. There seemed to be every prospect that Andhra would become India's first Communist-ruled State. It had long been a center of Communist strength. This time, however, the Congress mobilized its biggest guns and had considerable success in working with minor parties and independent candidates to form a united front against the Communists.

The voting took place over a five-day period in late February 1955, and the outcome was an overwhelming debacle for the Communists. The Congress and its allies gained a decisive majority of 196 seats in the new States Assembly, while the Communists were reduced to a feeble minority. Even the leader and deputy leader of the Communist Party in Andhra were defeated.[4] Since 1955 the Communists have

[4] For a summary of the results of the Andhra elections of 1955, see A. M. Rosenthal, "India Reds Routed in Andhra Voting," dispatch from New Delhi, March 2, 1955, in the *New York Times,* March 3, 1955. For background information, see Selig S. Harrison, *India: The Most Dangerous Decades* (Princeton, N.J., 1960), pp. 237–245.

never regained the political strength in Telegu-speaking areas which they had in the troubled years when the new State of Andhra was born.

Before the second general elections were held a major feat of political surgery was carried out in India by the reorganization of the Indian States, and the reduction of their number from 29 to 14. This reorganization became effective on November 1, 1956, only a few weeks before the second elections were scheduled to be held. After the Congress Ministry yielded on the issue of the creation of a new State of Andhra Pradesh, thus giving the Telegu-speaking peoples a State of their own, the linguistic demands in other areas could hardly be denied. Once Nehru and his associates were convinced that it was unavoidable, they tried to evolve some pattern of reorganization which would be generally acceptable to the linguistically oriented peoples of the South, in particular, without destroying the bases of Indian unity; and they were anxious to effect the reorganization soon so as not to interfere with the second general elections or with the prospects of the Congress Party in those elections. In this effort they were largely successful. Linguistic issues were not decisive factors in the general elections, with the notable exception of Bombay State and to a lesser degree of the Punjab — the only parts of India where linguistic demands had not been largely satisfied by the reorganization of the States.

## The Second General Elections, 1957

Whereas the first general elections were extended over a period of nearly four months, with most of the voting in January 1952, the second general elections were confined — except for a few remote areas where special problems existed — to a period of three weeks, from February 24 to March 14, 1957.[5] With the experience of the first nationwide elections, many by-elections, and three State elections behind it, the Election Commission was able to prepare for the second general elections with greater ease and dispatch than for the first,

[5] For the background of the second general elections, see S. L. Poplai, ed., *National Politics and 1957 Elections in India* (Delhi, 1957); note especially the excellent bibliography which is included as Appendix "C" (pp. 169–172). For the details of the second general elections see Myron Weiner and Rajni Kothari, eds., *Indian Voting Behavior: Studies of the 1962 General Elections* (Calcutta, 1965); R. James Roach, "India's 1957 Elections," *Far Eastern Survey*, XXVI (May, 1957), 65–78; Bodh Raj Sharma, "Some Reflections on the Second General Elections in India," *The Indian Journal of Political Science*, XIX (January–March, 1958), 73–77; "India's Second Elections," *The World Today*, XIII (June, 1957), 232–241; Phillips Talbot, "The Second General Elections: Voting in the States," a report, dated Bombay, April 28, 1957, issued by the American Universities Field Staff; "Analysis of Election Results," *India News*, April 15, 1957.

even though the number of eligible voters had increased by nearly 20,000,000. The 2,600,000 ballot boxes which had been assembled for the first general elections were available for the second, so that only an additional 500,000 were required. Nearly one million government officials, including teachers and police, were needed to supervise the voting, but many of those who were recruited for the task had served in 1951–52 and thus were generally familiar this time with their duties. It was still a gigantic task, however, to hold "the world's largest election."

Even more than in 1951–52 the second general election was an election without issues, as far as national politics were concerned. Except for the communalist parties and the Communists, most of the parties which had any pretensions to functioning on a nationwide basis were agreed on basic approaches to national and international issues. Most of the voters and parties were concerned with local issues and grievances, and on this level a number of issues did exist. Some of these centered more on differences in personalities than on issues, but a number of rather influential local parties or alliances, such as the Ganatantra Parishad in Orissa, the Dravida Munnetra Kazhagham in Madras, and, above all, the Samyukta Maharashtra Samiti and the Mahagujarat Janata Parishad in Bombay, took positions which were opposed to the official policies of the Congress in certain fundamental respects. Writing shortly after the second elections an American political scientist who had observed the elections remarked:

> The campaign was rich in clichés and rigorous in avoiding issues. . . . In India this is, at least in part, the result of a general attitude . . . of uncritical, unexamined acceptance of the correctness of the decisions of those who govern. . . . [There is] a certain lack of reality in Indian politics in that the public concern with politics is rarely with anything fundamental.[6]

As in 1951–52, electoral alliances and arrangements were formed in a few States, often composed of heterogeneous elements whose only apparent bond of unity was the desire to defeat Congress candidates. The most elaborate of these alliances were those in West Bengal and in Bombay State. Within some of the parties considerable divergence of opinion developed over the wisdom and desirability of entering into electoral arrangements with other groups which were hardly ideological bedfellows. In the Punjab, where linguistic and religious issues were fairly significant, the major Sikh political organization, the Akali Dal, agreed to support Congress candidates. The best known leader of the

[6] Roach, "India's 1957 Elections," p. 76.

Akali Dal, Master Tara Singh, repudiated this agreement on the eve of the voting, but most of the members of his party refused to follow his advice. A heated debate raged within the top circles of the PSP regarding the question of entering into electoral arrangements with the Communists. Jayaprakash Narayan favored such arrangements, on the ground that this was the only way to build up an effective opposition to the Congress. Asoka Mehta, however, was strongly opposed, on the ground that entering into alliances with the Communists was playing into the hands of a group which was basically opposed to the democratic system. The compromise which the PSP reached was strictly a pragmatic one. The party took a stand of general opposition to the arrangements with the Communists, but authorized them where local leaders deemed them to be necessary. As a result in some States, notably in Bombay State, the PSP joined with the Communists and often with other parties in anti-Congress arrangements.

Shortly before the voting was held in Bombay State *The Times of India* predicted confidently: "National and economic issues rather than regional or linguistic appeals will sway the vote with the great mass of the electorate in the new composite State of Bombay in the coming general elections." No prediction could have been more wrong. As Phillips Talbot observed, "The voters of Bombay entered this election campaign in the wake of an unprecedented, protracted emotional jag over group loyalties based on regional cultures and languages."[7] On the linguistic issue virtually all the opposition parties in Maharashtra joined in a united front called the Samyukta Maharashtra Samiti; and in the Gujarat section of Bombay State some of the parties joined in a looser and less inclusive anti-Congress arrangement which was called the Mahagujarat Janata Parishad.

In West Bengal there were three separate electoral arrangements: (1) the United Election Committee, composed of the five main leftist parties, the Communists, the PSP, the Revolutionary Socialists, the Forward Bloc, and the Marxist Forward Bloc; (2) the United Left Front, composed of eight other small leftist parties; and (3) the United Democratic People's Front, composed of a coalition within a coalition called the National Democratic Party (the Hindu Mahasabha, the Jana Sangh, and the Ram Rajya Parishad), plus a section of the Revolutionary Communist Party of India and some dissident Congressmen.

In 1957 the Indian people voted with more confidence and, presumably, with greater understanding and judgment than they had in 1951–52. Many of the fears and suspicions which had kept thousands of eligible voters from registering properly, or from casting valid ballots,

[7] Talbot, "The Second General Elections: Voting in the States."

were removed by 1957. Most of the women who had refused to give their own names now understood why this personal concession was necessary and were at last convinced that this was not a betrayal of confidence to which their husbands alone should be privy. Voters who had previously placed ballots outside instead of inside the ballot boxes, or who had stuffed the boxes with flowers or grass as votary offerings, now generally understood what the boxes symbolized and where they were expected to deposit their ballots. To be sure, there were still a fair number of cases of attempted impersonation and other irregularities, and more of misunderstanding.

The second general elections did not change the political complexion of India, either on the national or on the State levels; but some of the results were unexpected and even startling. Approximately 60.5 per cent of the 193 million eligible voters actually voted. The Congress got 47.66 per cent of the popular vote. It gained a few seats in the Lok Sabha, but lost 300 to 400 seats in the State Legislative Assemblies. Its heaviest losses in popular votes as well as in Assembly seats were in Kerala and Uttar Pradesh. In Bombay, Bihar, and West Bengal it also lost a number of Assembly seats, even though its percentage of the popular vote increased. So effective were the coalition tactics of the opposition, and so strong was the anti-Congress feeling on the linguistic issue, that six State ministers and three Central Ministers were defeated in Maharashtra and Gujarat. The Congress markedly increased its percentage of the total vote in Assam, Madras, the Punjab, and Rajasthan, as well as in West Bengal and the Telegana district of Andhra. It still retained a clear majority in every Indian State, except in Kerala and Orissa.

The CPI retained about the same number of members in the Lok Sabha, but greatly increased its percentage of the total vote and won substantially more seats in the State Assemblies. It won striking successes in Kerala, West Bengal, and Bombay. In Uttar Pradesh it increased its strength from one in 1952 to nine, and it placed at least one member in every other State Assembly. In Kerala its popular vote was less than that of the Congress, but it won 60 seats as compared with 43 for the Congress, and with the help of five Independents whom it had supported it had a narrow majority in the Kerala Assembly. Soon after the results of the election were known, the Communists were invited to form a Government in Kerala, with E. M. S. Namboodiripad as Chief Minister.

The PSP received a considerably lower percentage of the popular vote than had the Socialists and the KMPP in 1951–52, but it retained the same number of seats in the Lok Sabha. It lost a few seats in the elections for members of the State Assemblies, despite some unexpected gains in West Bengal. The Hindu Mahasabha lost two of its four seats in the Lok Sabha; its President, N. C. Chatterjee, and its General Secretary, V. G. Deshpande, were defeated. The Ram Rajya Parishad was unable to elect a single candidate to the national Parliament, and it placed very few in any of the State Assemblies. The number of Independents in the Lok Sabha was also less than before.

In their own localities, and only there, a number of local parties or groupings scored impressive victories. Notable among these were the Ganatantra Parishad in Orissa, the Dravida Munnetra Kazhagam in Madras, the Jharkhand Party in Bihar, and, as has been noted, the Samyukta Maharashtra Samiti and the Mahagujarat Janata Parishad in the Maharashtra and Gujarat sections of Bombay State, respectively.

Speculating on the results of the second general elections a writer in the *Radical Humanist* found two tendencies which stood out above all others:

> First, the prestige and strength of the Congress is steadily declining. It has lost its hold in urban-industrial areas, and more particularly over the middle class. . . . Secondly, there is no powerful democratic alternative to the Congress. . . . [The] "shift in the mass mood toward radicalisation" will continue, and the C.P.I. with its militant organisation, effective techniques of manipulating mass-psychology and an alluring radical programme appears . . . as the most potent threat to democracy and freedom. . . . If the elections have any lesson to offer, it is that the future of democracy in this country is dark, because appreciation of its values is lamentably lacking.[8]

### The Election in Kerala in 1960

The main event in India's electoral history between the second and third general elections was the election in Kerala in February 1960. With the possible exception of the election in Andhra in 1955, this was the most bitterly contested and the most highly publicized State election in the history of independent India. In July 1959, after a long period of indecision and because of reports of growing troubles in the State, the Government of India intervened in a deteriorating situation, and the Communist government of Kerala was superseded by President's rule, until new elections could be held. Determined not to be outmaneuvered this time by the Communists, the Congress took the initiative in forming a Triple Alliance wth the PSP and the Muslim

---

[8] "The Ballot Box: A Pointer," *The Radical Humanist,* XXI (May 19, 1957), 248.

League (which still had some strength in that part of India), and it conducted a vigorous electoral campaign, with Nehru and other top leaders participating. Principally as a result of these tactics and of the changing views of the voters regarding the Communists, the Triple Alliance emerged with 94 of the 127 seats in the Kerala Assembly. The Congress alone won 63 seats, while the PSP won 20, and the Muslim League 11. Before the voting the Congress had 43 seats and the PSP had 9. Communist membership in the Assembly plummeted from 60 to 26 (plus three Communist-supported Independents.) The voter turnout was nearly 85 per cent, a record high for any Indian State.[9]

The results of the Kerala election of February 1960 were widely hailed as a resounding Communist setback, and the changed composition of the State Assembly seemed to justify this interpretation. A more careful examination of the results, and especially of the general situation in Kerala, would lead to a less optimistic view. The Communists in Kerala actually increased their popular vote substantially over the figures in 1957; in fact, their popular vote was even greater than that of the Congress. The substantially improved position of the Congress in Kerala, therefore, could not be attributed to any lessening of support for the Communists, or any marked increase of support for the Congress, but rather to more effective electoral tactics on the part of the Congress and other relatively ephemeral factors.

## The Third General Elections

Before the third general elections, held between February 16 and 25, 1962 (except for a few remote constituencies),[10] the electoral rolls in most constituencies were "intensively revised," and the Two-Member Constituencies (Abolition) Act was passed by the Lok Sabha in January 1961. In the second general elections there had been 91 two-member Lok Sabha constituencies and 584 two-member Assembly constituencies, in each of which one seat was reserved for either the scheduled tribes or the scheduled castes. After 1962 some seats in

[9] "Final Tally and Party Positions in Kerala Elections," *Indiagram*, Feb. 19, 1960. For a detailed breakdown, see K. P. Bhagat, *The Kerala Mid-Term Election of 1960* (Bombay, 1962). For an account of the conditions in Kerala which led to the overthrow of the Communist Government in July 1959 and to the elections in that State in February 1960, see Benjamin N. Schoenfeld, "Kerala in Crisis," *Pacific Affairs*, XXXII (September, 1959), 235–248. For an analysis of the 1960 elections, see K. R. Rajgopalan, "Elections in Kerala," *The Indian Journal of Political Science*, XXI (April–June, 1960), 165–183.

[10] See Election Commission, Government of India, *Report on the Third General Elections in India, 1962*, 2 vols. (Delhi, 1966); Myron Weiner, "India's Third General Elections," *Asian Survey*, II (May, 1962), 3–18; and Surindar Suri, *1962 Elections: A Political Analysis* (New Delhi, 1962).

the Lok Sabha and the State Assemblies were reserved for these under-privileged groups, but all constituencies were made single-member.

Until the third general elections the Election Commission recognized any party that polled at least 3 per cent of the total valid votes in Parliamentary elections as a national party, and as a State party any party which obtained the same minimum percentage in certain States. In 1952 there were four recognized national parties — the Congress, the Praja Socialist Party, the Communist Party, and the Jana Sangh — and 19 other parties which were recognized as State parties. In the electoral revision the distinction between national and State parties was dropped, and parties which obtained more than 3 per cent of the total vote in 1962 were allotted reserved symbols in those States where they had obtained the minimum vote. Sixteen parties were so recognized for the third general elections.

In the 1962 elections the marking system of voting, as contrasted with the balloting system, was used for the first time on a nationwide scale, except in a few constituencies. This system had previously been used in a number of by-elections and in the elections to the Legislative Assembly in Kerala in 1960. It was in many respects an improvement over the balloting system, and although it was a somewhat more sophisticated and complicated system it proved to be so successful that it has been used ever since in most constituencies.

The electioneering techniques in the third general elections were roughly the same as in the second. Except in certain constituencies the campaign was rather dull, featuring local issues, grievances, and factional and caste differences.

The overall results of the polling contained few surprises, although some individual results did. The Congress lost a few seats in the Lok Sabha as compared with the 1957 elections (from 371 to 361), and its percentage of the votes polled declined slightly (from nearly 48 per cent in 1957 to just under 45 per cent). The Communist Party retained its position as the second largest party in the Lok Sabha, but it won only 29 seats, followed by the Swatantra, contesting for the first time in a general election, with 22, the Jana Sangh with 14, and the PSP with 12. The Congress won a clear majority of seats in all of the State Assemblies except Madhya Pradesh, where the Congress Chief Minister, Katju, was beaten. In Rajasthan it had a majority of only one. The results indicated that Congress support was declining in the Hindi "heartland" states of the North, formerly the center of its strength, and was increasing in several non-Hindi States, where strong State leaders — notably Atulya Ghosh in West Bengal, Y. B. Chavan in Maharashtra, Kamaraj Nadar in Madras, and B. Patnaik in Orissa — were emerging as increasingly important forces in Congress politics.

As a result of the elections, several of the best known opposition M.P.'s lost their seats in the Lok Sabha. These included Acharya Kripalani, who, running as an Independent, was defeated by Krishna Menon in North Bombay in the most publicized centest of the third elections, Asoka Mehta and N. G. Goray of the PSP, S. A. Dange of the CPI, Balraj Madhok of the Jana Sangh, and N. G. Ranga of the Swatantra Party.

The 1962 elections were the last of the Nehru era, the last to conceal the changes which were taking place in Indian politics — changes which were leading to the slow erosion of Congress strength without a corresponding increase in strength in any other parties of national importance. These changes became more evident only after the traumatic events of the following years, notably the Chinese attack of late 1962 and the Indian reverses, the death of Nehru, the war with Pakistan in 1965, and the bad seasons and economic setbacks of the mid-1960's; and they were dramatically highlighted in the fourth general elections in 1967.

## The Election in Kerala in 1965

Between the third and fourth general elections, as between the second and third, an election was held in Kerala. In September 1964, the Congress Government was forced to resign after it had been defeated in the Legislative Assembly, as a result of the defection of some dissident Congress members. President's Rule was imposed, as it had been in 1959 when the Communists were forced out of office. In the elections of March 1965, the Congress was faced with formidable opposition, not only from the Communists but also from the Kerala Congress, formed by a group of Congress dissidents. As a result the Congress won only 36 seats in the Assembly, compared to the 51 which it held prior to the election. The Communists won 40 seats, and the Kerala Congress 24. Because no one party or coalition could form a Government, President's Rule continued until the fourth general elections.

## The Fourth General Elections, 1967

A new complexion was given to the Indian political scene by the fourth general elections, held between February 15 and 21, 1967.[11]

[11] For accounts of the fourth general elections, see Norman D. Palmer, "India's Fourth General Elections," *Asian Survey*, VII (May, 1967), 275–291, and "Revolution by Ballot: The Fourth General Elections in India," *Midway* (Autumn, 1967), 83–97. S. P. Varma, Iqbal Narain and Associates, eds., *Fourth General Election in India*, 2 vols. (Bombay: Orient Longmans, 1968 and 1969); and Election Commission, Government of India, *Report on the Fourth General Elections in India, 1967*, 2 vols. (Delhi, 1968).

These elections marked the end of one party dominance, a process which had been under way for some time, and ushered in a new era of political instability, coalition politics, and uncertain political alignments.

Since the third general elections, India had experienced a series of disturbing developments, at home and abroad. Tensions with China, quite obvious by the time of the third general elections, reached a climax in October–November 1962 with the Chinese invasion of the North East Frontier Agency and Ladakh and the border war that followed. Tensions with Pakistan reached a climax in 1965, first with limited hostilities in the Rann of Kutch and then with the three-week war in September, preceded by Pakistani infiltration of Kashmir and a military push in Jammu, and followed by the Tashkent Conference of January 1966, and the Tashkent Agreement, signed by President Ayub Khan, and the Prime Minister of India, Lal Bahadur Shastri (a few hours before his sudden death). The death of Jawaharlal Nehru in May 1964 deprived the Congress of its charismatic leader and ushered in a period of weaker and more divided leadership. Shastri's death in January 1966 was another blow. His successor, Mrs. Indira Gandhi, was a compromise choice, and her first months in office were unusually trying ones.

The campaign preceding the elections was held in an atmosphere of despondency, frustration, and almost continuous agitation. Two of the worst seasons in living memory had created a serious economic situation, with rising prices, food shortages, and near-famine conditions in Bihar and parts of other States. The threat to law and order was particularly serious, with increasing resort to *bandhs, gheraos,* strikes, and other forms of public protest and mass agitation. In such a deteriorating situation the Congress Government seemed to be inept and ineffective. Under these circumstances some responsible observers expressed the view that the elections would have to be postponed, or possibly could not be held at all.

Not surprisingly, the campaign witnessed more acts or violence and more instances of extra-constitutional methods of protest than usual. The most highly publicized, but by no means the worst, acts of violence were a stone-throwing episode in a meeting in Bhubaneshwar in Orissa, which inflicted a minor wound on Mrs. Gandhi's nose, and the beating of a prominent leader of the Samyukhta Socialist Party, Madhu Limaye. Among the typically Indian forms of protest were a demonstration in New Delhi on November 7, 1966, when a mob numbering in the hundreds of thousands, led by naked sadhus (holy men) carrying tridents, spears, and other symbols of their calling, tried to storm the Parliament House on the anti-cow-slaughter issue, burned

**Results of General Elections in India, 1951–1967
House of the People (Lok Sabha)**

| Parties | 1951–52 | | 1957 | | 1962 | | 1967 | |
|---|---|---|---|---|---|---|---|---|
| | Number of seats won | % valid votes polled | Number of seats won | % valid votes polled | Number of seats won | % valid votes polled | Number of seats won | % valid votes polled |
| Congress Party | 364 | 45.0 | 371 | 47.78 | 361 | 44.72 | 283 | 40.73 |
| Socialist Party | 12 | 10.6 | — | — | — | — | — | — |
| Kisan Mazdoor Praja Party | 9 | 5.8 | — | — | — | — | — | — |
| Praja Socialist Party | — | — | 19 | 10.41 | 12 | 6.84 | 13 | 3.06 |
| Socialist Party of India | — | — | — | — | 6 | 2.49 | — | — |
| Samyukta Socialist Party | — | — | — | — | — | — | 23 | 4.92 |
| Communist Party of India | 16 | 3.3 | 27 | 8.92 | 29 | 9.96 | 23 | 5.19 |
| Communist Party of India (Marxist) | — | — | — | — | — | — | 19 | 4.21 |
| Jana Sangh | 3 | 3.1 | 4 | 5.93 | 14 | 6.44 | 35 | 9.41 |
| Swatantra | — | — | — | — | 18 | 7.89 | 44 | 8.68 |
| Dravida Munnetra Kazhagam | — | — | — | — | 7 | 2.02 | 25 | 3.90 |
| Other Parties | 44 | 16.4 | 34 | 7.57 | 30 | 7.37 | 20 | 6.15 |
| Independents | 41 | 15.8 | 39 | 19.39 | 20 | 12.27 | 35 | 13.75 |
| Total | 489 | 100.0 | 494 | 100.0 | 497 | 100.0 | 520 | 100.0 |

Source: Adapted from reports on the Election Commission, Government of India.

buses and cars, inflicted serious damage to buildings, and created such a disturbance that several persons were killed; and two "fasts unto death" which fortunately did not end in tragedy, one by the Shankacharya of Puri on the cow slaughter issue, the other by Sant Fateh Singh, a leader of the Akali Dal in the Punjab, on the Punjabi Suba issue. In spite of such acts of violence and protest the campaign as a whole was remarkably calm, especially in view of the disturbed state of the country. Except in some constituencies where the contests were keen, it was in fact a rather dull campaign, at least until the final stages.

The selection of candidates was particularly difficult in the 1967 elections.[12] Even more than in previous elections, dissatisfaction with party nominations led disappointed candidates to work against official candidates, and in several States dissident Congressmen formed rival political organizations. Since the third general elections the boundaries of most of the Lok Sabha and State Legislative Assembly constituencies had been redrawn, and the number of Lok Sabha constituencies had been raised to 520, and of State Assembly constituencies to 3,383. As usual, the Congress was the only party to name candidates for most of the Lok Sabha and Assembly seats. The techniques of campaigning were generally the same as in the previous elections, but there was greater emphasis on smaller meetings, and house-to-house canvassing.

Nationally, the main issues were economic — the food shortage, rising prices, the after-effects of devaluation, etc. — and psychological — the general dissatisfaction with the Congress. Foreign policy issues did not figure prominently in the campaign. For a time the cow slaughter issue seemed to be assuming major proportions, but after the Shankacharya of Puri was persuaded to break his "fast unto death" the issue became less significant. In several States and many constituencies local issues were dominant. The fact that the Congress was threatened with the loss of two or more States and with a greatly reduced majority in the Lok Sabha lent an element of excitement and uncertainty to the election results.

Contrary to many predictions, the elections went off smoothly, with only a few irregularities and cases of violence. The turnout of voters was the highest ever — about 61 per cent, as compared with 45 per cent in the first general elections, 46.6 per cent in the second, and 55.4 per cent in the third.

When the ballots were counted, it was learned that the political scene in India had indeed changed. Although the Congress remained

[12] See Stanley Kochanek, "Political Recruitment in the Indian National Congress: The Fourth General Elections," *Asian Survey,* VII (May, 1967), 292–304.

the only real national party, its reverses were even greater than had been predicted. Its share of the popular vote fell by some 5 percentage points, and its representation in the Lok Sabha from 361 to 283. It failed to win a majority of the seats in the Assemblies of eight States, containing three-fifths of the population of India. Its losses were particularly severe in Bihar, Madras, the Punjab, and West Bengal. In Kerala it returned only one of 19 Lok Sabha members, and only nine of 133 members of the Legislative Assembly, so few that it could not even be recognized as an opposition party. Many of its outstanding leaders, including the President of the Congress, the secretary and treasurer, two key members of the Syndicate (S. K. Patil and Atulya Ghosh), 9 Union ministers, 4 Chief Ministers, and several State ministers, were defeated. Among the opposition parties the largest gains were registered by the Swatantra, the Jana Sangh, the SSP, the CPI(M) in Kerala, the CPI(M) and the Bangla Congress in West Bengal, and the DMK in Madras. In the Lok Sabha the Swatantra Party emerged as the largest single opposition group (44 members), followed by the Jana Sangh (35), the DMK (which put up 25 candidates for the Lok Sabha and elected all 25), the SSP (23), the CPI (23), and the CPI(M) (19).

While the swing away from the Congress was unmistakable, its losses in seats in both the Lok Sabha and many States were greater than its decline in popular vote. This phenomenon may be accounted for largely by a series of unusually effective electoral alliances, often comprising strange bedfellows, such as the effective alliance of seven parties, including the CPI(M), the CPI, and the Muslim League in Kerala, and two multi-group alliances in West Bengal, with the CPI in one and the CPI(M) in another.

The election results may be interpreted as a partial repudiation of the Congress, and as an expression of frustration, disillusionment, and a desire for change, but they revealed no clear alternatives. E. P. W. da Costa, managing director of the Indian Institute of Public Opinion, pointed out that the elections indicated a loss of important groups of voters by the Congress: "The Indian electorate, believed inert and incapable of independent dramatic choice between sophisticated political alternatives, has exhibited marks of revolutionary change. The young, . . . the less educated, . . . the minorities, particularly the Muslims and the Sikhs and perhaps at last the lowest income groups whose patience is wearing thin are rewriting their basic loyalties."[13] Both left and right parties gained substantially in some States, but no clear ide-

---

[13] E. P. W. de Costa, "Roots of Change in Popular Vote," *The Hindu,* March 17, 1967.

ological patterns or swings could be discerned nationally. One conclusion might be that the Indian voter was becoming more pragmatic and more willing to change his political affiliation; he was becoming less nationalist and more regionalist and parochial. "The short answer for the people who ask where India is going is not 'more left' or 'more right,' but 'more local.' "[14]

## The Mid-Term Elections of 1969

The results of the 1967 general elections were soon reflected in political changes and confusion in many of the States. Political defections — often referred to as "floor-crossing" — occurred with bewildering rapidity. In the year following the elections "one out of every 7 legislators in the States . . . changed his political affiliation at least once [several more than once] . . . an average of more than one legislator changing his party each day."[15] In the same period there were 14 changes of government in the States, 4 of them in a single State (Bihar). In 1967–69 six of the Indian States were under President's Rule for varying lengths of time. At one time 9 of the 17 States had non-Congress Governments. All but one (Madras) were coalition governments of many different complexions. With few exceptions the coalition regimes proved to be quite unstable, and many of them soon fell, giving way to Congress governments, to other coalitions, or to President's Rule, which after February 1967 was a recurrent phenomenon in Indian political life.

In 1967 President's Rule was imposed in Rajasthan for a brief period (in March–April) until Mohanlal Sukhadia, long-time Congress Chief Minister, was able to get the support of a majority in the Legislative Assembly; in the Union Territory of Manipur in October, and in Haryana in November. President's Rule was continued in Haryana until May 1968, when the Congress Party, in a mid-term poll, won 48 of the 81 seats in the Assembly and was then able to form a government.

In 1968 four States — Bihar, the Punjab, Uttar Pradesh, and West Bengal — and the Union Territory of Pondicherry were placed under President's Rule. This situation continued until February 1969, when mid-term elections were held in all these States and Pondicherry, plus Nagaland.

This mini-general election involved nearly two-fifths of the entire Indian electorate, and a major part of the Hindi "heartland." The

[14] By a commentator in the *Spectator;* quoted in *The Statesman,* Feb. 12, 1967.
[15] Subhash C. Kashyap, *The Politics of Defection: A Study of State Politics in India* (Delhi, 1969), pp. 5, 6.

Congress Party was in a precarious position in the four key States. In West Bengal it was faced with the opposition of a coalition of several parties, spearheaded by the CPI(M), the Bangla Congress, and the CPI; in Bihar it was opposed by a variety of ill-assorted parties and groups; in U.P. it was challenged by a formidable dissident group, the Bhartiya Kranti Dal (BKD), and by the Jana Sangh and SSP; in the Punjab it was on the defensive because the Akali Dal, which had been divided, had united and entered into a strange alliance with the Jana Sangh. It seemed that the Congress was still vulnerable to the same forces, changes, and tactics which had led to such shattering reverses in 1967.

Although the Congress showed greater strength than was anticipated in U.P., where it actually won ten more seats than it had in 1967, it suffered a real rout in West Bengal, declining from 127 to 55 seats in the Assembly, whereas the CPI(M) increased its strength from 43 to 80, the CPI from 16 to 30, and the Forward Bloc from 13 to 21. In U.P. the BKD won 98 seats, mostly at the expense of the Jana Sangh, the SSP, Swatantra, and the CPI, all of which lost heavily. In Bihar the Congress lost 10 seats and the SSP 16, whereas the Jana Sangh gained 8, and the CPI and PSP held their previous positions. In the Punjab Congress also lost 10 seats, but the Akali Dal gained 20, giving it 6 more seats than the Congress.

After the February elections a United Front of 14 parties, headed by Ajoy Mukherjee, leader of the Bangla Congress, formed a ministry in West Bengal, in which the two Communist parties — especially the CPI(M) — were the major components. It was a shaky coalition at best. In Bihar the Congress for the first time headed a coalition government, but this fell after four months, and President's Rule was again proclaimed. In U.P. the BKD, led by Charan Singh, formerly a leading Congressman, formed a coalition government, but within a few weeks this government was defeated, and C. B. Gupta, former Congress Chief Minister, again formed a Congress government of uncertain future. In the Punjab the Akali Dal, supported by the Jana Sangh, formed a government, which seemed to offer some prospect for continuance for more than a few months. In 1970 further political changes occurred in all of these States, and also in Kerala.

Coalition politics had obviously become a regular feature of the political scene in the Indian States. After the split in the Congress Party in the latter part of 1969 it seemed likely to become a regular feature of the national political scene as well.

# 11 *

# Foreign Relations

Economically and militarily India is far from being a major power, and it faces serious political and social problems which threaten its national unity and its cultural cohesiveness; but at the same time it has great present influence and even greater potential power. It is the most populous of the non-Communist nations of the world. It is the largest and probably the most important of the underdeveloped countries in an age when "the revolution of rising expectations" in underdeveloped areas is one of the most potent forces in international relations. It is the leading nation in the "uncommitted world," a position which gives it a far greater influence than it would have if it were closely associated with any "power bloc." It is still perhaps the single most influential member of the Asian-African Group in the United Nations, although its relative influence has declined with the emergence of many new states and the rise of other centers of influence and power in Asia and Africa. Its past connections with Great Britain and its present associations through the Commonwealth and the sterling area give it an added importance in world affairs.

On the other hand, a number of recent developments in both international affairs and in India have diminished India's international position and role. These include the diminishing intensity of the "cold war," increasing polycentrism in both the Communist and non-Communist worlds, an "inward turning" by many nations, including the United States and India, India's loss of prestige following its humiliation by the Chinese in late 1962, the death of Nehru, and growing internal stresses and political instability.

In a sense, India's foreign policy can be divided into two main periods, the Nehru and the post-Nehru eras. As long as Jawaharlal Nehru was Prime Minister, he was the chief architect and spokesman of Indian policy, abroad as well as at home. He was one of the most vocal and best known of international statesmen. For a time he seemed to be the chief spokesman of Asia and of the "Third World," as well as of India. Although his influence and international role declined in the last years of his life, due to the changing world situation, the reverses at the hands of the Chinese, growing domestic problems, and fading health and energy, he retained much of his prestige to the end. After his death, most of the new leaders of India were men of little international experience, almost unknown abroad. As his constant companion his daughter, Mrs. Indira Gandhi, is well-known in international circles, but she lacks the international status of her father. Since she became Prime Minister in January 1966, she has had to concentrate on internal problems and has not been very active in foreign policy, even though she has traveled widely and for a time was her own Foreign Minister.

India's foreign policy has been variously described as one of "neutrality," "nonalignment," or "independence." Most Indian spokesmen prefer to describe it as independent, a policy based on the consideration of each issue on its own merits.[1] Indians like to feel that their past traditions of tolerance, the influence of their great leader, Mahatma Gandhi, and their policy of nonalignment or independence place them in a favorable position to play a mediating and conciliatory role in international relations, to contribute to the lessening of international tensions and to the development of a "climate of peace." Without claiming any special moral superiority over other peoples, most Indians seem to feel that their country can contribute greatly to improving the standards of diplomatic behavior and to "sweetening" international relations.

## Factors Shaping India's Foreign Policy

The foreign policy of India is determined by the same factors that shape the foreign policy of any country. Some of these factors are tangible, such as geographic and economic and demographic factors,

[1] In the first statement which he made when he became Member for External Affairs in the Interim Government in September 1946, Nehru said: "In the sphere of foreign affairs, India will follow an independent policy, keeping away from power politics of groupings aligned against the other." In an address to the United Nations General Assembly, on October 17, 1960, V. K. Krishna Menon, Nehru's chief adviser on foreign policy, declared: "We are not a neutral country. . . . We are not neutral in regard to war or peace. We are not neutral in regard to domination by imperialist or other countries. We are not neutral with regard to ethical values. We are not neutral with regard to the greatest economic and social problems that may arise. . . . Our position is that we are an unaligned and uncommitted nation in relation to the cold war. . . ." Fifteenth Session, General Assembly, United Nations, *Provisional Verbatim Record of the Nine Hundred and Sixth Plenary Meeting,* 17 October 1960 (A/PV.906, 17 October 1960), pp. 44–46.

while others are intangible, such as morale and leadership. In India's case three factors deserve special emphasis, namely geographical and strategic position, historical experience, involving traditional patterns and foreign impact, and domestic forces and pressures.

A glance at a map will be a sufficient reminder that India occupies a position of great geographic and strategic importance, in a local, regional, and global sense.[2] In 1903 Lord Curzon, then Governor-General of India, predicted that the geographical position of India would more and more push it into the forefront of international affairs. In 1948 Nehru spoke of India as the pivotal center of South, Southeast, and Western Asia.

Flanked by the world's highest mountains on the north and by the Indian Ocean and its vast reaches, the Arabian Sea and the Bay of Bengal, on the south, east, and west, the western frontiers of India border on West Pakistan, while to the east Indian territory almost surrounds East Pakistan and extends to the frontiers of Burma. India has something like 3,500 miles of seacoast and 8,200 miles of land frontier, if all the borders with Pakistan are included. Because of its strained relations with its sister nation of the subcontinent, India is faced with a security problem in its own front yard; yet ironically Pakistan has sometimes been called India's first line of defense, for India has to rely largely upon Pakistan for the defense of those parts of the subcontinent in the Northwest Frontier area which were the traditional avenues of entry by one invader after another across the centuries. Hostile activities of the Chinese Communists, including a military attack in late 1962, have reminded India that it has other security problems along its Himalayan frontier. Including Nepal, Sikkim, and Bhutan, as well as Ladakh and the Northeast Frontier Agency within India's strategic frontiers, India has more than 1,500 miles of frontier with Communist China — the longest frontier of any non-Communist state with a Communist state; and in the northern part of Kashmir it is separated from Soviet territory by only a few miles. India has a vital security interest in Nepal and Bhutan, and many of its policies attest to this fact. Sikkim, between Nepal and Bhutan, is a protectorate of India.[3]

India is also deeply concerned with the control of the Indian Ocean region, but for the moment at least it has no major fears from this quarter, as effective control of the entire Ocean is in the hands of States with which India is on friendly terms. Nevertheless, India views

[2] See P. P. Karan, "India's Role in Geopolitics," *India Quarterly,* IX (April–June, 1953), 160–169; K. M. Panikkar, *India and the Indian Ocean* (London, 1945).

[3] See Leo E. Rose, "Sino-Indian Rivalry and the Himalayan Border States," *Orbis,* V (Summer, 1961), 199–215.

with some alarm the changing power situation in the Indian Ocean area, a consequence of a number of major developments, including a large measure of British withdrawal East of Suez, the likelihood of a lesser American presence after Vietnam, and growing Soviet activity in the Indian Ocean, as in the littoral states of the Middle East and South and Southeast Asia. It doubts that a "power vacuum" will exist after the British withdrawal, and it insists that to the extent that such a vacuum will be created the indigenous states of the area, and no outside powers, will fill it.

The long, rich, and complicated historical experience of the Indian people has done much to condition Indian attitudes and outlook. Some knowledge of this experience, extending over many centuries, is essential for an understanding of the contemporary Indian scene as well as of India's past. In analyzing India's behavior in foreign as well as in domestic affairs, it is well to remember, as Nehru wrote in *The Discovery of India,* that "we are very old, and trackless centuries whisper in our ears."[4]

The predominant civilization of India has always been the Hindu, although in more recent centuries the Muslims and later the British have made a great impact. Some of the characteristics and practices of Hindu civilization have a very noticeable influence on Indian attitudes and policies today. Among these are a kind of other-worldly attitude toward life and an emphasis on nonmaterial factors, and a spirit of tolerance, detachment, mediation, and compromise which perhaps is best exemplified in Buddhism, an offshoot of Hinduism.

The British remained in India for more than three hundred years, and for well over a century, through direct and indirect rule, they were in effective control of virtually the entire subcontinent. While much can be said about British contributions to India, and while Indians reacted favorably to the way in which the British left in 1947, the many decades of Western "imperialism" left deep scars. They account in large measure for the sensitivity of independent India to any evidences, real or imagined, of imperialism and colonialism, of racial superiority and discrimination, of Western manipulation, of disregard of the interests and wishes of the newly independent nations of Asia and Africa.

It would be interesting to speculate on the extent to which India's present policy of nonalignment and its emphasis on the "middle way" in world affairs can be traced to ancient roots. Or are they rather attributable to the teachings and example of Gandhi? Or can they be explained largely by the practical assessment of India's present leaders of the wisest course for India to follow in world affairs?

[4] Jawaharlal Nehru, *The Discovery of India* (New York, 1946), p. 144.

India's role and influence in world affairs are greatly handicapped by its internal weaknesses and divisions, by its economic under-development, its confused political situation and generally weak leadership since the death of Nehru, and the internal pressures and forces which impinge upon its foreign as well as domestic policy. Domestic considerations have obviously colored the Indian approach to foreign policy and international developments.

In the post-Nehru era the "linkages" between foreign and domestic policy have become more evident. Since 1964 India has played a lesser international role; it has given much more attention to its relations with near neighbors, notably Pakistan, China, and the Soviet Union; and it has followed much more pragmatic policies abroad and at home. India's leaders have had little experience in foreign affairs and have, in any event, had to concentrate on a host of internal problems. Opposition parties and interest groups of a communal, regional, or professional nature have become more vocal and more influential. These are concerned primarily with domestic, not foreign, policy and problems.

In the Nehru era Indian public opinion, to the extent that it could be discerned, was generally supportive of India's foreign policy. Only rarely, as in the Hungarian crisis in 1956, did public opinion seem to be at variance with Nehru's position; and in the Hungarian case Nehru eventually came around to a position more acceptable to vocal elements of the Indian public. In the post-Nehru years the gap between official policy and public opinion has often been wider. This was shown in the Six-Day War in the Middle East in 1967, when the Indian Government took a strongly pro-Arab stand whereas Indian public opinion was sharply divided, and in the Soviet military move into Czechoslovakia in 1968, when the official position was cautious and "neutral" whereas some elements of public opinion strongly condemned the Soviet move.

Internal weaknesses have not only muted India's voice in international circles, but they explain, at least in part, India's policy of nonalignment and its efforts to strike a delicate balance between enforced dependence on other countries, notably the United States and the Soviet Union, for economic aid and perhaps ultimately for defense against nuclear attack, and the desire to avoid excessive influence and pressures upon it by outside countries, particularly the superpowers.

## Foreign Policy of the Indian National Congress
### Before Independence

The positions taken by the Indian National Congress on many issues of international import during the sixty-two years of its existence prior to independence are the bases for the foreign policy of independent

India. This is particularly true after World War I, when the Congress became more articulate and outspoken in its views, Mahatma Gandhi gave a unique twist to the work of the Congress, and the organization developed a kind of foreign office of its own, with Nehru in charge. "It is well to remember," said Nehru in 1955, "that our foreign policy is not a sudden growth but a natural outcome of our thinking for many years past."

A study of the resolutions passed by the Indian National Congress reveals that the Congress took a deep interest in certain external questions from its inception, and that it based its positions on certain fundamental principles which still shape Indian foreign policy.[5] A resolution passed at the first session of the Congress in 1885 deprecated the annexation of Upper Burma by the British. In 1892 the Congress objected to "the military activity going on beyond the natural lines of the defences of this country, in pursuance of the Imperial policy of Great Britain in its relation with some of the Great Powers of Europe." Increasingly the Congress objected to the use of India as a base for political maneuvering or military moves against surrounding areas such as Tibet, Burma, Afghanistan, and Persia. A resolution of 1904 asserted that an expedition to Tibet was "but part of a general forward policy, which . . . threatens to involve India in foreign entanglements." "This resolution," states Dr. N. V. Rajkumar, a "Foreign Secretary" of the Indian National Congress who compiled the major resolutions of the Congress relating to foreign affairs, "was perhaps the earliest expression of India's dislike of getting involved in unnecessary foreign entanglements and favouring a neutral stand on matters that did not concern her."

During World War I the Congress passed several resolutions of loyalty to the British and of support for the use of Indian troops in the war effort. After the war it began to take a more active interest and a more independent line on foreign issues. It was intensely interested in the Khilafat question.[6] In 1920 it sent "a message of sympathy to the Irish people in their struggle for independence." The meeting of the All-India Congress Committee in Delhi in 1921 was "a landmark in the history of India's foreign relations." For the first time the Congress passed a general resolution on foreign policy, which included the statement that "the present Government of India in no way represents Indian opinion." "This resolution," explains Rajkumar,

[5] All of the Congress resolutions cited in this section are given in full in N. V. Rajkumar, ed., *The Background of India's Foreign Policy* (New Delhi, 1952).

[6] This refers to the Allied decision to dismember the Ottoman Empire and to disband the office of Kaliph. In India this resulted in an alliance between the Congress and the Muslims.

"is important in as much as it was the first significant declaration on the part of nationalist India that its interests in the field of foreign policy were diametrically opposed to those of Britain. It further laid down the bases of an independent India's foreign policy. An analysis of this historic declaration would show that the fundamental principles guiding Free India's foreign policy today can be traced back to it." The Congress Session in Madras in 1927 passed a resolution of protest against the use of Indian troops in China, Mesopotamia, and Persia and deplored the "extensive war preparations which the British Government is carrying on in India." Nearly thirty years later Nehru stated that the foundations of India's foreign policy had been laid down at the Madras session of the Congress in 1927.

A resolution of the Congress in 1925 authorized the A.I.C.C. to open a Foreign Department "to look after the interests of Indians abroad and to carry on educative propaganda in the country regarding their position in the British Empire and foreign countries." Three years later the A.I.C.C. did set up a Foreign Department, with Jawaharal Nehru as head. From that time until his death nearly forty years later, Nehru was India's voice in foreign affairs. This record, unparalleled among the leading democratic statesmen of the twentieth century, helps to explain the remarkable consistency in Indian foreign policy, and serves as a reminder that that policy had evolved in most of its fundamentals well before 1947.

The 1928 Congress session at Calcutta sent its greetings to the people of Egypt, Syria, Palestine, and Iraq "in their struggle for emancipation from the grip of Western imperialism" and authorized the appointment of a representative to the Second World Congress of the League Against Imperialism, to be held in 1929. "These resolutions," states Rajkumar, "gave the first indication that India's national leaders were thinking in terms of a Pan-Asian movement to resist European imperialism."

In many resolutions in the late 1930's the Congress condemned the aggressive acts of the Nazis and Fascists, but it also declared that it would not be a party to "imperialist war." At the Tripura session in 1939 the Congress strongly disapproved of British foreign policy and dissociated itself from it. "In the opinion of the Congress, it is urgently necessary for India to direct her own foreign policy as an independent nation, thereby keeping aloof from both imperialism and fascism, and pursuing her path of peace and freedom." When the war came the Working Committee of the Congress, in a lengthy resolution, stated the attitude of the Congress toward the war: "The issue of war and peace for India must be decided by the Indian people. . . . Their sympathy is entirely on the side of democracy and freedom. But India cannot associate herself in a war said to be for democratic freedom when that very freedom is denied to her." The Congress ministries in the provinces resigned in protest against British policy, and the Congress refused to support the war effort. Under the influence of Gandhi, organized nonviolence was advocated as an alternative to war. The "Quit India" resolution of August 1942 marked the final parting of the ways, and thereafter, as Rajkumar notes, "the Congress went into the wilderness for the duration of the war."

With the release of most of its leaders early in 1945, the Congress resumed its demands for Indian independence and it spoke out strongly for the freedom of all countries and "the elimination of all traces of imperialist control by whatever name it may be called." While it welcomed the formation of the United Nations, from the outset it expressed certain major points of dissatisfaction with the kind of organization that had been formed. A resolution of the Working Committee of the Congress in July 1945 raised two major objections: one against the dominant role of the Great Powers in the new organization, with the consequence that "the position allotted to the smaller nations in the Charter is one lacking all effectiveness," the other against the "vague and unsatisfactory" declaration in the Charter regarding non-self-governing territories, instead of "a full and frank recognition of national independence." In subsequent resolutions in 1945 and 1946 the Working Committee voiced apprehensions regarding the consequences of the atomic bomb and the growing tensions in international relations, "resulting in open recrimination between the Great Powers and attempts on their part to secure or hold onto colonial areas and vantage points and create satellite states." The Congress was especially concerned over the many evidences that "the imperialist powers are again engaged in the old contest for dominion over others." It demanded the end of foreign domination over the countries of Asia and Africa, and it expressed its strong sympathy and support for the independence movements in Indonesia, Indo-China, and elsewhere. It was particularly insistent on the early granting of independence for India. A resolution of the Working Committee in March 1946 declared: "India still remains the crux of the problem of Asian freedom and on the independence of India depends the freedom of many countries and the peace of the world."

## Basic Principles of India's Foreign Policy

Shortly after India became an independent nation, the Congress called attention to the importance of the freedom struggle in shaping the foreign policy of free India, and it stated the basic principles of that policy:

The foreign policy of India must necessarily be based on the principles that have guided the Congress in past years. The principles are the promotion of world peace, the freedom of all nations, racial equality and the ending of imperialism and colonialism. In particular, the Congress is interested in the freedom of the nations and peoples of Asia and Africa who have suffered under various forms of colonialism for many generations.

In an address at Columbia University on October 17, 1949, Nehru summed up the main objectives of Indian foreign policy in a single sentence. "The main objectives of that policy are: the pursuit of peace, not through alignment with any major power or group of powers but through an independent approach to each controversial or disputed issue, the liberation of subject peoples, the maintenance of freedom, both national and individual, the elimination of racial discrimination and the elimination of want, disease and ignorance, whch afflict the greater part of the world's population."

**The Panchsheel.** Nehru and other Indian spokesmen attached great importance to the *Panch Shila,* or *Panchsheel.*[7] The famous "five principles of peace," which were first enunciated in specific form in the Sino-Indian treaty on Tibet in April 1954, were restated in the joint declaration issued by Nehru and Chou En-lai at the end of the visit of the Chinese Premier to India in June of the same year and in many joint statements and pronouncements by Indian spokesmen in the months and years immediately following. The five principles were: (1) mutual respect for each other's territorial integrity and sovereignty; (2) nonaggression; (3) noninterference in each other's internal affairs; (4) equality and mutual benefit; and (5) peaceful co-existence.

While even Nehru admitted that "there is nothing wonderful about the *Panchsheel"* and that "no one could disagree with them," they had real meaning for him. At a civic reception in Calcutta for Bulganin and Khrushchev on November 30, 1955, he explained the relationship of the *Panchsheel* to India's foreign policy:

Peaceful coexistence is not a new idea for us in India. It has been our way of life and is as old as our thought and culture.

[7] The words *Panch Shila* are derived from Sanskrit, and mean the five foundations or the five principles. Nehru first used the term *Panch Shila* at a State banquet given to him by the Prime Minister of Indonesia in Djakarta, on September 23, 1954. Apparently "the credit for calling these principles, for the first time in public, as *Pancha Sila* (or the five bases of conduct which India had consistently preached and attempted to follow in her international relations) should go to K. M. Panikkar, who used it in a broadcast talk over the All India Radio on 28 July 1954. He was commenting on the Nehru-Chou joint statement." M. S. Rajan, *India in World Affairs, 1954–56* (New York, 1964), p. 52, n. 6.

. . . We welcome association and friendship with all and the flow of thought and ideas of all kinds, but we reserve the right to choose our own path. That is the essence of "Panch Shila." . . . These principles form the basis of our relations with other nations. If Panch Shila were fully and sincerely accepted by all countries, then peace would be assured to everyone and cooperation would follow.

Enthusiasm for *Panchsheel* faded with the growth of tension in relations with Communist China and the multipolarity of the general international situation.

**Nonalignment.** The term which is most often used to characterize the foreign policy of India is "nonalignment." As has been noted, nonalignment was espoused by the Indian National Congress, and especially by Nehru, long before independence. It became, as Nehru observed in 1960, "a distinguishing mark of India," and in the mid-1950's virtually an article of faith. Nehru, Krishna Menon, and other spokesmen of India rang the changes on this theme in innumerable speeches and official pronouncements. They often joined with other nonaligned states in joint communiques and conferences, including the first conference of nonaligned states in Belgrade in 1961. They insisted that nonalignment was the only correct policy for India to follow, and that it was not a negative policy, but a positive and dynamic one. Nehru maintained his faith in this policy to the very end, and Krishna Menon is still proclaiming its virtues. In 1967 he told Michael Brecher that "there is no alternative to what is called nonalignment, which is called independence of policy; this has to continue." His views on this theme led Brecher to observe: "Although he would deny the emotional implication, this is an article of faith which has not been shaken by events affecting the position of India or the character of international politics from 1950 to 1965."[8]

The leaders of India since Nehru's death have invariably and consistently reaffirmed their faith in nonalignment as the basis of India's foreign policy, even though they have shown less emotional attachment to it and have not hesitated to espouse measures which would have been regarded by some of the early spokesmen of nonalignment as inconsistent with this basic principle. In January 1969, for example, Mrs. Gandhi said: ". . . we feel that the premises on which we built our nonalignment policy have proved so correct that more and more nations . . . are veering toward nonalignment. . . . In a bipolar world, nonalignment may have been easier to understand, but in a multipolar

[8] Michael Brecher, "Elite Images and Foreign Policy Choices: Krishna Menon's View of the World," *Pacific Affairs,* XL (Spring and Summer, 1967), 84.

world it is even more relevant."[9] India was one of forty-four countries which participated in a Consultative Meeting of Special Government Representatives on Non-Aligned Countries, held in Belgrade in July 1969, and joined in a joint communique reaffirming "the dedication of their states to the principles of the policy of non-alignment."

Spokesmen of all nations tend to be rather nebulous when attempting to enunciate principles of foreign policy. Indian spokesmen are past masters of this art, as their use of the term "nonalignment" well illustrates. The term is such a vague one as to be virtually meaningless. Even Nehru admitted that it "in itself is not a policy; it is only part of a policy." It could be more accurately described as an approach or as a guiding principle, rather than a policy. It has obviously taken on a very different context and perhaps a very different meaning since its heyday in the mid-1950s. The words may be the same, but the emotional and contextual framework are quite different.

Even in the Nehru era nonalignment was often criticized in India, especially by spokesmen of opposition parties, business, journalism and other professions. As relations with Communist China became more tense and as the international situation changed from stark bipolarity to a more obvious multipolarity, India was forced to adopt policies and approaches which would have been regarded as inconsistent with nonalignment a decade before. Increasing numbers of Indians began to question nonalignment in the light of changing conditions. This view was frequently voiced in the Indian press. An editorial in *The Statesman* of October 8, 1969, for example, calling for "A Policy, Please," contained this statement: "Nonalignment it has been said and needs to be said again is an attitude, if even that. Its relevance in a situation where cold war blocs are no longer identifiable is doubtful." Another editorial in the same journal two months later, on December 2, 1969, declared: "Since the years when nonalignment was preached by Mr. Nehru in a world context that made it meaningful, it has been rapidly reduced to a label with no apparent relevance to the international situation today."

However, official adherence to the "policy" of nonalignment has never wavered. Mrs. Gandhi stated the official view in January 1969 that "in a multipolar world it is even more relevant." Clearly the truth lies somewhere between the extremes of official adherence and the "convenient label" analysis. A seasoned American observer wrote in early 1969: "While the creed of nonalignment remains, its exciting days are over, and its great figures . . . are gone or embroiled in their

[9] Reply to a questionnaire by *India Weekly* of London; reprinted in *India News,* Feb. 14, 1969.

own difficulties. And two wars, along with the domestic strains of this decade, seem to have led Indians to look to their involvement in world affairs more closely in terms of their national interests."[10] Under existing circumstances one might argue that the key word for characterizing Indian foreign policy is not "nonalignment" but "pragmatic."

## Phases of India's Foreign Policy

Obviously there have been many aspects of both continuity and change in the foreign policy of India since independence. As Richard L. Park has pointed out, "The main lines of India's foreign policy were established by Jawaharlal Nehru and they have been continued, with some alterations in emphasis."[11] Within the broad framework of general principles and underlying conditioning, India's foreign policy went through several phases during the Nehru era, and the changes have been more marked since Nehru's death, an event which marked a watershed in India's foreign as well as domestic policy. A less clearly defined but perhaps even more significant watershed came in the late 1950's or early 1960's, epitomized by changes in the international situation and particularly in Sino-Indian relations, and culminating with the Chinese attack in late 1962.

A distinguished Indian journalist, Inder Malhotra, has suggested that Indian foreign policy can be divided into three main phases. The first phase, from 1947 to 1954, was one of "idealism" and "achievement," during which "India was able to play in international affairs a role out of all proportion to its intrinsic strength." Nehru seemed to enjoy his role as spokesman of the new Asia, as an opponent of colonialism, and as a champion of world peace, but he paid little attention to more immediate questions of foreign policy, including the threats posed to India by the Chinese occupation of Tibet in 1950. The second phase, from 1954 to 1961, was "a strange and contradictory" one. It was the heyday of the *Panchsheel* and of nonalignment. Relations with the Soviet Union and with Communist China until 1959 were cordial, at least on the surface, and those with the United States went through a series of ups and downs. "The biggest failure of the 1954–61 period, however, was the Government's . . . utter inability to correlate foreign policy with the needs of national security." This is a problem which has continued to bedevil India. The third phase, since 1961, has been a "period of confusion," during which India has been unable to adjust

[10] Phillips Talbot, "Half-Empty or Half Full? Impressions of India Revisited," American Universities Field Staff, South Asia Series XIII, No. 2 (India), March, 1969 (PT–2–'69), p. 12.

[11] Richard L. Park, "India's Foreign Policy: 1964–1968," *Current History,* LIV (April, 1968), 244.

to the consequences of the border war with China in 1962 and the war with Pakistan in 1965 or "fully to comprehend the bewildering complexities of the international situation." It has taken unrealistic attitudes on problems of Asian security, and its "excessive dependence" on the Soviet Union for arms and on the United States for food and economic aid "has made the country vulnerable to pressures from both the Super Powers."[12]

"India's current foreign policy is less concerned with the issues of the cold war than was Nehru's policy. Although a world of 'peaceful coexistence' remains prominent in India's world view, the new Indian foreign policy places greater stress on securing friends nearby and promoting a more viable intra-Asian sense of self-reliance."[13] India is clearly attempting, as Dilip Mukerjee has observed, to "diversify" its foreign relations in order to "gain greater leverage in a multipolar world."[14] Since the change for the worse in its relations with China, and particularly since the war with Pakistan in 1965, there have been repeated demands within India for more realistic policies and for "fresh thinking in foreign policy."[15]

### Relations with Pakistan

In view of the past relationships of the people who now inhabit the two countries and in view of their inescapable intimacy, despite their limited contacts and strained relations, the relations between India and Pakistan might well be treated as aspects of domestic rather than of foreign policies. Pakistan is at once India's "first line of defense" and closest neighbor, and at the same time the source or the object of some of India's deepest concerns in foreign matters. Indeed, India's relations with Pakistan have been the most absorbing aspect of its foreign relations; they have colored almost every phase of its foreign policy, and its entire international outlook and approach.

In their attitudes toward each other, India and Pakistan are influenced by a communal past, the tragedy of partition, two major armed conflicts (in 1948 and 1965) and many minor clashes and confrontations, limited diplomatic and personal contacts, mutual recriminations and propaganda exchanges, and continuously strained relations. Feel-

12 Inder Malhotra, "Three Phases of Foreign Policy," *The Statesman,* Aug. 15, 1969.

13 Park, "India's Foreign Policy: 1964–1968," p. 244.

14 Dilip Mukerjee, "P.M.'s Tours Should Be Better Linked with Foreign Policy," *The Statesman Weekly,* Oct. 5, 1968.

15 See, for example, Mukerjee, *ibid.;* Girilal Jain, "Soft Line Towards China," *The Times of India,* Feb. 19, 1969; and Bimla Prasad, "A Fresh Look at India's Foreign Policy," *International Studies,* VIII (January, 1967), 277–299.

ings of suspicion and distrust have been exacerbated by differences on a long list of specific issues, notably settlement of property claims of persons who were forced to move from one country to the other and abandon much of their property in so doing, disposition of stores and assets after partition, trade relations, exchange and currency difficulties, differing attitudes and policies in foreign affairs, the canal waters and other water disputes, and the Kashmir question.

Of the many specific issues in dispute between India and Pakistan the most vexing have been those relating to canal waters and to Kashmir. In 1960, after years of intermittent negotiation, India and Pakistan, through the good offices of the International Bank for Reconstruction and Development (the World Bank), reached an agreement on the use of the waters of the Indus River system; but the Kashmir question seems to be as far from solution as ever, and it remains the major issue in Indo-Pakistan relations.

**The Canal Waters Question.**  Whereas most of East Pakistan has too much water and experiences frequent and devastating floods, large parts of West Pakistan get too little water and are dependent on the rather uncertain supplies which are made available through some half dozen of the rivers which make up the Indus River system, the vital artery of West Pakistan. Three of these rivers — the Jhelum, the Chenab, and the Indus itself — rise either in Tibet or in remote parts of Kashmir, but three others — the Beas, the Ravi, and the Sutlej — flow through northwest India into West Pakistan and can therefore be diverted for India's uses.

As a consequence of partition the question of the use of the waters of these rivers, whose annual flow is twice that of the Nile, became crucial for Pakistan, but for some years no progress was made in resolving this life-or-death issue. In 1951 David Lilienthal, former Chairman of the Tennessee Valley Authority, suggested a solution, involving the working out of a comprehensive engineering plan for the use of the waters of the Indus River system and financial assistance by the World Bank. In March 1952, both India and Pakistan accepted an offer of good offices from the President of the Bank. Representatives of the two countries negotiated intermittently for many months, in Washington and elsewhere,[16] but not until the spring of 1959 was agreement reached on the main issues in dispute. The drafting of the treaty required further negotiations, over a period of a year and a half. Finally, on September 19, 1960, the Indus Waters Treaty was signed in Karachi by Prime Minister Nehru, President Mohammad Ayub

[16] See Eugene Black, "The Indus: A Moral for Nations," *New York Times Magazine,* Dec. 11, 1960. Mr. Black was President of the World Bank in 1960.

Khan, and W. A. B. Iliff, Vice-President of the World Bank. Subject to certain exceptions, the treaty allocated the waters of the eastern rivers — the Ravi, the Beas, and the Sutlej — for the use of India, and of the three western rivers — the Indus, the Jhelum, and the Chenab — for the use of Pakistan. Simultaneously an international financial agreement was signed by representatives of Australia, Canada, West Germany, New Zealand, Pakistan, the United Kingdom, the United States, and the World Bank. This agreement created the Indus Basin Development Fund of about $900 million to finance the construction of irrigation and other works in Pakistan provided for in the Indus Waters Treaty. Approximately $640 million was to be supplied by the participating governments, $174 million by India under the Indus Waters Treaty, and $80 million by a World Bank loan to Pakistan.[17]

**The Kashmir Question.** Prime Minister Nehru hailed the signing of these agreements as "a unique occasion," and he expressed the hope "that this will bring prosperity to a vast number of the people on both sides and will increase the goodwill and friendship for India and Pakistan." Many people in India and elsewhere hoped that the agreement on the canal waters issue, and the improved relations between India and Pakistan which this symbolized, might make it possible for the two countries to reach some amicable understanding regarding the even more complicated and much more highly publicized question of Kashmir. "In many ways," however, as Aloys Michel has pointed out, the Kashmir question "is the antithesis of the Indus Water Dispute. For the Kashmir problem is not *essentially* a question of land or water, but of people and prestige."[18]

From the beginning of the dispute shortly after the two countries began their independent existence, the disagreements between India and Pakistan have been complete.[19] They have not even been able to agree on the facts of the dispute, not to mention the proper interpretation of these facts. The Indian position is based on the "fact" of the accession of the Maharaja of Kashmir to India in 1947, the

[17] See Aloys A. Michel, *The Indus Rivers: A Study of the Effects of Partition* (New Haven, 1967), pp. 254–265.

[18] *Ibid.*, p. 518.

[19] For details of the complicated developments in and relating to Kashmir since 1947, see Michael Brecher, *The Struggle for Kashmir* (New York, 1953); Josef Korbel, *Danger in Kashmir* (Princeton, N.J., 1954); Lord Birdwood, *Two Nations and Kashmir* (London, 1956); J. B. Das Gupta, *Indo-Pakistan Relations, 1947–1955* (Amsterdam, 1958), Chaps. III and IV; Sisir Gupta, *Kashmir: A Study in Indo-Pakistan Relations* (Bombay, 1966); J. B. Das Gupta, *Jammu and Kashmir* (The Hague, 1968); and G. W. Choudhury, *Pakistan's Relations with India, 1947–1966* (New York, 1968), especially Chap. 3.

"fact" of Pakistani aggression in Kashmir, the "fact" of the manifest desire of the post-partition governments of that part of Kashmir on the Indian side of the cease-fire line to associate Kashmir with India. Indian spokesmen point out that India brought the question before the Security Council of the United Nations early in 1948, and they criticize the Security Council, and especially the United States and Britain which are permanent members, for allowing Pakistan to befog the issue and for taking an unduly critical position with regard to the Indian claims ever since. They have been maintaining for some years, certainly since 1952, that "the accession of Kashmir to India is complete in law and in fact," and they seem to imply that, in spite of the contrary views of Pakistan, the Security Council, and vocal segments of world public opinion, the Kashmir issue is in fact settled. Presumably they are willing to settle for effective Indian control of the Valley of Kashmir and of other parts of the former princely State on the Indian side of the cease-fire line, while at the same time they have not abandoned their theoretical claims to all of Jammu and Kashmir.

When Pakistanis call attention to India's pledge to hold a plebiscite in Kashmir to determine the wishes of the inhabitants as to their political future, Indians argue that this "pledge" was contingent on certain preconditions that have not been realized, that the offer was not a standing one, and that a plebiscite is no longer feasible or desirable. In an address in New York on March 31, 1966, Mrs. Indira Gandhi reaffirmed the Indian position on a plebiscite, and cited two additional reasons for this position. "It is now too late to talk of a plebiscite. The second invasion of Kashmir by Pakistan last summer has destroyed whatever marginal or academic value the old United Nations resolution might have had. Kashmir is also vital to the defense of India in Ladakh against China." India also maintains that the present government in Kashmir represents the popular will, and that a plebiscite would only tend to raise old issues and divisions and might produce communal tensions between Hindus and Muslims, not only in Kashmir but throughout India. To the Pakistani contention that the majority of the people, who are Muslims, are living in a police state and would much prefer to be a part of Pakistan, Indians emphasize the concept of the secular state and point to the many millions of Muslims who are living peacefully within the Republic of India.

Following the border war between India and China in October-November 1962, India and Pakistan agreed, under pressure from the United States and Britain, and with considerable reluctance, at least on India's part, to hold a series of talks on the Kashmir issue. Five rounds of talks — the most comprehensive exchanges on Kashmir between the two countries — were held between December 1962 and May 1963, but no progress was made in resolving the impasse. The Tashkent Declaration of January 10, 1966 (see below), sidestepped the Kashmir issue, stating simply that "Jammu and Kashmir was discussed, and each of the sides set forth its respective position." Since then, in spite of some proposals by well-known Indians for fresh overtures to Pakistan on the issue, in spite of continued Pakistani demands and protests, and in spite of occasional discussion in the UN Security Council or General Assembly and criticism in some countries, the Indian position on Kashmir has remained frozen and inflexible. As Mrs. Gandhi said in 1968, "India has nothing to negotiate with Pakistan on Kashmir."[20]

The existence of a major dispute between two of the most important nations along the periphery of the Communist-dominated world, involving a strategically important territory deep in Asia and close to both Russian and Chinese territories, creates a situation of weakness in an already vulnerable part of the world. The dispute also raises embarrassing problems for Western states, particularly Britain and the United States, which would like to be on close terms with both India and Pakistan. This goal is made more difficult by the inclination of both of these South Asian countries to test the attitudes of other states by the position which they take on the Kashmir issue and by the dissatisfaction which both have expressed, for different reasons, with the position taken by the United Nations, and especially by Britain and the United States, on Kashmir.

**Indo-Pakistan Relations since 1960.** The signing of the Indus Waters Treaty in 1960 may be regarded as the high point in Indo-Pakistan relations. Since then, and especially since the 1965 war, relations between the two countries have deteriorated badly. India was very critical of Pakistan's allegedly unfriendly attitude during its difficulties with China in late 1962 and of Pakistan's border and other agreements with China in 1963. In the last months of his life Nehru took a number of steps which seemed to indicate a renewed desire to improve relations with Pakistan. For example, Sheikh Abdullah, former Prime Minister of Kashmir, was released from custody and, with Nehru's approval, visited Pakistan to confer with Ayub Khan.

[20] One of the best studies of the Kashmir question by an Indian scholar, published in 1968, contained the following statement: "It is useless . . . to examine the various alternative solutions proffered for the settlement of the Kashmir question. No solution can be imposed from without, and Pakistan would do well to be satisfied with a bilateral solution, instead of hoping to gain from any third party support, or from a possible twist in the unpredictable Asian balance of power." Das Gupta, *Jammu and Kashmir,* p. 385.

His visit was hastily concluded, without results, by Nehru's death. Nehru's successor, Lal Bahadur Shastri, was believed to be equally desirous of reversing the trend in Indo-Pakistan relations, but, after a few months, it was apparent that no improvement was in sight.

The events of 1965 brought relations to a new low. In the spring the two countries engaged in limited military exchanges in the desolate Rann of Kutch, and in September, following infiltration of guerrillas into Indian-held Kashmir, some limited Indian advances across the cease-fire line, and a movement of Pakistani troops into Jammu, India and Pakistan became involved in a genuine war, but it was limited in scope, area, and duration.[21] Although both sides claimed a "glorious victory," the war, which was terminated through the good offices of the United Nations Security Council, was militarily a stalemate and had disastrous effects on the international reputations, the economies, and the mutual relations of the two combatants. Both accepted a Russian invitation to meet at Tashkent in January 1966 and, with Kosygin's good offices, were induced to reach agreements to withdraw their military forces to positions they had held prior to August 5, 1965, and to restore "normal and peaceful" relations, including economic and trade relations, communications, and cultural exchanges, as well as diplomatic relations. The military provisions were speedily implemented, but most of the others were not.

India was not happy with the decision of a three-man arbitration commission, announced in 1968, regarding the Rann of Kutch, although the commission awarded India all but 300 square miles of the Rann. In the same year India refused to agree to Pakistan's demand to mediate the question of the use of the waters of the Ganges River — a question precipitated by India's plans to build a dam across the Ganges at Farakka, about ten miles from the border of East Pakistan. India played down the whole issue, claiming that Pakistan was using it for domestic political reasons.[22]

In 1968, also, India was greatly disturbed by the decision of the Soviet Union to provide limited arms aid to Pakistan, and by other evidences that the Soviet Union, while continuing to aid India, was establishing new ties with Pakistan. Indian newspapers frequently asserted that Pakistan was spending relatively more on defense than was India, with less reason, and was also benefiting from arms from both the Soviet Union and Communist China.

---

[21] See Russell Brines, *The Indo-Pakistan Conflict* (London, 1968).

[22] See Joseph Lelyveld, "Ganges Dispute Still Unsolved," *The New York Times,* July 28, 1968. Lelyveld reported that "In recent months the Farakka dispute has been a major issue in the Pakistan press, even dwarfing Kashmir."

In 1969 Indian and Pakistani representatives in the United Nations General Assembly engaged in bitter exchanges, and India was humiliated by the refusal of President Yahya Khan of Pakistan to sit with an Indian delegation to the Islamic summit conference in Rabat in September. Pakistan further aroused India by pointing to the Hindu-Muslim riots in Ahmedabad in the same month, the worst communal rioting and killing since the partition period, as added proof of its oft-asserted charges of discrimination against and persecution of Muslims in India.

In June 1969, Mrs. Gandhi wrote to the new leader of Pakistan, Yahya Khan, proposing the establishment of a joint Indo-Pakistani body to work out the "normalisation and improvement of relations" between the two countries, and renewing the long-standing offer of a no-war pact. In reply the President of Pakistan wrote that "We have always been, and continue to remain, ready to enter into a dialogue as long as it is not only understood but made clear by both sides that it would encompass all outstanding issues," and he referred specifically to "our two outstanding disputes regarding Jammu and Kashmir and the Ganges waters."

### Relations with Other Non-Communist States of Asia

India is also concerned with its relations with other neighbors, which, in spite of certain sources of friction, are much happier than its relations with Pakistan. India has shown a special interest in the Himalayan states of Nepal and Bhutan, which lie between it and Tibet, now under the direct control of Communist China, and which form a part of India's strategic Himalayan frontier. Indian troops have from time to time entered Nepal, and Indian advisers have been conspicuous in that country. Since 1966 India has made special efforts to improve relations with Nepal; it has increased its economic aid, and has made trade and other concessions to the Himalayan kingdom. Nehru's rather arduous visit to Bhutan in late 1958 was evidence of the gradual and partial emergence of that isolated state into the modern world and of India's special ties with Bhutan, at a time when India is troubled over the possibility of penetration of the area from the north by agents of the Chinese Communists.

Leaders of India and Ceylon have worked hard to accentuate the positive in the relations of their two countries, but these relations have been strained by the differences arising from the treatment of the Tamil-speaking people of Ceylon, some of whom emigrated from India long ago while others are relatively recent arrivals whose status is still uncertain. In 1964 the two countries finally concluded an agreement for the repatriation over a 15-year period of 500,000 Indian immigrants from Ceylon and for the granting of Ceylonese citizenship to more than 300,000 persons of Indian origin in Ceylon; but not until 1969 were the first significant but slow steps taken to implement this pact.

Geographic and historical ties with Burma have always been close. Until 1935, in fact, Burma was associated with India, under the general supervision of the British Viceroy. Burma achieved independence a few months after India, but unlike the larger state it chose to opt out of the Commonwealth. Economic and political bonds between free India and Burma have been numerous, and the natural friendship of the two countries was deepened by the personal friendship of Nehru and U Nu, who was Prime Minister of Burma from 1948 to 1958, and again in 1960–62. Major differences have arisen over Burmese treatment of the large Indian minorities in Burma. Burmans resent the privileged position which many Indians have managed to achieve in the economic life of Burma, and India has shown a special concern for persons of Indian origin in Burma, even though it has urged these people to give their primary loyalties to the state in which they live and work. The attitude of India toward persons of Indian origin in Ceylon and Burma is typical of its general attitude towards the millions of Indians overseas, in many parts of the world.

India has shown a special interest in other countries of Southeast Asia, where in the past Indian cultural and political influence has been strong. It supported the independence struggles in Indonesia and Indochina. In the latter years of the Sukarno era its relations with Indonesia were limited and strained, but since 1965 they have again been cordial. India strongly supported the Geneva agreements of 1954 made with respect to Indochina; it has been consistently critical of the policies of various governments in South Vietnam and of most American actions in Vietnam; it is a leading proponent of United States military withdrawal and an end to the fighting. It has not extended official recognition to either North or South Vietnam, but it has maintained Consulates-General in both Hanoi and Saigon, and it has had *de facto* diplomatic and other relations with both Vietnams, particularly with North Vietnam. Its relations with Laos and Cambodia have been closer.[23] India has had a special, and difficult, role in the former Indochina area, embracing Laos, Cambodia, and North and South Vietnam, as chairman of the International Control Commission, whose other members are Canada and Poland. It has gradually developed

[23] D. R. Sar Desai, *Indian Foreign Policy in Cambodia, Laos, and Vietnam 1947–1964* (Berkeley, Calif., 1968), p. 252.

closer relations with Malaysia and Singapore, where large numbers of Indians live in plural societies composed mainly of Chinese and Malays. Its relations with Thailand and the Philippines, the two Southeast Asian members of SEATO, have been less cordial and less close, but they are improving.

India's growing interest in Southeast Asia is evidenced by increasing contacts and cooperation on many fronts. In 1968 Mrs. Gandhi made state visits to Malaysia and Singapore, and in 1969 to Indonesia. India has even shown some interest in regional cooperation in this area, of a nonmilitary nature.

In the Far East and the Middle East, too, India has special interests and concerns. India, China, and Japan form what is sometimes called the Asian triangle. It is clear that the relative evolution and mutual relations of these three most important Asian states are of special significance in world affairs. Communist China exercises an almost hypnotic influence on India, which does not even recognize the existence of the Nationalist regime on Formosa and which until 1959 was a leading champion of Communist China in the councils of the nations.

The visit of the President of India to Japan in late 1958 was symbolic of the growing awareness of the two most important non-Communist states of Asia of each other. Since then official and unofficial contacts have been more frequent. In a joint communique issued at the end of a five-day state visit to Japan in June 1969, Prime Minister Indira Gandhi joined with Japan's Prime Minister Sato in making special reference to "the growing scope for economic cooperation between the two countries." Actually relations between India and Japan have been rather distant, and their growing contacts are somewhat affected by rivalries in trade and in influence in Southeast Asia and other parts of the continent.

India has been generally more successful than its Muslim neighbor, Pakistan, in its relations with the Muslim states of the Middle East, except Turkey and possibly Iran. Possibly its special interest in Afghanistan and its special efforts to cultivate the spokesmen of Arab nationalism, especially Nasser, have been prompted in part by a desire to counteract Pakistani influence in this part of the world; but these attitudes may also be explained by other basic considerations of Indian foreign policy. Nehru established close ties with Nasser, and his daughter, Mrs. Gandhi, has obviously been influenced by the Nehru-Nasser relationship. Nasser allowed Indian contingents, but not Pakistani, in the United Nations Emergency Force in the Middle East. Although India recognized Israel, it has never accredited an Ambassador to Israel, and during the Arab-Israeli war in 1967 the official Indian position was strongly pro-Arab. Mrs. Gandhi and her colleagues were widely criticized for their stand, in India as well as in many Western countries. India's relations with the Arab countries became cooler as a result of the exclusion of the Indian delegation from the Islamic summit conference in Rabat in September 1969, on the insistence of Pakistan. Nasser favored Indian participation, but, in addition to Pakistan, the position of two Arab countries, Morocco and Jordan, was regarded as so hostile that India withdrew her Ambassadors from these two countries.

India sponsored two of the major Asian conferences in the postwar period, namely the Asian Relations Conference in 1947 and the conference on Indonesia in 1949, and it was one of the sponsors of the greatest of all Asian conferences, that at Bandung in April 1955. While in a sense Chou En-lai and not Nehru was the "star" of the Bandung Conference, the Indian Prime Minister was certainly one of the major luminaries at this meeting, which was hailed in India as marking a new era for Asia in world affairs. India has been in fact a leader in most of the Asian associations in which it has participated — the "Colombo Powers," the Colombo Plan, the Economic Commission for Asia and the Far East, and many other specialized organizations — and it was the prime mover in the loose association of Asian and African members of the United Nations which is now referred to as the Asian-African or the Afro-Asian Group.

After Bandung India seemed to lose interest in Asian cooperation, and its influence and prestige in Asia, and in world affairs generally, were greatly reduced as a result of the humiliation inflicted on it by Communist China in 1962. Since the late 1960's, however, India has shown a renewed interest in unilateral and regional, as well as bilateral, cooperation with the other Asian countries, especially those in Southeast Asia.

### Relations with Communist China

Because of their vast size, large and rapidly expanding populations, economic growth and unlimited potentials, relations between India and China will do much to shape the future of Asia and indeed of the world. The Communist leaders of China and the democratic leaders of India are trying to deal with essentially similar problems of political unity and stability, economic development, and social uplift in fundamentally different ways, and much will depend on their comparative success or failure. If China under communism makes great economic progress and is able to demonstrate convincingly that Communist techniques, however ruthless, do produce results in terms of individual living standards and national strength, while at the same time the Indian experiment in economic and political development and social change does not produce sufficiently convincing results, the prospects for democracy in Asia and in the world will be dim indeed, whereas the attractive power of the Asian brand of communism centering in Peking will vastly increase. In this sense there is, in spite of all the protestations in India to the contrary, a fundamental rivalry between democratic India and Communist China, with very high stakes at issue. The leaders of India are probably well aware of this basic test, but at the same time they appear to believe that they are on the right path, and that an increasingly powerful India can co-exist with an increasingly powerful China, whatever their differences in ideological outlook.

Until 1959 official relations between India and China were generally close and friendly, and there were few major disagreements between them. Nehru and his associates were markedly conciliatory in their approach to Communist China — "nobody on earth," observed Vincent Sheean, "has tried harder to make friends with the Chinese than Jawaharlal has"[24] — and public opinion generally was favorably disposed toward the Communist regime in China.

India was the leading champion of the claims of Communist China for admission to the United Nations and for its "rightful place" in world affairs. It was outspokenly critical of the China policies of the United States, which, in its view, was mainly responsible for propping up "the so-called Kuomintang regime on Formosa" and for keeping the Communist Government of China out of the UN. Indian and Chinese leaders frequently exchanged visits and usually received warm receptions. As has been indicated, the statement of the famous "five principles of peace" — the *Panchsheel* — was first made in a Sino-Indian treaty on Tibet and in the Nehru–Chou En-lai declaration of 1954; and spokesmen of Communist China often referred to these principles.

Until 1959, at least, the prevailing climate of opinion in India was markedly sympathetic toward the "New China." Chinese Communist literature was available in India in large quantities and at very low prices. A number of Indian organizations helped to promote the favorable climate regarding China. The great majority of members of these organizations were non-Communists who were nevertheless so favorably disposed toward the New China that they tended to become Chinese apologists and defenders; or perhaps it would be fairer to state that they were so impressed with the apparent progress of China under Communist control and so indignant at what they regarded as insulting treatment by outside powers of a fellow-Asian nation that

[24] Vincent Sheean, *Nehru: The Years of Power* (New York, 1960), p. 185. For a brief summary of Indo-Chinese relations in recent years, see Brecher, *Nehru,* pp. 588–592.

they tended to accept a roseate picture of actual conditions in the New China and to overlook the human and social costs of whatever progress was being made.

For all the professions of friendship and brotherhood, it is not difficult to find evidences of open differences and fundamental rivalry between the two great Asian states. Undoubtedly the low point in Sino-Indian relations prior to 1959 came in the fall of 1950, when without warning Chinese Communist troops moved into Tibet. India's protest against this action led only to an exchange of blunt notes. Two years later another low point in Sino-Indian relations was reached when an Indian formula to resolve the prisoner exchange issue in Korea, which was introduced in the Political Committee of the General Assembly of the United Nations in early November 1952 and approved by the Committee in December, was scathingly rejected by the U.S.S.R. and Communist China.

Even before 1959 the presence of Chinese Communist forces along the borders of India, and of Nepal and Bhutan, which India regards as falling within its security zone, and the increased Chinese activities along the Himalayan frontier were viewed by India with many misgivings. India repeatedly protested to the Chinese Government because Chinese maps still showed parts of Assam and Kashmir as belonging to China. The battle of the maps was an indication of India's great sensitivity to any real or alleged violations of her northern territories and of her acute security consciousness.

The actions of the Chinese Communists in Tibet and along the Indo-Chinese borders in 1959 hit India like an icy blast from the high Himalayas, and seemed to provoke a marked change in public moods and attitudes, as well as in official policy. In March a widespread rebellion in Tibet against the Chinese was ruthlessly suppressed by Chinese Communist troops. Shortly afterward the young Dalai Lama, and some 13,000 other Tibetans, escaped from Tibet and arrived in India, where they were given asylum. In August the occupation of the frontier post of Longju in India's Northeast Frontier Agency by Chinese Communist troops, which was followed by a whole series of border incidents, aroused strong anti-Chinese feelings in India and strong criticisms of the foreign policy of India.[25] Nehru called the Chinese occupation of Longju a "clear case of aggression," and he announced his firm intention "to defend our borders and to strengthen them and thus to protest the integrity of India"; but he also recalled the long friendship between India and China, and he indicated that "the door

[25] For an account of the Sino-Indian border dispute in late 1959 and the Indian reactions to it, see *Indian Affairs Record* (New Delhi), V (December, 1959), 279–288.

is always open to accommodation." When Parliament met in November Nehru defended himself vigorously against criticisms that he did not take the Chinese challenge seriously enough.

In the fall of 1959 the Government of India issued two White Papers on the crisis with China, consisting of the texts of the exchanges of notes and memoranda with China over border issues and related matters. Two more White Papers were issued in 1960, in March and November, and seven more by 1965. These White Papers clearly revealed that the Indian Government had protested in the strongest terms against the Chinese violations of the Sino-Indian frontiers, but that, as Nehru said in the Lok Sabha in April 1960 after talks with Chou En-lai, India and China "always came up against the hard rock of a different set of facts." These differences were highlighted in two very divergent reports, submitted in December 1960, after several weeks of fruitless negotiations between Indian and Chinese representatives.[26]

Many observers in India and in the West were convinced that the crisis with China was a watershed in the history of India's foreign relations and orientation. Vincent Sheean, a sympathetic Western observer with close contacts with Gandhi as well as with Nehru and many other leaders of modern India, expressed this view eloquently in his biography of Nehru, published in 1960:

> Politically speaking, the India-China relationship of the late summer and autumn of 1959 seems very nearly to dominate the mind of India. It certainly dominates every other consideration in foreign affairs. . . . The passionate resentment against China which inhabits the very air of India today is a political reality of the greatest importance. It flows in upon almost every other consideration, even the most distant; it pervades the intellectual and emotional climate of the hour. It has required every resource of Nehru's personal supremacy to ride out this storm without disaster, and it casts the chilliest and most somber fog over the future.[27]

Tensions between India and China mounted, and in 1962 they reached a new and even more serious climax. In September and October 1962, Indian and Chinese troops along the borders of India and Tibet in the Northeast Frontier Agency (NEFA) and Ladakh engaged in limited skirmishes. On October 20 large numbers of Chinese troops launched attacks in both NEFA and Ladakh and soon

[26] *Report of the Officials of the Governments of India and the People's Republic of China on the Boundary Question* (New Delhi, 1961).

[27] Sheean, *Nehru,* pp. 186–187.

occupied large tracts of Indian territory. Indian forces were able to give a good account of themselves in Ladakh, but in NEFA they were routed, and within three weeks the Chinese had moved over the mountain passes and threatened the plains of Assam. Just as India seemed about to face a major invasion, the Chinese abruptly terminated the fighting and announced that as of December 1 they would withdraw to the positions they had occupied on November 7, 1959. Thus the threatened invasion turned out to be no more than a border war; but India had suffered severe reverses, militarily, diplomatically, politically, and psychologically. Even Nehru admitted that "we have been living in an artificial atmosphere of our own creation," and 'he insisted that India had been shocked into reality by the Chinese actions.[28]

Since the Chinese attack in 1962 India has been faced with the unpleasant prospect of two hostile neighbors. In many respects it seems to regard the Chinese threat as more serious than the continuing threat from Pakistan. After all, China is stronger than India, while Pakistan is weaker. The danger of Sino-Pakistan "collusion" is a specter which haunts Indian minds, and they see plentiful evidence that this is more than a specter. For example, they point to the border agreement between Pakistan and China in 1963 concerning territory which they regard as within India's security zone; to the Chinese "ultimatum" and threatening moves in the Nathu La Pass area between Sikkim and Tibet during the Indo-Pakistan war of 1965; to the increasingly close relations between Pakistan and China since 1963, including Chinese support for Pakistan on the Kashmir issue and Chinese military aid to Pakistan; and to alleged Chinese assistance in building roads from northern Pakistan (Gilgit, Hunza, and parts of Pakistan-held Kashmir) to connect with Chinese roads to Kashgar in Sinkiang and between Sinkiang and Tibet.

A new dimension to the Chinese threat has existed since October 16, 1964, when China exploded its first atomic bomb. Since then it has successfully tested several more nuclear devices, apparently including hydrogen bombs, and it is developing intermediate, and perhaps intercontinental, ballistic missiles as well. On April 24, 1970 it launched its first space satellite, thus confirming its growing technological and missile delivery capabilities. Thus, at a time when it has been shocked into awareness of its increasing security needs and has been rapidly building up its conventional military forces and defenses, India is faced with the threat of nuclear blackmail, or worse.

[28] See John Rowland, *A History of Sino-Indian Relations: Hostile Co-existence* (Princeton, N.J., 1967); and W. F. Van Bekelen, *India's Foreign Policy and the Border Dispute with China* (The Hague, 1964).

The dilemma faced by India is that whereas her government favors the reduction in the world of the nuclear threat and has consistently supported efforts leading towards disarmament, the national interests of India demand that non-nuclear powers, such as India, be protected from the direct threat of nuclear weapons, and be allowed to develop nuclear power for peaceful purposes. . . . some Indians, though not the government, . . . believe that India may have to build nuclear weapons in the interests of national security. The government has opposed nuclear arming of India and the proliferation of nuclear capability and delivery systems to other countries, but not at the expense of a lack of safeguards that might result in the nuclear blackmail of India.[29]

India was very critical of the nuclear non-proliferation treaty, originally presented to the Eighteen Nation Disarmament Committee in Geneva in August 1967, and later submitted in revised form by both the Soviet Union and the United States for general ratification, and it refused to ratify it, on the grounds that (1) the treaty sought to ban nonnuclear nations forever from the nuclear club without giving them adequate guarantees, (2) it did not assure compensatory concessions and limitations on the part of the nuclear states, and (3) China would obviously not adhere to the treaty.

India is disturbed not only by the close relations between Pakistan and China, by Chinese arms aid to Pakistan, and by the evidence of the Chinese development of a nuclear weapons systems, but also by the open and clandestine encouragement and support which China is giving to dissident tribal groups inside India, particularly the Nagas, and to extreme Communist groups in India, particularly the "Naxalites." Several hundred Naga "hostiles" have gone to China for indoctrination and training in guerrilla warfare, and China has supplied them with arms, military equipment, and supplies on a fairly large scale. It has given similar, if more limited, support to other tribal groups in sensitive areas, such as the Mizos in the Manipur-Assam-Tripura region, and perhaps some tribal groups in NEFA. Peking has given considerable support to the Communist Party of India (Marxist), since the split in the Indian Communist Party in 1964, but it has also been critical of some of the tactics and leaders of the CPI(M), including the leading figures in the party in West Bengal and Kerala, the two Indian states where coalition regimes dominated by the CPI(M) have been in power.

[29] Park, "India's Foreign Policy: 1964–1968," p. 244. The first sentence in the quotation appears in Professor Park's original manuscript, but not in the published version.

When more radical Communists stirred up a revolt of peasants and tribal peoples in Naxalbari and two adjoining villages in the Darjeeling district of West Bengal in the summer of 1967, a writer in *People's Daily* hailed the uprising as the "prelude to a violent revolution by hundreds of millions of people throughout India," and declared that "The Indian revolution must take the road of relying on the peasant, establishing base areas in the countryside, persisting in protracted armed struggle, and using the countryside to surround the cities."[30] The *Peking Review* professed to see "dozens of Naxalbaris" springing up "in all parts of the Indian countryside."[31] Clearly Peking has laid down a "Maoist line" for India.[32]

Peking's policy towards India," wrote Dr. V. P. Dutt, a leading Indian authority on China, "is predicated on the presumption that India has entered a period of decline and disintegration, . . . and that therefore all that China has to do is to sit pretty, giving a violent push now and then. . . . The Chinese are consequently not interested in any political reconciliation with India." Dr. Dutt argued that "The trouble with India's Chinese policy is that it is always reacting and never acting. . . . An effective Chinese policy would be one which stands up to Peking's aggressive chauvinism and at the same time leaves room for an honourable settlement at a suitable time when Peking curbs its xenophobic nationalism, shows some appreciation of the nationalism of other countries, realises that India is not a house of cards about to collapse and that it is in China's interest to show a spirit of accommodation and to end its conflict with her."[33]

Most Indians still seem to want to be friends with China, if the Chinese will reciprocate. The desire for a renewed "dialogue" with China has often been voiced by Indians in official and unofficial positions and by the Indian press. Mrs. Gandhi expressed this desire in a press conference on New Year's Day, 1969. Thus India may be willing, but China apparently is not.

### Relations with the Soviet Union

Indians are favorably disposed toward China not because but in spite of the Communist orientation of its leadership. The same comment may be made about Indian attitudes toward the Soviet Union. Indians are not very familiar with what is happening in the Soviet

[30] "The Darjeeling Peasant Armed Struggle," *People's Daily,* July 5, 1967.
[31] "Dozens of Naxalbaris," *Peking Review,* Aug. 11, 1967.
[32] See Bhabani Sen Gupta, "A Maoist Line for India," *China Quarterly* (January–March, 1968), 3–16; and same author, "Moscow, Peking, and the Indian Political Scene after Nehru," *Orbis,* XI (Summer, 1968).
[33] Vidya Prakash Dutt, "India and China: Case for Policy Reappraisal," *The Times of India,* July 4, 1967.

Union, and they are inclined to ignore the seamier aspects of the Soviet experiment in Russia. They are profoundly impressed by Russia's obvious economic progress. Many think that the Soviet experience offers a model for them to follow. They are also impressed by the apparent absence of racial and color consciousness in the multinational U.S.S.R., and by the treatment of minority groups; by the flattering attention which the Russian Communists pay to Asia and Asians; by the Soviet encouragement of their independence struggles and their opposition to imperialism, "capitalism," and racialism; and by the Soviet propaganda "offensives" in the era of the "new look" — peace "offensives," economic "offensives," anti-imperial and anti-capitalist "offensives," and cultural "offensives." They do not accept the thesis of a Soviet-Communist threat, nor do they recognize the existence of a Soviet form of imperialism.

Until Stalin's death in 1953 — an event which was officially mourned in India — India's relations with the Soviet Union were confined almost exclusively to the official level; but in the more open and relaxed period of the "new look" India was wooed more directly and more ardently by the Soviets, and the Indian response was quite cordial. The visits of Nehru to the Soviet Union in June 1955, and of Bulganin and Khrushchev to India in November and December of the same year, were high points in the new cordiality. During sixteen days in the Soviet Union Nehru (who was accompanied by Mrs. Indira Gandhi) was given a tremendous welcome and special concessions which had not been extended to any other non-Communist leader. In the joint communiqué at the conclusion of his visit he and the Soviet Prime Minister affirmed their "profound faith that states of different social structures can exist side by side in peace and work for the common good." At the airport in Moscow on his departure, he is reported to have said: "I am leaving my heart behind." Some American commentators "feared that Nehru had also left some of his common sense behind in Moscow."[34] The visit of the Soviet leaders to Afghanistan, India, and Burma was the first such trip for any Soviet leader. During three hectic weeks in India they were greeted by tremendous crowds, and they won many friends by adopting Indian forms of greeting, using the Hindi expression, "Hindi-Russi bhai-bhai," and taking to "native food, customs, and costumes . . . with gusto."[35] The Soviet visitors used Indian platforms to attack Western policies, as well as to support Indian views; and Nehru shared the platform with them on several occasions, although he reaffirmed the determination of India to follow a policy of

[34] Arthur Stein, *India and the Soviet Union: The Nehru Era* (Chicago, 1969), p. 67.
[35] K. P. S. Menon, *The Flying Troika* (London, 1963), pp. 130–131.

nonalignment. The Soviet Union gained a great deal of good will in India by a public espousal of the Indian position on Kashmir and Goa, two issues dear to the heart of official and unofficial India.

During the second half of the 1950's, official Indian policy seemed to be definitely pro-Soviet and pro-Chinese, and to some extent anti-American. Nehru was quick to criticize the British and French for their military operations against Egypt in 1956, but he was slow and tentative in criticizing the almost simultaneous Soviet moves in Hungary. "The Indian government and public media were far more involved emotionally with Suez than with the Hungarian situation."[36] There was, however, considerable opposition to the government's vacillation during the Hungarian crisis, especially noteworthy because this "marked the first time Nehru's foreign policy had ever been subjected to serious, sustained criticism within India."[37] However, in June 1958 the Soviets were annoyed by Nehru's criticism of the execution of the Hungarian leader, Imre Nagy, and by a famous article by Nehru, entitled "The Basic Approach," published in May of the same year, in which the Indian leader referred to "the growing contradictions within the rigid framework of Communism itself."[38] In reply Soviet academician Pavel Yudin, Russia's Ambassador to China, made caustic remarks about Nehru's concept of socialism and India's domestic policies, but he praised Nehru as "the leader of the national liberation struggle of the Indian people" and "the outstanding leader of the world against the warmongers today."[39]

As the Sino-Soviet dispute broke out into the open and as India's relations with China underwent a sharp reversal, Nehru began to distinguish between Soviet communism and Chinese communism and what he called "the broad approach of the USSR to world problems and the Chinese approach."[40] But some critics within India thought that his effusive references to the Soviet Union and his pro-Soviet inclinations were endangering India's security.

In February 1960, Khrushchev visited India en route to Indonesia. His reception, while good, was far less enthusiastic than it had been during his previous visit in late 1955 or President Eisenhower's two months earlier. A number of strains in Indo-Soviet relations developed in 1960 and 1961. These included Soviet annoyance over India's dis-

[36] Stein, *India and the Soviet Union,* p. 89.

[37] *Ibid.,* p. 91.

[38] Jawaharlal Nehru, "The Basic Approach," *A.I.C.C. Economic Review,* V (May 15, 1958).

[39] Pavel Yudin, "Can We Accept Pandit Nehru's Approach?," *World Marxist Review,* I (December, 1958).

[40] Statement in the Rajya Sabha, Nov. 27, 1959.

patch of troops to the Congo and Indian criticisms of the resumption of nuclear testing by the Soviet Union on the eve of the first conference of nonaligned states in Belgrade; but any Indian reservations regarding the Soviet Union were at least temporarily forgotten as a result of the strongly favorable Soviet attitude toward the military annexation of Goa in December 1961.

When India and China became involved in the border war in late 1962, the Soviet Union was placed in a very difficult position. India was disturbed by the original Soviet reactions, including a call for a cease-fire and negotiations with China, but gradually the Soviets adopted a position that was more welcome in India. The Soviets did not cancel plans to assist India in building several factories to build and assemble MIG–21 jet fighters in India, they gave India strong support on Kashmir, and they continued to provide substantial economic aid, which by February 1965 amounted to over one billion dollars, mostly in loans for development projects, including the huge steel mill at Bhilai.

"In the post-Nehru, post-Khrushchev period, the leaders of India and the Soviet Union continue to minimize the differences and emphasize the similarities in their respective positions on international political issues."[41] During the Indo-Pakistan war in 1965 Kosygin played an intermediary role. Both India and Pakistan accepted his invitation to send their top leaders to the Soviet city of Tashkent, and in January 1966, with Kosygin available for personal mediation, Ayub Khan and Lal Bahadur Shastri signed agreements to withdraw their military forces to positions occupied before the fighting began and to work for the "normalisation and improvement" of their relations. The Soviet Union was given a great deal of credit in India for helping to make these agreements possible, and a public opinion poll taken shortly after the Tashkent conference showed that Soviet popularity in India had risen to a new high.

Soon, however, India became rather disillusioned with the fruits of Tashkent and increasingly disturbed by what seemed to be a major change in the Soviet approach to South Asia, from almost complete support of the "special relationship" with India to a more "balanced" position. The new Soviet policy combined continued special support of and interest in India with the establishment of new ties with Pakistan. India was particularly disturbed by the 1968 Soviet decision to extend some arms aid to Pakistan. In the wake of this decision, prominent Indian political leaders and journalists called for a reappraisal of

[41] Stein, *India and the Soviet Union,* p. 260.

India's foreign policy, with particular reference to policy toward the Soviet Union. A marked coolness set in in official Indo-Soviet relations and in public attitudes in India toward the Soviet Union.

These developments, however, did not affect the heavy dependence of India on the Soviet Union and the sympathetic attitude of Mrs. Gandhi and her associates toward Russia. The Soviets have gained an increased leverage as the main supplier of arms to India, especially since the Indo-Pakistan war which led the United States and Britain to suspend all arms aid to both India and Pakistan. Other ties are "the shared concern of Moscow and New Delhi about Communist China and Prime Minister Indira Gandhi's apparent ideological preference for Russian socialism over American capitalism." The result, in the opinion of a correspondent of *The New York Times,* "has been that India's policy on nonalignment has come to mean a policy with a pro-Soviet anti-West bias."[42] Mrs. Gandhi and her group within the Congress Party were often accused of a pro-Soviet bias, or worse. In 1968 an Indian lawyer-journalist referred to "the hapless dependence on Russia which is our foreign policy today."[43] The opposition group to Mrs. Gandhi in the Congress Party often raised the pro-Soviet charge, accusing Mrs. Gandhi of "being a Soviet sycophant" and of "subordinating some of India's policies to the Soviet Union in order to gain the support of the Communists at home." These charges were of course strongly denied by Mrs. Gandhi and her supporters.

The general picture that emerges is that since 1955 India has developed extensive relations with and a considerable dependence upon the Soviet Union, that leaders of India, especially Nehru and Mrs. Gandhi, have been favorably disposed toward the Soviet Union, and that on the whole, subject to many ups and downs and many qualifications, Soviet influence and penetration have been growing. "The forms and techniques of access and penetration" which the Soviet Union has employed have been many. "Its main reliance has been on diplomatic relations, economic and military aid, educational and cultural exchange programs, propaganda, and special ties and contacts with various organizations and groups in India," including front organizations, sympathetic journalists, and the CPI.[44]

[42] Sydney H. Schanberg, "An Indian-Soviet 'Misunderstanding'," *The New York Times,* Dec. 28, 1969.

[43] A. G. Noorani, "Russia and Kashmir," *Opinion,* May 14, 1968, p. 5.

[44] Norman D. Palmer, *Recent Soviet and Chinese Penetration in India and Pakistan: A Study in Formal and Informal Access* (McLean, Va., 1969), p. 36. See also Stein, *India and the Soviet Union,* Chap. 8, and Peter Sager, *Moscow's Hand in India: An Analysis of Soviet Propaganda* (Bombay, 1967).

## India, Britain, and the Commonwealth

In spite of bitter memories of the past and strong anti-imperial sentiments and policies, the prevailing Indian attitudes toward Britain and toward Englishmen have been remarkably good. This was partly due to the orientation of India's leaders, many of whom were educated in Britain or in the British system of education in India, and as a result were often more familiar with British history, literature, and political thought than they were with the culture and institutions of their own country. It was also partly due to the circumstances of the British withdrawal; although independence came only after a long struggle, in the final stages the British speeded up the timetable and withdrew with a considerable amount of grace and dignity.

Contacts with India and Britain have remained close since 1947. India has benefited from its continued associations with Britain in the Commonwealth, the sterling area, the Colombo Plan organization, and other multilateral associations. Thousands of Englishmen still live and work in India, and much larger numbers of Indians live and work in Britain, and many Indians still study in British universities and other educational institutions.

The British impact on India is still clearly visible in many tangible and intangible ways. India's parliamentary system, most of its other political institutions, its judicial and legal structure and practices, its administrative organization, its educational system, its military organization, and to a large extent its business and professional life are patterned after British models. British political and economic ideas are still pervasive and influential in India, although they mingle with other foreign and a widening stream of indigenous ideas. About half of all foreign investment in India is British. For many years Britain was the most important of India's trading partners, although today it shares that position with the United States. British economic aid to India has been substantial, although again it has been overshadowed by American aid. As compared with the British influence in and impact on India, however, the United States is a parvenu.

Official and unofficial Indian attitudes toward Britain have, of course, varied greatly among different groups and at different times. India's decision to remain in the Commonwealth, under a special formula, came as something of a surprise, in view of the long struggle of the leaders of the new nation against the British connection. Some Indians criticized Nehru for going to London for the coronation of Queen Elizabeth in 1953 and marching in the procession, along with other Commonwealth Prime Ministers; but the coronation received considerable favorable attention in India, almost as if the imperial tie still remained.

A major crisis developed in Indo-British relations at the time of the Suez crisis in 1956, when India severely criticized the British military moves against Egypt as an attempt to revive evil imperial ways. In 1961 Queen Elizabeth was very well received during a state visit in India, but shortly afterwards new tensions developed over a number of issues, including conflicting policies in the Congo, especially Katanga, British restrictions on Commonwealth immigrants — a recurrent and very sensitive issue with racial overtones — and British criticisms of the Indian military take-over of Goa. India was continually unhappy over what it alleged to be an unfriendly British position toward its stand on Kashmir, as reflected in the votes of the British representative in the Security Council whenever the Kashmir question was raised and in comments in Parliament and the British press. It appreciated prompt British military assistance when it was attacked by China in late 1962, but it was less appreciative of the combined British and American pressure to enter into negotiations with Pakistan on the Kashmir question. It was generally satisfied with British support and understanding in its protracted crisis with Communist China.

A new low in Indo-British relations came in the fall of 1965, when, at the beginning of the conflict with Pakistan, Prime Minister Harold Wilson made a statement that was interpreted in India as very unsympathetic and unfriendly, showing a markedly pro-Pakistan bias, and when similar "anti-Indian" statements appeared in the British press or were made by BBC commentators. The halt of British economic and military aid added to India's sense of grievance. Even as late as December 3, 1968, a leading Indian newspaper, *The Indian Express,* declared that "Since Mr. Harold Wilson's mischievous and disastrous intervention in Indo-Pakistan affairs, relations between Britain and India have been at an all-time low." The comment appeared in an editorial prompted by the visit of the British Foreign Secretary, Michael Stewart, which apparently did much to place Indo-British relations on a better footing.

Whenever Indian and British policies have sharply diverged, some demands have been voiced in India for the severance of the Commonwealth tie. These demands were quite vocal at the time of the Suez crisis of 1956, the Goa occupation, and particularly the Indo-Pakistan war, when Mr. Wilson's statement aroused such a storm of protest in India. On each such occasion the Congress leaders have defended the Commonwealth association, have emphasized the benefits India derives from it, and have pointed out that the Commonwealth is an association of many nations, mostly in Asia and Africa, in which Britain is a leading but not dominant member. Many Indians have been impressed with the fact that in recent years the gloomiest views on the future of the Commonwealth seem to come from Britishers, and that recent British policies, more than those of any other member, are weakening what was once referred to as the British Commonwealth.

A typical statement of the official Indian position on the Commonwealth was made by Foreign Minister Dinesh Singh in the Lok Sabha on April 8, 1969: ". . . the point is often missed that it is not India which is weakening the Commonwealth; it is the action of the UK which is weakening the Commonwealth today. . . . We shall continue to be there. . . . We are not in favour of liquidation. We are in favour of a useful association. Therefore, it will be our effort to try to work in the Commonwealth so long as it is compatible with our interests and our principles." But he also said: "There is nothing sacrosanct about the Commonwealth. The moment we feel that it is not in our national interest to stay on in the Commonwealth, we shall not hesitate to come out."

## Relations with the United States

Prior to independence few Americans had direct contact with India and most of these were traders, missionaries, and consular officials.[45] Americans took considerable interest in the Indian struggle for independence. This interest was enhanced by occasional visits to the United States of outstanding Indian leaders, notably Vivekananda in the 1890's and Rabindranath Tagore on five occasions between 1912 and 1930. One prominent leader of the Indian Nationalist movement, Lala Lajpat Rai, lived in the United States for several years (1913–19). Another, Jayaprakash Narayan, spent an equal period of time in the United States in the 1920's, working at odd jobs in several States and studying at several American universities. Gandhi captured the hearts and imagination of the American people, as he did of people in many other parts of the world, but he never visited the United States. Nehru was well-known in America well before 1947, although he did not visit the United States until 1949. The American image of India was a mixed one, formed by conflicting impressions of Gandhi and Maharajas, the Taj Mahal and the burning ghats at Benares, glamor and the terrible economic and social conditions pictured so vividly in Katherine Mayo's best-selling shocker, *Mother India*.[46] The Indian image of America was

[45] See E. R. Schmidt, *American Relations with South Asia, 1900–1940* (unpublished doctoral dissertation, University of Pennsylvania, 1955).
[46] See Harold R. Isaacs, *Scratches on Our Minds: American Images of China and India* (New York, 1958), pp. 239–378.

equally mixed, reflecting a confused kaleidoscope of vast material progress and exploitative capitalism, of the Declaration of Independence and Abraham Lincoln and racial discrimination in the South and imperialism in Latin America, of gratitude for the American interest in India's independence struggle and resentment at the picture of Indian life presented in *Mother India.*

As long as India was under British control the official policy of the United States was largely a stand-offish one. This became less true during World War II. Thousands of American GI's were stationed in India — most of them in rather undesirable places such as Karachi and Calcutta and the jungles of Assam — and the Roosevelt administration, convinced that the tough British policy toward the Indian National Congress was interfering with the objectives of the combined war effort in Asia and was sowing the seeds of later troubles, showed enough interest in the situation in India to alarm the British and to gain the lasting appreciation of the Indian leaders and people.[47]

Since the end of the war Indians and Americans have got to know each other better, on both official and unofficial levels.[48] These closer contacts have not erased the great areas of ignorance and misunderstanding of the past; they have even added new tensions arising from differences in approaches and in policies. But fundamentally the relations between India and the United States have been good, based as they are on shared objectives and on mutual friendship and respect. "Our two republics," said Nehru in a radio and television address to the American people in December 1956, during his second visit to the United States, "share a common faith in democratic institutions and the democratic way of life, and are dedicated to the cause of peace and freedom." "What is important," he stated nearly a year later, "is the basic approach between one country and another. In regard to that I am quite convinced that the basic approach of India and the United States, in spite of often hard criticism on either side, is a friendly ap-

[47] See *ibid.,* p. 300.

[48] For commentaries on Indo-American relations since World War II, see L. K. Rosinger, *India and the United States: Political and Economic Relations* (New York, 1950); Phillips Talbot and S. L. Poplai, *India and America* (New York, 1958); Selig S. Harrison, ed., *India and the United States* (New York, 1961); N. D. Palmer, "Ups and Downs in Indo-American Relations," *The Annals of the American Academy of Political and Social Science,* CCXCIV (July, 1954), 113–123, "The United States and India," *Current History,* XXVIII (January, 1955), 43–50, "India and the United States: Maturing Relations," *Current History,* XXXVI (March, 1959), 129–134, *South Asia and United States Policy* (Boston, 1966); Chester Bowles, *A View from New Delhi: Selected Speeches and Writings* 1963–1969 (Bombay, 1969); and John Kenneth Galbraith, *Ambassador's Journal: A Personal Account of the Kennedy Years* (Boston, 1969).

proach, is an appreciative approach, an approach with a desire to understand and improve relations with each other." The most thorough study of Indian-American relations that has yet been made — based on two years of discussions by thirty-four Indian and American specialists and written by an Indian and an American — reached this conclusion: "Despite the differences of approach and of policy that have so far troubled Indian-American relations and that may for some time continue to do so, this study has shown that the mutual interests of India and the United States far outweigh the differences, that it is strongly in the interests of both India and the United States for the two countries to cooperate effectively on important world problems, and that the mutual advantage of cooperation is being increasingly recognized in both countries as their policy interests touch at a growing number of points."[49]

However, in the January 1954 issue of *Foreign Affairs* an Indian writer who signed himself simply as "P," later identified as the well-known scholar-diplomat, K. M. Panikkar, warned that "there is a growing difference between South Asian opinion and the United States in matters affecting world policy." On three issues, in particular, the differences in the mid-1950's were great and disturbing. These issues were: (1) approaches to peace, (2) the seriousness and reality of the Soviet-Communist threat, and (3) policies toward Communist China.[50]

During the cold war era the United States placed emphasis upon national security and collective security arrangements, of which NATO was the outstanding example. This policy was viewed with real alarm in India. Nehru repeatedly criticized the reliance on collective security arrangements, which in his judgment had created "insecurity, uncertainty, and instability," and had heightened rather than lessened international tensions. He was particularly critical of SEATO, which he insisted had "no reality" and increased the danger of Asian involvement in the power struggle between the two rival giants of the contemporary world. He was quite bitter about Pakistan's adherence to SEATO, on the ground that this had brought the cold war to the very gates of India. In 1954 he said that there were "two approaches to the question of war and peace": to consider war inevitable and to prepare for it; or the course he chose to follow, to consider that war "must be avoided if not at all costs, almost at all costs." Thus Indian spokesmen were

[49] Talbot and Poplai, *India and America*, p. 193.
[50] "P," "Middle Ground Between American and Russia: An Indian View," *Foreign Affairs*, XXXII (January, 1954), 259–269. See also Taya Zinkin, "Indian Foreign Policy: An Interpretation of Attitudes," *World Politics*, VII (January, 1955), 179–208.

fearful that the security policies of the United States tend to increase the danger of nuclear war and mutual destruction, and they therefore questioned the basic approach of the United States to the problem of war and peace. "The great difference between America and India," wrote the veteran Indian leader, C. Rajagopalachari, in the *Hindustan Times* of March 3, 1955, "is that the means America is adopting for establishing peace on earth do not appeal to India."

Few Americans need to be convinced of the reality and seriousness of the Soviet-Communist threat; most Indians seem either not to believe in the threat at all or to assign it a relatively low priority in their list of present problems and dangers. This difference in viewpoint helps to explain many of the differences in the foreign policies of the United States and India. It springs from a basic difference in both internal and external position, as well as in general outlook. India is a relatively weak nation, beset by a multitude of internal problems which are so pressing that they tax the resources of the country and the energies of its leaders. It cannot afford to antagonize the Soviet Union. The United States is the most powerful nation of the non-Communist world, and therefore is inescapably the major bulwark of defense of that world against the further encroachments of the Soviet Union or of international communism. It is quite natural, therefore, that the United States should be more directly concerned than India with the problem of resisting the Soviet-Communist pressures and should be inclined, out of sheer necessity, to give less attention to other and perhaps in the long run more important problems of international life.

In the mid-1950's India and the United States were poles apart in their attitudes toward Communist China. India was the leading advocate of a conciliatory approach to the regime which controlled the destinies of more than one-fifth of the human race, and it favored the full acceptance of that regime in the councils of the nations. The United States, on the other hand, was the leading advocate of the non-recognition of Communist China, and the leading supporter of the Nationalist Government of China, which India did not recognize at all. Indian leaders were outspoken in their criticisms of United States China policy, which they regarded as based on an inexcusable refusal to face "the facts of life" and as being in effect a barrier to international cooperation and virtually an insult to a fellow-Asian people.

With the change for the worse in Sino-Indian relations in 1959, China ceased to be a major irritant in Indo-American relations. India continued to favor the admission of China to the United Nations and the United States continued to oppose it, but India ceased to press this issue, and the United States showed signs of some flexibility. India seemed to look to the United States for support in various tangible and intangible ways in its unwelcome protracted conflict with its giant Asian neighbor.

Relations between the United States and India have, as Robert Trumbull once stated, gone up and down like a yo-yo in the postwar years. At all times there has been a strong undercurrent of common interests and mutual good will, but this has often been tempered by mutual recriminations and mutual criticisms regarding both the general approach to foreign policy and regarding specific isues. Many influential Americans have been outspokenly critical of India's "neutralist" orientation, which they interpret as neutralism in favor of the Communists. Nehru was often criticized for his alleged pro-Soviet and anti-American orientation. Nehru's chief foreign policy spokesman, V. K. Krishna Menon, was one of the least popular of foreign diplomats in the United States. Indians have been equally critical of America's cold war mentality and approach to world problems, and they have been appalled by the views of such prominent American politicians as former Senator Knowland. They were highly critical of the late American Secretary of State, John Foster Dulles. The ups and downs in Indo-American relations can be traced in reactions to specific issues. Indians responded very favorably to such American acts or policies as the substantial wheat loan to India at a time of dire need in 1951 (although India's gratitude was somewhat lessened by the long debate on the wheat loan question in the United States Congress and by some of the critical comments that were made during that debate), the American policies in the Suez crisis in 1956, the warm reception extended to Nehru when he visited the United States in late 1956, the substantial American economic assistance to India and the emergency military aid following the Chinese attack in late 1962. On the other hand, Indians reacted very unfavorably to a variety of American acts and policies, notably American arms aid to Pakistan, the American sponsorship of various security arrangements, notably SEATO, and the whole gamut of America's China policy. India has been generally unhappy with the position of the United States on the Kashmir question. On many international issues, India and the United States have been on different sides in the majority of votes in the United Nations General Assembly.

"On a government-to-government level," as Richard L. Park has pointed out, "India has not appreciated the anti-Communist stand and the substantial involvement of the United States in Asian affairs since the end of World War II."[51] On these broad approaches, as on many

---

[51] Richard L. Park, "India's Foreign Policy: 1964–1968," *Current History,* LIV (April, 1968), 244.

issues of a general or specific nature, the Indian reactions, even on an official level and more obviously on unofficial levels, have been mixed. For example, there are some Indians who have been just as anti-Communist as the most anti-Communist Americans, and some whose views on American actions and policies in Vietnam would be gratifying to the most belligerent American "hawks." But there can be no doubt that the prevailing views, especially on the official level, have been those indicated by Professor Park.

The differences between India and the United States on such broad approaches, however, have tended to be lessened and muted in recent years. The world situation has changed greatly from that which prevailed at the height of the cold war era, and the prevailing American views, official and unofficial, toward the Soviet Union and world communism have become more relaxed and flexible. The emphasis has been on detente and on "negotiation not confrontation," which has brought the United States closer to India's position. Meanwhile Indian outlooks have become more pragmatic and realistic as their experiences with Communists inside their own country, with Communist China, and even to a lesser extent with the Soviet Union, have somewhat dampened whatever enthusiasm they may have had for communism and the Communist countries.

American operations in Vietnam have created problems in the relations of the United States with India, as in almost every other aspect of American foreign relations. The prevailing opinion in India has been sharply critical of American policy in Vietnam. Mrs. Gandhi and other Indian spokesmen have repeatedly called for an end of the fighting in Vietnam and for complete American withdrawal. "The Vietnam war and its ramifications tend to place in jeopardy other aspects of Indo-American cooperation, at least within official circles."[52] Actually there was more ambivalence in official Indian circles on American policy in Vietnam and more support for the American position in unofficial circles than would appear from casual analysis; and the differences became less serious after the beginning of significant American de-escalation in 1969. Apparently India, like most non-Communist countries of South and Southeast Asia, wanted the withdrawal of the American military presence in Vietnam and elsewhere in the area, but not of American interest, aid, trade, and nonmilitary contacts generally.

American economic aid has reached such dimensions and has had so many ramifications that it has tended to distort and to overshadow the whole nexus of Indo-American relations.[53] Beginning with the

[52] *Ibid.*, p. 201.
[53] See Norman D. Palmer, *South Asia and United States Policy* (Boston, 1966), Chap. 6, "Foreign Aid in United States-South Asian Relations."

wheat loan in 1951, American economic aid has been a continuing aspect of these relations, and it reached substantial proportions in the decade of the 1960's. For some years India has been the chief recipient of American foreign economic assistance. By the end of the 1960's nearly $9 billion dollars of aid had been extended, in the form of loans and grants and shipments of wheat and other agricultural commodities under the "Food for Peace" Program (Public Law 480). But by 1970 the United States Congress, reflecting an aid weariness and a concern for other problems at home and abroad on the part of most Americans, was reducing the amounts of aid appropriations. This naturally led to decreased appropriations to India, the largest recipient, at a time when India's need for external assistance was still great and when other sources of aid were also declining.

No action of the United States has done more to exacerbate Indo-American relations than its arms aid to Pakistan, first extended in 1954 and continued on a fairly substantial scale until the Indo-Pakistan war of 1965. India flatly refused an offer of similar aid as inconsistent with its policy of nonalignment (avoidance of military alliances and commitments). When its unpreparedness was starkly revealed with the Chinese attack in late 1962, however, Nehru did not allow his basic convictions and policies to stand in the way of a prompt appeal to the United States, Britain, and other friendly powers to provide military assistance immediately. This was done, and the result was a new era of good feeling between India and America. In addition to emergency military assistance valued at approximately $60 million, the United States in 1963 and 1964 entered into agreements to provide limited military aid on a more regular basis in the amount of $200 million. However, the 1965 war between India and Pakistan led the United States to cut off all military aid to both countries. Except for limited amounts of spare parts and "nonlethal" weapons, the ban on military aid has been continued. India has not protested very strongly against this, probably because it hits Pakistan harder than it does India, but the American and British ban has forced India to turn to the Soviet Union for its outside arms supply, a situation which has aroused some apprehensions in the United States and in some quarters in India as well.

Since World War II, and especially since India's independence in 1947, contacts between Indians and Americans have been growing rapidly, and mutual interest is visibly increasing. Thousands of Americans have been in India in various official and unofficial capacities. In addition to missionaries, the largest single group, who represent an older relationship and apparently an increasingly controversial one, there have been large numbers of official representatives — diplomatic, information, educational and cultural affairs, and aid personnel and their families, Peace Corps Volunteers, and others; and even larger numbers of Americans in unofficial capacities — businessmen, technical specialists, journalists, professors, students, employees of the Ford, Rockefeller, Asia, and other foundations, tourists, and many others. The flow has not been one-way. In fact, larger numbers of Indians have come to the United States than Americans to India. Between 1950 and 1965, for example, according to Chester Bowles, "more than 68,000 Indian citizens . . . travelled to the United States for technical training or education," and smaller but still substantial numbers came in other capacities. "At this moment," said Bowles in a lecture in Ahmedabad in 1965, "there are some 8,000 Indian students in American universities — far more than the number who are studying in any other foreign country. Moreover, more than 4,000 Indian professors are now teaching in our universities."[54] Special programs of Indian studies have been developed at several American universities, and almost every American university and college gives some special attention to India. The same observation, *mutatis mutandi,* could be made of programs in American studies and special attention to the United States in India.

For all of the increasing contacts and growing awareness, however, "United States-South Asian contacts are still more extensive than intensive. . . . Too often ignorance is compounded by indifference, irritation and sensitivity. . . . The relative superficiality of the United States-South Asian encounter . . . need not be a serious barrier in the way of satisfactory relations; but obviously a greater knowledge of each other on a widespread popular scale, and especially among elite opinion-making groups, would create a better background for more meaningful encounters at many levels."[55]

Late in 1949 Nehru made his first "voyage of discovery" to the United States. Unfortunately it was more of a voyage of disenchantment, for himself and for his American hosts. "By any standards this first visit to America was a failure. Nehru came away empty-handed. American leaders were not over-impressed with him, primarily because of his refusal to 'stand up and be counted.' And he was decidedly unhappy at his experience."[56] His second visit, however, seven years later, was another story. India and the United States had learned to understand each other better, and Indian reactions to the United States

---

[54] This observation was made in an address entitled "Candid Comments on Indo-American Relations" at the Harold Laski Institute of Political Science. *A View from New Delhi,* p. 180.

[55] Palmer, *South Asia and United States Policy,* pp. 7–8.

[56] Brecher, *Nehru,* pp. 419–420.

stand on the Anglo-French-Israeli military intervention in Suez a few weeks before had been most favorable. Nehru was warmly received in New York, Washington, and wherever he went, and he made a very favorable impression upon American officials and, through the medium of television, upon the American people generally.

Three years later President Eisenhower, on the first visit which an American President had ever made to Asia while in office, returned the visit of the Indian Prime Minister. He came at an opportune time, while the Indian Government and people were still smarting from the actions of the Chinese Communists in Tibet and along the India-China borders. New Delhi, accustomed to welcoming world leaders of all types and orientation, staged a welcome which was described as exceeding any other in modern Indian history. In Delhi the American President addressed perhaps the largest crowd that had ever assembled in the shadow of the nation's capital. Nehru and Eisenhower seemed to get along famously, and the Eisenhower smile, very much in evidence, was infectious. Eisenhower himself was profoundly moved by his experience in India. Undoubtedly his visit marked a high point in Indo-American relations.

Another high point came during the period of the Kennedy administration (1961–63). Kennedy was known to be especially interested in India. As Senator he had often spoken favorably of India and had joined others with similar interests, including former Ambassadors John Sherman Cooper and Chester Bowles, in championing aid and other measures of concrete assistance to India. Indians, like people throughout the world, were attracted by the Kennedy image — the young, dynamic, far-seeing leader who seemed to speak not only for his own country but for a "new generation" everywhere. Indians were also pleased by his appointment to key positions of persons who were also known to be good friends of India. These included Chester Bowles as Under Secretary of State, later as a Special Representative and Adviser on African, Asian, and Latin American Affairs, and in 1963 as Ambassador to India; Professor John Kenneth Galbraith, known as a liberal economist and close friend of the President, as Ambassador to India; and Phillips Talbot, an old hand in the subcontinent, as Assistant Secretary of State for Near Eastern and African Affairs. The prompt response of the American President to India's appeal for military and other help at the time of the Chinese attack in late 1962 was greatly appreciated, although American and British pressure on Nehru to enter into high-level negotiations with Pakistan on Kashmir was less welcome. President Kennedy himself was not able to visit India during his short period in the White House, although he probably would have done so if he had lived. The "unofficial" visit of Mrs. Kennedy in 1962, however, was a major event.

Since 1963 much of the temporary warmth in Indo-American relations has been missing. Official relations have remained good, thanks in part to the efforts of Chester Bowles during his second tenure in the post of American Ambassador to India (1963–69). Contacts between Indians and Americans have continued to increase, but not always with happy results. Indians were resentful of the suspension of both military and economic aid to India as a result of the September 1965 war with Pakistan, and of the intermittent and, in general, declining economic aid. President Johnson was an enigma to most Indians, and President Nixon has been viewed with doubt and apprehension. Americans generally either ignored India, because other foreign and a host of domestic issues seemed to be more pressing, or were highly critical of India's leaders and India's economic, social, and political policies and developments.

Two brief comments by informed American observers in 1969 well summed up the general state of Indo-American relations: (1) "India's association with the United States is active and correct, but cordiality is only occasionally present";[57] (2) "As for Indian desires to maintain firm and friendly relations with the United States, I am persuaded they remain strong in spite of some synthetic and some real Indian complaints about American policies."[58]

[57] Park, "India's Foreign Policy: 1964–1968," p. 201.
[58] Phillips Talbot, "Half-Empty or Half Full?," p. 14.

# EPILOGUE:
# THE FIFTH GENERAL ELECTIONS

On December 27, 1970, at the request of Prime Minister Gandhi, the President of India dissolved the Lok Sabha and announced that new general elections would be held in the near future. In a radio broadcast Mrs. Gandhi said that she sought a "fresh mandate" from the people to make possible "proper and effective implementation of our secularist socialist policies and programs through democratic processes."

The fifth general elections were the first to be held since the Congress split in 1969, the first to be called before the expiration of a five-year term for the Lok Sabha, the first to be held separately from State elections (only three States — Orissa, Tamil Nadu, and West Bengal — held elections concurrently with the national elections in 1971). The election campaign was marked by a much higher incidence of violence than any previous campaign; more than 200 political murders were committed in West Bengal alone.

Eight national and some forty regional parties contested the elections. Four of the main parties in opposition to the Congress(R) — the Congress(O), the Swatantra Party, the Jana Sangh, and the SSP — joined in a unique electoral alliance, but the "grand alliance" proved to be anything but grand. The campaign was notably devoid of real issues, even though each party insisted that the future of democracy was at stake. As many observers noted, Mrs. Gandhi herself was about the only real issue.

Voting in seventeen States and all eight Union Territories took place between March 1 and 7, 1971, and in West Bengal on March 10. From the time the first results became known, it was apparent that Mrs. Gandhi's party had scored a landslide victory, much more sweeping than had been generally predicted, giving it a decisive majority in the new Lok Sabha. One party dominance of the type enjoyed by the undivided Congress was not restored, but the Congress(R) under Mrs. Gandhi clearly had a commanding position in the new system of "competitive dominance." Mrs. Gandhi had scored an impressive personal triumph, and she had been given the clear mandate she had sought. In a larger sense, the fifth general elections had again demonstrated the resilience and the unpredictability of the Indian political system.

# SELECTED BIBLIOGRAPHY

BIBLIOGRAPHIES

*Government Administration in South Asia: A Bibliography.* Compiled by Paul E. Menge. Papers in Comparative Administration, Special Series No. 9, Comparative Administration Group, American Society of Public Administration. Washington, D.C., 1968.

*Government and Politics of India and Pakistan, 1885–1955; a Bibliography of Works in Western Languages.* Compiled by Patrick Wilson. Modern India Project, Bibliographical Study No. 2, Institute of East Asiatic Studies, University of California. Berkeley, Calif., 1956.

*Government Archives in South Asia. A Guide to National and State Archives in Ceylon, India and Pakistan.* Compiled by D. A. Low; J. C. Iltis; and M. D. Wainwright. New York, 1969.

*India: A Critical Bibliography.* Compiled by J. Michael Mahar. Tucson, Ariz., 1964.

*Introduction to the Civilization of India; South Asia, an Introductory Bibliography.* Compiled by Maureen L. P. Patterson and Ronald B. Inden. Chicago, 1962.

*The Journal of Asian Studies.* Annual bibliographical issues (since 1956).

*South Asia: A Selected Bibliography on India, Pakistan, Ceylon.* Compiled by Patrick Wilson. New York, 1957.

*South Asian History, 1750–1950: A Guide to Periodicals, Dissertations, and Newspapers.* Compiled by Margaret H. Case. Princeton, N.J., 1968.


GENERAL AND HISTORICAL

Basham, A. L. *The Wonder That Was India: A Survey of the Culture of the Sub-Continent Before the Coming of the Muslims.* 3rd ed. New York, 1968.

Brown, W. Norman. *The United States and India and Pakistan.* 2nd ed. Cambridge, Mass., 1953.

*The Cambridge History of India.* 6 vols. Cambridge, 1922–32.

Griffiths, Percival. *Modern India.* 3rd ed. New York, 1962.

Ikram, S. M. *Muslim Civilization in India.* Edited by Ainslee Embree. New York, 1964.

Lamb, Beatrice Pitney. *India: A World in Transition.* 3rd ed. New York, 1968.

Majumdar, R. C., general editor. *The History and Culture of the Indian People.* Bombay, 1951–  . Volumes already published: Vol. I, *The*

*Vedic Age;* Vol. II, *The Age of Imperial Unity;* Vol. III, *The Classical Age;* Vol. IV, *The Age of Imperial Kanauj;* Vol. V, *The Struggle for Empire;* Vol. VI, *The Delhi Sultanate;* Vol. IX, *British Paramountcy and Indian Renaissance, Part I;* Vol. X, *British Paramountcy and Indian Renaissance, Part II;* Vol. XI, *Struggle for Freedom.*

Majumdar, R. C.; H. C. Raychaudhuri; and K. Datta. *An Advanced History of India.* London, 1950.

Moreland, W. H. and A. C. Chatterjee. *A Short History of India.* 4th ed. London, 1957.

Nehru, Jawaharlal. *The Discovery of India.* New York, 1946.

O'Malley, L.S.S., ed. *Modern India and the West, a Study of the Interaction of Their Civilizations.* London, 1941.

Radhakrishnan, S. *The Hindu View of Life.* London, 1927.

Radhakrishnan, S. *Indian Philosophy.* 2 vols. New York, 1922–27.

Riencourt, Amaury de. *The Soul of India.* New York, 1960.

Smith, Vincent A. *The Oxford History of India.* 3rd ed. Edited by Percival Spear. Oxford, 1961.

*Sources of Indian Tradition.* Compiled by William Theodore de Bary; Stephen Hay; Royal Weiler; and Andrew Yarrow. New York, 1958.

Spear, Percival. *India, Pakistan and the West.* 4th ed. London, 1967.

Zimmer, Heinrich. *Philosophies of India.* Edited by Joseph Campbell. Princeton, N.J., 1967.

## BIOGRAPHIES AND AUTOBIOGRAPHIES

Ashe, Geoffrey. *Gandhi.* New York, 1968.

Azad, Maulana Abul Kalam. *India Wins Freedom: An Autobiographical Narrative.* Calcutta, 1959.

Bolitho, Hector. *Jinnah: Creator of Pakistan.* London, 1954.

Brecher, Michael. *Nehru: A Political Biography.* London, 1959.

Erikson, Erik H. *Gandhi's Truth: On the Origins of Militant Nonviolence.* New York, 1969.

Fischer, Louis. *Gandhi: His Life and Message for the World.* New York, 1954.

Gandhi, M. K. *An Autobiography, or the Story of My Experiments with Truth.* 2nd ed. Ahmedabad, 1940.

Moraes, Frank. *Jawaharlal Nehru.* New York, 1956.

Munshi, K. M. *Indian Constitutional Documents.* Vol. I, *Pilgrimage to Freedom.* Bombay, 1967.

Nanda, B. R. *The Nehrus: Motilal and Jawaharlal.* New York, 1963.

Nehru, Jawaharlal. *Toward Freedom: The Autobiography of Jawaharlal Nehru.* New York, 1941.

Norman, Dorothy, ed. *Nehru: The First Sixty Years.* 2 vols. New York, 1965.

Tendulkar, D. G. *Mahatma: Life of Mohandas Karamchand Gandhi.* 8 vols. Bombay, 1951–54.

Tennyson, Hallam. *India's Walking Saint: The Story of Vinoba Bhave.* Garden City, N.Y., 1955.

Wolpert, Stanley A. *Tilak and Gokhale: Revolution and Reform in the Making of Modern India.* Berkeley, Calif., 1961.


GOVERNMENT AND POLITICS IN THE PRE-BRITISH PERIOD

Altekar, A. S. *State and Government in Ancient India.* Benares, 1949.

Brown, D. Mackenzie. *The White Umbrella: Indian Political Thought from Manu to Gandhi.* Berkeley, Calif., 1953.

Ghoshal, U. N. *A History of Indian Political Ideas: The Ancient Period and the Period of Transition to the Middle Ages.* London, 1959.

Jayaswal, K. P. *Hindu Polity — A Constitutional History of India in Hindu Times.* Calcutta, 1924.

Kautilya. *Arthasastra.* Trans. by R. Shamasastry. 4th ed. Mysore, 1951.

Prasad, Beni. *The State in Ancient India — A Study in the Structure and Practical Working of Political Institutions in North India in Ancient Times.* Allahabad, 1928.

Sarkar, Sir Jadunath. *The Mughal Administration.* 3rd ed. Calcutta, 1935.

Sharma, Sri Ram. *Mughal Government and Administration.* Bombay, 1951.

Sherwani, H. K. *Studies in Muslim Political Thought and Administration.* 4th ed. Lahore, 1963.

Spellman, John W. *Political Theory of Ancient India.* Oxford, 1964.

Srivastava, A. L. *The Mughal Empire (1526–1803).* 5th ed. Agra, 1966.


GOVERNMENT AND POLITICS IN THE BRITISH PERIOD

Banerjee, A. C., ed. *Indian Constitutional Documents, 1758–1945.* 2 vols. Calcutta, 1945–46.

Birdwood, Lord. *A Continent Experiments.* London, 1946.

Campbell-Johnson, Alan. *Mission with Mountbatten.* London, 1951.

Coupland, Sir Reginald. *The Indian Problem: Report on the Constitutional Problem in India.* Three vols. in one: Vol. I, *The Indian Problem,*

*1833–1935;* Vol. II, *Indian Politics, 1936–1942;* Vol. III, *The Future of India.* London, 1944.

Dodwell, H. H. F., ed. *The Indian Empire, 1858–1919, with Chapters on the Development of Administration, 1818–58.* The Cambridge History of India, Vol. VI. Cambridge, 1932.

Edwardes, Michael. *British India, 1772–1947.* New York, 1967.

Furber, Holden. *John Company at Work: A Study of European Expansion in India in the Late Eighteenth Century.* Cambridge, Mass., 1948.

Griffiths, Percival. *The British Impact on India.* London, 1952.

Keith, A. B. *A Constitutional History of India, 1600–1935.* 2nd ed. London, 1926.

Menon, V. P. *The Transfer of Power in India.* Princeton, N.J., 1957.

Metcalf, Thomas R. *The Aftermath of Revolt: India, 1857–1870.* Princeton, N.J., 1964.

Phadnis, Urmila. *Towards the Integration of Indian States, 1919–1947.* New York, 1968.

*Proceedings of the Round Table Conference* (3 sessions, 1931–32). Cmd. 3378, 3997, 4238.

*Report of the Indian Statutory Commission* (the Simon Commission), 1930. Cmd. 3568–9.

*Report on Indian Constitutional Reforms* (the Montagu-Chelmsford Report), 1918. Cmd. 9109.

Singh, Gurmukh Nihal. *Landmarks in Indian Constitutional and National Development.* Vol. I: *1600–1919.* 3rd ed. Delhi, 1952.

Suda, J. P. *Indian Constitutional Development and National Movement,* Meerut, 1951.

Thompson, Edward and G. T. Garrett. *Rise and Fulfilment of British Rule in India.* London, 1934.

Tinker, Hugh R. *The Foundations of Local Self-Government in India, Pakistan, and Burma.* London, 1954.

Woodruff, Philip (pseud. for Philip Mason). *The Men Who Ruled India.* Vol. I, *The Founders of Modern India.* London, 1953. Vol. II, *The Guardians.* London, 1954.

## THE NATIONALIST MOVEMENT

Andrews, C. F. and G. Mookerji. *The Rise and Growth of the Congress of India.* London, 1938.

Bandyopadhyaya, J. *Social and Political Thought of Gandhi.* Bombay, 1969.

Banerjea, Surendranath. *A Nation in the Making: Being the Reminiscences of Fifty Years of Public Life.* London, 1925.

Bondurant, Joan. *Conquest of Violence; the Gandhian Philosophy of Conflict.* Princeton, N.J., 1958.

Buch, M. A. *Rise and Growth of Indian Militant Nationalism.* Baroda, 1940.

Chand, Tara. *History of the Freedom Movement in India.* 2nd ed., Vol. I, Delhi, 1965. Vol. II, Delhi, 1967.

Desai, A. R. *Social Background of Indian Nationalism.* Bombay, 1948.

Gupta, D. C. *Indian National Movement.* Delhi, 1970.

Heimsath, Charles H. *Indian Nationalism and Hindu Social Reform.* Princeton, N.J., 1964.

Lajpat Rai, Lala. *Young India: An Interpretation and a History of the Nationalist Movement from Within.* New York, 1916.

Lovett, Sir Harrington Verney. *A History of the Indian Nationalist Movement.* London, 1920.

Majumdar, R. C. *History of the Freedom Movement in India.* 3 vols. Calcutta, 1962–63.

Martin, Briton, Jr. *New India, 1885: British Official Policy and the Emergence of the Indian National Congress.* Berkeley, Calif., 1970.

Mukherjee, Haridas and Uma. *The Growth of Nationalism in India, 1857–1905.* Calcutta, 1957.

Pal, Bipin Chandra. *The Spirit of Indian Nationalism.* London, 1910.

Seal, Anil. *The Emergence of Indian Nationalism: Competition and Collaboration in the Later Nineteenth Century.* Cambridge, 1968.

Sitaramayya, P. B. *A History of the Indian National Congress (1885–1935).* Allahabad, 1935.

Sitaramayya, P. B. *The Nationalist Movement in India.* Bombay, 1950.

Smith, William R. *Nationalism and Reform in India.* New Haven, 1938.

Varma, V. P. *Modern Indian Political Thought.* 2nd ed. Agra, 1964.

## INDIA SINCE INDEPENDENCE: GENERAL

Birdwood, Lord. *India and Pakistan: A Continent Decides.* New York, 1954.

Chopra, Pran. *Uncertain India: A Political Profile of Two Decades of Freedom.* Cambridge, Mass., 1969.

Harrison, Selig S. *India: The Most Dangerous Decades.* Princeton, N.J., 1960.

Mason, Philip, ed. *India and Ceylon: Unity and Diversity: A Symposium.* New York, 1967.

Menon, V. P. *The Story of the Integration of the Indian States.* New York, 1956.

Philips, C. H., ed. *Politics and Society in India.* London, 1963.

Rudolph, Lloyd I. and Susanne H. *The Modernity of Tradition: Political Development in India.* Chicago, 1967.

Smith, Donald E. *India as a Secular State.* Princeton, N.J., 1963.

Smith, Donald E., ed. *South Asian Politics and Religion.* Princeton, N.J., 1966.

Srinivas, M. N. *Caste in Modern India and Other Essays.* Bombay, 1962.

THE CONSTITUTIONAL AND POLITICAL SYSTEM

Austin, Granville. *The Indian Constitution: Cornerstone of a Nation.* London, 1966.

Basu, D. D. *Commentary on the Constitution of India.* 8 vols. 5th ed. Calcutta, 1965–68.

Basu, D. D. *Shorter Constitution of India.* 5th ed. Calcutta, 1967.

Bombwall, K. R. *The Foundations of Indian Federalism.* Bombay, 1967.

Brecher, Michael. *Nehru's Mantle: The Politics of Succession in India.* New York, 1966.

Brecher, Michael. *Political Leadership in India: An Analysis of Elite Attitudes.* New York, 1969.

Chanda, Asok. *Federalism in India.* London, 1968.

Chanda, Asok. *Indian Administration.* London, 1958.

Douglas, William O. *We the Judges: Studies in American and Indian Constitutional Law from Marshall to Mukerji.* Garden City, N.Y., 1956.

Gledhill, Alan. *The Republic of India: The Development of Its Laws and Constitution,* 2nd ed. London, 1964.

Hardgrave, Robert L., Jr. *India: Government and Politics in a Developing Nation.* New York, 1970.

Indian Institute of Public Administration. *The Organisation of the Government of India.* Bombay, 1958.

Jain, H. M. *The Union Executive.* Allahabad, 1969.

Joshi, G. N. *The Constitution of India.* 5th ed. Bombay, 1966.

Kothari, Rajni. *Politics in India.* Boston, 1970.

Lal, A. B., ed. *The Indian Parliament.* Allahabad, 1956.

Majumdar, B., ed. *Problems of Public Administration in India.* Patna, 1954.

Morris-Jones, W. H. *The Government and Politics of India.* Garden City, N.Y., 1964.

Morris-Jones, W. H. *Parliament in India.* Philadelphia, 1957.

Munshi, K. M. *The President under the Indian Constitution.* Bombay, 1963.

Park, Richard L. *India's Political System.* Englewood Cliffs, N.J., 1967.

Park, Richard L. and Irene Tinker, eds. *Leadership and Political Institutions in India*. Princeton, N.J., 1959.

Pylee, M. V. *Constitutional Government in India,* 2nd ed. Bombay, 1965.

Rao, B. Shiva, ed. *Framing of the Constitution.* 5 vols. Delhi, 1968.

Rau, B. N. *India's Constitution in the Making.* Edited by B. Shiva Rao. Bombay, 1960.

Santhanam, K. *Union-State Relations in India.* Bombay, 1960.

Seervai, H. M. *Constitutional Law of India, a Critical Commentary.* Bombay, 1967.

Sen, D. K. *A Comparative Study of the Indian Constitution.* 2 vols. New York, 1968.

Srinivasan, N. *Democratic Government in India.* Calcutta, 1954.

Tiwary, Uma K. *The Making of the Indian Constitution.* Allahabad, 1967.

Venkateswaran, R. J. *Cabinet Government in India.* London, 1967.

Weiner, Myron. *The Politics of Scarcity: Public Pressure and Political Response in India.* Chicago, 1962.

STATE AND LOCAL GOVERNMENT AND POLITICS

Bailey, F. G. *Politics and Social Change: Orissa in 1959.* Berkeley, Calif., 1963.

Braibanti, Ralph, ed. *Asian Bureaucratic Systems Emergent from the British Imperial Tradition.* Durham, N.C., 1966.

Franda, Marcus. *West Bengal and the Federalizing Process in India.* Princeton, N.J., 1968.

Hardgrave, Robert L., Jr. *The Dravidian Movement.* Bombay, 1965.

Kashyap, Subash C. *The Politics of Defection: A Study of State Politics in India.* Delhi, 1969.

Khanna, R. L. *Municipal Government and Administration in India.* Chandigarh, 1967.

Khera, S. S. *District Administration in India.* Bombay, 1964.

Maddick, Henry. *Panchayati Raj: A Study of Rural Local Government in India.* London, 1969.

Narain, Iqbal, ed. *State Politics in India.* Meerut, 1968.

Nayar, Baldev Raj. *Minority Politics in the Punjab.* Princton, N.J., 1966.

Potter, David C. *Government in Rural India: An Introduction to Contemporary District Administration.* London, 1964.

Retzlaff, Ralph H. *Village Government in India: A Case Study.* New York, 1962.

Sharma, M. P. *Local Self-Government in India.* 2nd ed. Bombay, 1951.

Turner, Roy, ed. *India's Urban Future.* Berkeley, Calif., 1962.

Weiner, Myron, ed. *State Politics in India.* Princeton, N.J. 1968.

## POLITICS PARTIES AND ELECTIONS

Bahadur, Lal. *The Muslim League: Its History, Activities, and Achievements*. Agra, 1954.

Baxter, Craig. *The Jana Sangh: A Biography of an Indian Political Party*. Philadelphia, 1969.

Brass, Paul. *Factional Politics in an Indian State: The Congress Party in Uttar Pradesh*. Berkely, Calif., 1965.

Burger, Angela S. *Opposition in a Dominant Party System: A Study of the Jan Sangh, the Praja Socialist Party and the Socialist Party in Uttar Pradesh, India*. Berkeley, Calif., 1969.

Curran, J. A., Jr. *Militant Hinduism in Indian Politics: A Study of the R.S.S.* New York, 1951.

Election Commission, Government of India. Reports on all Indian elections.

Erdman, Howard L. *The Swatantra Party and Indian Conservatism*. Cambridge, 1967.

"Fourth General Elections in India," *Political Science Review* (Department of Political Science, University of Rajasthan). Part I, Vol. 6, Nos. 3 and 4 (July–September and October–December, 1967) and Vol. 7, Nos. 1 and 2 (January–March and April–June, 1968); Part II, Vol. 7, No. 3 (July–September, 1968).

*India Votes: A Source Book on Elections*. Edited and compiled by R. Chandidas, Leon Clark, Richard Fontera, and Ward Morehouse, Bombay, 1966.

Jhangiana, Motilal A. *Jana Sangh and Swatantra: A Profile of the Rightist Parties in India*. Bombay, 1967.

Kochanek, Stanley. *The Congress Party of India: The Dynamics of One-Party Democracy*. Princeton, N.J., 1968.

Kogekar, S. V. and Richard L. Park, eds. *Reports on the Indian General Elections, 1951–52*. Bombay, 1956.

Kothari, Rajni, ed. *Party Systems and Election Studies*. Bombay, 1967.

Masani, M. R. *The Communist Party of India: A Short History*. London, 1954.

Overstreet, Gene D. and Marshall Windmiller. *Communism in India*. Berkeley, Calif., 1959.

Prakash, Indra. *A Review of the History and Work of the Hindu Mahasabha and the Hindu Sanghatan Movement*. New Delhi, 1952.

Ram, Mohan. *Indian Communism: Split Within a Split*. Delhi, 1969.

Sirsikar, V. M. *Political Behaviour in India: a Case Study of the 1952 General Elections*. Bombay, 1965.

Varma, S. P. and Iqbal Narain, eds. *Fourth General Elections in India*. Part One. Bombay, 1968.

Weiner, Myron. *Party Building in a New Nation: The Indian National Congress*. Chicago, 1967.

Weiner, Myron. *Party Politics in India: The Development of a Multi-Party System*. Princeton, N.J., 1957.

Weiner, Myron and Rajni Kothari, eds. *Indian Voting Behaviour: Studies of the 1962 General Elections*. Bombay, 1965.


## ECONOMIC PLANNING AND DEVELOPMENT

Bhagwati, Jagdish N. and Padma Desai. *India: Planning for Industrialization; Industrialization and Trade Policies since 1951*. London, 1970.

Chandra, J. G. *India's Socialist Pattern of Society*. Delhi, 1956.

Gadgil, D. R. *Economic Policy and Development*. New York, 1955.

Hanson, A. H. *The Process of Planning: A Study of India's Five Year Plans, 1950–1964*. London, 1966.

Lewis, John P. *Quiet Crisis in India*. Garden City, N.Y., 1964.

Malenbaum, Wilfred. *Prospects for Indian Development*. London, 1961.

Mayer, Albert, and Associates, in collaboration with McKim Marriott and Richard L. Park. *Pilot Project, India*. Berkeley, Calif., 1958.

Myrdal, Gunnar. *Asian Drama: An Inquiry into the Poverty of Nations*. 3 vols. New York, 1968.

*The New India: Progress Through Democracy*. New York, 1958.

Planning Commission, Government of India. Texts of all the Five Year Plans, and numerous supplementary reports.

Programme Evaluation Organization, Planning Commission. Various evaluation reports.

Rosen, George. *Democracy and Economic Change in India*. 2nd ed. Berkeley, Calif., 1967.

Streeten, Paul and Michael Lipton, eds. *The Crisis of Indian Planning: Economic Planning in the 1960s*. London, 1968.

Venkatasubbiah, H. *The Anatomy of Indian Planning*. Bombay, 1969.

Woytinsky, W. S. *India, the Awakening Giant*. New York, 1957.


## FOREIGN RELATIONS

Aiyar, S. P. *The Commonwealth in South Asia*. Bombay, 1969.

Bandyopadhyaya, J. *The Making of India's Foreign Policy*. Bombay, 1970.

Berkes, Ross N. and Mohinder S. Bedi. *The Diplomacy of India*. Stanford, Calif., 1958.

Brecher, Michael. *India and World Politics: Krishna Menon's View of the World*. New York, 1968.

Brines, Russell. *The Indo-Pakistani Conflict*. London, 1968.

Choudhury, G. W. *Pakistan's Relations with India, 1947–1966*. New York, 1968.

Das Gupta, J. B. *Indo-Pakistan Relations (1947–1955)*. Amsterdam, 1958.

Das Gupta, J. B. *Jammu and Kashmir*. The Hague, 1968.

Eldridge, P. J. *The Politics of Foreign Aid in India*. New York, 1969.

Gupta, Karunakar. *India in World Politics: A Period of Transition*. Calcutta, 1969.

Gupta, Sisir. *Kashmir: A Study in India-Pakistan Relations*. Bombay, 1966.

Harrison, Selig S., ed. *India and the United States*. New York, 1961.

Heimsath, Charles H. and Surjit Mansingh. *A Diplomatic History of Modern India*. Bombay, 1970.

*India in World Affairs*. Vol. I, *August, 1947, to Januray, 1950*, by K. P. Karunakaran. Bombay, 1952, Vol. II, *February, 1950 to December, 1953*, by K. P. Karunakaran. Bombay, 1958. Vol. III, 1954–56, by M. S. Rajan. Bombay, 1964.

*The Indian Year Book of International Affairs*. Annual volumes, beginning in 1952, published under the auspices of the Indian Study Group on International Law and Affairs, Madras University.

"India's Relations with Pakistan," *International Studies*, VIII (July–October, 1966).

Kavic, Lorne J. *India's Quest for Security: Defense Policies, 1947–65*. Berkeley, Calif., 1967.

Kundra, J. C. *Indian Foreign Policy, 1947–1954: A Study of Relations with the Western Bloc*. Groningen, 1955.

Mallik, Deva Narayan. *The Development of Non-Alignment in Indian Foreign Policy*. Allahabad, 1967.

Maxwell, Neville. *India's China War*. London, 1970.

Misra, K. P., ed. *Studies in Indian Foreign Policy*. Delhi, 1969.

Nehru, Jawaharlal. *India's Foreign Policy—Selected Speeches, September 1946–April 1961*. Delhi, 1961.

Palmer, Norman D. *South Asia and United States Policy*. Boston, 1966.

Prasad, Bimla. *The Origins of Indian Foreign Policy: The Indian National Congress and World Affairs*. 2nd ed. Calcutta, 1962.

Rajkumar, N. V., ed. *The Background of India's Foreign Policy*. New Delhi, 1952.

Rao, P. V. R. *Defence Without Drift*. Bombay, 1970.

Reddy, T. Ramakrishna. *India's Policy in the United Nations*. Rutherford, N.J., 1968.

Rowland, John. *A History of Sino-Indian Relations: Hostile Co-existence*. Princeton, N.J., 1967.

SarDesai, D. R. *Indian Foreign Policy in Cambodia, Laos, and Vietnam, 1947–1964*. Berkeley, Calif., 1968.

Stein, Arthur. *India and the Soviet Union: The Nehru Era.* Chicago, 1969.

Talbot, Phillips and S. L. Poplai. *India and America.* New York, 1958.

Varma, S. P. and K. P. Misra, eds. *Foreign Policies in South Asia.* Bombay, 1969.

SCHOLARLY JOURNALS (A SELECTED LIST)

*Asian Survey* (Berkeley, Calif., monthly)

*Economic and Political Weekly* (Bombay, weekly)

*The Far Eastern Economic Review* (Hong Kong, weekly)

*The Indian Journal of Political Science* (quarterly; journal of the Indian Political Science Association)

*The Indian Journal of Public Administration* (New Delhi, quaterly; journal of the Indian Institute of Public Administration)

*The Indian Political Science Review* (Delhi, quarterly; published by the Department of Political Science, University of Delhi)

*India Quarterly* (New Delhi, quarterly; journal of the Indian Council of World Affairs)

*International Studies* (New Delhi, quarterly; journal of the School of International Studies, Jawaharlal Nehru University)

*The Journal of Asian Studies* (Ann Arbor, Mich., quarterly; journal of the Association for Asian Studies)

*The Journal of Commonwealth Political Studies* (London, quarterly; journal of the Institute of Commonwealth Studies)

*The Journal of Constitutional and Parliamentary Studies* (New Delhi, quarterly; journal of the Institute for Constitutional and Parliamentary Studies)

*Modern Asian Studies* (Cambridge, quarterly; published by Cambridge University)

*Monthly Public Opinion Surveys* of the Indian Institute of Public Opinion (New Delhi, monthly)

*Pacific Affairs* (Vancouver, British Columbia, quarterly; journal of the Institute of Pacific Relations)

*Political Science Review* (Jaipur, biennally; published by the Department of Political Science, University of Rajasthan)

*Seminar* (New Delhi, monthly)

*South Asian Studies* (Jaipur, quarterly; journal of the South Asian Studies Centre, University of Rajasthan)

# INDEX

Abdullah, Sheikh, 280–81
Administrative Reforms Commission, 153, 189–90
*ahimsa*, 28, 84
Akali Dal, 18, 117, 209, 235–36, 263
Akbar, 38–39
All-India Congress Committee (A.I.C.C.), 95, 214
All-Party Hill Leaders' Conference, 6, 237
Ambedkar, Dr. B. R., 15, 103, 110, 128, 234
Andhra Pradesh, 115, 249–50
Annadurai, C. N., 234–35
Aryans in India, 26
Asoka, 34
Attlee, Clement, 67, 95
Azad, Maulana Abul Kamal, 91

*bandhs*, 7
Bandung Conference (1955), 285
Banerjea, Surendranath, 78, 80
Bentinck, Lord William, 42–43
*Bhagavad Gita*, 32
Bharatiya Kranti Dal (BKD), 209, 239, 263
Bhave, Vinoba, 4, 5, 11, 207
Bhoodan Yagna movement, 11, 200
Bhutan, 282
Bombay State, division of, 115–16
Bose, Subhas Chandra, 59, 87, 89, 211
Bowles, Chester, 304, 306, 307
British in India, 11, 39–72, 74, 267
British Cabinet Mission, 66
British East India Company, 40–42, 47
Buddhism, 30–31
Burma, 283

Calcutta Indian Association, 76, 77–78
Canal Waters question, 277–78
castes in India, 29–30; caste associations, 14; caste system, 13; and politics, 13–15; scheduled castes, 15; untouchables, 29–30, 234
Ceylon, 282
Chandragupta II, 34
China: early Indian contacts with, 35; Communist, and nuclear weapons, 289, 290; Communist, and Pakistan, 289; Communist,

relations with India, 284, 301–02
Cholas, 36
Clive, Robert, 41
Commonwealth, India in the, 107–08
communal parties, 18, 111, 224–28
communalism, 17–18, 37, 54, 110–11, 224
Communist parties in India, 206–07, 228–33; CPI, 229–33, 238, 253; CPI(M), 229–33; CPI(M-L), 231–32; Maoist, 232–33; non-Maoist, 232–33
Community Development Program, 153, 192–94
Congress (O), 134
Congress Parliamentary Party, 214
Congress Party. See Indian National Congress
Constituent Assembly, 100, 103, 106
cooperatives, 180, 194–96
Council of Ministers, 125–26
Council of States (Rajya Sabha), 127–29
Cripps, Sir Stafford, 65
Curzon, Lord, 53, 81, 266

Dange, S. A., 229, 231, 238
Delhi Sultanate, 37–38
democracy in India, 21–24, 99–100, 180–81
*dharma*, 28, 33
*dharnas*, 7
Dhebar, U.N., 213
district officers, 49, 160–63
districts, 49, 160–64
Dravida Kazhagam, 234–35
Dravida Munnetra Kazhagam, 235
Dravidians, 27, 234
"dyarchy", 56–57

Eisenhower, Dwight D., 306
Election Commission, 240, 242
Elections, 113–14, 240–63; *1937*, 63–64; *1945*, 66; *1946*, 66; *1951–52*, 227, 242–48; *1957*, 235, 250–54; *1962*, 223, 224, 232, 255–57; *1967*, 223–24, 227, 232, 234, 235, 237, 257–62; *1969*, 205, 224, 228, 232, 239, 262–63; Constitutional provisions regarding, 240–42; electoral alliances and coalitions, 237–39, 251, 261; electoral procedures, 242–44, 256, 260, 263; State